Chinese Language Learning Sciences

This book series investigates several critical issues embedded in fundamental, technical, and applied research in the field of Chinese as second language (CSL) learning and teaching, including learning mechanism in the brain, technology application for teaching, learning and assessment. The book series discusses these issues from the perspectives of science (evidence-based approach) and technology. The studies in the book series use the methods from the fields of linguistics (such as corpus linguistics and computational linguistics), psychological and behavioural sciences (such as experimental design and statistical analyses), informational technology (such as information retrieval and natural language processing) and brain sciences (such as neuroimaging and neurolinguistics). The book series generally covers three main interdisciplinary themes: (1) fundamental investigation of Chinese as a first or second language acquisition, (2) development in Chinese language learning technology, and (3) applied research on Chinese language education.

More specifically, the book series involves seven research topics:

- Language transfer mechanism in Chinese as a second language
- Factors of Chinese as a second language acquisition in childhood
- Cultural influence on Chinese acquisition
- Information technology, corpus
- Teaching material design
- Teaching strategies and teacher training
- Learning models
- Assessment methods

More information about this series at http://www.springer.com/series/13176

Xiaofei Lu · Berlin Chen
Editors

Computational and Corpus Approaches to Chinese Language Learning

Springer

Editors
Xiaofei Lu
Department of Applied Linguistics
The Pennsylvania State University
University Park, PA, USA

Berlin Chen
Department of Computer Science
and Information Engineering
National Taiwan Normal University
Taipei, Taiwan

ISSN 2520-1719 ISSN 2520-1727 (electronic)
Chinese Language Learning Sciences
ISBN 978-981-13-3569-3 ISBN 978-981-13-3570-9 (eBook)
https://doi.org/10.1007/978-981-13-3570-9

Library of Congress Control Number: 2018964227

This Springer imprint is published by the registered company Springer Nature Singapore Pte Ltd.
The registered company address is: 152 Beach Road, #21-01/04 Gateway East, Singapore 189721, Singapore

Preface

The past few decades have witnessed much progress in the construction of Chinese corpora oriented towards Chinese language pedagogy as well as the development of computational tools for annotating and analyzing Chinese texts and educational natural language processing (NLP) applications for Chinese language learning and assessment. Chinese language teachers, learners, and testers stand to benefit from such resources, tools, and applications in numerous productive ways. This volume brings together some of the most recent theoretical, empirical, methodological, and technological developments in applying computational and corpus approaches to teaching, learning, and assessing Chinese as a second or foreign language. It is our hope that the insights from these developments will help advance the state of the art in theorizing, designing, and implementing research and practice in corpus-informed and NLP-enabled Chinese language teaching, learning, and assessment.

We owe a special thanks to the co-editors of the Springer book series on Chinese Language Learning Sciences, Prof. Yao-Ting Sung and Prof. Ping Li, for their inspiring trust, support, and guidance from the very beginning of this process through the end. Thanks also go to many colleagues and friends who have helped shape the direction of the book in various ways, directly or indirectly. To name just a few: Marjorie Chan, Howard Ho-Jan Chen, Hsiao-Tsung Hung, Tan Jin, Zhuo Jing-Schmidt, Detmar Meurers, Hongyin Tao, Ming-Han Yang, and many others.

Last but not least, we would like to sincerely thank Lawrence Liu and Lay Peng Ang at Springer for their impressively professional and efficient support and the anonymous reviewers of the book proposal and manuscript for their highly insightful and constructive comments.

University Park, USA — Xiaofei Lu
Taipei, Taiwan — Berlin Chen

Contents

Part I
Introduction

Computational and Corpus Approaches to Chinese Language Learning: An Introduction

Xiaofei Lu and Berlin Chen

Abstract In this introductory chapter, we first provide a discussion of the rationale and objectives of the book. We then offer a brief review of the body of corpus linguistics research that intersects with Chinese language pedagogy and acquisition. This is followed by an overview of the state of the art of research in computational linguistics and natural language processing that pertains to Chinese language teaching, learning, and assessment. We conclude with a description of the organization of the book.

1 Rationale and Objectives of the Book

The past a few decades have witnessed remarkable progress in the construction of large corpora of spoken and written language produced by both first language (L1) and second language (L2) speakers and writers. In addition to their proven value in a vast range of linguistic research (McEnery and Hardie 2011), language corpora have increasingly been used to inform second and foreign language teaching, learning, and assessment (Aijmer 2009). The plethora of language corpora have also facilitated the development of natural language processing (NLP) technologies with various language understanding and production capabilities (Jurafsky and Martin 2008). Two types of NLP technologies that are especially useful in second and foreign language pedagogy and research are computational tools designed to automate corpus annotation and analysis at specific linguistic levels (Lu 2014) and educational NLP applications designed to facilitate different aspects of language teaching and learning or to assist with the assessment of different aspects of language production (Lu 2018).

X. Lu (✉)
The Pennsylvania State University, University Park, USA
e-mail: xxl13@psu.edu

B. Chen
National Taiwan Normal University, Taipei, Taiwan
e-mail: berlin@ntnu.edu.tw

X. Lu and B. Chen (eds.), *Computational and Corpus Approaches to Chinese Language Learning*, Chinese Language Learning Sciences,
https://doi.org/10.1007/978-981-13-3570-9_1

Second and foreign language teachers, learners, and testers, particularly those who practice computer-assisted language learning (CALL), stand to benefit from computational and corpus resources, tools, and methods in numerous productive ways. For example, different types of first or expert language corpora can serve as resources for teaching material selection and adaptation (Jin and Lu 2018) and for deriving pedagogically relevant lists of words, collocations, and various kinds of multiword expressions (Xiao et al. 2009). Corpora also allow for the extraction of large quantities of authentic examples of language use that can be utilized by teachers to explicate patterns of language use or by learners to discover and generalize patterns of language use (Flowerdew 2009). Analyses of learner corpora can help teachers identify characteristics, patterns, as well as individual variation of learner language use, acquisition, and development, which in turn can be used to inform the adjustment and individual customization of the emphasis of pedagogical intervention (Díaz-Negrillo et al. 2013). Computational tools designed to automate corpus annotation and analysis can be used to dramatically increase the scale and efficiency of these and other ways to exploit corpora for pedagogical purposes. At the same time, intelligent computer-assisted language learning (ICALL) systems that integrate various types of NLP capabilities have the potential to enhance learning in a myriad of ways (Lu 2018). For example, ICALL systems may automatically analyze input texts at various linguistic levels to facilitate text selection and sequencing, textual enhancement, and visualization of relationships and differences among different linguistic concepts and elements. They may also integrate technologies to automatically diagnose errors, problems, and challenges in learners' spoken or written responses to learning tasks and provide learners with individualized feedback and assistance in real time. Finally, computational systems designed to automatically assess learners' spoken or written performance can be of considerable help to language testers and teachers alike, as they help alleviate the time- and labor-intensiveness involved in scoring learner task performance, particularly in large-scale and time-sensitive assessment scenarios.

While a large proportion of computational and corpus linguistics research to date has centered on English, much progress has been made in constructing Chinese corpora oriented towards Chinese language pedagogy as well as in developing computational tools for annotating and analyzing Chinese texts and educational NLP applications for Chinese language learning and assessment. The goal of this volume is to bring together some of the most recent theoretical, empirical, methodological, and technological developments in applying computational and corpus approaches to teaching, learning and assessing Chinese as a second or foreign language. Given that research efforts in this area are still emerging, the volume does not focus on a specific, targeted aspect of Chinese language teaching and learning, nor does it cover the full range of topics in this area. Nevertheless, it is our hope that the insights from the studies included here will help advance the state of the art in theorizing, designing, and implementing research and practice in corpus-informed and NLP-enabled Chinese language teaching, learning, and assessment.

In the rest of this chapter, we first provide a brief review of the body of corpus linguistics research that intersects with Chinese language pedagogy and acquisition. This is followed by an overview of the state of the art of research in computational linguistics that pertains to Chinese language teaching, learning, and assessment. We conclude with a description of the organization of the book.

2 Corpus Linguistics and Chinese Language Learning

Corpus resources and findings from corpus-based research into L1 and L2 use and acquisition have found increasingly broad applications in language teaching and learning. We do not intend to cover the full spectrum of such applications here; nor do we intend to repeat the same information that has been covered in the body of works on the same subject for English and other languages (e.g., Aijmer 2009; Flowerdew 2009). Instead, we focus on five specific types of applications in the context of Chinese as a second or foreign language that are touched upon in some of the chapters in this volume.

A long-standing use of corpus resources has been the derivation of pedagogically useful lists of words, multiword expressions, and the like (e.g., Xu this volume). Work in this area requires large-scale general-purpose or specialized corpora that are representative of the language being targeted (in terms of mode, register, genre, etc.) and that have been annotated with necessary linguistic information (e.g., parts of speech and lemmas of the words), a clear operationalization of the linguistic items or units to be extracted (e.g., collocations, phrasal verbs, lexical bundles, etc.), as well as a set of procedures and corpus statistics to be used to extract, filter, and organize the linguistic items or units to be included in the list. A good example of this line of research is Xiao et al.'s (2009) work on deriving a frequency dictionary of Mandarin Chinese from a large corpus of close to 50 million Chinese words. In this volume, Chen and Tao describe several efforts in deriving lists of academic vocabulary and lexical bundles from specialized corpora of academic Chinese.

Another well-established use of corpus resources has been in-depth analyses of specific language phenomena using corpus-based methods. Such analyses can generate valuable insights into the nature of the linguistic phenomena in question, which in turn can be used to inform the teaching and learning of those phenomena. Two chapters in this volume report work that exemplifies new advances in this area. Zhang shows how corpus-based analysis and visualization of differences among Chinese near-synonyms using Correspondence Analysis can yield highly useful information for teaching and learning Chinese near-synonyms. Gong and Hong illustrate the usefulness of corpus-based analysis of neologisms originated from Chinese new media in helping Chinese learners acquire not only lexical and morphological knowledge but also sociocultural knowledge that underlies the construction and emergence of such neologisms.

Parallel corpora, i.e., corpora consisting of texts in the original language as well as their translations in one or more other languages, have found their way into corpus-informed language pedagogy as well. As detailed by Bluemel in this volume, while such corpora were initially designed to facilitate research in contrastive linguistics and translation studies, they have been shown to be particularly useful in helping learners develop conceptual knowledge of complex linguistic constructions in Chinese. His novel design of the Parallel Corpus Teaching Tool and successful application of it in beginning-level Chinese classes break new ground in theory-informed integration of parallel corpora in Chinese language pedagogy.

Text corpora and various types of corpus-derived lists are now also being used as benchmarks to inform reading text selection and adaptation. This line of research involves establishing benchmarks of text complexity features of collections of texts of different grade, readability, or difficulty levels and using such benchmarks to assist the processes of selecting and/or adapting additional reading texts for learners at different proficiency levels (Jin and Lu 2018). In this volume, Bo et al. describe the development of an online text adaptation system that uses linguistic features mined from a large corpus of Chinese textbooks to provide real-time assistance to teachers who use the system to adapt Chinese texts.

Finally, with the increasing availability of learner corpora, i.e., corpora of language samples produced by second or foreign language learners, investigations of patterns of as well as individual variation in learner language use, acquisition, and development have flourished. Findings from such investigations have clear values for helping teachers understand learners' abilities, challenges, and developmental trajectories. A good example of this line of research in the current volume is Xu et al. analysis of Chinese learners' acquisition of the Chinese particle *le* using data from the Guangwai-Lancaster Chinese Learner Corpus.

3 Computational Linguistics, Natural Language Processing, and Chinese Language Learning

Computational linguistics, also referred to as natural language processing, is a scientific discipline under the larger field of artificial intelligence that works on problems involving human languages from a computational perceptive (Manning and Schütze 1999). The general objective of computational linguistics is to use computers to construct formal models, either rule-based or statistical, to explain different kinds of linguistic phenomena and to automatically perform tasks that involve the processing, understanding, and/or generation of natural language. Notably, the last two decades have seen a surge of research in developing statistical modeling paradigms from researchers and practitioners in the computational linguistics community, due largely to the explosion of available text and speech data, amid the rapid advancement of machine learning techniques and exponential growth in computing power. These statistical modeling paradigms have been used in many academic prototype and practical product systems, providing such wide-ranging functionalities as syntactic and semantic analysis of text content, automatic speech recognition, information retrieval, document summarization, machine translation, and question answering, among others. For example, various forms of hidden Markov models (HMM) have been applied to part-of-speech (POS) tagging and speech recognition (Gales and Young 2007), serving as simple and effective frameworks for modeling time-evolving word-level tag sequences and speech vector sequences, respectively. As another illustration, latent Dirichlet allocation (LDA) (Blei et al. 2003) and its two prominent precursors, namely latent semantic analysis (LSA) (Deerwester et al. 1990) and probabilistic latent semantic analysis (PLSA) (Hofmann 1999), have been put to good use in semantic analysis of text content, query-document relevance assessment in information retrieval, and salient sentence selection in extractive document summarization. More recently, deep learning, embodied also as disparate deep neural networks (DNN) and representation learning techniques (Goodfellow et al. 2016), has emerged as the dominant statistical modeling paradigm. The record-breaking performance achieved by this paradigm on a vast array of speech and language processing tasks has exerted a catalytic effect on reviving interest in computational linguistics. One attractive advantage of deep learning is that the associated statistical models can be trained in an end-to-end manner, alleviating the need for specific domain knowledge or human-engineered features while being easily modifiable to accommodate new domains.

Numerous state-of-the-art theories and models of computational linguistics have been applied with good success to computer-assisted language teaching, learning, and assessment, notably in the context of Chinese as a second or foreign language. For example, near-synonym sets, which represent groups of words with similar meanings, are useful knowledge resources for computer-assisted language learning. Recent work has exploited LSA as a context analysis technique to identify useful latent context features for near-synonyms through indirect associations between words and sentences, represented by low-dimensional latent vectors. Classifiers trained on top of such latent vectors can then be used to distinguish among near-synonyms (Wang and Hirst 2010). As a second illustration, computer-assisted pronunciation training (CAPT) systems that are able to pinpoint and diagnose erroneous pronunciations in the utterances produced by L2 learners in response to given text prompts can serve as a surrogate for or supplement to classroom instruction by teachers. A common practice for mispronunciation detection is to extract decision features (attributes) from the prediction output of phone-level acoustic models, which are normally estimated based on certain criteria that maximize the automatic speech recognition performance. The extracted decision features are then fed into a pretrained classifier (decision function) for identifying mispronounced speech segments (Chen and Li 2016). In addition, there have been many attempts to employ long short-term memory (LSTM), a particular type of recurrent neural network (RNN), to detect inappropriate linguistic usage, including character-level confusions (commonly known as spelling errors) and word-, sentence-, or discourse-level grammatical errors (Yeh et al. 2016). Others still, for the task of automated essay scoring (AES), various linguistic features that align with the criteria specified in rating rubrics (e.g., lexical diversity, syntactic complexity, coherence, among others) have been used as predictors of writing quality. Alternatively, some approaches to AES employ LSA to convert a given essay into a semantic vector (Peng et al. 2010), which represents the location of the essay in a latent semantic space. Close proximity of the semantic vectors representing different essays then implies a high degree of similarity of the semantic content of the essays. Several chapters in this volume detail recent developments in these and other educational NLP applications for Chinese language teaching, learning, and assessment.

4 Organization of the Book

This book is thematically organized into four parts. Part 1, "Introduction," includes two additional introductory chapters beyond the current overview chapter. The second chapter in this part, "Corpus and Computational Methods for Usage-Based Chinese Language Learning: Toward a Professional Multilingualism," starts with a discussion of the main tenets of the usage-based model of language, the theoretical model underlying much of the research presented in this volume. It then illustrates the necessity of corpus and computational methods as tools for usage-based second language acquisition research and the criticality of the voice such methods constitute in the professional multilingualism that informs Chinese language teaching, learning, and assessment.

Xu's chapter, "The Corpus Approach to the Teaching and Learning of Chinese as an L1 and an L2 in Retrospect," reviews the historical development of research into the use of corpora in teaching and learning Chinese. This chapter synthesizes the insights from corpus-based Chinese studies into Chinese textbook compilation and syllabus design, the range and types of important vocabulary items and grammatical patterns to be taught, and the order in which such items and patterns are best to be presented. It further illustrates how some of these insights have found their way into Chinese language pedagogy in the form of data-driven learning and calls for additional research in transforming such insights into pedagogical practices.

Part 2, "Tools, Resources and General Applications," includes three chapters that each introduces a specific type of corpus resource or computational tool with broad pedagogical applications. The first chapter in this part, "Academic Chinese: From Corpora to Language Teaching," describes two written academic Chinese corpora constructed by researchers at National Taiwan Normal University and University of California Los Angeles, respectively. The chapter also reports the outcomes of research on developing lists of academic vocabulary and multiword expressions based on these corpora and discusses applications of the corpora and related research outcomes in teaching material design and pedagogical practices.

Bluemel's chapter, "Pedagogical Applications of Chinese Parallel Corpora," starts with a thorough discussion of the ways in which parallel corpora can be used in language pedagogy in general and then takes a close look at the application of a Chinese-English parallel corpus in a beginning-level Chinese as a foreign language course for L1 English learners. The chapter also includes a review of various parallel corpus resources along with recommendations for their pedagogical uses.

Bo et al.'s chapter, "Data-Driven Adapting for Fine-Tuning Chinese Teaching Materials: Using Corpora as Benchmarks," examines how teachers adapt Chinese texts using an online data-driven text adaptation system, *Chi-Editor*. The system is designed to automatically assess text complexity, to annotate a text for difficult words and long sentences based on features mined from a large textbook corpus, and to dynamically reassess the complexity of the text as it is being modified. The chapter reports evidence that teachers can benefit from the data-driven text adaptation system and discusses how it can be integrated in regular teaching material preparation.

Part 3, "Specific Applications," includes three chapters that each addresses a specific application of a computational tool or corpus resource in Chinese language teaching and learning. The first chapter in this part, "Context Analysis for Computer-Assisted Near-Synonym Learning," reports on the design and performance of a prototype computer-assisted near-synonym learning system for Chinese and English. The system integrates a number of context analysis techniques that can be used to automate the selection of near-synonyms in a given context and to provide useful contextual information to help learners understand different usages of near-synonyms.

Zhang's chapter, "Visualizing Stylistic Differences in Chinese Synonyms," demonstrates the use of Correspondence Analysis to visualize stylistic differences in near-synonyms as two-dimensional bi-plots. The pedagogical advantages of such an approach in promoting Chinese learners' stylistic awareness are showcased using five groups of Chinese near-synonyms.

Gong and Hong's chapter, "Using Corpus-Based Analysis of Neologisms on China's New Media for Teaching Chinese as a Second or Foreign Language," explicates how Chinese neologisms on new media can constitute a productive resource for helping learners acquire and reinforce lexical and sociocultural knowledge. The pedagogical value of information about word-formation strategies of Chinese neologisms is demonstrated through a detailed analysis of a small corpus of authentic usage samples of 50 neologisms originated from Chinese new media.

The fourth part, "Learner Language Analysis and Assessment," includes four chapters that report research on the use of computational and corpus methods for analyzing or assessing learner production. The first chapter in this part, "Acquisition of the Chinese Particle *le* by L2 Learners: A Corpus-Based Approach," uses the spoken subcorpus of the large-scale Guangwai-Lancaster Chinese Learner Corpus to investigate the frequency and accuracy with which Chinese learners at different proficiency levels use the Chinese particle *le* and the developmental pattern of their acquisition of this particle.

Chen and Hsu's chapter, "Mandarin Chinese Mispronunciation Detection and Diagnosis Leveraging Deep Neural Network based Acoustic Modeling and Training Techniques," focuses on automatic mispronunciation detection and diagnosis. Following a review of recent developments on this front with state-of-the-art automatic speech recognition methodologies, the chapter presents a training approach for deep neural network based acoustic models as well as a series of empirical experiments designed to evaluate the effectiveness of the approach.

Lee et al.'s chapter, "Resources and Evaluations of Automated Chinese Error Diagnosis for Language Learners," introduces the HSK Dynamic Composition Corpus and the TOCFL Learner Corpus as useful resources for understanding patterns of Chinese learners' grammatical errors as well as a series of bakeoffs and shared tasks that utilized these corpora to evaluate computational systems for Chinese spelling checking and grammatical error identification.

The final chapter, "Automated Chinese Essay Scoring Based on Multilevel Linguistic Features," discusses critical issues concerning the task of automated Chinese essay scoring, followed by a detailed description of the design of a novel automated system for scoring Chinese essays along with experimental results indicating superior stability and reliability of its performance.

References

Aijmer, K. (Ed.). (2009). *Corpora and language teaching*. Amsterdam/Philadelphia: John Benjamins.

Blei, D. M., Ng, A. Y., & Jordan, M. I. (2003). Latent Dirichlet allocation. *Journal of Machine Learning Research, 3*(4–5), 993–1022.

Chen, N. F., & Li, H. (2016). Computer-assisted pronunciation training: From pronunciation scoring towards spoken language learning. In *Proceedings of the Asia-Pacific Signal and Information Processing Association Annual Summit and Conference*.

Deerwester, S., Dumais, S. T., Furnas, G. W., Landauer, T. K., & Harshman, R. (1990). Indexing by latent semantic analysis. *Journal of the American Society for Information Science, 41*(6), 391–417.

Díaz-Negrillo, A., Ballier, N., & Thompson, P. (Eds.). (2013). *Automatic treatment and analysis of learner corpus data* (pp. 249–264). Amsterdam/Philadelphia: John Benjamins.

Flowerdew, L. (2009). Applying corpus linguistics to pedagogy. *International Journal of Corpus Linguistics, 14*(3), 393–417.

Gales, M., & Young, S. (2007). The application of hidden Markov models in speech recognition. *Foundations and Trends in Signal Processing, 3*(1), 195–304.

Goodfellow, I., Bengio, Y., & Courville, A. (2016). *Deep learning*. Cambridge: The MIT Press.

Hofmann, T. (1999). Probabilistic latent semantic indexing. In *Proceedings of the Annual International ACM SIGIR Conference on Research and Development in Information Retrieval* (pp. 50–57).

Jin, T., & Lu, X. (2018). A data-driven approach to text adaptation in teaching material preparation: Design, implementation and teacher professional development. *TESOL Quarterly, 52*(2), 457–467.

Jurafsky, D., & Martin, J. (2008). *An introduction to natural language processing, computational linguistics, and speech recognition* (2nd ed.). Englewood Cliffs, NJ: Prentice Hall.

Lu, X. (2014). *Computational methods for corpus annotation and analysis*. Dordrecht: Springer.

Lu, X. (2018). Natural language processing and intelligent computer-assisted language learning (ICALL). In J. I. Liontas (Ed.), *The TESOL encyclopedia of english language teaching*. Chichester, UK: Wiley Blackwell.

Manning, C., & Schütze, H. (1999). *Foundations of statistical natural language processing*. Cambridge: MIT Press.

McEnery, T., & Hardie, A. (2011). *Corpus linguistics: Method, theory and practice*. Cambridge: Cambridge University Press.

Peng, X., Ke, D., Chen, Z., & Xu, B. (2010). Automated Chinese essay scoring using vector space models. In *Proceedings of the International Universal Communication Symposium* (pp. 149–153).

Wang, T., & Hirst, G. (2010). Near-synonym lexical choice in latent semantic space. In *Proceedings of the International Conference on Computational Linguistics* (pp. 1182–1190).

Xiao, R., Rayson, P., & McEnery, T. (2009). *A frequency dictionary of Mandarin Chinese: Core vocabulary for learners*. London: Routledge.

Yeh, J.-F., Hsu, T.-W., & Yeh, C.-K. (2016). Grammatical error detection based on machine learning for Mandarin as second language learning. In *Proceedings of the 3rd Workshop on Natural Language Processing Techniques for Educational Applications* (pp. 140–147).

Corpus and Computational Methods for Usage-Based Chinese Language Learning: Toward a Professional Multilingualism

Zhuo Jing-Schmidt

Abstract Language is a complex functional adaptive system (Beckner et al. in Lang Learn 59:1–26, 2009; Ellis in Usage-based perspectives on second language learning, De Gruyter, Berlin/Boston, pp 49–73, 2015). Language learning is learning to use a complex system Larsen-Freeman (Alternative approaches to second language acquisition, Routledge, London, pp 47–72, 2011). It is a multidimensional task involving social cognitive processes that interact both in time and space MacWhinney (Usage based perspectives on second language learning, De Gruyter, Berlin, pp 19–48, 2015). Language learning in the twenty-first century is "enmeshed in globalization, technologization, and mobility" and hence "emergent, dynamic, unpredictable, open ended, and intersubjectively negotiated" (The Douglas Fir Group in Mod Lang J 100:19–47, 2016: 19). Accordingly, the field of language teaching is more interdisciplinary than ever. It requires not only knowledge of language as a functional system and knowledge of language learning as a human socio-cognitive endeavor but also expanded communication across domains traditionally separated by differences in the methodology of knowledge construction. This chapter focuses on the usage-based model of language and language learning within a broader cognitive theory of linguistic knowledge and its development. The goal is to establish a theoretical relevancy and methodological necessity of corpus and computational methods to the knowledge base for language pedagogy as a practical field. In doing so, this chapter serves to ground the application of such methods as part of a professional multilingualism that informs the learning, teaching, and assessment of Chinese as a second language.

Z. Jing-Schmidt (✉)
University of Oregon, Eugene, USA
e-mail: zjingsch@uoregon.edu

X. Lu and B. Chen (eds.), *Computational and Corpus Approaches to Chinese Language Learning*, Chinese Language Learning Sciences,
https://doi.org/10.1007/978-981-13-3570-9_2

1 Introduction

Language is a complex functional adaptive system (Beckner et al. 2009; Ellis 2015). Language learning, including adult second language learning, involves multidimensional social cognitive processes that interact both in time and space (Larsen-Freeman 2011; MacWhinney 2015). More than ever before, language learning in the twenty-first century is "enmeshed in globalization, technologization, and mobility," and therefore "emergent, dynamic, unpredictable, open ended, and intersubjectively negotiated" (The Douglas Fir Group 2016: 19). Accordingly, the field of language teaching is more interdisciplinary than ever, requiring not only knowledge of language as a functional system and knowledge of language learning as a human socio-cognitive endeavor but also expanded communication across domains traditionally separated by differences in the methodology of knowledge construction. The discussion of knowledge base and methodology of knowledge construction inevitably involves the discussion of the place and role of linguistic theory and second language acquisition (SLA) research in second language teaching. The complexity and the contested nature of that relationship is evident in the discourse about second language teaching in general (Byrnes 2000), and in the discourse about knowledge base in the field of teaching Chinese as a second language (TCSL) in particular (Han 2016; Jing-Schmidt 2015; Jing-Schmidt and Peng 2018; Ke et al. 2015).[1]

Treating *Modern Language Journal* as a site of observing the discursive history of the language teaching profession throughout the twentieth century, Byrnes (2000: 489–490) viewed that history as one of identity construction and negotiation in a community striving for professionalization. That history is a symbiosis between "affective-holistic" "grassroots" movements that come and go, and powerful "top-down" "rational-analytical" theoretical constructs, especially in linguistics, that have themselves undergone major revolutions and paradigm shifts. At the same time, Byrnes observed that the professional discourse on language teaching "has increasingly become as multivoiced as the languages we teach and as multilayered as are the societies within which we practice, powerful unifying, centralizing, and standardizing moves notwithstanding." Warning of the danger of misrepresenting "important aspects of our past identities, both of our own individual identities and of the field as a whole" by characterizing "contingent ways of knowing as deviations, as positions that need to be corrected," she contended that professionalization of the language teaching field "can also mean professional multilingualism" (ibid.: 492).

What has transpired in the larger landscape of discipline formation and identity construction of second language teaching as a field in general is mirrored in the history of TCSL as a developing field. Tracing the evolution of TCSL and the impact of discipline inquiries on this field in the last two decades, Jing-Schmidt and Peng (2018: 64) noted that central to that evolution "are efforts to define and delimit TCSL as an academic discipline, to identify and specify its theoretical foundations and guiding principles" for pedagogical decision-making. These efforts eventually led to a recognition of the interdisciplinary nature of TCSL, and negotiations of the

[1] In this chapter, I use the term "second language" in a broad sense that includes "foreign language".

place of disciplines that contribute to its formation, in particular, that of linguistics. The inchoation of a positive interaction between TCSL and linguistics is evident in the increasing "dialogue and synergy between theoretical linguistics and pedagogical practice, motivated by a desire to professionalize TCSL as well as to test linguistic theories" (ibid.). This positive tendency is enabled by the increasing number of CSL instructors who are trained in linguistics or applied linguistics research, which "fortifies the knowledge structure of the field by adding discipline knowledge to existing practical expertise in language teaching," and "rebalances the discursive power in the field through the authorial voice and disciplinary authority of the teachers-cum-researchers" (ibid.: 65).

While the enthusiastic embracement of the various linguistic theories in the recent history of TCSL may have been a strategy of coping with the uncertainty in a developing field, it is also an unmistakable sign of an "open-minded optimism" about professional growth (Jing-Schmidt and Peng 2018: 72). Despite the mistakes and detours that naturally accompany the multitude of choices, that growth mindset has led to "a powerful hybridity of intellectual resources" that have contributed to the professionalization of TCSL in one way or another (ibid.). Not only is the history of TSCL as a field one that has nurtured professional multilingualism, there is strong indication that the synergy will continue. Tao (2016) presented recent examples of research and practice meeting each other in the middle toward continuing mutual integration, and illustrated how various empirical efforts can contribute to sustained professional multilingualism for TCSL. Ke et al. (2015) provided a model of standardizing and assessing the integration of theoretical knowledge in pedagogical practice in CSL teacher professional development.

These positive developments in the integration of disciplinary inquiry and pedagogy notwithstanding, tension remains in the field with regard to the relationship between research and practice. While factors contributing to the tension may be many, there is one that has been overlooked. That is the misunderstanding that knowledge of how a second language is learned, the central concern of SLA research, is complete and free of controversy, and should be trusted as the basis of authoritative guidelines for L2 instruction. Consequently, suspicions of the applicability of certain SLA findings are perceived as irrational. For example, in a recent call for rationality and corrective intervention in TCSL, Han (2016: 238–239) referred to five "broad facts" about L2 learning, which she characterized as "firmly established," and ten generalizations derived therefrom. She urged the field to hold on to the "guiding principles" based on "the robustness of the empirical facts." What Han failed to acknowledge is that knowledge of L2 learners and L2 learning is far from "firmly established." Consider as an example the construct of fossilization as permanent cessation of learning, which is the cornerstone of the Interlanguage Hypothesis proposed by Selinker (1972), the mother theory that gives rise to the five "facts" referred to in Han (2016).

The Interlanguage Hypothesis was born in the generativist tradition that denies the learnability of language from experience in favor of a modular view of language as acquired through an innate language learning device (LAD). It arose in response to the many complications of SLA that could not be accounted for by the construct of the LAD, which presumably explains child language acquisition. Instead of challenging the empirical status of the LAD, Selinker (1972) found a way around it by proposing that interlanguage, the linguistic system produced by adult L2 learners while learning the L2, is distinct from both the learners' native language and the target language. As such its development is not governed by LAD. The defining feature of interlanguage is fossilization, initially defined as a global "permanent cessation" of learning (Selinker and Lamendella 1978: 187), later modified to be "permanent local cessation of development" (Han and Odlin 2006: 8). Both definitions dwell on the permanence of fossilization as resulting from maturation-related innate constraints, and attribute interlanguage development to a putative latent psychological structure the central component of which is L1 transfer. Thus, L1 transfer was posited as an underlying cognitive process to explain fossilization while what exactly causes L1 transfer itself was never explained.

The fundamental problem, however, is that the exact cognitive mechanisms will remain inexplicable within a modular theory of learning that denies the role of domain-general cognitive capacities essential to language learning, and the effect of language experience on learning. Insisting on the permanency of fossilization, Selinker and his followers consistently described the condition as impervious to experience and intervention, "no matter what the age of the learner or the amount of instruction he receives in the target language" (Selinker 1972: 229), and "no matter what the input or what the learner does" (Han 2004: 20). These universalistic "no matter what" statements are extraordinary claims that were never backed up by extraordinary evidence, and remain central to the fatalism of fossilization despite accumulating counterevidence. When Han (2004) offered "abundant exposure to input," "adequate motivation to learn," and "plentiful opportunity for communicative practice" as the preconditions of fossilization identification, she was negligent of the empirical duty to provide quantitative data to support the quantitative statements made by her adjectives. Namely, how is "abundant," "adequate," and "plentiful" quantified?

The last two decades saw accumulating evidence of learner variability, domain selectivity, and non-inevitability of fossilization (e.g., Abrahamsson and Hyltenstam 2009; Bongaerts 1999; Byrnes 2012; MacWhinney 2006). But what has transpired in the field is bigger and deeper than the discovery of successful L2 learners whose language development defies the notion of fossilization.[2] Mounting converging evidence supports the consensus that both domain-general cognitive capacities and experience with language shape language development, both L1 and L2. Thus, the very premise of the innatist model is shaken. When this happens, a paradigm shift

[2]The 10-year learning results in the Language Flagship Program, a model of undergraduate advanced foreign language education designed to produce professionals with superior proficiency in a critical target language, demonstrate that attainment of professional proficiency is possible. However, it takes high expectations, realistic goal setting, rigorous student-centered and individualized intervention, immersion experience, and accountability at the institutional level (Nugent and Slater 2016). The proportion of students in the program that reach the professional level are not the 5% outliers Selinker (1972) deemed ignorable as data. For example, in 2015, 39.4% of the students who completed the program reached IRL level 3 in three modalities. See the Flagship Annual Reports Archive for data: https://www.thelanguageflagship.org/content/reports.

ensues: on the horizon is an emergentist view of language (Cook et al. 2006; Ellis 1998; MacWhinney 1999). A central part of this shift is the consolidation of the usage-based model of language and language learning (Behrens 2009; Ellis 2010, 2015; Ellis and Wulff 2015; Ibbotson 2013; Tomasello 2003; Wulff 2010). In essence, taking seriously the transformative role of adaptive learning as a lifelong process, the usage-based model rejects the notion of fossilization in the sense of permanent cessation of learning. This, however, does not mean that the enormous difficulty of L2 learning should be ignored. Within the usage-based model, L1 transfer and other risk factors related to the entrenchment of L1 knowledge can be explained by a combination of domain-general factors such as cue strength, cue competition, salience, prototypicality, etc., that influence selective attention and perceptual learning (Ellis 2006, 2008), and factors pertaining to individual aptitude (Winke 2013). In addition, language learning is sensitive to frequency effects (Arnon and Snider 2010; Behrens and Pfänder 2016; Bybee 2006, 2010; Dąbrowska 2008; Ellis 2002; Ellis and Ferreira-Junior 2009; Reali 2014; Wolter and Gyllstad 2013). Converging with evidence of usage-based language learning is neurophysiological evidence of a structural plasticity of the adult brain in adaptation to environmental enrichments (Belzung and Wigmore 2013; Hofman 2002; Sale 2016). Such converging evidence should give cause for concern to adherents of the notion of the imperviousness of language development to exposure, experience, and intervention.

The example of fossilization as a theoretical construct offers a cautionary tale that conveys the need to distinguish established facts from received wisdom, and to evaluate research by examining its theoretical assumptions and the evidence behind those assumptions. SLA research must be grounded in an empirically tested theory of language and language learning. Only in this way can research properly inform teaching. To talk about adhering to SLA research before examining its underlying theoretical assumptions puts the cart before the horse. Teachers would be ill-advised to “hold on” to implications of research the theoretical assumptions of which fail to stand up to empirical evidence.

Given the ongoing construction of knowledge of SLA processes, and given the continuing emergence of counterevidence against received wisdom, future explorations will benefit from a professional multilingualism that embraces research on usage data and learner data. The remainder of this chapter will discuss the central tenets of the usage-based model of language, its application in and impact on SLA and L2 pedagogy, and why corpus and computational methods as essential tools for usage-based approaches to SLA constitute an important voice in the professional multilingualism that informs pedagogical decision-making in TCSL.

2 The Usage-Based Model of Language

Language is learned in social interaction through shared experience and practice. This intuition, tracing back to the works of Quine (1960), has increasingly consolidated into a model of linguistic representation and language learning generally referred to as the usage-based theory. As briefly noted in the previous section, this theory views linguistic knowledge as emergent from knowledge of usage and generalizations over usage events in interaction (Barlow and Kemmer 2000; Bybee 2006, 2010; Ellis 2002; Ellis and Wulff 2015; Ellis et al. 2016a; Goldberg 2006; Tomasello 2000, 2003). In first language acquisition, knowledge of usage comes from the child's language experience, which consists of encountering utterances that people in the child's surroundings produce in communicative context. Early language learning begins with high-frequency utterances as unanalyzed wholes, which are associated with particular functions. This is the formulaic speech stage of language learning. Learning at this stage is input-sensitive and exemplar-based, and produces an "inventory of item-based utterance schemas" (Tomasello 2000: 70) paired with specific communicative intentions and functions (Ambridge and Lieven 2011; Ellis 2011; Lieven et al. 1997; Pine et al. 1998; Tomasello 1992, 2000).

However, unanalyzed language experience is insufficient for learning grammar, which is in essence a system of generalizations. As the unanalyzed formulas become entrenched over repeated usage events, incoming utterances are sorted based on their similarity to these high-frequency exemplars. Generalization of schemas takes place in this sorting process, which allows prediction of novel exemplars and the acquisition thereof. The abstraction of schemas may occur at different levels within the hierarchical category of a construction (Barlow and Kemmer 2000; Kapatsinski 2014; Tummers et al. 2005). The more different incoming utterances in the input are, the more schematic and productive the schema becomes (Bybee 2010). In the L1 acquisition of verb-centered constructions, high-frequency exemplars with perceptually salient or prototypical verbs are learned first. As "pathbreakers," these prototypical exemplars lead the consolidation of abstract schemas and constructional meanings (Goldberg 1995; Goldberg et al. 2004). Thus, the early holistic learning of formulaic speech is followed by the abstraction of construction meaning from entrenched prototype meaning, and the generalization of abstract patterns over experienced type variations in the input. In these processes, high token frequency of a prototypical exemplar facilitates the learning of constructional meaning (Goldberg et al. 2004), and high type frequency contributes to the productivity of a pattern (Bybee and Hopper 2001; Goldberg 2006; MacWhinney 1999; Tomasello 2000). Induction or generalization involves unconscious statistical inference over utterances encountered and stored in memory (Bybee 2013; Kapatsinski 2014).

The usage-based view of language and language learning is part of a broader cognitive theory of learning that recognizes the following general cognitive strategies critical to learning:

(1) The cognitive system tracks individual items across usage events and establishes integrated representations of them as episodic memory (Barsalou et al. 1998).
(2) The stored representations of individual items in the form of episodic memory have long-term influence on the categorization and learning of items subsequently encountered (Medin and Schaffer 1978; Medin and Smith 1981; Nosofsky 1988; Smith 1991; Smith and Zarate 1992).

(3) Frequency as a structural property of a category has effects on the learning of a category (Anderson 2000; Ebbinghaus 1913; Rosch and Mervis 1975).

In addition to these general cognitive strategies, prelinguistic social cognitive capacities unique to humankind are indispensable in the acquisition of language. Such a "nonlinguistic infrastructure" (Tomasello 2008: 58) consists of:

(1) Understanding communicative intentions in intersubjectively shared context and reality (Rossano et al. 2015; Schulze and Tomasello 2015; Tomasello 1999, 2003)
(2) Joint attention of child and caregiver as scaffolding for language learning (Bruner 1981; Carpenter et al. 1998, 2002; Tomasello 2003; Tomasello and Farrar 1986).

Contra the words-and-rules theory, which assumes the modular innateness of abstract rules that guide the combination of learned words in the lexicon in developing grammatical competence, the usage-based theory explains the rapid development of child grammatical competence from input by drawing on domain-general learning mechanisms and prelinguistic capacities of social cognition, thereby obviating the need to postulate innate grammatical rules (e.g., Chomsky 2002; Pinker 1999).

3 The Usage-Based Model of SLA and Its Pedagogical Impact

SLA is an interdisciplinary field that focuses on the mechanisms by which a second or foreign language is learned. SLA research developed from child language acquisition research in the 1970s in response to the need to teach English as a second language (ESL) around the world, and has since expanded to the learning and teaching of other second and foreign languages (Kramsch 2000). It subsequently became the research base for language teaching in the United States (Byrnes 1998), though SLA researchers have recognized the role of SLA as lying primarily in informing teacher's practice rather than ensuring competent practice (Ellis 1997; Tragant and Muñoz 2004).

In its earlier years, SLA research was heavily influenced by the generative framework and focused on whether and how Universal Grammar (Chomsky 1965) constrains adult L2 acquisition and interlanguage development (Schachter 1989, 1990; Selinker 1972). In the last two decades in which generative linguistics has been increasingly challenged as a theory of linguistic knowledge, its influence on SLA has been on the wane. At the same time, the usage-based model of language acquisition has resonated with researchers in SLA and increasingly gained ground. There is now accumulating evidence that many of the usage-based mechanisms underlying L1 acquisition operate in L2 language learning:

(1) The learning of L2 grammar is data-driven and depends on the properties of input (Blom et al. 2012; Gass 1997; Madlener 2016). Cue strength in the input influences cue validity (Ellis 2006; MacWhinney 2005a, b, 2015).
(2) The learning of L2 grammar is exemplar-based and prototype-driven, and abstract patterns emerge from the generalization of language experience in communication context (Ellis 2013; Ellis and Ferreira-Junior 2009; Eskildsen 2008; Goldberg and Casenhiser 2008; Larsen-Freeman 2011).
(3) The learning of L2 grammar relies on statistical learning and is sensitive to the frequency of use (Ellis 2002; Eskildsen 2012; Medlener 2016; Rebuschat and Williams 2012; Sockett and Kusyk 2015).

Recognizing the common mechanisms underlying L1 and L2 development, the usage-based model of language unifies accounts of L1 and L2 acquisition under a broader cognitive theory of language learning. Using common concepts and relying on similar explanations allow for a more systematic comparison of the psychology of language acquisition in different settings. However, despite the shared learning strategies and mechanisms, it is a recognized fact that L2 acquisition is in general more effortful and less successful than L1 acquisition. The reason is that there are many ways in which SLA differs from L1 acquisition. Ellis (2002, 2015) points out that SLA distinguishes itself from L1 acquisition in that it draws on adult conceptual knowledge, and qualitatively and quantitatively limited language input in a non-naturalistic environment, and is subject to the influence and interference from preexisting L1 knowledge and the learned attention to both L1 form and L1 function (Ellis 2013). Similarly, MacWhinney (2012, 2015: 23) attributes the reduced success of SLA to the "set of risk factors" faced by adult learners "that reduce the effectiveness of mere exposure to L2 input." These include L1 related factors of entrenchment, negative transfer, parasitism, misconnection, and the social factor of isolation that limit language input. Importantly, although the same learning mechanisms are available to both L1 and L2 learners, SLA is complicated by the interference of learners' existing L1 experience and by their insufficient exposure to, and limited meaningful interaction in, the target language. All of these differences have implications for SLA research and L2 instruction.

The insights into the general learning mechanisms underlying L1 and L2 acquisition, as well as the recognition of L2-specific learning conditions have profound impact on L2 pedagogy. Notably, usage-based SLA research has become the empirical base of language pedagogy in many languages. Pedagogical strategies have been proposed in keeping with the usage-based model of language learning (Barcroft 2013; DeKeyser 2003; Fotos 2002; Jing-Schmidt et al. 2015; Medlener 2016; Skehan 1998; Verspoor and Nguyen 2015). Protective or compensatory interventions have also been developed in L2 pedagogy for the purpose of offsetting the negative effects of L2-specific risk factors, including conscious registration of the input and explicit "noticing" of L2 features and patterns (Schmidt 1990, 1993), explicit or form-focused instruction (Ellis 2001), corrective feedback (Ellis 2009; Lyster and Mori 2006; Lyster and Ranta 1997; Sato and Lyster 2012; Van Beuningen et al. 2012), technology-assisted learning (Peterson 2006, 2010), among many other methods and resources. In TCSL, attempts to translate the usage-based theory of language into an overall philosophy of teaching and professional development have been made (Jing-Schmidt 2015).

The usage-based model of language has reenergized SLA research and infused empirically derived insights and information into L2 language teaching. In doing so, it has pushed the field toward a higher level of professionalism and professional multilingualism. With the usage-based view of language and language learning becoming ever more vocal in SLA, it is necessary to look at the methodological tools essential to its commitment to the study of how language is learned through experience, and to understand how these tools can be part of the solution to the challenges in usage-based SLA and TCSL, and as such contribute to sustained professional multilingualism essential to the advances of our field.

4 Corpus and Computational Methods as Part of Professional Multilingualism

SLA research has traditionally preferred "experimental and introspective data over the exploration or analysis of corpus data" (Gries 2015: 159). This situation is changing. The usage-based theory of language learning has started to impact the methodology for SLA research. As a result, corpus-based methods are on the forefront of providing useful tools of data analysis in SLA research. The same can be said of computational methods. Although in itself not intellectually or theoretically affiliated with usage-based approaches to language, computational linguistics offers powerful algorithms in processing and modeling language use and learning, and therefore has affinity to the usage-based framework at the methodological level.

Corpus Linguistics investigates "relations between frequency and typicality, and instance and norm" based on a body of naturally occurring discourses or texts (Stubbs 2001: 151). It is a "major methodological paradigm in applied and theoretical linguistics" (Gries 2006: 191). Gries (2015: 195) noted that, despite a general neglect of corpus research in SLA, corpus data have become a "major source of data" in SLA research, "both on their own and in combination with experimental data." This change was enabled by the availability of large-scale language corpora including L2 learner language corpora, as well as advances in computational tools and statistical methods. It occurred in response to the call for data-driven studies of the learning of language (Gries and Ellis 2015). Corpus linguistics offers quantitative methods for exploring L2 language production and development by enabling the examination of frequency of use, frequency of collocation, and error patterns in learner corpora. Corpus research also illuminates how L2 production differs from native language use (in terms of patterns of overuse and underuse) by comparing learner corpora with native language corpora (Jing-Schmidt 2011; Li 2014; Xu 2016; Zhang and Lu 2013), and by using descriptive and inferential statistics to analyze learner data (Gries 2015). Although language use and language experience cannot be reduced to pure frequency effects (Behrens and Pfänder 2016), learner corpora studies have shown that frequency information extracted by corpus methods sheds important light on many notions central to language learning in SLA research. For example, Jing-Schmidt (2011) compared the uses of zero anaphors in Chinese L2 heritage and non-heritage written corpora and those in a native Chinese corpus, and discovered differential learning patterns between the two learner populations, which indicates the need of a differential instructional approach to addressing varying learning needs. Zhang and Lu (2013) compared numeral classifier uses by L2 Chinese learners and native speakers by examining a longitudinal corpus of L2 written samples from two proficiency levels in contrast to a native writing corpus. They found that L2 development in numeral classifier usage is nonlinear and highly variable for the three dimensions examined—fluency, diversity, and accuracy, which suggests the potential benefits of individualized and collocation-based instructional strategies. The application of corpus-based studies goes beyond SLA research. Frequency-based reference books (e.g., Jiao et al. 2011; Xiao et al. 2009) provide useful tools of strategizing the teaching of lexical and idiomatic expressions in Chinese. Multiple chapters in this volume demonstrate as well the utilization of corpus methods in other areas of TCSL.

Computational linguistics as an interdisciplinary field was born from the synergies of multiple related fields concerned with getting computers to perform human-centered, language-related complex tasks (Huang and Lenders 2005; Jurafsky and Martin 2008). Computational linguistics focuses on developing algorithms and software for processing and modeling speech and language. Just as corpus linguistics emerged and gained power at the auspices of the availability of large-scale language data, so is computational linguistics making great strides in speech and language processing thanks to a "startling increase in computing resources available to the average computer user, thanks to the rise of the Web as a massive source of information, and thanks to the increasing availability of wireless mobile access" (Jurafsky and Martin 2008: 8). In SLA, computational methods allow researchers to probe, test, and refine theories by reliably and efficiently detecting patterns of language use in the vastness of naturally occurring linguistic materials, and modeling and explaining mechanisms of language learning and factors that impact learning. Much of the research has found application in TCSL and is revolutionizing the field by incorporating computer-assisted learning and assessment. For example, Hoshino and Yasuda (2013) developed an automatic system of discriminating Chinese retroflex and dental affricates using VOT measurement algorithm and breathing power measurement algorithm. The system can be applied in automatic speech training of L2 Chinese learners who have difficulty distinguishing and pronouncing those sounds. Hsiao et al. (2016) developed The Chinese Listening and Speaking Diagnosis and Remedial Instruction (CLSDRI) system, which employs computerized diagnostic tests to diagnose L2 Chinese learner errors in listening comprehension and speaking, and delivers remedial instruction materials to learners to assist learning (see Chen and Hsu this volume; Lee et al. this volume). Automatic Essay Scoring technologies have also been introduced to TCSL where the assessment of L2 writing has been a perennial challenge (see Chang and Sung this volume).

Corpus and computational methods intersect. Corpus linguistic methods are computational to the extent that the processing and analysis of data from large corpora rely on digital and computational technology. When used for processing large bodies of computerized language materials, computational methods converge with corpus research. By analyzing natural language data in large quantities, computational and corpus methods provide powerful quantitative analysis inaccessible by intuition and introspection, and can provide a level of objectivity or "a layer of order" in the data "where none was previously suspected" (Stubbs 2001: 169). Such methods also complement experimental psycholinguistic research that can reveal what learners know or what they think they know about language but fails to reveal patterns in large-scale naturally occurring language (Fillmore 1992; Gries 2009; Gries et al. 2005). Based on data from the British National Corpus, Ellis et al. (2016b) analyzed the usage patterns of English verb argument constructions. They employed computational tools to investigate the verb selection preferences of these constructions and mapped out the semantic network structure of the verbs. They also explored factors that influence the learning of these constructions by measuring frequencies, semantic prototypicality and cohesion, as well as cue salience related to polysemy. The findings of Ellis et al. (2016b) strongly indicate that the use, processing, and learning of language are nonarbitrary, and opened up the problem space for future research to investigate the complexity of the interaction among the patterns, and to fine-tune our understanding of that complexity. At the operational level, when aimed directly to inform language learning and teaching, computational and corpus methods provide useful resources for L2 instruction. For example, using computational and corpus tools, Shih and Hsieh (2016) constructed a word dependency profile tool through automatically sketching syntagmatic relations of words in an untagged corpus based on dependency parses. The system provides a useful tool for learners of Chinese to visualize the collocation behavior of words, the knowledge of which is essential to the comprehension and production of linguistic conventions of Chinese.

The usage-based theory of language is still evolving, and the tasks of understanding the complexity of language and explicating mechanisms of language learning, which require increased data recording and increased sophistication in data analysis, are far from accomplished. Take input as an example. Researchers from various theoretical camps agree that input matters in learning a second language (Gass 1997; Piske and Young-Scholten 2008). There is the assumption that input flood, a teaching technique designed to inundate learners with massive input containing a target form, facilitates their intake of that form (Sharwood Smith 1985, 1991). However, as Madlener (2016) pointed out, there is no consensus as to exactly what kind of input structure effectively facilitates learning. Thus, everyone takes input for granted as a magic potion, yet no one is quite sure how to concoct one with a reliable measure of ingredients, and in practice, everyone makes their own from scratch, and hopes for the best. Essentially, there is great arbitrariness in how input is handled in L2 instruction. Madlener (2016) wanted to take a closer look at the structure and distributions of input and their effects on incidental learning. She designed a classroom training paradigm that manipulates input type frequency, token-type ratios, and surface structural similarity in authentic learning conditions to test the exact effects played by these measures on learners' ability to detect and extend pattern in learning. She found "consistent effects of more fine-grained input features" in terms of token and type frequency distributions, which suggests the inadequacy of a simplistic view of input flood.

Madlener's study highlights several important points. First, it shows how specific and testable hypotheses can be formulated within the usage-based model to test SLA constructs and pedagogical strategies that are taken for granted but poorly understood at a greater granularity. Second, it shows the possibility of developing teaching methods that are theoretically grounded and empirically tested and demonstrates what it takes to get there. Third, it reminds us that a full and fine-grained understanding of the complexity of language and language learning is far from a reality. Lastly, the discrepancy between Madlener's classroom training results and those obtained in Artificial Language Learning (ALL) experiments indicates the need for the triangulation of research methods and more work on the replicability of results in usage-based approaches.

The need to drum up the effort to explore language learning at a deeper level and the criticality of methodological triangulation are being recognized. Ellis (2017: 41–42) identified three future priorities that necessitate the triangulation of evidence from the complementary areas of research in Cognitive, Corpus, and Computational Linguistics, and require more sophisticated corpus and computational methods. These are:

(1) Analyzing the distributional characteristics of linguistic constructions and their meanings in large collections of language that are representative of the language that learners experience
(2) Conducting longitudinal analyses of learner language
(3) Conducting Natural Language Processing (NLP) or computational analyses of the dimensions of language complexity.

These tasks, Ellis emphasized, require increased effort in data recording and increased sophistication in data analysis. Ke (2012, 2018) envisioned an interdisciplinary research agenda for Chinese SLA. He articulated the need for international cooperation in building large-scale corpora with "broad scope of genres, registers, styles, text types, and learner backgrounds" including learner corpora with discourse data as part of that agenda, and stressed the importance of raising the "standard of selection and utilization of statistical analysis procedures" in the field. Similarly, Zhang and Tao (2018) called for more quantitative studies on learner corpora, to be triangulated with other kinds of empirical data for corroboration and validation. Without a doubt, corpus and computational methods, with their proven empirical strengths in detecting and modeling patterns of language use and learning, are essential tools for tackling these tasks of corpora construction, data recording, and analysis. As such they are crucial voices in the professional multilingualism that invigorates SLA research and informs instructed second language learning.

5 Conclusion

As a community of practice, we need to recognize the collective journey that has taken us so far. At the same time, we need to acknowledge the persisting barriers in the continuing professionalization of our field. These include the inaccessibility of SLA research to teachers and the lack of direct pedagogic utility of isolated research findings. These problems were raised two decades ago (Crookes 1997; Ellis 1997; Markee 1997) but continue to hinder the integration of research and practice today. Given these barriers, a call for a rational approach to TCSL must not put the blame and burden firstly and solely on the teaching practitioners, and must reflect on the accessibility and utility of theory and research. More important, as a community of practice, we must evaluate the theoretical and empirical soundness of research before we jump at its pedagogical implications in order for a professional multilingualism to be productive.

Because our knowledge of L2 learning is still incomplete, more robust empirical data are needed. The twenty-first century is witnessing an unprecedented boom of digital technology, the direct impact of which can be readily seen in the methodological sophistication of quantitative research based on large bodies of corpora, including L2 corpora. Corpus and computational methods developed in Corpus Linguistics and Computational Linguistics and NLP are making inroads into the field of SLA to throw light on how language is used and learned, and on the contingencies of usage and learning. The data processing and pattern detecting power of these methods make them indispensable for SLA research. With results from this fecund area of exploration gradually entering TCSL, a field with a history of professional multilingualism, and an eagerness to explore methodological innovations, we will likely see an increased interest in learner data, an increased interest in experimenting with usage-based instruction, and an increased demand for computational technology enabled methods for error detection and correction, as well as assessment of learning results, among many other application potentials.

References

Abrahamsson, N., & Hyltenstam, K. (2009). Age of onset and nativelikeness in a second language: Listener perception versus linguistic scrutiny. *Language Learning, 59*(2), 249–306.

Ambridge, B., & Lieven, E. V. M. (2011). Child language acquisition: Contrasting theoretical approaches. Cambridge: Cambridge University Press.

Anderson, J. R. (2000). *Learning and memory* (2nd ed.). New York: Wiley.

Arnon, I., & Snider, N. (2010). More than words: Frequency effects for multi-word phrases. *Journal of Memory and Language, 62*(1), 67–82.

Barcroft, J. (2013). *Input-based incremental vocabulary instruction for the L2 classroom: Innovative research and practices in second language acquisition and bilingualism*. New York: John Benjamins.

Barlow, M., & Kemmer, S. (2000). *Usage-based models of language*. Stanford, CA: CSLI Publications, Center for the Study of Language and Information.

Barsalou, L. W., Huttenlocher, J., & Lamberts, K. (1998). Basing categorization on individuals and events. *Cognitive Psychology, 36*(3), 203–272.

Beckner, C., Blythe, R., Bybee, J., Christiansen, M. H., Croft, W., Ellis, N. C., et al. (2009). Language is a complex adaptive system. Position paper. *Language Learning, 59*(S1), 1–26.

Behrens, H. (2009). Usage-based and emergentist approaches to language acquisition. *Linguistics, 47*(2), 383–411.

Behrens, H., & Pfänder, S. (2016). *Experience counts: Frequency effects in language*. Berlin: Walter de Gruyter.

Belzung, C., & Wigmore, P. (2013). *Neurogenesis and neural plasticity*. Dordrecht: Springer.

Blom, E., Paradis, J., & Duncan, T. (2012). Effects of input properties, vocabulary size, and L1 on the development of third person singular –s in child L2 English. *Language Learning, 62*(3), 965–994.

Bongaerts, T. (1999). Ultimate attainment in L2 pronunciation. The case of very advanced L2 learners. In D. Birdsong (Ed.), *Second language acquisition and the critical period hypothesis* (pp. 133–159). Mahwah, NJ: Lawrence Erlbaum.

Bruner, J. (1981). The social context of language acquisition. *Language & Communication, 1*(2), 155–178.

Bybee, J. (2006). From usage to grammar: The mind's response to repetition. *Language, 82*(4), 711–733.

Bybee, J. (2010). *Language, usage and cognition*. Cambridge: Cambridge University Press.

Bybee, J. (2013). Usage-based theory and exemplar representations of constructions. In T. Hoffmann & G. Trousdale (Eds.), *The Oxford handbook of construction grammar* (pp. 49–69). Oxford: Oxford University Press.

Bybee, J., & Hopper, P. J. (Eds.). (2001). *Frequency and the emergence of linguistic structure*. Amsterdam/Philadelphia: John Benjamins.

Byrnes, H. (1998). *Learning foreign and second languages: Perspectives in research and scholarship*. New York: Modern Language Association of America.

Byrnes, H. (2000). Shaping the discourse of a practice: The role of linguistics and psychology in language teaching and learning. *The Modern Language Journal, 84*(4), 472–494.

Byrnes, H. (2012). Advanced language proficiency. In S. M. Gass & A. Mackey (Eds.), *The Routledge handbook of second language acquisition* (pp. 506–521). London: Routledge.

Carpenter, M., Nagell, K., & Tomasello, M. (1998). Social cognition, joint attention, and communicative competence from 9 to 15 months of age. *Monograph of the Society for Research in Child Development, 63*(4), Serial no. 255.

Carpenter, M., Pennington, B., & Rogers, S. (2002). Interrelations among social-cognitive skills in young children with autism. *Journal of Autism and Developmental Disorders, 32*(2), 91–106.

Chomsky, N. (1965). *Aspects of the theory of syntax*. Cambridge: MIT Press.

Chomsky, N. (2002). *On nature and language*. Cambridge: Cambridge University Press.

Cook, G., Kasper, G., Ellis, N. C., & Larsen-Freeman, D. (2006). Language emergence. *Applied Linguistics, 27*(4), 554–740.

Crookes, G. (1997). SLA and language pedagogy. A socioeducational perspective. *Studies in Second Language Acquisition*, 19(1), 93–116.

Dąbrowska, E. (2008). The effects of frequency and neighbourhood density on adult speakers' productivity with Polish case inflections: An empirical test of usage-based approaches to morphology. *Journal of Memory and Language, 58*(4), 931–951.

DeKeyser, R. (2003). Implicit and explicit learning. In C. Doughty & M. Long (Eds.), *Handbook of second language acquisition* (pp. 313–348). Oxford: Blackwell.

Ebbinghaus, H. (1913). *Memory; a contribution to experimental psychology*. New York City: Teachers College, Columbia University.

Ellis, N. C. (1998). Emergentism, connectionism and language learning. *Language Learning, 48*(4), 631–664.

Ellis, N. C. (2008). The dynamics of second language emergence: Cycles of language use, language change, and language acquisition. *Modern Language Journal, 92*(2), 232–249.

Ellis, N. C. (2011). Implicit and explicit SLA and their interface. *Georgetown University Round Table on Languages and Linguistics*, 35–47.
Ellis, N. C. (2002). Frequency effects in language processing: A review with implications for theories of implicit and explicit language acquisition. *Studies in Second Language Acquisition, 24*(2), 143–188.
Ellis, N. C. (2006). Selective attention and transfer phenomena in L2 acquisition: Contingency, cue competition, salience, interference, overshadowing, blocking, and perceptual learning. *Applied Linguistics, 27*(2), 164–194.
Ellis, N. C. (2013). Second language acquisition. In G. Trousdale & T. Hoffmann (Eds.), *Oxford handbook of construction grammar* (pp. 365–378). Oxford: Oxford University Press.
Ellis, N. C. (2015). Cognitive and social aspects of learning from usage. In T. Cadierno & S. W. Eskildsen (Eds.), *Usage-based perspectives on second language learning* (pp. 49–73). Berlin/Boston: De Gruyter.
Ellis, N. C. (2017). Cognition, corpora, and computing: Triangulating research in usage-based language learning. *Language Learning, 67*(S1), 40–65.
Ellis, R. (1997). *SLA research and language teaching*. Oxford: Oxford University Press.
Ellis, R. (Ed.). (2001). *Form-focused instruction and second language learning*. Malden, MA: Blackwell.
Ellis, R. (2009). Correct feedback and teacher development. *L2 Journal, 1,* 3–18.
Ellis, N. C., & Ferreira, F., Jr. (2009). Construction learning as a function of frequency, frequency distribution, and function. *Modern Language Journal, 93*(3), 370–386.
Ellis, N. C., & Wulff, S. (2015). Usage-based approaches to SLA. In B. VanPatten & J. Williams (Eds.), *Theories in second language acquisition: An introduction* (2nd ed., pp. 75–93). New York: Routledge.
Ellis, N. C., Romer, U., & O'Donnell, M. B. (2016a). Constructions and usage-based approaches to language acquisition. *Language Learning, 66*(S1), 23–44.
Ellis, N. C., Romer, U., & O'Donnell, M. B. (2016b). Computational models of language usage, acquisition, and transmission. *Language Learning, 66*(S1), 241–278.
Eskildsen, S. W. (2008). Constructing another language—Usage-based linguistics in second language acquisition. *Applied Linguistics, 30*(3), 335–357.
Eskildsen, S. W. (2012). L2 Negation constructions at work. *Language Learning, 62*(2), 335–372.
Fillmore, C. J. (1992). "Corpus linguistics" or "Computer-aided armchair linguistics". In I. Svartvik (Ed.), *Directions in corpus linguistics* (pp. 35–60). Berlin: Mouton de Gruyter.
Fotos, S. (2002). Structure-based interactive task for the EFL grammar learner. In E. Hinkel & S. Fotos (Eds.), *New perspectives on grammar teaching in second language classrooms* (pp. 135–154). Mahwah, NJ: Lawrence Erlbaum.
Gass, S. M. (1997). *Input, interaction, and the second language learner*. Mahwah, NJ: Lawrence Erlbaum.
Goldberg, A. E. (1995). *Constructions: A Construction Grammar approach to argument structure*. Chicago: University of Chicago Press.
Goldberg, A. E. (2006). *Constructions at work: The nature of generalization in language*. Oxford: Oxford University Press.
Goldberg, A. E., & Casenhiser, D. (2008). Construction learning and second language acquisition. In P. Robinson & N. C. Ellis (Eds.), *Handbook of cognitive linguistics and second language acquisition* (pp. 197–215). New York: Routledge.
Goldberg, A. E., Casenhiser, D., & Sethuraman, N. (2004). Learning argument structure generalizations. *Cognitive Linguistics, 15*(3), 289–316.
Gries, S. T. (2006). Introduction. In S. T. Gries & A. Stefanowitsch (Eds.), *Corpora in Cognitive Linguistics: Corpus-based approaches to syntax and lexis* (pp. 1–17). Berlin: de Gruyter.
Gries, S. (2009). What is corpus linguistics? *Language and Linguistics Compass, 3*(5), 1–17.
Gries, S. (2015). Statistical methods in learner corpus research. In G. Gilquin, S. Granger, & F. Meunier (Eds.), *The Cambridge handbook of learner corpus research* (pp. 159–181). Cambridge: Cambridge University Press.

Gries, S., & Ellis, N. (2015). Statistical measures for usage-based linguistics. *Language Learning, 65*(S1), 228–255.

Gries, S., Hampe, B., & Schönefeld, D. (2005). Converging evidence: bringing together experimental and corpus data on the association of verbs and constructions. *Cognitive Linguistics, 16*(4), 635–676.

Han, Z.-H. (2004). *Fossilization in adult second language acquisition*. Clevedon, UK: Multilingual Matters.

Han, Z.-H. (2016). Research meets practice: Holding off and holding on. *Chinese as a Second Language, 51*(3), 236–251.

Han, Z.-H., & Odlin, T. (2006). Introduction. In Z.-H. Han & T. Odlin (Eds.), *Studies of fossilization in second language acquisition* (pp. 1–20). Clevedon, UK: Multilingual Matters.

Hofman, M. (2002). Plasticity in the adult brain: From genes to neurotherapy. In *Proceedings of the 22nd International Summer School of Brain Research*. Amsterdam/Boston: Elsevier.

Hoshino, A., & Yasuda, A. (2013). Automatic discrimination of pronunciations of Chinese retroflex and dental affricates. In M. Sun, M. Zhang, D. Lin, & H. Wang (Eds.), *Chinese computational linguistics and natural language processing based on naturally annotated big data* (pp. 303–314). Berlin/Heidelberg: Springer.

Hsiao, H.-S., Chang, C.-S., Lin, C.-Y., Chen, B., Wu, C.-H., & Lin, C.-Y. (2016). The development and evaluation of listening and speaking diagnosis and remedial teaching system. *British Journal of Educational Technology, 47*(2), 372–389.

Huang, C.-R., & Lenders, W. (2005). Computational linguistics and beyond: An introduction. In C.-R. Huang & W. Lenders (Eds.), *Computational linguistics and beyond* (pp. 1–16). Taipei: Academia Sinica.

Ibbotson, P. (2013). The scope of usage-based theory. *Frontiers in Psychology, 4,* 255.

Jiao, L., Kubler, C. C., & Zhang, W. (2011). *500 common Chinese idioms: An annotated frequency dictionary*. London/New York: Routledge.

Jing-Schmidt, Z. (2011). Zero anaphora in higher level Chinese writings across learner backgrounds. *Chinese Teaching in the World, 25*(2), 258–267.

Jing-Schmidt, Z. (2015). The place of linguistics in CSL teaching and teacher education: Toward a usage-based constructionist theoretical orientation. *Journal of Chinese Language Teachers Association, 50*(3), 1–22.

Jing-Schmidt, Z., & Peng, X. (2018). Linguistics theories and teaching Chinese as a second language. In C. Ke (Ed.), *The Routledge handbook of Chinese second language acquisition* (pp. 63–81). London: Routledge.

Jing-Schmidt, Z., Peng, X., & Chen, J.-Y. (2015). From corpus analysis to grammar instruction: Toward a usage-based constructionist approach to constructional stratification. *Journal of Chinese Language Teachers Association, 50*(2), 109–138.

Jurafsky, D., & Martin, J. (2008). *Natural language processing, speech recognition, and computational linguistics* (2nd ed.). Upper Saddle River, NJ: Prentice-Hall.

Kapatsinski, V. (2014). What is a grammar like? A usage-based constructionist perspective. *Linguistic Issues in Language Technology, 11*(1), 1–41.

Ke, C. (2012). Research in second language acquisition of Chinese: Where we are, where we are going. *Journal of the Chinese Language Teachers Association, 47*(3), 43–113.

Ke, C. (2018). Chinese SLA: Introduction and future directions. In C. Ke (Ed.), *The Routledge handbook of Chinese second language acquisition* (pp. 1–8). London: Routledge.

Ke, C., Lu, Y., & Pan, X. (2015). 汉语教师教学技能及二语习得理论知识的评估模式. (Assessing international Chinese language teachers' second language acquisition theoretical foundation and language pedagogy). *《世界汉语教学》(Chinese Teaching in the World), 29*(1), 111–129.

Kramsch, C. (2000). Second language acquisition, applied linguistics, and the teaching of foreign languages. *Modern Language Journal, 84*(3), 311–326.

Larsen-Freeman, D. (2011). A complexity theory approach to second language development/acquisition. In D. Atkinson (Ed.), *Alternative approaches to second language acquisition* (pp. 47–72). London: Routledge.

Li, X. (2014). Variation in subject pronominal expression in L2 Chinese. *Studies in Second Language Acquisition, 36*(1), 39–68.

Lieven, E. V. M., Pine, J. M., & Baldwin, G. (1997). Lexically-based learning and early grammatical development. *Journal of Child Language, 24*, 187–219.

Lyster, R., & Mori, H. (2006). Interactional feedback and instructional counterbalance. *Studies in Second Language Acquisition, 28*(2), 269–300.

Lyster, R., & Ranta, L. (1997). Corrective feedback and learner uptake: negotiation of form in communicative classrooms. *Studies in Second Language Acquisition, 19*(1), 37–66.

MacWhinney, B. (Ed.). (1999). *The emergence of language*. Mahwah, NJ: Lawrence Erlbaum Associates.

Macwhinney, B. (2005a). The emergence of linguistic form in time. *Connection Science, 17*(3–4), 191–211.

MacWhinney, B. (2005b). Extending the competition model. *International Journal of Bilingualism, 9*(1), 69–84.

MacWhinney, B. (2006). Emergent fossilization. In Z.-H. Han & T. Odlin (Eds.), *Studies of fossilization in second language acquisition* (pp. 134–156). Clevedon, UK: Multilingual Matters.

MacWhinney, B. (2012). The logic of the Unified Model. In S. Gass & A. Mackey (Eds.), *The Routledge handbook of second language acquisition* (pp. 211–227). New York, NY: Routledge.

MacWhinney, B. (2015). Multidimensional SLA. In T. Cadierno & S. W. Eskildsen (Eds.), *Usage-based perspectives on second language learning* (pp. 19–48). Berlin: De Gruyter.

Madlener, K. (2016). Input optimization: effects of type and token frequency manipulation in instructed second language learning. In H. Behrens & S. Pfänder (Eds.), *Experience counts: Frequency effects in language* (pp. 133–174). Berlin: De Gruyter.

Markee, N. (1997). Second language acquisition research: A resource for changing teachers' professional cultures? *The Modern Language Journal, 81*(1), 80–93.

Medin, D. L., & Schaffer, M. M. (1978). Context theory of classification learning. *Psychological Review, 85*(3), 207–238.

Medin, D. L., & Smith, E. E. (1981). Strategies in classification learning. *Journal of Experimental Psychology: Human Learning and Memory, 7*(4), 241–253.

Nosofsky, R. (1988). On exemplar-based exemplar representations: Reply to Ennis (1988). *Journal of Experimental Psychology: General, 117*(4), 412–414.

Nugent, M., & Slater, R. (2016). The language flagship: Creating expectations and opportunities for professional-level language learning in undergraduate education. In D. Murphy & K. Evans-Romaine (Eds.), *The U.S. language flagship program: Professional competence in a second language by graduation* (pp. 1–9). Clevedon, UK: Multilingual Matters.

Peterson, M. (2006). Learner interaction management in an avatar and chat-based virtual world. *Computer Assisted Language Learning, 19*(1), 79–103.

Peterson, M. (2010). Computerized games and simulations in computer-assisted language learning: A meta-analysis of research. *Simulation and Gaming: An Interdisciplinary Journal, 41*(1), 72–93.

Pine, J. M., Lieven, E. V. M., & Rowland, C. F. (1998). Comparing different models of the development of the English verb category. *Linguistics, 36*, 807–830.

Pinker, S. (1999). *Words and rules*. New York: Harper Perennial.

Piske, T., & Young-Scholten, M. (2008). *Input matters in SLA*. Clevedon: Channel View Publications.

Quine, W. (1960). *Word and object*. Cambridge, MA: MIT Press.

Reali, F. (2014). Frequency affects object relative clause processing: Some evidence in favor of usage-based accounts. *Language Learning, 64*(3), 685–714.

Rebuschat, P., & Williams, J. (2012). Implicit and explicit knowledge in second language acquisition. *Applied Psycholinguistics, 33*(4), 829–856.

Rosch, E., & Mervis, C. B. (1975). Family resemblances: Studies in the internal structure of categories. *Cognitive Psychology, 7*(4), 573–605.

Rossano, F., Fiedler, L., Tomasello, M., & Eccles, J. S. (2015). Preschoolers' understanding of the role of communication and cooperation in establishing property rights. *Developmental Psychology, 51*(2), 176–184.

Sale, A. (2016). *Environmental experience and plasticity of the developing brain*. Hoboken, NJ: Wiley/Blackwell.

Sato, M., & Lyster, R. (2012). Peer interaction and corrective feedback for accuracy and fluency development. *Studies in Second Language Acquisition, 34*(4), 591–626.

Schachter, J. (1989). Testing a proposed universal. In S. Gass & J. Schachter (Eds.), *Linguistic perspectives on second language acquisition* (pp. 73–88). Cambridge: Cambridge University Press.

Schachter, J. (1990). On the issue of completeness in second language acquisition. *Second Language Research, 6*(2), 93–124.

Schmidt, R. (1990). The role of consciousness in second language learning. *Applied Linguistics, 11*(2), 129–158.

Schmidt, R. (1993). Awareness and second language acquisition. *Annual Review of Applied Linguistics, 13*, 206–226.

Schulze, C., & Tomasello, M. (2015). 18-month-olds comprehend indirect communicative acts. *Cognition, 136*, 91–98.

Selinker, L. (1972). Interlanguage. *International Review of Applied Linguistics, 10*(2), 209–231.

Selinker, L., & Lamendella, J. (1978). Two perspectives on fossilization in interlanguage learning. *Interlanguage Studies Bulletin, 3*(2), 143–191.

Sharwood Smith, M. (1985). From input to intake: On argumentation in second language acquisition. In S. Gass & C. Madden (Eds.), *Input in second language acquisition* (pp. 394–403). Rowley, MA: Newbury House.

Sharwood Smith, M. (1991). Speaking to many minds: On the relevance of different types of language information on the L2 learner. *Second Language Research, 7*(2), 118–132.

Shih, M.-H., & Hsieh, S.-K. (2016). Word dependency sketch for Chinese language learning. *Concentric, 42*(1), 45–72.

Skehan, P. (1998). Task-based instruction. *Annual Review of Applied Linguistics, 18*, 268–286.

Smith, E. R. (1991). Illusory correlation in a simulated exemplar-based memory. *Journal of Experimental Social Psychology, 27*(2), 107–123.

Smith, E. R., & Zarate, M. A. (1992). Exemplar-based model of social judgment. *Psychological Review, 99*(1), 3–21.

Sockett, G., & Kusyk, M. (2015). Online informal learning of English: Frequency effects in the uptake of chunks of language from participation in web-based activities. In T. Cadierno & S. W. Eskildsen (Eds.), *Usage-based perspectives on second language learning* (pp. 153–177). Berlin: De Gruyter Mouton.

Stubbs, M. (2001). Texts, corpora, and problems of interpretation: A response to Widdowson. *Applied Linguistics, 22*(2), 149–172.

Tao, H. (Ed.). (2016). *Integrating Chinese linguistic research and language teaching and learning*. Amsterdam: John Benjamins.

The Douglas Fir Group. (2016). A transdisciplinary framework for SLA in a multilingual world. *Modern Language Journal, 100*(S1), 19–47.

Tomasello, M. (1992). *First verbs: A case study of early grammatical development*. Cambridge/New York: Cambridge University Press.

Tomasello, M. (1999). *The cultural origins of human cognition*. Cambridge, MA: Harvard University Press.

Tomasello, M. (2000). First steps toward a usage-based theory of language acquisition. *Cognitive Linguistics, 11*(1–2), 61–82.

Tomasello, M. (2003). *Constructing a language: A usage-based theory of language acquisition*. Cambridge, MA: Harvard University Press.

Tomasello, M. (2008). *Origins of human communication*. Cambridge, MA: MIT Press.

Tomasello, M., & Farrar, M. J. (1986). Joint attention and early language. *Child Development, 57*(6), 1454–1463.

Tragant, E., & Muñoz, C. (2004). Second Language acquisition and language teaching. *International Journal of English Studies, 4*(1), 197–219.

Tummers, J., Heylen, K., & Geeraerts, D. (2005). Usage-based approaches in Cognitive Linguistics: A technical state of the art. *Corpus Linguistics and Linguistic Theory, 1*(2), 225–261.

Van Beuningen, C. G., De Jong, N. H., & Kuiken, F. (2012). Evidence on the effectiveness of comprehensive error correction in second language writing. *Language Learning, 62*(1), 1–41.

Verspoor, M., & Nguyen, T. P. H. (2015). A Dynamic usage-based approach to second language teaching. In T. Cadierno & S. Eskildsen (Eds.), *Usage-based perspectives on second language learning* (pp. 305–328). Berlin: De Gruyter.

Winke, P. (2013). An investigation into second language aptitude for advanced Chinese language learning. *Modern Language Journal, 97*(1), 109–130.

Wolter, B., & Gyllstad, H. (2013). Frequency of input and L2 collocational processing: A comparison of congruent and incongruent collocations. *Studies in Second Language Acquisition, 35*(3), 451–482.

Wulff, S. (2010). *Rethinking idiomaticity: A usage-based approach*. London: Continuum.

Xiao, R., Rayson, P., & McEnery, T. (2009). *A frequency dictionary of Mandarin Chinese: Core vocabulary for learners*. London: Routledge.

Xu, Q. (2016). Item-based foreign language learning of give ditransitive constructions: Evidence from corpus research. *System, 63,* 65–76.

Zhang, J., & Lu, X. (2013). Variability in Chinese as a foreign language learners' development of the Chinese numeral classifier system. *Modern Language Journal, 97*(S1), 46–60.

Zhang, J., & Tao, H. (2018). Corpus Linguistics and Chinese SLA. In C. Ke (Ed.), *The Routledge handbook of Chinese second language acquisition* (pp. 48–63). London: Routledge.

The Corpus Approach to the Teaching and Learning of Chinese as an L1 and an L2 in Retrospect

Jiajin Xu

Abstract The use of corpora in the teaching and learning of Chinese has a history of nearly a century. Pedagogically oriented Chinese corpus studies have originated on a solid methodological footing before computers were available. The creation of concordances and character/word lists, coupled with quantitative analyses of sentence patterns, have offered fascinating insights into Chinese textbook compilation and syllabus design. Such corpus findings have illuminated what lexical items and grammatical patterns should be taught, and in what order vocabulary and grammar points should be presented. Over the last few decades, the craze for Chinese interlanguage corpora has been largely motivated by China's growing global influence. The lexico-grammatical performance in the spoken and written production of Chinese as a second language (CSL) learners has been systematically investigated. Both corpus-based L1 and L2 Chinese studies have been fairly successful in terms of the description of the Chinese (inter)language, but there is still much room for pedagogical implementation, that is, to transform the research into classroom friendly teaching materials.

1 Preamble

A corpus is now commonly understood as a large collection of a representative sample of natural texts, based on which language studies, theoretical or applied, can be conducted with the aid of computer tools (Biber et al. 1998; Hunston 2002). It is safe to say that corpora and corpus methodology have secured a solid niche in present-day linguistics and applied linguistics. The main appeal of the corpus approach to language studies is characterised by the potential of quantitative profiling of actual language use.

J. Xu (✉)
Beijing Foreign Studies University, Beijing, China
e-mail: xujiajin@bfsu.edu.cn

X. Lu and B. Chen (eds.), *Computational and Corpus Approaches to Chinese Language Learning*, Chinese Language Learning Sciences,
https://doi.org/10.1007/978-981-13-3570-9_3

The term 'corpus linguistics' appeared as early as 1959 (Voegelin 1959: 216), 'but its roots go way back, unless we restrict the term to the use of texts in electronic form' (Johansson 2011: 115). The early non-machine readable corpora are variously called 'pre-computer corpora', 'pre-electronic corpora', or 'corpora B.C.[1]' (Francis 1992). Thus, the concept of 'corpus' and its related 'corpus method(ology)' and 'corpus approach' in this chapter will refer broadly to both pre-electronic and electronic language databases and their respective theoretical constructs.

Before the advent of computers, the idea of a 'corpus methodology' or a 'corpus approach' has long been experimented and practiced in applied linguistics. For example, around 1820 John Freeman (1843) compiled a frequency list of English words based on approximately 20,000 words to teach adults to read. In 1838,[2] Issac Pitman devised the alphabetic and numerical arrangements of frequent words based on 10,000 words taken from 20 books, 500 from each. Pitman's word list was meant to facilitate the learning of stenography, the practice of writing English words in shorthand. Similar stenography-oriented corpus work was published by German scholar Fredrick Kaeding (1897). Early corpus work better known to the field of language education is Thorndike's (1921, 1931, 1944) corpus-based word books for language teachers.

In this review chapter, both pre-electronic and computerised corpus work will be considered with due reverence. Corpus methodology in pre-computer age may well account for the notion of 'innovation' in language teaching and learning. Admirable to contemporary scholars, early corpus workers tallied individual occurrences of language items all by hand, and formulated probabilistic claims about language use and applied them to pedagogic praxis.

Previous reviews on Chinese corpus linguistics aimed at a comprehensive introduction to the construction of corpora and the corpus research of all kinds (e.g. Feng 2006; McEnery and Xiao 2016; Xu 2015), in which the account on corpus-based Chinese language teaching and learning were cursory. This article, however, will mainly focus on the corpus approach to language teaching and learning of Chinese, both as a mother tongue and a second language. Moreover, pedagogically informed Chinese corpus research and practice in Chinese mainland, Hong Kong, Taiwan and overseas will all be addressed *passim* in this chapter.

---

[1] 'B.C.' here is Nelson Francis' play on words, meaning 'Before Computer' rather than its literal sense 'Before Christ'.

[2] Issac Pitman's word frequency list was published in 1843 in *The Phonotypic Journal*, but the research was done in 1838 (Pitman 1843: 161).

2 Key Corpus Projects in Teaching and Learning Chinese as an L1

2.1 First Concordance Projects for Chinese Classics Exegesis

The earliest Chinese corpus projects commenced in China around the 1920s and were motivated by classic exegesis and basic literacy. Back to the Qing Dynasty (A.D. 1644–1911), mainstream scholars worked on Chinese literary and metaphysical canons. After the downfall of China's last feudal dynasty, some elite Chinese scholars committed themselves to collating the myriad of Chinese classics. Stemming from dissatisfaction with the hundreds of contradicting and confusing annotations and interpretations of Chinese philosophical canon *Lao Tzu's Tao-Te-Ching*, the Western-educated Admiral 蔡廷干 Ting-Kan Tsai (1861–1935) compiled probably the first ever Chinese concordance 老解老 *Laojielao 'A Synthetic Study of Lao Tzu's Tao-Te-Ching in Chinese'* (1922). The text of *Tao-Te-Ching*, in this case, was considered a corpus, based on which a frequency list of all characters was created. The frequency count of a character and the original sentences and chapters in which it appeared were presented (as illustrated in Fig. 1 where the sixth character 無 occurs 102 times). One of the primary purposes of the concordance was meant to be a learning aid for younger generations to understand *Tao-Te-Ching*, especially when such key philosophical terms as 無 wu 'nothingness' was considered elusive and ambiguous given limited context.

Tsai's concordance initiative was acclaimed and shortly followed up by William Huang's (1893–1980) *Harvard-Yenching Institute Sinological Index Series* from the early 1930s (Hung 1931, 1932: 9–10). It was a gigantic enterprise which published a total of 64 titles in 77 volumes of concordances of Chinese classics from 1931 to 1950 (Huang 1962–1963: 8), such as the complete concordances of 易经 *Yijing* 'Book of Changes', 礼记 *Liji* 'The Classic of Rites', 论语 *Lunyu* 'The Analects', 孟子 *Mengzi* 'The Works of Mencius', and the like. The first volume of the index series is 说苑引得 *Shuoyuan Yinde* 'Index to Shuo Yuan' (Hung 1931), and the fourth volume (Hung 1932)—引得说 *Yinde Shuo* 'On Indexing'—of the series is a theoretical work in which Chinese concordance method 中国字庋擷 *Zhongguo zi guixie* 'Chinese character based retrieving' was formulated. Hung (ibid.: 8) explains that 引得 is the transliteration of English terminology 'index', and also known as 堪靠灯 *kenkaodeng* whose English equivalent is 'concordance'. Hung prefers the term 'index' to its synonymous counterpart 'concordance'; the two are not exactly the same though. The Index Series has become a key resource for learners and researchers of Chinese canons.

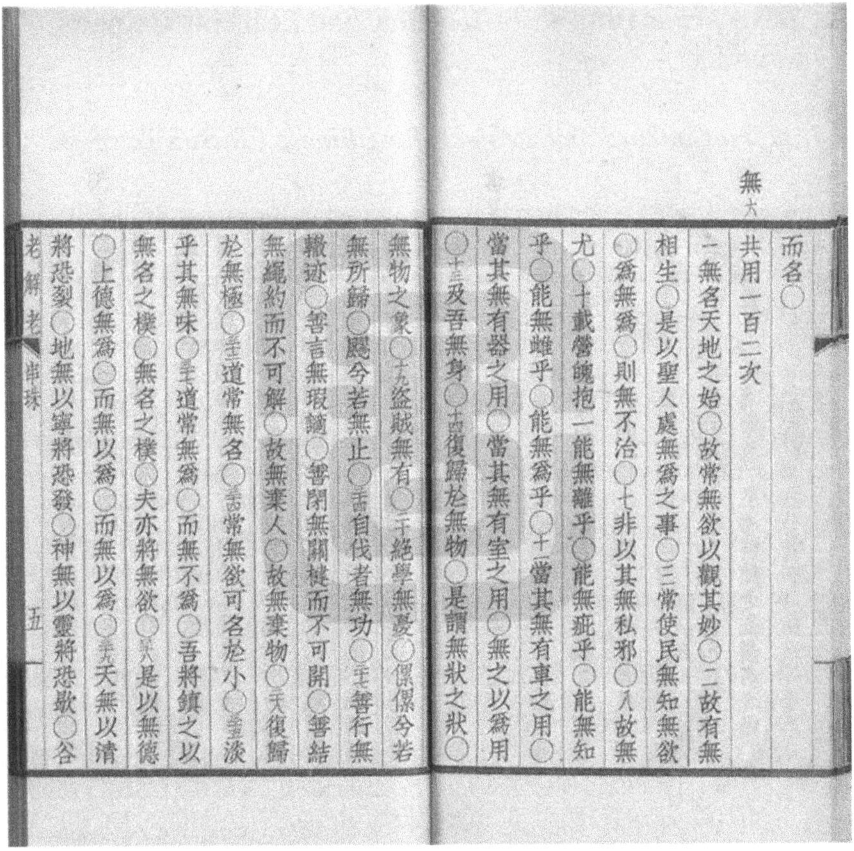

Fig. 1 A snapshot of *Laojielao 'A synthetic study of Lao Tzu's Tao-Te-Ching in Chinese'* concordances (p. 51) (The two pages shown here present part of the concordance of the 102 occurrences of 無 'Nothingness' in *Tao-Te-Ching*. The circles between the lines serve as the separator of 無 sentences. The smaller font size numerals attached to the initial position of some sentences, such as 一 before 無名天地之始, indicate the chapter number where the sentence can be found in *Tao-Te-Ching*)

2.2 *Pre-computer Chinese Corpus-Based Character Lists and Chinese Textbooks for Basic Literacy*

In the beginning years of the twentieth century, China experienced great political turbulence and instability. Against this backdrop, the massive number of illiterates turned out an imminent problem for the government at the time. The psychologist and educationalist 陈鹤琴 Heqin Chen addressed the critical social issue by virtue of a corpus-based project on compiling a Chinese character list. 'While the data used in Chen was not computerised, his list of basic Chinese characters was nevertheless corpus-based' (McEnery and Xiao 2016: 439). The intended goal of the project was to

育 教 新

A 字彙材料表

兒童用書類

同列於下：

專論 語體文應用字彙

書名	卷冊	字之數目
全世界的小孩子 (中)	第一集	4402
同上	第三集 第四集	9489
同上	第五集 第六集	9135
兒童文學故事 (中)	第一集	811
同上	第二集	1241
同上	第三集	1433
兒童文學小說 (中)	第一集	1030
兒童詩歌 (商)	第一冊	1267

Fig. 2 A snapshot of text sampling in *Yutiwen yingyong zihui* '*Characters used in vernacular Chinese*' (Chen 1922: 990)

survey, from a language education curriculum perspective, how many characters and in what sequence the characters should be exposed to illiterate learners of Chinese.

Chen and his nine associates, between 1919 and 1921, collected vernacular Chinese (rather than classical Chinese used by intellectuals and aristocrats) texts totalling 554,478 characters from a wide spread of genres, ranging from children's literature, news, magazines and vernacular Chinese fiction. A frequency list of characters (Chen 1922, see Figs. 2 and 3) was created and sorted in both radical and frequency order. Four thousand two hundred and sixty-one distinct characters were identified from the corpus. Chen's list was widely known as 语体文应用字汇 *Yutiwen yingyong zihui* 'Characters used in vernacular Chinese'. It was later expanded by Chen himself with a larger corpus of 902,678 characters (Chen 1928) and significantly updated by Liu (1926) and Ao (1929a, b) with more everyday and practical Chinese writing text samples.

Chen's corpus work was immediately hailed by Chinese educators and adopted in Chinese textbooks (Tao and Zhu 1923; Ao 1929a, b). Graded character lists based on Chen's 4261 characters became the vocabulary selection criterion for many Chinese textbooks. For instance, about one thousand frequent characters served as the word ladder, so to speak, for all series of the *Pingmin*[3] *Jiaoyu* 'Mass Education' textbooks. The series were sold for more than three million (Liu 1926: 1) copies after their publication in about 3 years. This was phenomenal given the population of 350 million Chinese people in the 1920s.

[3]*Pingmin* was defined by the leaders of the Mass Education Movement as illiterates (Tao and Zhu 1923: 43).

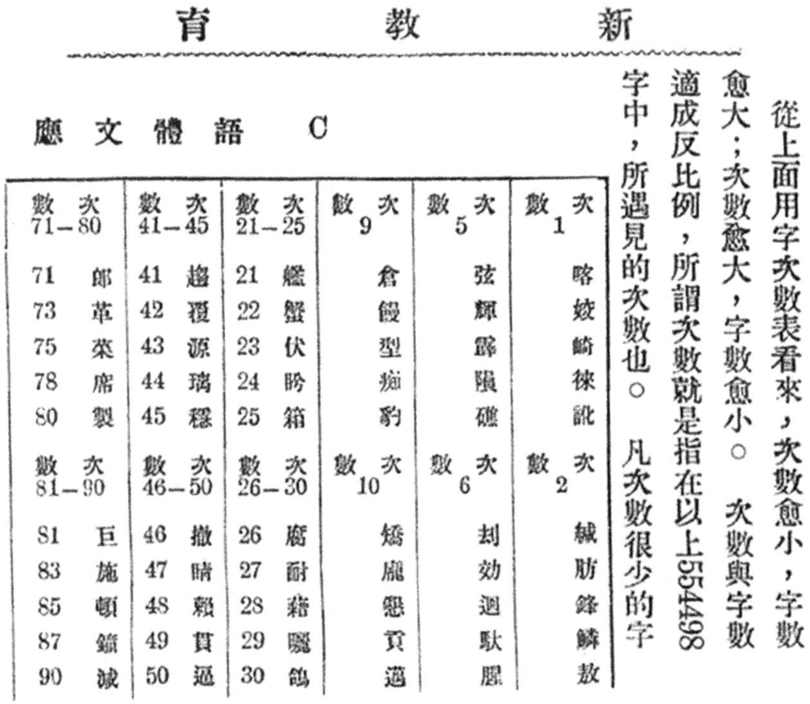

新教育

導論 語體文應用字彙

從上面用字次數表看來，次數愈小，字數愈大；次數愈大，字數愈小。次數與字數適成反比例，所謂次數就是指在以上554498字中，所遇見的次數也。凡次數很少的字

C 語體文應

次數 1	次數 5	次數 9	次數 21–25	次數 41–45	次數 71–80
喀	弦	倉	21 艦	41 趨	71 郎
姣	輝	餿	22 蟹	42 覆	73 革
崎	霹	型	23 伏	43 源	75 桨
徠	隕	痴	24 盼	44 璃	78 席
訛	礁	豹	25 箱	45 穩	80 製
次數 2	**次數 6**	**次數 10**	**次數 26–30**	**次數 46–50**	**次數 81–90**
絨	封	矯	26 瘸	46 撤	81 巨
肪	効	龐	27 耐	47 晴	83 施
鋒	迴	懇	28 籍	48 賴	85 頓
鱗	馱	貢	29 曬	49 貫	87 鎮
敖	腮	遒	30 鴿	50 涵	90 減

Fig. 3 A snapshot of character counting in *Yutiwen yingyong zihui* '*Characters used in vernacular Chinese*' (Chen 1922: 994)

The use of Chinese textbooks with careful vocabulary control was part of the nationwide mass education movement that attempted to educate the illiterates in an efficient manner. That is to say, the character list enabled instructors to teach the most common Chinese characters to illiterates in cities, in rural areas, and in the army during their limited time after work. Listed below are a few textbooks used at that time.

(1) Book 1–Book 3 of 平民千字课 *Pingmin qianzi ke* 'Foundation characters' by 晏阳初 Y. C. James Yen and 傅葆琛 Daniel C. Fu (1924) of the National Association of Mass Education Movement. About 300 characters were allocated to each book. The series were Romanised and translated into English under the name of '1000 Chinese Foundation Characters' by William White to be used by Western learners of Chinese. The 1000 Chinese characters were divided into four levels and 250 characters for each level. Its international students oriented edition was published by the University of Toronto in 1944.

(2) Book 1–Book 4 of 平民千字课 *Pingmin qianzi ke* 'Early Chinese lessons for illiterates' compiled by 陶知行 Zhixing Tao[4] and 朱经农 Jingnong Zhu. Book 1 was published in 1923 by the Commercial Press.
(3) Book 1–Book 4 of 市民千字课 *Shimin qianzi ke* 'Textbook of one thousand characters for townspeople' compiled by the National Association of Mass Education Movement (1928).
(4) Book 1–Book 4 of 农民千字课 *Nongmin qianzi ke* '1000 Chinese foundation characters for peasants' compiled by the National Association of Mass Education Movement (1922a).
(5) Book 1–Book 4 of 士兵千字课 *Shibing qianzi ke* '1000 Chinese foundation characters for servicemen' compiled by the National Association of Mass Education Movement (1922b).

Amongst them, in addition to the better-known Heqin Chen's (1922) character list and Zhixing Tao and Jingnong Zhu's corpus-informed texts, Y. C. James Yen and his language education projects merit special mention. Yen received his PhD from Yale University. Upon his graduation in 1918 which was the time of World War I, he went to France as a volunteer for the Y.M.C.A. to teach the 20,000 illiterate Chinese labourers to read. Yen developed a basic Chinese vocabulary of about 1300 characters in his interaction with the coolies. His basic Chinese vocabulary was integrated into his Foundation Chinese textbooks. Yen and Chen developed their 1000 basic characters independently, and luckily two character lists share over 80% of the characters (Yen 1922: 1012).

Yen and Tao were close partners in the so-called National Association of Mass Education Movements which was first organised by Yen in Beijing in 1923. In 1921, Zhixing Tao and other educationists founded the China Education Improvement Society in Nanjing, the then capital of China at the time. The two leading educationalists and activists of China at the time joined hand in the national campaign to combat illiteracy. The like-minded twin-star scholars tried their utmost to ameliorate the overall literacy situation on a 'maximum vocabulary and minimum time' basis. The core vocabulary formed the basis of their syllabus of Chinese teaching, and the 1000 characters came from their experimental method of collecting frequently used characters in real life. The underlying idea here is none other than corpus methodology.

Heqin Chen's character list can be regarded as a general purpose common core Chinese vocabulary. Specialised vocabulary was also counted up in existing compilations of Chinese textbooks for different target readerships. For instance, James

---

[4]陶知行 Zhixing Tao was an early alias of the better-known Chinese educationalist 陶行知 Xingzhi Tao. The difference in name says something about the transformation of his philosophy. Influenced by Chinese Confucianist scholar 王阳明 Wang (1472–1529), Tao (1891–1946) took his name *Zhixing* (meaning knowledge-action) in the 1910s and *Xingzhi* (meaning action-knowledge) in 1934 (Tao 1934: 286–287). Both names, *Zhixing* and *Xingzhi*, showed Tao's identification with Yangming Wang's theory of 知行合一 *zhi xing he yi* 'unity of knowledge and action'. When *Xingzhi* was adopted, Tao seemed to prioritise *xing* (action) over *zhi* (knowledge), which suggested that knowledge was derived from empirical engagement (Boorman 1970: 243–244; Browning and Bunge 2009: 388).

Yen's collaborator Daniel Fu collected plenty of texts of farming, gardening, contracts, almanacs, invitation letters, and other practical writings by Chinese farmers and discovered more characters which were not on Heqin Chen's and James Yen's lists, when he prepared the Chinese textbooks for farmers. The new characters that Fu found could successfully distinguish general Chinese from farming Chinese, and served the very learning need of illiterate farmers.

To summarise the early, pre-computer corpus-based language education, it is clear to see that 100 years ago in China the most pressing concern was the eradication of illiteracy. The empirically grounded character lists and the corresponding textbooks proved to be extremely effective and helpful to common people of all walks of life. The textbooks had been popular for about two decades, but the momentum was suspended and discontinued due to the power change in 1949.

2.3 Computer Corpus-Based Lexical Studies for the Teaching and Learning of Chinese

Chen and Yen type of corpus-based language teaching and learning endeavour were unheard of until the years after the Cultural Revolution (1966–1978). From 1979 onwards, corpus projects started to grow along a clearly uphill trajectory in different parts of China, and computer corpora played a central role in it.

Since the late 1970s and the early 1980s, an increasing number of corpus projects contributed to the teaching of Chinese language in one way or another. The greatest number of new character lists and tokenised word lists had been made available based on larger updated corpora.

The following list serves as a quick overview of the key corpus-based Chinese lexical frequency lists. Please refer to Xu (2015) for a comprehensive review.

(1) Liu (1973). Frequency Dictionary of Chinese Words.
(2) Bei and Zhang (1988). Hanzi Pindu Tongji [Frequency Calculation of Chinese Characters].
(3) Liu et al. (1990). Xiandai Hanyu Changyong Ci Cipin Cidian [A Dictionary of Frequency of Modern Chinese Words].
(4) China State Language Commission and China State Bureau of Standards. (1992). Xiandai Hanyu Zipin Tongji Biao [A Frequency List of Modern Chinese Characters].
(5) Huang et al. (1996). The Academia Sinica Balanced Corpus for Mandarin Chinese.
(6) Tsou et al. (1997). LIVAC (LInguistic VAriation in Chinese communities) Synchronous Corpus.
(7) Zhang (1999). The Dynamic Circulation Corpus (DCC).
(8) Xiao et al. (2009). A Frequency Dictionary of Mandarin Chinese.

The latest national achievement of the corpus-based Chinese lexical project is 通用规范汉字表 *Tongyong Guifan Hanzi Biao* 'A General Service List of Chinese

Characters'. The character list was compiled by the Chinese State Language Commission and officially released by China's State Council in June 2013. The general service character list is made up of three graded character lists: 3500 basic characters as Level One, 3000 characters as Level Two, and Level Three with 1605 proper nouns, technical, domain-specific and archaic Chinese characters. The lists, especially the first two levels, are based on the frequency counts of the Chinese National Corpus. Other character lists, such as Bei and Zhang (1988) and Zhang (1999), were also integrated into the list.

Once an officially approved character list is in place, language pedagogy professionals, and scholars do not need to build a corpus or create character lists on their own, as the national character is based on a large and balanced corpus of modern Chinese—the Chinese National Corpus.

Most Chinese corpus projects reviewed so far focus on the creation of a lexical frequency list, and some of them produce both frequency lists and their document frequency, namely, the distribution across different genres or text types. However, this is still insufficient from a language curriculum perspective.

2.4 Computer Corpus-Based Grammatical Studies for the Teaching and Learning of Chinese

Corpus-based grammatical studies are far fewer than that of corpus-based lexical studies. During pre-computer time, the quantitative analysis of sentence patterns was seldom, if ever seen. When computer technology is available, the calculation of sentence patterns is still an underdeveloped field. Amongst the very few corpus-based grammatical studies for Chinese pedagogic purposes, Shuhua Zhao's 现代汉语基本句型 *Xiandai Hanyu Jiben Juxing* 'Basic Sentence Patterns of Modern Chinese' (The Sentence Pattern Research Group at Beijing Language Institute 1989a, b, c, 1990, 1991)[5] is a project that deserves special attention. Zhao and her project team made an exhaustive counting of all major sentence patterns in some elementary and secondary school Chinese textbooks as well as in some intensive Chinese reading textbooks used for college students.

The occurrence and distribution across different programme levels of broad sentence types in Chinese textbooks, such as declaratives, general interrogatives, rhetorical questions, imperatives, exclamatory, and negative sentences were systematically tallied and reported. One of their statistical reports is reproduced in Table 1.

In a similar fashion, grammatical categories were computed, for instance, the use of sentences with a lexical verbal phrase predicate, focus constructions 是…的 *shi…de*, existential sentences, 把 *ba*-constructions, 被 *bei*-constructions, serial verb constructions, and so forth.

[5]赵淑华 Shaohua Zhao was the lead scholar and director of the Sentence Pattern Research Group at Beijing Language Institute.

Table 1 An example of Zhao's statistical tables of Chinese sentence patterns (Zhao et al. 1995: 16)

Sent. type	Textbook								
	College Chinese (Elementary)					College Chinese (Intermediate)			
	Bk 1	Bk 2	Bk 3	Subtotal	% of all sent.	Bk 1	Bk 2	Subtotal	% of all sent.
Declarative	415	801	1660	2885	83.45	1837	2854	4691	89.3
General interrogative	148	128	150	426	12.32	67	151	218	4.15
Rhetorical question	1	3	29	33	0.96	52	87	139	2.65
Imperative	38	21	10	69	2.00	46	79	125	2.38
Exclamatory	3	13	28	44	1.27	30	50	80	1.52
Total	605	966	1886	3457		2032	3221	5253	
Negative[a]	42	73	173	290	8.39	257	424	681	12.96

[a]The negative sentence frequency counts were not included in the total number of the sentence types, but placed underneath the Total row. This last row featuring the negative sentences has been transcribed exactly as found in the source table

This comprehensive sentence pattern project proves to be a solid and sound resource for the understanding of the general patterns of Chinese language use at the syntactic level in primary, secondary and tertiary Chinese language textbooks. It is needless to say that Zhao's research is a great resource for Chinese as a second language teaching and learning as well. As a matter of fact, the project was largely meant to serve the purpose of language teaching for CSL in the first place. Essentially, the description of grammatical patterns goes far beyond the teaching of Chinese as a second language (TCSL). As Zhao claimed in the Sentence Pattern Research Group at Beijing Language Institute (1989a), the results of the project would become an important resource for Chinese textbook compilation, Chinese syntactic studies in general, as well as natural language processing applications such as machine translation.

The sentence pattern database has been chiefly employed to look for and sort out frequent and less frequent, typical simple and complex sentence patterns for language educators and language teachers. As it is commonly observed, grammatical change is far less dramatic than it is in the case of lexis. This means that research conducted around 1990 is still of currency and validity for language education today.

2.5 L1 Chinese Production Corpora: Collections of School Pupils' Essays

The Chinese corpus projects discussed so far can be understood as the 'input corpus' (Sugiura 2002: 316; Nesselhauf 2004: 146)[6] work. The language input here refers to Chinese language teaching textbooks and/or newspapers, fiction, essays etc. that learners are likely to read in real life. The corpus compliers can gather texts from different input sources, make statistical claims about Chinese characters, words, phrases and sentences, and eventually turn them into teaching and learning resources. However, the language output, or production, of native Chinese speakers has not been attended to in real earnest in corpus-based Chinese studies. The Chinese school pupil's essay corpus developed at the Institute of Modern Educational Technology, Beijing Normal University was an important undertaking of L1 Chinese output corpus (Wei et al. 2008). In the project report, as of August 2007, the corpus contained over 11 million characters of Chinese texts from elementary and secondary school pupils of five grades (i.e. first to fifth graders) across China. 162 schools (148 elementary schools and 14 secondary schools) were involved, and seven cities were covered (namely Beijing, Fengning, Dalian, Guangzhou, Shenzhen, Xiamen and Hong Kong). To a large extent, the databank was developmental in the sense that Chinese essays of the same groups of pupils were archived and arranged in a chronological order (Table 2).

---

[6]The term 'input corpus' is used by some learner corpus linguists meaning the collection of learners' language exposures such as teachers' talk in class as well as the written texts that the learners are confronted with in learning. In this article, input corpora mainly refer to the written texts, textbooks in particular.

Table 2 Some key information of the school pupil essays

Categories	Statistics
Number of essays	79,244
Chinese characters	11,456,403
Number of pupils	2164

A query system was developed for the corpus; both standard queries and queries with sociolinguistic variables (e.g. region, school type, year of entering grade one, date of writing, grade, etc.) were enabled. All the texts were tagged for part of speech and annotated for syntactic patterns; therefore, word-class and grammatical category based queries were also available. Unfortunately, the corpus is not publicly accessible. The construction of learner production corpora of this kind should be encouraged, and it would be very much desirable to promote the sharing of corpus resources among language researchers and practitioners at large.

Quantitative analysis of Chinese language proudly emerged nearly a century ago at a very high standard in terms of the quality of research and the theoretical and practical impact they had on Chinese language education. Over the years, the majority of pedagogically oriented Chinese corpus research has been on the building of lexical frequency lists, viz. character lists and tokenised word lists. The corpus texts focus more on Chinese language input, e.g. Chinese textbooks or newspapers, magazines, popular readings and fiction. Less attention was directed to native Chinese learners' L1 production. Besides, corpora of Chinese for specific and academic purposes need special attention (cf. Chen and Tao this volume).

3 Key Corpus Projects in Teaching and Learning Chinese as an L2

The last two decades have seen a development boom in corpus-based Chinese studies for Teaching Chinese as a Second Language due to China's growing global influence. As such, the construction of Chinese interlanguage corpora has become very popular in the wake of the augmented enrolment of international learners of Chinese. Learner corpora started to emerge in the West around 1993, according to Granger (2015: 7). The first Chinese learner corpus project began at Beijing Language and Culture University also in 1993 independently without any scholarly communication with the Western corpus linguists. Unlike the development of L1 Chinese corpus research, L2 Chinese corpus research, from its onset, prioritised learner production data. Chinese L2 input corpora only caught up at a later stage. Note that most L1 Chinese lexical frequency list projects, including some recent ones such as Xiao et al. (2009), may well be adopted for the teaching and learning of Chinese as an L2.

3.1 L2 Learner Chinese Corpora

The earliest corpus-based interlanguage Chinese studies date back to 1993 at the Beijing Language Institute, now Beijing Language and Culture University (BLCU) (Chu and Chen 1993). The corpus, consisting of the first Chinese interlanguage dataset, was described at length in Chen (1996). The overall corpus size was about 3.5 million characters, and a re-sampled core L2 Chinese learner corpus was about one million characters. 23 textual and sociolinguistic variables were marked up. All the student essays in the Chu and Chen's corpus were sentence segmented, tokenised and tagged for part of speech categories (Table 3).

BLCU's Chinese interlanguage corpus construction was followed up in the late 1990s and the early 2000s by the hitherto most frequently cited L2 Chinese learner corpus, *HSK (Hanyu Shuiping Kaoshi) Dongtai Zuowen Yuliaoku 'Chinese Proficiency Test Dynamic Essay Corpus'* (Zhang 2003). The first release of the HSK corpus contained more than 20,000 essays written by HSK test-takers starting in 1992, and as the corpus keeps growing, the modifier 'dynamic' is added to the corpus name.

BLCU's L2 Chinese learner corpus work is now being upgraded to a globally-oriented interlanguage Chinese corpus project—the International Corpus of Learner Chinese. The projected corpus size will be 50 million characters, including 45 million written interlanguage Chinese and five million spoken interlanguage Chinese (Cui and Zhang 2011).

BLCU has been the leader in L2 Chinese learner corpus research. Other research teams in the field, however, have developed their own distinctive Chinese interlanguage corpus projects, such as learner corpora with intensive annotation on character misspelling as well as more balanced corpora of spoken and written learner Chinese.

The writing of Chinese characters is supposedly the hardest part of Chinese learning. The L2 Chinese learner corpus developed at the National Taiwan Normal University (Teng et al. 2007) is arguably the earliest Chinese interlanguage corpus which has a specific focus on (traditional) Chinese character writing errors. In Phase I of the project, 2457 instances of misspelling were collected from 72 learners of Chinese from 22 countries. An additional 52 learners' data were archived and 1858 misspellings were annotated for Phrase II. All the misspellings were classified into one of nine error types (i.e. *quesheng* 'omission', *zengbu* 'addition', *daihuan*

Table 3 Information on the first interlanguage Chinese corpus by Chu and Chen (1993)

Attributes (partial)	Value
L1 background	59 countries
Age range	16–35
Male/female	50.93%/47.93% (remaining unstated)
Task types	Homework essays (63.45%), exam essays (15.31%), writing after reading or listening (19.21%)

'substitution', *fenhe* 'division/combination', *cuowei* 'misplacement', *chutou* 'cross-the-border', *jingxiang* 'flip', *bianxing* 'transformation', *hezi* 'blending', *jianhuazi* 'simplification', *xingsizi* 'deja vu'). The image files of the errors were stored alongside each entry in the corpus. The National Taiwan Normal University corpus (Teng et al. 2007) might be disqualified as a corpus because its size is too small, and only individual characters, rather than running texts, were recorded in the database.

Hanzi Pianwu Biaozhu de Hanyu Lianxuxing Zhongjieyu Yuliaoku 'The Continuity Corpus of Chinese Interlanguage of Character-error System' developed at the Sun Yat-sen University is another important corpus that deals with the misspelled (simplified) Chinese characters. The interlanguage writing samples were complete texts, and all tokenised and part of speech tagged. The misspelled characters were inserted into the texts using the Microsoft Windows Font Creator Program—a TrueType Chinese character/font editing application. More importantly, all the originally hand-written essays were scanned as image files. Users of the corpus can view the scanned essays for more contextualised analysis of what the non-native Chinese writers actually wrote (Zhang 2017).

Some recent Chinese interlanguage corpus projects aim at a more balanced design covering both spoken and written interlanguage. Jinan University Chinese learner corpus (JCLC) (Wang et al. 2015) and Guangwai-Lancaster Chinese Learner Corpus[7] are two cases in point. The JCLC written corpus contains 5.91 million Chinese characters across 8739 texts, and the spoken part is composed of 350,000 characters. Guangwai-Lancaster Chinese Learner Corpus is more balanced in terms of spoken and written data proportion. It is a 1.2-million-word corpus of interlanguage Chinese with a spoken (621,900 tokens, 48%) and a written (672,328 tokens, 52%) part, covering a variety of task types and topics. The entire corpus is tagged for errors as well.

A few other Chinese interlanguage corpora cited in the literature include those developed at Ludong University (Hu and Xu 2010), the University of Hong Kong (Tsang and Yeung 2012), Nanjing Normal University (Xiao and Zhou 2014), and many other universities.

The construction of L2 Chinese learner corpora has become the empirical basis for many doctoral theses and research articles and monographs. The usage patterns of interlanguage Chinese at morphosyntactic and textual levels have been investigated. However, the overwhelming focus of Chinese interlanguage corpus studies has been on error analysis. This might be accounted for by the strong impetus of language praxis.

Another indicator of the progress of L2 Chinese corpus research is that a biennial Chinese learner corpus research conference series 'The International Symposium on the Construction and Application of Chinese Interlanguage Corpora' has been in place since 2010.

[7]The corpus is freely available at https://www.sketchengine.co.uk/guangwai-lancaster-chinese-learner-corpus/.

3.2 L2 Chinese Learners' Input Corpora

Apart from the corpus-based Chinese interlanguage studies, there are some projects on L2 learners' input corpora. For instance, the corpus of Chinese textbooks for international students (CSL textbooks hereafter) developed at Xiamen University (Su 2010) has been made publicly available online,[8] which has become a useful resource for researchers and teachers of Chinese. Eleven types of Chinese textbooks published between 1992 and 2006 were digitised, and modelled into a corpus format. The total running characters of the corpus is 771,350. Besides, Sun Yat-sen University has constructed an updated CSL textbook corpus, which includes 1752 textbooks (54.5% of the total 3212 textbooks) published after 2006. 1802 out of 3212 textbooks (56.1%) were published outside China (Zhou et al. 2017). The two corpus teams have conducted a series of research on the coverage of vocabulary and grammar points across different CSL textbooks.

3.3 Applications of Data-Driven Teaching and Learning of Chinese

Chu's (2004) ChineseTA is probably one of the best known Chinese teaching software packages that integrate corpus linguistics functionalities. For instance, it can compute the occurrences and distribution of characters and words for the loaded Chinese teaching materials, and identify new words against the built-in level lists (e.g. HSK lists) as well as new word proportion. Such corpus-based data-driven features provide quantitative measures for Chinese texts that teachers can adopt for students of certain proficiency levels (Fig. 4).

Kilgarriff et al. (2015) demonstrate how Chinese teaching and learning can benefit from the data-driven methods with the assistance of the online system Sketch Engine. The system provides both Chinese corpora (together with a large number of corpora in other languages) and corpus analysis tools (e.g. concordance, word sketch, sketch difference, thesaurus, etc.). Word sketches—a different name for collocations—are key to the tool. Sketch diff (the shortened form on the system interface for sketch difference) is an often cited feature applicable to meaning distinction of ambiguous near-synonyms. Figure 5 shows the different collocational patterns between 形成 *xingcheng* 'to form' and 造成 *zaocheng* 'to cause' computed by Sketch Engine. Apparently, *xingcheng* tends to co-occur with neutral words like 共识 *gongshi* 'consensus', while *zaocheng* tends to co-occur with negative words, such as 伤亡 *shangwang* 'casualties' and 损失 *sunshi* 'loss'.

The data-driven learning trials on Chinese are still scarce. More collaboration between language practitioners, materials developers, publishers and corpus linguists should be encouraged to produce some corpus-informed computer-assisted language learning tools and mobile or cloud-enhanced learning applications.

[8]http://ncl.xmu.edu.cn/shj/Default.aspx. Chinese textbooks for native Chinese students were also collected alongside the CSL textbook data.

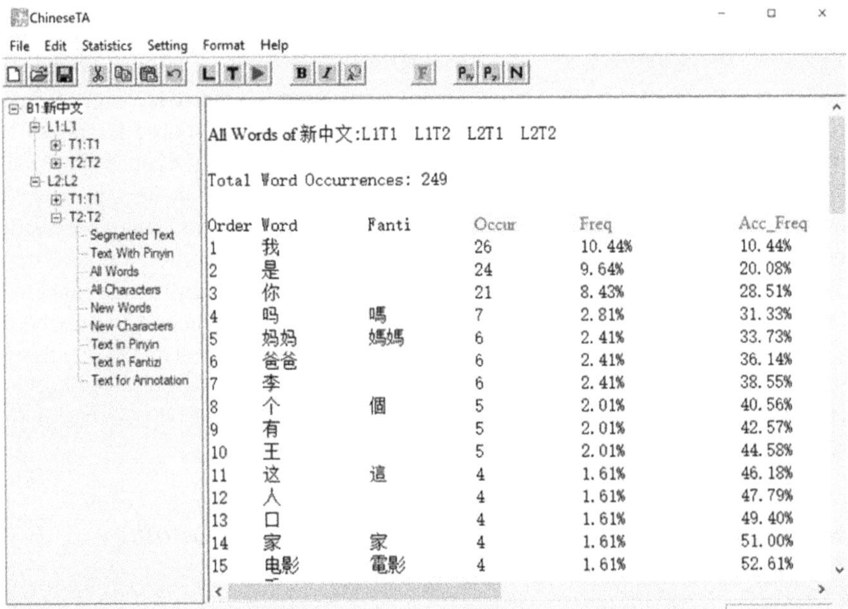

Fig. 4 The frequency list feature of ChineseTA

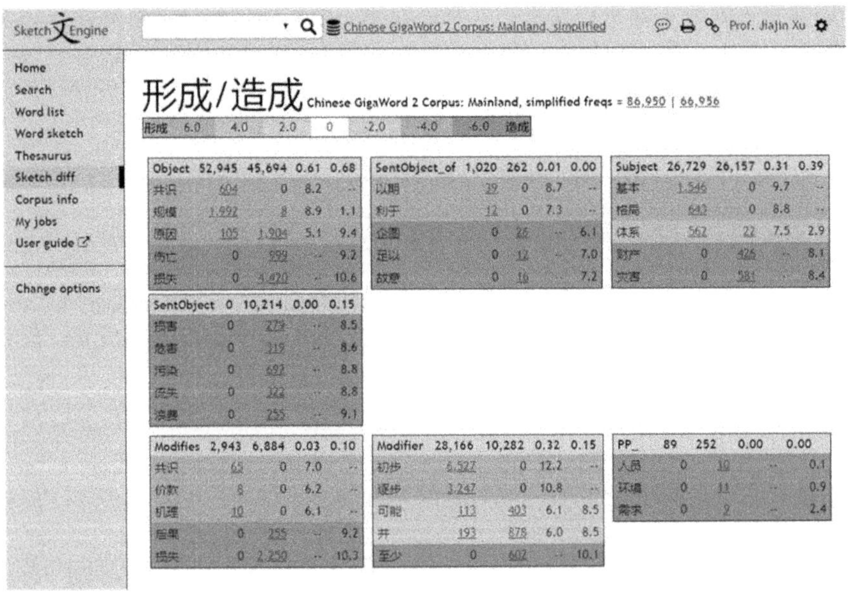

Fig. 5 The sketch diff feature of Sketch Engine: an example of 形成 versus 造成

4 Concluding Remarks

The use of corpora in the teaching and learning of Chinese has a history of nearly a century. Pedagogically oriented Chinese corpus studies originated on a solid methodological foundation prior to computer use. The creation of concordances, character/word lists, and the quantitative analyses of sentence patterns have offered fascinating insights into Chinese textbook compilation and syllabus design, the range and types of lexical items and grammatical patterns that should be taught, as well as the order in which vocabulary and grammar points should be presented.

The adoption of a corpus approach to the teaching and learning of Chinese is innovative in the sense that it relies on a quantitative methodology to look at Chinese. The corpus approach highlights the exhaustive account of all lexical, grammatical and textual features. This methodological innovation, nonetheless, should not be reduced to a technological advancement alone. According to Willis (1990a, b), what underlies the corpus approach to language teaching and learning is a descriptivist view of language, an inductive way of learning, and a task-based lexical syllabus. The notions have been best materialised in data-driven learning (Johns 1991). Corpus-based L1 and L2 Chinese studies have been fairly successful in terms of the description of the Chinese (inter)language, but there is still much room for pedagogical implementation, that is, to transform the research findings into classroom friendly teaching materials.

In this regard, we can find notable examples in English, such as corpus-based learner dictionaries, e.g. *Collins COBUILD English Dictionary* (Sinclair 1987), pedagogical grammar books, e.g. *Longman Student Grammar of Spoken and Written English* (Biber et al. 2002) and *Real Grammar: A Corpus-Based Approach to English* (Conrad and Biber 2009), English textbooks, e.g. *Collins COBUILD English Course* series (Willis 1990a, b) and Cambridge University Press' *Touchstone* and *Viewpoint* series (McCarthy and McCarten 2012; McCarthy et al. 2004), ESP and EAP teaching and learning materials e.g. *Academic Vocabulary in Use* (McCarthy and O'Dell 2008), classroom concordancing or data-driven learning tasks and activities, e.g. Tribble and Jones (1990), and the theorising about corpus-based language teaching, e.g. *The Lexical Syllabus* (Willis 1990a, b) and *The Lexical Approach* (Lewis 1993).

Acknowledgements The research was supported in part by the key project of the National Research Centre for Foreign Language Education (MOE Key Research Institute of Humanities and Social Sciences at Universities) (Ref No.: 17JJD740003) at Beijing Foreign Studies University. The author gratefully acknowledges the funding of the Fulbright Visiting Scholar grant during the writing up of the article. The author would also like to thank the referees and editors for their constructive comments, Professor Chengzhi Chu for providing helpful resource of ChineseTA, and Professor Eniko Csomay and Dr. Lu Lu for proofreading the manuscript.

References

Ao, H. (1929a). Yutiwen yingyong zihui yanjiu baogao: Chen Heqin shi *Yutiwen yingyong zihui* zhi xu [A study of characters used in vernacular Chinese: Extending Chen's character list]. *Jiaoyu Zazhi [Journal of Education], 21*(2), 77–101.

Ao, H. (1929b). Yutiwen yingyong zihui yanjiu baogao (Xu): Chen Heqin shi Yutiwen yingyong zihui zhi xu [A study of characters used in vernacular Chinese: Extending Chen's character list (continued)]. *Jiaoyu Zazhi [Journal of Education], 21*(3), 97–113.

Bei, G., & Zhang, X. (1988). *Hanzi pindu tongji [Frequency calculation of Chinese characters]*. Beijing: Publishing House of Electronics Industry.

Biber, D., Conrad, S., & Reppen, R. (1998). *Corpus linguistics: Investigating language structure and use*. Cambridge: Cambridge University Press.

Biber, D., Conrad, S., & Leech, G. (2002). *Longman student grammar of spoken and written English*. London: Longman.

Boorman, H. (1970). *Biographical dictionary of republican China* (Vol. 3). New York: Columbia University Press.

Browning, D., & Bunge, M. (Eds.). (2009). *Children and childhood in world religions: Primary sources and texts*. New Brunswick: Rutgers University Press.

Chen, H. (1922). Yutiwen yingyong zihui [Characters used in vernacular Chinese]. *Xin Jiaoyu [New Education], 5*(5), 987–995.

Chen, H. (1928). *Yutiwen yingyong zihui [Characters used in vernacular Chinese]*. Shanghai: The Commercial Press.

Chen, X. (1996). Hanyu zhongjie yu yuliaoku xitong jieshao [Introducing the Chinese interlanguage corpus system]. In the *proceedings of the 5th International Chinese Language Teaching conference* (pp. 450–458). Beijing.

China State Language Commission and China State Bureau of Standards. (1992). *Xiandai hanyu zipin tongji biao [A frequency list of modern Chinese characters]*. Beijing: Language and Culture Press.

Chu, C. (2004). *ChineseTA (1.0). Stanford university and the silicon valley language technologies*. San Jose, CA: LLC.

Chu, C., & Chen, X. (1993). Jianli hanyu zhongjieyu yuliaoku xitong de jiben shexiang [The initial considerations of creating a Chinese interlanguage corpus system]. *Shijie Hanyu Jiaoxue [Chinese Teaching in the World], 7*(3), 199–205.

Conrad, S., & Biber, D. (2009). *Real grammar: A corpus-based approach to English*. New York: Pearson.

Cui, X., & Zhang, B. (2011). Quanqiu hanyu xuexizhe yuliaoku jianshe fangan [A proposal for the building of the International Learner Corpus of Chinese]. *Yuyan Wenzi Yingyong [Applied Linguistics], 19*(2), 100–108.

Feng, Z. (2006). Evolution and present situation of corpus research in China. *International Journal of Corpus Linguistics, 11*(2), 173–207.

Francis, N. (1992). Language corpora B.C. In J. Svartvik (Ed.), *Directions in corpus linguistics* (pp. 17–32). Berlin: Mouton de Gruyter.

Freeman, J. (1843). On grammalogues: To the editor of the Phonotypic Journal. *The Phonotypic Journal, 2*(24), 170–171.

Granger, S. (2015). Contrastive interlanguage analysis: A reappraisal. *International Journal of Learner Corpus Research, 1*(1), 7–24.

Hu, X., & Xu, X. (2010). Mianxiang zhongwen dianhua jiaoxue de hanguo liuxuesheng hanyu zhongjieyu yuliaoku de kaifa yu jianshe [The development of a computer-assisted Chinese language teaching oriented Korean students' interlanguage Chinese corpus]. In the *Proceedings of the Seventh International Conference on Computer-assisted Chinese Language Teaching*.

Huang, C, Chen, K., & Chang, L. (1996). Segmentation standard for Chinese natural language processing. In *Proceedings of the 1996 International Conference on Computational Linguistics*. Copenhagan: Denmark.

Huang, W. (1962–1963). An annotated, partial list of the publications of William Hung. *Harvard Journal of Asiatic Studies, 24*, 7–16.
Hung, W. (1931). *Shuoyuan yinde [Index to Shuo Yuan]*. Peiping: Harvard-Yenching Institute Sinological Index Series, Peking University Library.
Hung, W. (1932). *Yinde shuo [On indexing]*. Peiping: Harvard-Yenching Institute Sinological Index Series, Peking University Library.
Hunston, S. (2002). *Corpora in applied linguistics*. Cambridge: Cambridge University Press.
Johansson, S. (2011). A multilingual outlook of corpora studies. In V. Viana, S. Zyngier, & G. Barnbrook (Eds.), *Perspectives on corpus linguistics* (pp. 115–129). Amsterdam: John Benjamins.
Johns, T. (1991). From printout to handout: Grammar and vocabulary teaching in the context of data-driven learning. *ELR Journal, 4*, 27–45.
Kaeding, F. (1897). *Häufigkeitswörterbuch der Deutschen Sprache*. Berlin: Self-publication.
Kilgarriff, A., Keng, N., & Smith, S. (2015). Learning Chinese with the Sketch Engine. In B. Zou, M. Hoey, & S. Smith (Eds.), *Corpus linguistics in Chinese contexts* (pp. 63–73). Basingstoke: Palgrave Macmillan.
Lewis, M. (1993). *The lexical approach: The state of ELT and a way forward*. Hove: LTP.
Liu, D. (1926). Pingjiao zonghui 'gaibian qianzi ke' jianzi gongzuo de jingguo [The process of vocabulary selection for the *Revised Edition of 1000 Foundation Characters* by the National Association of Mass Education Movement]. *Jiaoyu Zazhi [Journal of Education], 18*(12), 1–14.
Liu, E. (1973). *Frequency dictionary of Chinese words*. The Hague: Mouton.
Liu, Y., Liang, N., Wang, D., Zhang, S., Yang, T., Jie, C., et al. (1990). *Xiandai hanyu changyong ci cipin cidian [A dictionary of frequency of modern Chinese words]*. Beijing: Astronautic Publishing House.
McCarthy, M., & O'Dell, F. (2008). *Academic vocabulary in use*. Cambridge: Cambridge University Press.
McCarthy, M., McCarten, J., & Sandiford, H. (2004). *Touchstone (Student's Book 1)*. Cambridge: Cambridge University Press.
McCarthy, M., & McCarten, J. (2012). *Viewpoint (Level 1 Student's Book)*. Cambridge: Cambridge University Press.
McEnery, T., & Xiao, R. (2016). Corpus-based study of Chinese. In S. Chan (Ed.), *The Routledge encyclopedia of the Chinese language* (pp. 438–451). London: Routldge.
National Association of Mass Education Movement. (1922a). *Nongmin qianzi ke [1000 Chinese foundation characters for peasants]*. Shanghai: The Commercial Press.
National Association of Mass Education Movement. (1922b). *Shibing qianzi ke [1000 Chinese foundation characters for servicemen]*. Shanghai: The Commercial Press.
National Association of Mass Education Movement. (1928). *Shimin qianzi ke [Textbook of one thousand characters for townspeople]*. Shanghai: The Commercial Press.
Nesselhauf, N. (2004). Learner corpora and their potential for language teaching. In J. Sinclair (Ed.), *How to use corpora in language teaching* (pp. 125–152). Amsterdam: John Benjamins.
Pitman, I. (1843). List of words from which grammalogues may be selected. *The Phonotypic Journal, 2*(23), 161–163.
Sentence Pattern Research Group at Beijing Language Institute. (1989a). Xiandai hanyu jiben juxing [Basic sentence patterns of modern Chinese]. *Shijie Hanyu Jiaoxue [Chinese Teaching in the World], 3*(1), 26–35.
Sentence Pattern Research Group at Beijing Language Institute. (1989b). Xiandai hanyu jiben juxing (Xu yi) [Basic sentence patterns of modern Chinese (Continued I)]. *Shijie Hanyu Jiaoxue [Chinese Teaching in the World], 3*(3), 144–148.
Sentence Pattern Research Group at Beijing Language Institute. (1989c). Xiandai hanyu jiben juxing (Xu er) [Basic sentence patterns of modern Chinese (Continued II)]. *Shijie Hanyu Jiaoxue [Chinese Teaching in the World], 3*(4), 211–219.
Sentence Pattern Research Group at Beijing Language Institute. (1990). Xiandai hanyu jiben juxing (Xu san) [Basic sentence patterns of modern Chinese (Continued III)]. *Shijie Hanyu Jiaoxue [Chinese Teaching in the World], 4*(1), 27–33.

Sentence Pattern Research Group at Beijing Language Institute. (1991). Xiandai hanyu jiben juxing (Xu si) [Basic sentence patterns of modern Chinese (Continued IV)]. *Shijie Hanyu Jiaoxue [Chinese Teaching in the World], 5*(1), 23–29.

Sinclair, J. (1987). *Collins COBUILD English dictionary*. London: Collins.

Su, X. (2010). Jiaocai yuyan tongji yanjiu de duoweidu gongneng [The multi-dimensional function of the statistical research on textbook language]. In *Proceedings of the Innovation of International Chinese Teaching Theories and Models Conference*. Xiamen.

Sugiura, M. (2002). Collocational knowledge of L2 learners of English: A case study of Japanese learners. In T. Saito, J. Nakamura, & S. Yamazaki (Eds.), *English corpus linguistics in Japan* (pp. 303–323). Amsterdam: Rodopi.

Tao, X. (1934). Xing zhi xing [Action knowledge action]. *Shenghuo Jiaoyu [Life Education], 1*(11), 286–287.

Tao, Z., & Zhu, J. (1923). *Pingmin qianzi ke [Early Chinese lessons for illiterates]*. Shanghai: The Commercial Press.

Teng, S. Hong, Y. Chang, W. & Lu, C. (2007). Huayuwen xuexizhe hanzi pianwu shuju ziliaoku jianli ji pianwu leixing fenxi [The construction of Chinese learners' character writing error databse and the analysis of error types]. In *Proceedings of 2007 National Linguistics Conference* (pp. 313–325). Tainan: National Cheng Kung University.

Thorndike, E. (1921). *The teacher's word book*. New York: Teachers College, Columbia University.

Thorndike, E. (1931). *A teacher's word book of the twenty thousand words found most frequently and widely in general reading for children and young people*. New York: Teachers College, Columbia University.

Thorndike, E., & Lorge, I. (1944). *The teacher's word book of 30,000 words*. New York: Teachers College, Columbia University.

Tribble, C., & Jones, G. (1990). *Concordances in the classroom: A resource book for teachers*. London: Longman.

Tsai, T. (1922). *Laojielao [A synthetic study of Lao Tzu's Tao-Te-Ching in Chinese]*. Beijing: Self-publication.

Tsang, W., & Yeung, Y. (2012). The development of the Mandarin Interlanguage Corpus (MIC): A preliminary report on a small-scale learner database. *JALT Journal, 34*(2), 187–208.

Tsou, B., Lin, H., Chan, T., Hu, J., Chew, C., & Tse, J. (1997). A synchronous Chinese language corpus from different speech communities: Construction and application. *International Journal of Computational Linguistics and Chinese Language Processing, 2*(1), 91–104.

Voegelin, C. (1959). The notion of arbitrariness in structural statement and restatement I: Eliciting. *International Journal of American Linguistics, 25*(4), 207–220.

Wang, M., Malmasi, S. & Huang, M. (2015). The Jinan Chinese Learner Corpus. In *Proceedings of the Tenth Workshop on Innovative Use of NLP for Building Educational Applications* (pp. 118–123). Denver, CO: The Association for Computational Linguistics.

Wei, S., Zhao, P., Yang, X., & Chen, L. (2008). Daxing zhongguo xiaoxuesheng zuowen yuliaoku de shengcheng [The construction of a large-scale Chinese pupils' written language corpus]. *Modern Educational Technology, 18*(12), 45–48.

Willis, D. (1990a). *The lexical syllabus: A new approach to language teaching*. London: Collins ELT.

Willis, J. (1990b). *Collins COBUILD English course (First lessons, Student's edition)*. London: Collins ELT.

Xiao, R., Rayson, P., & McEnery, T. (2009). *A frequency dictionary of Mandarin Chinese: Core vocabulary for learners*. London: Routledge.

Xiao, X., & Zhou, W. (2014). Hanyu zhongjieyu yuliaoku biaozhu de quanmianxing ji leibie wenti [The exhaustiveness and taxonomy of Chinese interlanguage corpus annotation]. *Shijie Hanyu Jiaoxue [Chinese Teaching in the World], 28*(3), 368–377.

Xu, J. (2015). Corpus-based Chinese studies: A historical review from the 1920s to the present. *Chinese Language and Discourse, 6*(2), 218–244.

Yen, J. (1922). Pingmin jiaoyu xin yundong [A new movement of mass education]. *Xin Jiaoyu [New Education], 5*(5), 1007–1026.

Yen, J., & Fu, D. (1922). *Pingmin qianzi ke 'Foundation characters' (Books 1–3)*. Dingxian: National Association of Mass Education Movement.

Yen, J., & Fu, D. (1924). *Foundation characters* (2nd revised edition). Shanghai: National Committee of Y.M.C.A. of China.

Zhang, B. (2003). HSK (Hanyu Shuiping Kaoshi) dongtai zuowen yuliaoku jianjie [Introducing Chinese proficiency test dynamic essay corpus]. *Ceshi Yanjiu [Assessment Research], 1*(4), 37–38.

Zhang, P. (1999). Guanyu Yugan yu Liutongdu de Sikao [On Language Sense and Degree of Circulation]. *Yuyan Jiaoxue yu Yanjiu [Language Teaching and Linguistic Studies], 21*(2), 83–96.

Zhang, R. (2017). Hanyu zhongjieyu yuliaoku zhong de hanzi pianwu chuli yanjiu [The character errors in Chinese interlanguage corpora]. *Yuliaoku Yuyanxue [Corpus Linguistics], 3*(2), 50–59.

Zhao, S., Liu, S., & Hu, X. (1995). Beijing Yanyan Xueyuan xiandai hanyu jingdu jiaocai zhu kewen juxing tongji baogao [The BLCU report of the sentence patterns of the main texts of Modern Chinese Intensive Reading]. *Yuyan Jiaoxue yu Yanjiu [Language Teaching and Linguistic Studies], 17*(2), 11–26.

Zhou, X., Bo, W., Wang, L., & Li, Y. (2017). Guoji hanyu jiaocai yuliaoku de jianshe yu yingyong [The construction and application of international Chinese textbook corpus]. *Yuyan Wenzi Yingyong [Applied Linguistics], 25*(1), 125–135.

Part II
Tools, Resources and General Applications

Academic Chinese: From Corpora to Language Teaching

Howard Ho-Jan Chen and Hongyin Tao

Abstract The past several decades of research in Chinese applied linguistics have seen rapid developments in corpus infrastructure building and exploitation. However, one area in which systematic research is still lacking involves academic Chinese. In this chapter, we describe the construction of written academic Chinese corpora at the National Taiwan Normal University and University of California, Los Angeles and report preliminary results of research based on these corpora as well as their pedagogical applications in developing teaching materials for advanced Chinese language learning. Theoretical and practical issues in academic Chinese and the role of corpora in academic language pedagogy are discussed.

1 Introduction

The past several decades of research in Chinese applied linguistics have seen rapid developments in corpus infrastructure building and exploitation. For example, large-scale corpora such as the Chinese National Language Commission Corpus (中国国家语委现代汉语通用平衡语料库, http://www.cncorpus.org), the Beijing Language and Culture University corpus (BCC Corpus, http://bcc.blcu.edu.cn/), and the Peking University Center for Chinese Linguistics Corpus (CCL Corpus, http://ccl.pku.edu.cn:8080/ccl_corpus/) all have over several 100 million words. In Taiwan, the Academia Sinica Corpus of Balanced Chinese (台湾中央研究院的现代汉语平衡语料库, http://db1x.sinica.edu.tw/cgi-bin/kiwi/mkiwi/mkiwi.sh) contains many different written and spoken genres and can be searched in multiple ways. The CallHome and CallFriend corpora (Canavan and Zipperlen 1996) contain 100s of hours of telephone calls. Important publications based on corpora, such as the Dictio-

H. H.-J. Chen
National Taiwan Normal University, Taipei, Taiwan
e-mail: hjchen@ntnu.edu.tw

H. Tao (✉)
University of California, Los Angeles, USA
e-mail: tao@humnet.ucla.edu

X. Lu and B. Chen (eds.), *Computational and Corpus Approaches to Chinese Language Learning*, Chinese Language Learning Sciences,
https://doi.org/10.1007/978-981-13-3570-9_4

nary of Global Chinese Neologisms (Zou and You 2010) and Frequency Dictionary of Mandarin Chinese (Xiao et al. 2009), have also appeared.

However, one area in which systematic research is still lacking involves academic Chinese. Other than being a special genre in some of the large collections mentioned above, very little effort has been put into developing corpora of academic Chinese and developing teaching materials based on such data.

In this chapter, we first review the state of academic Chinese corpus building (Sect. 2). We then describe the construction of two written academic Chinese corpora developed at the National Taiwan Normal University (NTNU) and the University of California, Los Angeles (UCLA) (Sect. 3) and discuss preliminary results based on these corpora. We conclude by introducing pedagogical applications in developing teaching materials for advanced Chinese language learning.

2 Review of the State of the Art of Academic Chinese Corpus Building

Academic language generally refers to language used in academic settings and products such as textbooks, journal articles, research monographs, dictionaries, lab manuals, and so forth. Although spoken academic language has drawn increasing interest (see, e.g., Biber 2006; Simpson-Vlach 2006, 2013), most of the current work is on written academic language. The literature on corpus-based academic language research is extensive, but is mostly based on the English language. According to Coxhead (2000), as early as the 1970s, efforts have been made to compile academic word lists for the English language (Campion and Elley 1971; Ghadessy 1979; Lynn 1973; Praninskas 1972), where most of the work was done manually. Later, Xue and Nation (1984) created the University Word List (UWL) by combining four existing word lists, and the UWL became quite popular in English language education materials. It was not until the 2000s that large-scale corpus-based academic language research began to take center stage. In a landmark study, Coxhead (2000) develops an English Academic Word List (AWL) based on an academic corpus of 3.5 million words, covering four academic disciplines (arts, commerce, law, and science). Some recent studies in the area of academic word lists strive for even larger quantities of corpus data and more extensive coverage. For example, Gardner and Davies (2013) use a 100 million-word subcorpus of academic English, with more recent texts, to develop the Academic Vocabulary List (AVL), with a claimed better coverage of academic texts.

In the case of Chinese, academic language, traditionally referred to as scientific language (科学体 *kexueti*, Chen 1962/1997 or 科技汉语 *kejihanyu*, Li 1985), research based on corpora has been conspicuously lacking. Discussions of vocabulary (e.g., Han and Dong 2010) and grammatical features (e.g., Li 1985) of academic Chinese are mostly impressionistic. Most of the corpus-based studies are on general-purpose language use; and when special purpose corpora are constructed, on the other hand, most of them fall into a few disciplines such as business, education, and second language learning. Thus, in a review of the development of Chinese corpus linguistics from the 1920s through the early twenty-first century (Xu 2015), there is no entry on Chinese for Academic Purposes (CAP). Similarly, in a collection of introductions to Chinese for Specific Purposes (CSP, Peng 2016), there is no chapter on CAP.

However, this does not mean that collections of academic text do not exist. On the contrary, a considerable amount of data has been available, most of which is embedded in general corpus collections. For example, most of the written Chinese corpora inspired by the Brown Corpus (Francis and Kucera 1964), including the Lancaster Corpus of Modern Chinese (LCMC, McEnery and Xiao 2004), the UCLA corpus of written Chinese (Tao and Xiao 2007), and the ToRCH corpus (Xu 2017) contain the J/"learned" or "academic writing" category, which includes various kinds of academic texts. Online search mechanisms typically allow the end user to either select the entire corpus or only some specific genres/registers, such as learned or academic writing, when conducting searches, making it possible to do genre-based investigations and comparisons. An example of such a search interface can be found in the screenshot of the UCLA Corpus of Written Chinese in Fig. 1.

Other large-scale corpora have similar academic text categories. For example, the Academia Sinica Balanced Corpus of Modern Chinese (Huang and Chen 1992) has several categories that can be considered academic genres, including journal articles (學術期刊 *xueshu qikan*), reference works (工具書 *gongjushu*), and academic books/monographs (學術論著 *xueshu lunzhu*). A graphical user interface for genre selection in the Academic Sinica corpus website is shown in Fig. 2.

Similarly, a recent large-scale corpus developed by the Beijing Language and Culture University (BCC, Xun et al. 2016), also has an academic sub-register (科技 *keji*), as shown in Fig. 3.

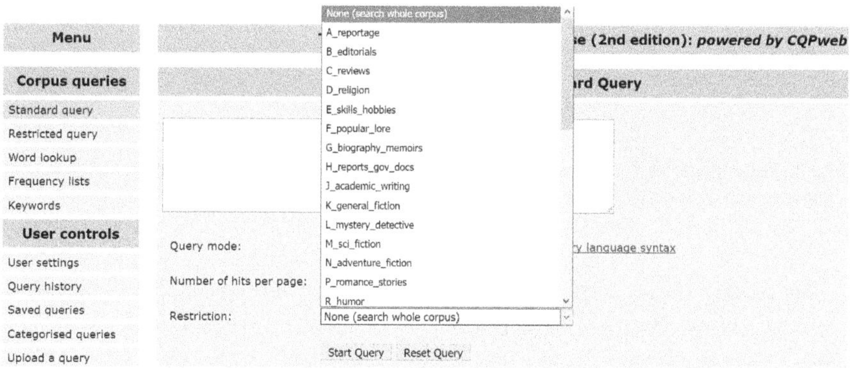

Fig. 1 Genres, including the J/Learned or academic writing category, in the UCLA Corpus of Written Chinese (hosted at the Beijing Foreign Studies University website) (last accessed August 30, 2017)

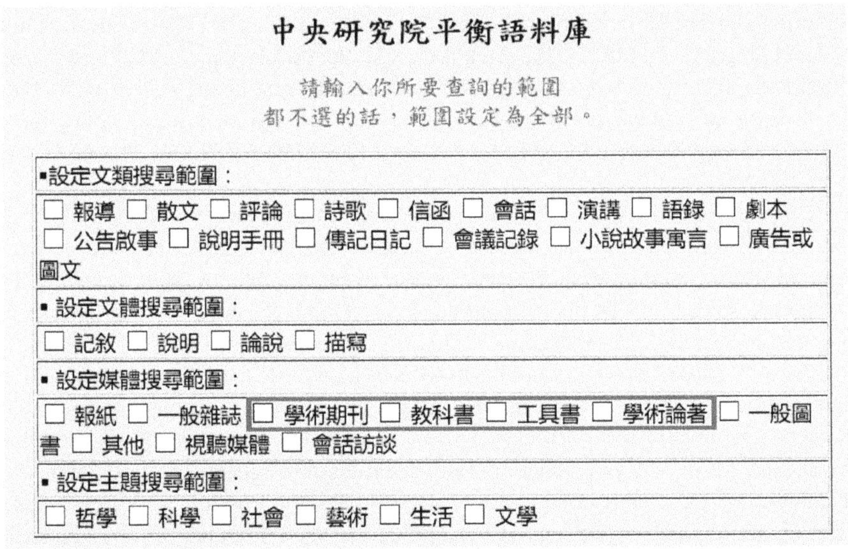

Fig. 2 Text types, including academic texts, shown at the online user interface of the Academia Sinica Balanced Corpus of Modern Chinese (last accessed August 30, 2017)

Fig. 3 Text categories, including academic texts, shown in the online user interface of the Beijing Language and Culture University Corpus (last accessed August 30, 2017)

Specialized large corpora of academic Chinese have been developed at the National Taiwan Normal University and UCLA, which we will discuss next.

3 Academic Chinese Corpora at NTNU and UCLA: Development and Research

As indicated earlier, most of the collections of academic Chinese texts have been developed in conjunction with larger general-purpose corpora. In recent years, however, research teams at both the National Taiwan Normal University and the University of California, Los Angeles have independently developed two academic Chinese corpora, which have begun to be put to use for language pedagogical purposes.

3.1 The NTNU Academic Chinese Corpus

3.1.1 Corpus Description

The NTNU Academic Chinese Corpus (Liu et al. 2016, 2017), compiled by a team led by the first author of this chapter, is specialized in two ways: first, it is a collection of academic journal articles; second, it focuses on the humanities and social sciences.

In the NTNU corpus, the journals from which research articles are culled are restricted to those that are designated in the locally authoritative Taiwan Humanities Citation Index Core (THCTC) and Taiwan Social Sciences Citation Index (TSSCI). In other words, the selected journals are all highly reputable publications published in Taiwan over the past few decades. Following the categorization scheme of the indexes, the articles in the corpus are also classified into ten subject areas: education, management, literature, history, political science, law, sociology, area studies and geography, linguistics, and economics. Journals published in English are filtered out, leaving a total of 106 qualified journals. The distribution of journals is given in Table 1.

Table 1 Distribution of journals and articles in the ten subject areas in the 9 million words NTNU Academic Chinese Corpus

Subject area	Journals	Articles
Education	20	100
Management	14	100
Literature	13	100
History	12	100
Political science	11	100
Law	7	100
Sociology	8	100
Area studies and geography	9	100
Linguistics	5	100
Economics	7	100
Total	106	1000

One hundred articles from each of the ten subject areas are randomly selected, resulting in a total of 1000 articles. The articles are processed with a tokenizer developed by the Academia Sinica for word segmentation and part-of-speech tagging. The total number of running words in the corpus is 9 million.

3.1.2 Research Based on the NTNU Corpus

Research based on the NTNU corpus has been performed in two areas: the compilation of an academic word list for Chinese and the compilation of frequent lexical bundles for academic Chinese.

For the academic word list, according to Liu et al. (2016), both frequency and range information are taken into consideration. A separate word list is first compiled for each of the ten subject areas; then high-frequency lexical items that also appear in at least eight of the ten subject areas are chosen as representative academic vocabulary. After the initial word lists are compiled, the overall word list is checked against a general-purpose word list of 8000 words, namely, the Teaching of Chinese as a Foreign Language (TOCFL) 8000 Word List (SCTOP 2016). This general-purpose word list was developed based on the Academia Sinica Balanced Corpus of Modern Chinese discussed earlier as well as some local Chinese language textbooks and learner corpus word lists. There are multiple bands of vocabulary in the TOCFL list intended to distinguish assumed different levels of difficulty. The lowest levels, the entry (入門級 *rumenji*), and the foundation (基礎級 *jichuji*) bands are used against the initial academic word list, where any words that are shared on both lists are eliminated in order to ensure that what is on the academic word list is genuinely academic in nature and not something that is also commonly used in everyday situations. The overall workflow, as just described, can be schematized in Fig. 4.

As a result, 2405 words are identified as meeting the requirements of both frequency and range. In comparison with the TOCFL word list, there is a difference of 557 lexical items that are not found to be on the latter, meaning that these are unique to the academic language.

With regard to the second project, identifying lexical bundles (multiword expressions) commonly used in academic Chinese, Liu et al. (2017) detail the identification process and criteria used based on the same corpus. This study follows the same general guidelines proposed in Biber et al. (1999) and adopts a cutoff of 10 occurrences per million words or 90 times per 9 million words for this particular corpus. Applying this criterion, the largest numbers of bundles are found to be three- and four-word bundles. A further criterion applied to the three-word bundles is that the multiword expressions must occur in at least 5% of the texts. For four-word bundles, however, the minimum textual occurrence is set at 2% due to their lower frequency compared to the three-word bundles. Additional filters applied include non-grammatical strings such as 的另一, 上所述, and 了一種, as well as subject-area-specific expressions, such as 日常生活的 "of daily life," 經濟發展的

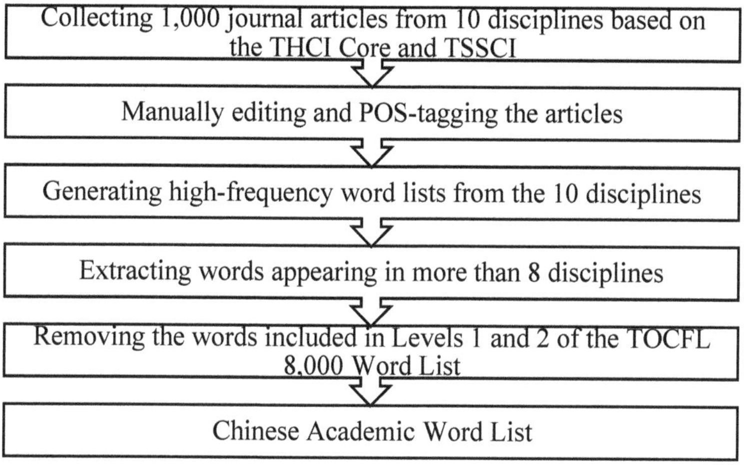

Fig. 4 Workflow for the NTNU academic word list

Table 2 Lexical bundle types and their distribution

Bundle type	195 three-word bundles (%)	105 four-word bundles (%)
Participant oriented	12	18
Research oriented	28	24
Text oriented	60	58
Total	100	100

"economic development," and 意識形態的 "ideological." The end result is 195 types of three-word bundles and 105 types of four-word bundles, totaling 300 bundles.

In addition to the bundles themselves, this study also provides a functional classification of commonly used multiword units. Following Hyland (2008) and Salazar (2014), common lexical bundles are categorized as research oriented (location, procedure, quantification, etc.), text oriented (transition signals, resultative signals, etc.), or participant oriented (stance features and engagement features). Overall distributional patterns show that text-oriented multiword expressions are the largest group among all three types for both three- and four-word bundles, followed by research-oriented bundles and finally participant oriented. Table 2 provides a breakdown of the functional types in both groups.

3.1.3 Suggested Applications in Language Learning and Teaching

Given these results, the NTNU team suggests a number of possibilities for language teaching. In the case of the academic word list, it is noted that teachers can take advantage of the list for course and materials design, and learners can work directly with the word list for self-study. It is suggested that even native speakers be trained in the use of the common academic words to improve professional writing skills. Other noted applications include developing learning-oriented dictionary entries involving the items on the academic vocabulary list, where it is suggested that synonyms, antonyms, as well as authentic examples be included for each entry. A sample dictionary entry is given below, in Fig. 5, showing the entry for the word 擴充 *Kuòchōng* "expand, expansion."

In addition to learning the word information which would be included in dictionary entries, such as definition, synonym, antonym, and example sentence, the collocation information of a word is another important aspect that students should learn about in order to master the usage of a word. Collocation information could allow students to further understand how one word is used with other words and further improve their language use. Collocation information based on actual language use, as shown in the sample collocation of the word 課題 *Kètí* "topic, issue" in Fig. 6, is another suggested way to enhance learning materials.

Conceivably, teachers and learners can explore the collocation patterns in, for example, writing exercises, and the sample passages, culled from actual corpora, can be used for pattern identification purposes. Similarly, lexical bundles discussed earlier can be used in vocabulary learning, as a way to supplement traditional teaching focus on individual words. Textbooks, on the other hand, can highlight the bundled patterns found in corpora and design exercises for the learner to understand and use them in various skill practices such as speaking and writing. Finally, some comparison can be made between individual lexical use and lexical items in bundles, such as the cases of "terms" versus "in terms of" and "sum" versus "to sum up."

In short, the NTNU corpus, with a large number of recent authentic journal articles selected, is a valuable resource for written academic Chinese, especially in the Taiwan Chinese language setting. While there is ongoing research to exploit this resource for advanced Chinese language teaching and learning in the area of academic Chinese, the suggested applications are practical and ready for implementation in actual learning environments. Meanwhile, the NTNU team also aims to compile a collocation list based on the high-frequency academic words to provide more potentially useful materials for the teaching and learning of Chinese for academic purposes.

擴充： 注音 (Bopomofo): ㄎㄨㄛ ㄔㄨㄥ; 漢語拼音 (Pinyin): Kuòchōng
解釋：伸張、擴展
Meaning: Expand, develop
同義詞：增加、擴大、推廣、擴張
Synonyms: *zengjia*, *kuoda*, *tuiguang*, *kuozhang*
反義詞：收縮、裁減、縮小
Antonyms: *shousuo*, *caijian*, *suoxiao*
例句：高等教育的快速擴充已經衍生一些高等教育本質與功能方面的問題。
Sample sentence: The rapid expansion of higher education has brought about issues in the nature and function of higher education.

Fig. 5 Sample dictionary entry for the word 擴充 *Kuòchōng* "expand, expansion"

課題: 注音 (Bopomofo): ㄎㄜ ㄊㄧ; 漢語拼音 (Pinyin): Kètí; 'topic, issue'

搭配詞：重要的～；探討的～；研究的～；研究～；首要～；重視的～；思考的～；實證～；教育～；學習～

Collocates: *zhongyao de~*; *tantao de~*; *yanjiu de~*; *yanjie~*; *shouyao~*; *zhongshi de~*; *sikao de~*; *shizheng~*; *jiaoyu~*; *xuexi~*

例句1: 大正後期文化主義與教育學研究的關聯成為重要的課題，使當時文化教育學的氣氛與精神科學派的思想合成一體。

Sample sentence 1: In the late period of Dazheng, the connection between culturalism and education studies became an important **topic**....

例句2. 假如把道德與國民放在同一課程內容內，我們就理應追求民族國家利益與普世道德標準的兼顧與平衡；這亦是近代道德哲學與政治哲學的一個重要研究課題。

Sample sentence 2: ...This is also an important research **topic** in ethics and political philosophy in the early modern time.

Fig. 6 Sample collocation: 課題 *Kètí* "topic, issue."

3.2 The UCLA Academic Chinese Corpus and Related Applications

3.2.1 The UCLA Corpus

The UCLA Corpus of Written Academic Chinese (CWAC), a joint project between UCLA (headed by Hongyin Tao, PI) and Peking University (headed by Weidong Zhan), is a 32-million-word collection of academic texts sampled from a wide range of sources such as journal articles, book chapters, laboratory manuals, course workbooks, and course notes, spanning over the period of 1990s to the beginning of the twenty-first century. Following the New Zealand Academic English Corpus (Coxhead 2000), CWAC is organized in terms of four different broad disciplinary fields—arts, commerce, law, and science—each with a number of subfields. As shown in Table 3, the arts subcorpus comprises 440 texts, the commerce section has 366 texts, the law section has 302 texts, and there are 356 texts in the science subcorpus. All of the texts are further divided into short texts (2000–5000 running words, 40% of the corpus), medium texts (5000–10,000 running words, 40% of the corpus), and long texts (over 10,000 running words, 20% of the corpus).

Due to the relatively large size of the corpus, a smaller sample, about one-third of the original collection, is assembled for ease of processing. The sampler version has 504 files, with over 20 million characters. It was processed, as with the larger corpus, with the Peking University Chinese tokenizer, resulting in over 5.4 million running words (or 78,537 word types). Table 4 gives a breakdown of the composition of each disciplinary area.

Table 3 General makeup of the UCLA Corpus of Written Academic Chinese

Discipline	Arts	Commerce	Law	Science	Total
Subfield	Education History Linguistics Philosophy Politics Psychology Sociology	Accounting Economics Finance Industrial relations Management Marketing Public policy	Constitutional law Criminal law Family law and medico-legal International law Pure commercial law Quasi-commercial law Rights and remedies	Biology Chemistry Computer science Geography Geology Mathematics Physics	
Texts	440	366	303	356	1465
Tokens	94,85,811	86,44,792	59,12,777	85,69,661	3,26,13,041

Table 4 Composition of the sampler version of the UCLA Corpus of Written Academic Chinese

Subject area	Files	Words	Characters	Percent
Arts	119	1,392,729	5134643	25%
Commerce	118	1,400,469	5390517	26%
Law	145	1,241,159	4847149	23%
Science	122	1,383,535	5283403	26%
Total	**504**	**5,417,892**	**20,655,712**	**100%**

The original corpus is open to the public at the Peking University Center for Chinese Linguistics (CCL) website (http://ccl.pku.edu.cn:8080/ccl_corpus/), under contemporary Chinese.

3.2.2 Research Based on the UCLA CWAC Corpus

This corpus was part of a larger research project sponsored by the US Department of Education in conjunction with the Center for Advanced Language Proficiency Education and Research (CALPER) at The Pennsylvania State University. The objectives in developing this corpus are threefold (Tao 2013): (1) To better understand the linguistic features of Chinese academic discourse as well as the typological similarities and differences of these features cross-linguistically and cross-culturally; (2) to explore the pedagogical implications of linguistics research that can foster language learning in such areas as grammar instruction, pragmatic competence as well as cultural understanding; and (3) to develop a set of L2 Chinese language teaching materials, for advanced Mandarin Chinese learners, that are educational, authentic, and pedagogically effective.

Research has been conducted with the sampler CWAC corpus on a number of issues. First, with regard to representative academic vocabulary, a set of criteria has been identified, with interesting results. The research team defines representative vocabulary based on both frequency and range, as is standard with this type of study.

Specifically, items must occur at least 500 times in the corpus (about 10 per million, the same as the cutoff suggested by Biber et al. (1999: 992) for most lexical bundles). It was decided that monosyllabic words be excluded. The reason for the exclusion is that, according to a prior study (Tao 2015), most monosyllabic words are found to be characteristic of everyday conversational Chinese. This exclusion eliminates a large number of (monosyllabic) words that may be part of the common vocabulary. Lastly, representative tokens must be found across all of the subfields of the corpus, which makes for a more conservative selection in terms of range and aims to ensure the maximum representativeness of the academic genre.

A multitiered approach is adopted following Coxhead (2000), with four sublists (A, B, C, and D), based on token frequencies found in the corpus. The four bands are established as follows: the top-tier group (A) consists of words with 10,000 occurrences or more; the second group (B), words with 5000–10,000 occurrences; the third group (C) with occurrences of 1000–5000; and the fourth group (D) with occurrences of 500–1000. The total number of tokens identified is 1158, and their distribution across the four sublists is given in Table 5.

The same result is represented graphically in Fig. 7.

Table 5 Distribution of the four sublists of high-frequency academic vocabulary in word type in the UCLA CWAC corpus

Band	10,000	5000–10,000	1000–5000	500–1000
Label	A	B	C	D
Word types	12	47	566	533

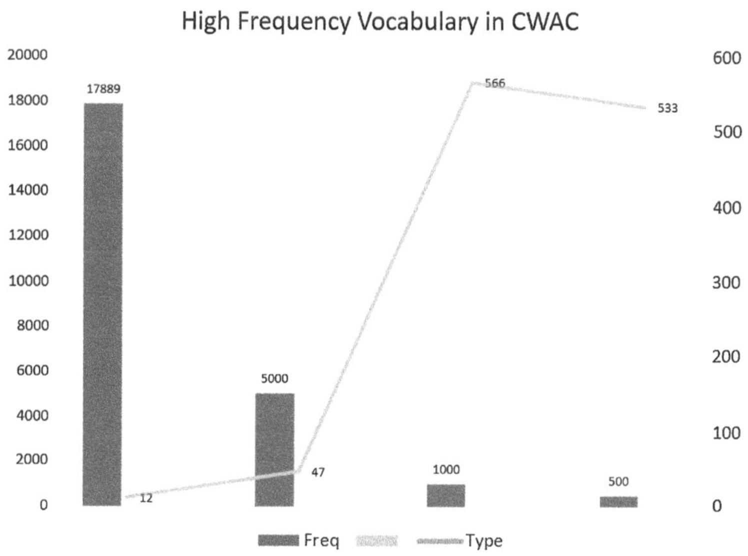

Fig. 7 High-frequency vocabulary types and tokens in CWAC

Table 6 Sublist A: > 10,000, N = 12

1	16	17889	社會
2	25	14158	可以
3	26	13823	一個
4	28	13242	發展
5	29	12318	管理
6	30	12016	研究
7	34	11592	企業
8	38	10816	國家
9	40	10629	關係
10	42	10564	規定
11	43	10331	問題
12	45	10106	進行

As is common with word frequency distribution cross-linguistically (Zipf 1935), there is an inverse relation between token frequency and the number of types: fewer word types have higher token frequencies (Tao 2015). Some sample vocabulary items[1] from the different sublists are given in Tables 6, 7, 8 and 9.

In addition to single lexical tokens, common lexical strings are also examined with an N-gram approach. The top high-frequency clusters, roughly 100 in number and shown in Table 10, are obtained based on the following criteria: the cluster can be any three- to five-word string, must have a minimum frequency of occurrence of five or more, and must be used in at least 10 subfields.

A quick glance at these clusters shows that most of them (是一种 "a type of," 的情况下 "in the case of," 的过程中 "in the process of," 另一种 "another type/kind (of)," etc.) may be categorized as discourse organizing (Biber et al. 1999) or text oriented (transition signals, resultative signals, etc.) (Hyland 2008). They also corroborate the findings reported by the NTNU team (Liu et al. 2017) in terms of the dominance of both three-word sequences and the text-oriented functional type, although Liu et al. (2016) considered only grammatically well-formed strings.

3.2.3 Developing Language Teaching Materials

The UCLA project has been an integral component in developing teaching materials. As is by now well known, corpus data are essential for authentic and accurate description and representation of language use (Biber et al. 1998; O'Keeffe et al.

[1] Some of the automated word segmentation results used here may be subject to different treatments based on different linguistic analyses. We have decided to preserve the original segmentation results in this paper due to the fact that many of the potentially controversial results (e.g. 一个, 这种, 第二, etc.) involve high frequency items, which may justify their status as a single item. We thank an anonymous reviewer for drawing our attention to this matter.

Table 7 Sublist B: 5000–9000, N = 47

13	48	9586	經濟	37	108	6106	政府
14	51	9103	公司	38	109	5953	需要
15	52	9039	行為	39	110	5915	存在
16	59	8371	組織	40	111	5862	基本
17	65	8021	工作	41	113	5732	影響
18	66	7996	法律	42	114	5699	權利
19	67	7955	教育	43	115	5582	作用
20	68	7950	中國	44	116	5539	分析
21	70	7915	不同	45	117	5444	情況
22	74	7711	或者	46	118	5423	根據
23	76	7680	我們	47	119	5376	活動
24	79	7536	主要	48	120	5369	條件
25	82	7308	理論	49	121	5362	方面
26	83	7294	市場	50	123	5301	結構
27	84	7282	過程	51	125	5280	這些
28	85	7268	方法	52	126	5257	如果
29	88	7081	制度	53	128	5157	認為
30	90	7030	通過	54	130	5090	科學
31	91	6925	政策	55	131	5065	要求
32	96	6707	其他	56	133	5034	單位
33	97	6619	沒有	57	134	5033	產生
34	98	6491	具有	58	135	5020	環境
35	99	6407	系統	59	136	5004	包括
36	106	6160	這種				

Table 8 Sublist C: 1000–5000, N = 566 (sample list)

60	137	4982	技術	98	181	4264	提供	136	244	3284	建立
61	138	4979	發生	99	182	4244	勞動	137	245	3277	程式
62	139	4977	作為	100	184	4209	有關	138	250	3241	特徵
63	140	4973	自己	101	185	4179	一定	139	253	3202	決定
64	141	4939	內容	102	186	4168	財產	140	254	3200	但是
65	142	4936	之間	103	187	4100	變化	141	255	3190	體系
66	143	4916	必須	104	191	4037	能力	142	256	3134	處理
67	144	4879	重要	105	193	3981	對於	143	257	3131	具體
68	145	4875	原則	106	194	3975	結果	144	258	3121	控制
69	146	4869	應當	107	195	3950	形式	145	259	3113	人類
70	147	4851	歷史	108	196	3941	文化	146	260	3109	美國
71	148	4836	形成	109	200	3786	利益	147	261	3094	心理
72	149	4824	憲法	110	201	3784	第一	148	264	3074	計算
73	150	4789	政治	111	203	3775	機構	149	266	3070	人民
74	151	4774	資源	112	206	3700	時間	150	269	3049	目的
75	154	4720	犯罪	113	207	3690	提出	151	270	3042	行政
76	156	4698	人員	114	211	3620	實現	152	271	3035	合同
77	157	4631	他們	115	213	3574	同時	153	272	3019	因素
78	158	4631	方式	116	214	3558	因為	154	274	2993	第二
79	159	4630	因此	117	216	3543	概念	155	275	2993	範圍
80	160	4627	產品	118	217	3506	部分	156	278	2969	貨幣
81	161	4618	由於	119	220	3487	各種	157	279	2954	得到
82	162	4607	以及	120	221	3483	一些	158	280	2952	成本
83	163	4583	基礎	121	222	3476	個人	159	281	2938	實驗

Table 9 Sublist D: < 1000, N = 533 (sample list)

626	883	998	處罰	670	932	943	策略	715	994	870	北京
627	884	996	刑事	671	934	941	國務院	716	995	869	錯誤
628	885	995	股票	672	936	940	主張	717	997	867	嚴格
629	886	994	外部	673	937	940	承認	718	999	866	事物
630	888	990	職業	674	938	938	運行	719	1000	866	同意
631	889	989	資本主義	675	939	935	參加	720	1001	865	國有
632	890	987	中華人民共	676	940	933	訴訟	721	1003	863	逐漸
和國				677	942	932	金額	722	1006	861	於是
633	891	986	處於	678	943	932	集體	723	1007	861	降低
634	892	985	最高	679	944	930	創新	724	1009	858	線性
635	893	985	調查	680	946	929	重視	725	1010	857	氣候
636	894	984	真正	681	948	925	轉讓	726	1011	856	有些
637	895	981	勞資	682	950	921	礦物	727	1012	855	矛盾
638	896	977	然後	683	952	920	專門	728	1013	854	那些
639	897	974	群體	684	953	918	還是	729	1014	853	安排
640	898	973	福利	685	954	917	必然	730	1016	851	審計
641	899	971	基金	686	955	917	成功	731	1017	849	位置
642	900	968	元素	687	956	913	德國	732	1018	846	連續
643	901	968	廣泛	688	957	913	轉移	733	1019	845	帶來
644	902	967	中央	689	958	912	工程	734	1020	844	具備
645	903	967	使得	690	959	912	擴大	735	1021	842	東西
646	904	965	情形	691	960	911	股份	736	1022	842	及時
647	905	964	代表大會	692	961	911	自我	737	1023	839	介紹
648	906	964	包含	693	962	910	教師	738	1025	838	試驗
649	908	962	存款	694	965	902	維護	739	1026	837	趨勢
650	909	962	系列	695	967	901	事項	740	1027	836	關鍵
651	910	961	原始	696	968	901	物理	741	1028	836	行動
652	912	960	變動	697	969	900	名稱	742	1029	834	擔保

Table 10 Sample high-frequency multiword cluster list

Rank	Freq	Range	N-gram	Rank	Freq	Range	N-gram	Rank	Freq	Range	N-gram
1	51	32	是 一 种	35	13	8	较 多 的	69	9	5	的 这 就
2	34	25	的 一 种	36	12	6	一定 程度 上	70	9	7	越来越 多 的
3	32	22	并 不 是	37	12	9	中 的 一	71	9	8	这 并 不
4	31	12	年 月 日	38	12	6	在 这样 的	72	9	6	长 的 时间
5	28	18	更 多 的	39	12	6	更 好 地	73	8	5	不同 程度 的
6	28	18	最 大 的	40	12	9	的 前提 下	74	8	6	世界 卫生 组织
7	27	8	很 大 的	41	12	9	的 基础 上	75	8	7	了 大量 的
8	27	12	的 过程 中	42	11	9	另 一 种	76	8	7	任何 一 种
9	25	14	也 就 是	43	11	6	在 一定 程度	77	8	7	完全 不同 的
10	24	5	技术 的 发展	44	11	6	在 一定 程度 上	78	8	6	已 知 的
11	24	9	的 情况 下	45	11	8	更 好 的	79	8	5	的 另 一
12	24	12	较 高 的	46	11	6	最 基本 的	80	8	6	的 问题 是
13	23	14	而 不 是	47	11	5	有 两 个	81	8	6	范围 内 的
14	22	8	所 说 的	48	11	5	每 一 次	82	8	5	较 低 的
15	22	12	最 重要 的	49	11	5	的 另 一个	83	8	8	这 也 是
16	20	8	这 两 个	50	11	7	的 这 一	84	7	6	也 不 是
17	20	16	这 就 是	51	11	7	这 一 过程	85	7	7	也 是 如此
18	19	8	有 一定 的	52	10	6	不 是 一个	86	7	7	了 一 种
19	19	11	重要 的 是	53	10	5	大 脑 中	87	7	6	因为 它 是
20	17	7	了 新 的	54	10	5	很 高 的	88	7	6	在 我们 的
21	17	7	所 需 的	55	10	5	所 处 的	89	7	7	在 短 时间
22	17	5	更 大 的	56	10	6	的 第一 个	90	7	5	就 有 了
23	17	8	这 两 种	57	10	5	过程 中 的	91	7	7	并 不 能
24	15	8	有 很 大	58	10	5	这 一 理论	92	7	5	很 好 的
25	15	8	的 条件 下	59	10	8	这 是 因为	93	7	6	所 占 的
26	14	7	所 具有 的	60	10	9	都 是 由	94	7	6	是 世界 上
27	14	9	注意 的 是	61	9	5	一 段 时间	95	7	6	最 重要 的 是
28	14	5	的 两 个	62	9	5	了 这 一	96	7	6	有 多 大
29	14	5	的 两 种	63	9	6	值得 注意 的	97	7	6	的 一 贯
30	14	9	被 认为 是	64	9	6	所 需要 的	98	7	7	的 同时 也
31	13	5	在 这 一	65	9	8	是 不 是	99	7	6	的 科学家 们
32	13	7	所 产生 的	66	9	7	最 好 的	100	7	6	短 时间 内
33	13	5	指 的 是	67	9	9	的 就 是	101	7	5	随着 时间 的
34	13	9	最 早 的	68	9	8	的 最 大	102	6	5	一个 巨大 的

2007; Sinclair 2004); as such they have potential in many ways to improve language learning and teaching in the area of academic language (Donley and Reppen 2001).

A set of teaching materials in academic Chinese has been developed for advanced learners of Mandarin Chinese based on the corpus data and research findings. This set of materials is designed on the basis of an advanced Chinese language course called Academic and Professional Chinese (APC), which has been offered at UCLA since 2013–14; however, the materials are meant to be eventually made available to the wider Chinese language teaching and learning community.

Past experience shows that students taking the APC class typically are (1) learners who have no Chinese background but who have moved from lower levels all the way to advanced levels in a college of Chinese language program environment; (2) heritage students who have various prior exposures to Chinese but whose formal and/or written Chinese needs the most attention; and (3) graduate students from various research disciplines who need to improve their professional Chinese for research and career advancement.

In response to student needs, APC has focused on a range of pedagogical features that are essential for learner language development in this area. Some of the major skill areas involve the ability and proficiency to summarize academic writing and lectures and to critique materials in their own language; gather research data (based on surveys, experiments, printed sources, interviews, natural recordings, etc.) and categorize and represent data in meaningful ways; follow standard Chinese writing conventions, as appropriate, and express ideas clearly and logically; find reference sources written in different times, formats, and media; participate and lead discussions in an academic and professional setting; and, finally, deliver oral presentations in a professional and effective manner.

On the basis of the corpus data and corpus findings, the UCLA research team has sought to develop materials with the following considerations: (1) balancing the length of the texts to include texts of various sizes; (2) combining printed and online lectures and speeches; (3) expanding the content areas to cover multiple disciplines: the arts and humanities, social sciences, science and technology, and professional fields; (4) including multiple text genres, e.g., essays, research articles, dictionary/encyclopedia entries, textbooks, guidebooks, etc.; (5) attending to a variety of pragmatic/rhetorical functions based on the functions of multiword expressions: research-oriented strategies (describing settings and procedures of projects, quoting and referencing, etc.), text structuring strategies (expressing reasoning, highlighting hierarchies, and connections), and participant-oriented strategies showing (dis)agreement, expressing (un)certainty, expressing author's affective stance (Ochs 1996); and (6) developing a wide range of pedagogical activities based on the texts selected. These activities include analyzing the structure of a text, crafting a fitting title for a text, analyzing themes of paragraphs, identifying signaling/linking elements, writing abstracts, condensing long texts, finding contradictions and missing elements, comparing similar texts with different styles, leading discussions on complex topics, and conveying research ideas to laypersons in easy-to-understand ways.

As of this writing, 18 units have been developed. Each unit contains the following components:

(1) Instruction to the teacher with information on:

   (a) The text: describing important content and textual features of the selected text.
   (b) Lesson focus: describing major learning goals and specific academic/professional language features.

(2) Text: original authentic texts with various lengths.
(3) Vocabulary representing important academic textual characteristics, focusing on collocation and lexical bundles.
(4) Teaching activities (classroom activities, homework assignments, and extracurricular activities).

The 18 units and their titles are shown in Table 11.

Sample lesson design (with partial text, sample classroom activities, and sample homework assignments):

Text

FDA批准突破性帕金森药物,可减少幻觉发生

作者:冷月如霜

4月29日,美国FDA宣布批准了一种用于帕金森患者的新药——匹莫范色林(pimavanserin,商品名Nuplazid)。和以往的药物不同,这是第一种获得批准用于帕金森患者、治疗幻觉和妄想症状的药物。

帕金森症是一种神经退化性疾病,说到它,我们总是会想到那些无法控制抖动的双手。确实,肢体不由自主的抖动是帕金森最典型的症状,但运动能力的障碍远不是患者面临的唯一问题。根据美国国立卫生研究院(NIH)的统计,全美每年约新增五万名帕金森症患者,患者总数近百万。其中,有约50%的帕金森症患者会出现幻觉或妄想的症状。他们会看见或听见实际上并不存在的事物(幻觉),或存有虚妄的信念(妄想)。这些症状会让患者出现错误的想法与情绪,伤害与身边亲友之间的关系,并使他们无法好好照顾自己。

在此之前,一些抗精神病药物也能减少幻觉,帮助患者恢复理智,但遗憾的是,它们并不适合帕金森患者使用。Nuplazid的获批上市让这一切成为了历史。这种药物作用在与幻觉有关的5-羟色胺2A受体上,它能够起到与致幻药物正好相反的作用:致幻药物提高受体的活性,使中枢系统兴奋,产生迷幻效果;而Nuplazid则降低受体的基础活性,减少中枢系统的兴奋程度,从而降低出现幻觉或妄想的风险。

……

Selected Classroom Activities

(1) Vocabulary practice (focusing on key academic vocabulary and their patterns)

   (a) Reading comprehension: practice understanding of the vocabulary and article content by reading the text and identifying key expressions.
   (b) Consult a corpus of academic texts if necessary when explaining lexical items, especially commonly used academic vocabulary.

Table 11 The 18 units developed at UCLA for academic and professional Chinese teaching and learning

01. FDA批准突破性帕金森藥物	01. FDA approves a drug for Parkinson's disease
02. 人为什么会做梦	02. Why people dream
03. 文献综述撰写的原则和方法	03. Academic literature review guidelines
04. 转基因技术有何利与弊	04. Genetic modification: Pros and cons
05. 英语词汇学习中的分类组织策略实验研究	05. Strategies in English vocabulary learning: An experimental study
06. 汉英公示语翻译	06. Translating Chinese and English public signs
07. 翻转课堂	07. Flipped classroom
08. 丝绸之路	08. The Silk Road (Wikipedia)
09. 儿童肥胖已不再是“城市病”副本	09. Curing child obesity
10. 全球智能教育或将来临	10. The dawning of the era of global smart education
11. 关于2011年度中国大学生婚恋观的调查报告	11. The 2011 survey of views on relationships and marriage among Chinese college students
12. 关于合作视角下的委婉语使用的研究	12. Use of euphemisms from the perspective of the cooperative principle
13. 关于论儒家道德思想及其当代价值副本	13. The Confucian philosophy of morality and its current societal relevance
14. 如何培养学生的美学素养副本	14. How to teach aesthetics to college students
15. 幽默的心理学研究	15. The psychology of humor
16. 美国枪支管制的困难	16. What makes American gun control laws so tough
17. 關於電視相親類節目存在的問題及原因探微	17. An investigation of current issues in dating TV shows
18. 青少年心理疾病與父母教養方式的關係	18. Probing into the relationship between mental problems among the young and parenting methods

(c) Have the students use the following fixed expressions:
- 根据……统计
- 有效性……
- 与……相比
- 显著降低/提高……
- 基于……结果

(2) Introduce a product (such as a phone or tablet) and practice speaking (focusing on text genre awareness and practices):

(a) Why should you buy and use this product?
(b) Why is the product updated every year or why are new generations of the product rolled out annually?
(c) Would using or not using this product have an impact on people's everyday life?

(3) Introduce this product's target users (further activities and practices related to genre features).

(a) What group is most suited to use this product?
(b) How would you allow a user without relevant experience or understanding of this product to obtain information about it?
(c) What should users of different age categories know about using this new product?

(4) Extended activities related to the text in question: Alzheimer's, otherwise known as senile dementia, is a disease with a serious impact on the elderly and their families. Please describe:

(a) Symptoms of Alzheimer's disease.
(b) Age of onset.
(c) Harm caused to families and society by Alzheimer's disease.
(d) How to care for people with Alzheimer's disease and their families?

(5) Analysis and description (focusing on transformation of formality and ensuing text features):

(a) Analyze and describe, in plain language, the difference between Nuplazid and anti-psychotic medicines that were already available on the market.

(6) Discussion (focusing on academic discussion activities):

(a) What are the causes and symptoms of Parkinson's disease?
(b) Compare the quality of life for people with Parkinson's disease to those with malignant tumors.
(c) If someone in the family develops this disease, what should the family do?

(d) Discuss the five most fatal diseases in the United States. What are the main causes of these diseases? How can they be prevented?

Homework Assignment (focusing on student and individual profession-centered activities)

Have students chose from any of the suggested topics and give an oral report in class or write an article to hand it to the teacher. Oral reports must be about 4 min long and articles must be 200–300 characters.

(1) General requirements:

 (1) Choose interesting content or a research finding from a field with which you are most familiar.
 (2) In the style of a news reporter, use plain language to "report on" this content or result.

(2) Topic Choice I:

 (1) An introduction to a product upgrade.
 (2) A comparison of the product before and after the upgrade, highlighting its pros and cons.

(3) Topic Choice II:

 (1) A disease that you have seen or heard of.
 (2) Early symptoms of the disease and disease treatments.

Finally, beyond the specifics, a few general observations can be made regarding the relationship between corpora and academic Chinese material development and language teaching based on our experience with this project. These observations, in general, point to both advantages and limitations with corpora.

First, some advantages of academic corpora for language pedagogy. (1) Corpora can be helpful in guiding text selection in terms of both the range and type of texts to select. This is because corpus building with academic texts has dealt extensively with genre and discipline issues (Flowerdew 2013), which can be translated into text selection for developing teaching materials. (2) Corpus findings can be used directly with material development and related curricular activities (Donley and Reppen 2001). As discussed earlier, high-frequency vocabulary items, collocation patterns, and lexical bundles are all important types of information that can be brought to bear on the efficient integration of lexical and grammatical learning (Conrad 2000) and can be incorporated into curriculum design. (3) Corpora can be part of the teaching tools that both teachers and students take advantage of. Corpus materials, for example, can be selected to represent suitable examples and can be used for explanations of usage patterns.

Of course, corpora and some of the common ways in which corpora are used have limitations for teaching and learning (see Flowerdew 2005 for a comprehensive review of some of the arguments leveled against corpus approaches). With academic texts, these limitations may manifest in several ways. First, large-scale or higher level text properties are not easily extractable from corpora (Swales 2002), and much of this has to be done by an experienced language teacher. A case in point would be the analysis of the logical relations among different segments of academic prose. Another example would be comparing different versions of compatible texts or the condensation of a larger text. Second, not all texts in a corpus are suitable for pedagogical use. This is because, among other reasons, teaching material preparation requires consideration of many factors, such as language difficulty levels, types of content, and stylistic attractiveness—features and issues that corpus construction efforts may not necessarily be concerned with.

4 Concluding Remarks

Academic language has been identified as a key area for advanced language proficiency for international learners (Flowerdew 2013). Corpora can provide the much needed resources and tools for both research and education in academic language. Yet, systematic studies of Chinese academic texts remain rare. The efforts by the teams at NTNU and UCLA, especially in corpus building, constitute the necessary first step in remedying the situation. In the meantime, we expect that more efforts will be put into developing teaching materials and other pedagogical applications, in addition to more in-depth research beyond vocabulary. For example, grammatical features in academic (or scientific) Chinese have been the focus of much of the previous studies that have been conducted without much corpus support (Du 2005; Li 1985; Shao 2010); the availability of corpora can only improve the situation. Another area that will be both theoretically interesting and pedagogically relevant would be comparing discourse strategies in academic writing across disciplines and across languages. Previous research has compared the use of hedges (ways in which authors qualify their claims or indicate levels of commitment to their arguments) across disciplines (Chang et al. 2012) and between Chinese and English (Hu and Gao 2011). Findings along these lines will be extremely valuable for learners. Finally, academic Chinese research can also shed new light on the nature of the Chinese language in general. For example, the role of syllabicity in characterizing spoken and written Chinese as well as differentiating Chinese genres (Lǚ 1963; Feng 2009; Tao 2015; Zhang 2017) is a unique issue that may not figure prominently in other languages but is important for research and teaching of written academic Chinese. In short, there is much to be done in this very much underexplored area of Chinese applied linguistics.

Acknowledgements Howard Chen would like to thank the Ministry of Sciences and Technology, Taiwan, for supporting the related corpus research. He is also very grateful that this research is partially supported by the "Aim for the Top University Project" of the National Taiwan Normal University, sponsored by the Ministry of Education, Taiwan.

Hongyin Tao wishes to acknowledge the following individual and institutional support: Weidong Zhan and his team at Peking University, Ying Yang, and Yan Zhou for assistance with the UCLA CWAC corpus; Danjie Su, Xiaoxin Sun, and Yu-Wen Yao for participating in the development of the teaching materials; Jiajin Xu for constructive comments on an earlier version of the paper; Elizabeth Carter for both the translation of the teaching materials into English and the editorial assistance with this article; National Taiwan Normal University for support with a Distinguished Chair Professorship (2015–17); the UCLA Academic Senate faculty research grant (AY2014-16); and the U.S. Department of Education, grant #P229A140026, to the Center for Advanced Language Proficiency Education and Research (CALPER), The Pennsylvania State University. However, the contents developed under the grant do not necessarily represent the policy of the U.S. Department of Education, and you should not assume endorsement by the Federal Government.
Finally, we are grateful to the editors and anonymous referees for the constructive comments and suggestions on an earlier version of the paper. Any remaining shortcomings are of course entirely our own.

References

Biber, D. (2006). *University language: A corpus-based study of spoken and written registers*. Amsterdam: John Benjamins.

Biber, D., Conrad, S., & Reppen, R. (1998). *Corpus linguistics: Investigating structure and use*. Cambridge: Cambridge University Press.

Biber, D., Johansson, S., Leech, G., Conrad, S., & Finegan, E. (1999). *Longman grammar of spoken and written English*. Harlow: Pearson.

Campion, M., & Elley, W. (1971). *An academic vocabulary list*. Wellington: New Zealand Council for Educational Research.

Canavan, A., & Zipperlen, G. (1996). *CALLFRIEND Mandarin Chinese-Mainland dialect*. Philadelphia: Linguistic Data Consortium.

Conrad, S. (2000). Will Corpus linguistics revolutionize grammar teaching in the 21st century? *TESOL Quarterly, 34*(3), 548–560.

Coxhead, A. (2000). A new academic word list. *TESOL Quarterly, 34*(2), 213–238.

Chang, M., Luo Y., & Hsu Y. (2012). Subjectivity and objectivity in Chinese academic discourse: How attribution hedges indicate authorial stance. *Concentric: Studies in Linguistics, 38*(2), 293–329.

Chen, W. (陈望道) (1962/1997). *Introduction to rhetoric* (《修辞学发凡》). Shanghai: Shanghai Education Press (上海教育出版社).

Donley, K., & Reppen, R. (2001). Using corpus tools to highlight academic vocabulary in SCLT. *TESOL Journal, 10*(2–3), 7–12.

Du, W. (杜文霞) (2005). *Ba* constructions in different registers and their pragmatic functions (把字句在不同语体中的分布、结构、语用差异考察). *Journal of Nanjing University Social Sciences Edition* (《南京师范大学报 (社会科学版)》), *2005*(1), 145–150.

Feng, S. (2009). On modern written Chinese. *Journal of Chinese Linguistics, 37*(1), 145–161.

Francis, W., & Kucera, H. (1964). *A standard corpus of present-day edited American English, for use with digital computers*. Providence, RI: Brown University.

Flowerdew, J. (2013). Introduction: Approaches to the analysis of academic discourse. In J. Flowerdew (Ed.), *academic discourse* (pp. 1–18). New York: Routledge.

Flowerdew, L. (2005). An integration of corpus-based and genre-based approaches to text analysis in EAP/ESP: Countering criticisms against corpus-based methodologies. *English for Specific Purposes, 24*(3), 321–332.

Gardner, D., & Davies, M. (2013). A new academic vocabulary list. *Applied Linguistics, 35*(3), 305–327.

Ghadessy, P. (1979). Frequency counts, words lists, and materials preparation: A new approach. *English Teaching Forum, 17,* 24–27.

Han, Z., & Dong, J. (韓志剛、董傑). (2010). Vocabulary selection for scientific Chinese (《科技漢語教材編寫中的選詞問題》), *Cultural and Teaching Materials* (文教资料), *2010*(9), 51–53.

Huang, C., & Chen, K. (1992). A Chinese corpus for linguistics research. In *Proceedings of the 1992 International Conference on Computational Linguistics* (pp. 1214–1217). Nantes, France.

Hu, G., & Cao, F. (2011). Hedging and boosting in abstracts of applied linguistics articles: a comparative study of English- and Chinese-medium journals. *Journal of Pragmatics, 43*(11), 2795–2809.

Hyland, K. (2008). As can be seen: Lexical bundles and disciplinary variation. *English for Specific Purposes, 27*(1), 4–21.

Hyland, K. (2012). Bundles in academic discourse. *Annual Review of Applied Linguistics, 32,* 150–169.

Li, Y. (李裕德). (1985). *Grammar of scientific Chinese* (科技汉语语法). Beijing: Metallurgical Industry Press (冶金工业出版社).

Liu, C.(劉貞妤), Chen, H.(陳浩然), & Yang, H. (楊惠媚) (2016). Compiling a Chinese academic wordlist based on an academic corpus (藉學術語料庫提出中文學術常用詞表: 以人文社會科學為例). *Journal of Chinese Language Teaching* (華語文教學研究), *13*(2), 4–87.

Liu, C.(劉貞妤), Chen, H.(陳浩然), & Yang, H. (楊惠媚) (2017). Study on the lexical bundles in Chinese academic writing (中文人文社會科學論文常用詞串之研究). *Journal of Chinese Language Teaching* (華語文教學研究), *14*(1), 119–152.

Lǘ, S. (吕叔湘) (1963). Monosyllables and disyllables in modern Chinese (现代汉语单双音节问题初探). *Chinese Language* (《中国语文》), *1963*(1), 11–23.

Lynn, R. (1973). Preparing word lists: A suggested method. *RELC Journal, 4*(1), 25–32.

McEnery, A., & Xiao, Z. (2004). The Lancaster corpus of Mandarin Chinese: A corpus for monolingual and contrastive language study. In *Proceedings of the Fourth International Conference on Language Resources and Evaluation* (pp. 1175–1178). Lisbon, Portugal.

Ochs, E. (1996). Linguistic resources for socializing humanity. In J. Gumperz & S. Levinson (Eds.), *Rethinking linguistic relativity* (pp. 407–437). Cambridge: Cambridge University Press.

O'Keeffe, A., McCarthy, M., & Carter, R. (2007). *From corpus to classroom: Language use and language teaching*. Cambridge: Cambridge University Press.

Peng, N. (彭妮丝) (Ed.). (2016). *Introduction to professional Chinese* (專業華語概論). Taipei: New Sharing Publishing Company Ltd. (新學林出版股份有限公司).

Praninskas, J. (1972). *American university word list*. London: Longman.

Salazar, D. (2014). *Lexical bundles in native and non-native scientific writing: Applying a corpus-based study to language teaching*. Amsterdam: John Benjamins.

SCTOP (Steering Committee on the Test of Proficiency—Huayu. 國家華語測驗推動工作委員會). (2016). Introducing the Mandarin TOCFL 8000 word list (華語八千詞表説明). Taipei. Available online from http://www.sc-top.org.tw/download/8000_description.pdf. Last accessed September 2, 2017.

Shao, C. (邵长超). (2010). Adjectival predicates in literary and scientific registers (文艺语体和科技语体形谓句状语差异研究). *Jinan University Journal* (《暨南学报 (哲学社会科学版)》), 2010(2), 123–127.

Simpson-Vlach, R. (2006). Academic speech across disciplines: Lexical and phraseological distinctions. In K. Hyland & M. Bondi (Eds.), *Academic discourse across disciplines* (pp. 295–316). Bern: Peter Lang.

Simpson-Vlach, R. (2013). Corpus analysis of spoken English for academic purposes. In C. Chapelle (Ed.), *The encyclopedia of applied linguistics*. Chichester, UK: Blackwell.

Sinclair, J. (Ed.). (2004). *How to use corpora in language teaching*. Amsterdam: John Benjamins.

Swales, J. (2002). Integrated and fragmented worlds: EAP materials and corpus linguistics. In J. Flowerdew (Ed.), *Academic discourse* (pp. 150–164). London: Longman.

Tao, H. (2013). *Corpus of Written Academic Chinese*. ACTFL CALPER Brochure. State College, PA: Pennsylvania State University.

Tao, H. (2015). Profiling the Mandarin spoken vocabulary based on corpora. In W. Wang & C. Sun (Eds.), *Oxford handbook of Chinese linguistics* (pp. 336–347). Oxford: Oxford University Press.
Tao, H., & Xiao, R. (2007). *The UCLA Chinese Corpus*. UCREL: Lancaster.
Xiao, R., Rayson, P., & McEnery, T. (2009). *A frequency dictionary of Mandarin Chinese: Core vocabulary for learners*. London/New York: Routledge.
Xu, J. (2015). Corpus-based Chinese studies: A historical review from the 1920s to the present. *Chinese Language and Discourse, 6*(2), 218–244.
Xu, J. (许家金) (2017). *ToRCH2014 Corpus* (ToRCH2014现代汉语平衡语料库). Beijing: Beijing Foreign Studies University.
Xue, G., & Nation, I. (1984). A university word list. *Language Learning and Communication, 3*(2), 215–229.
Xun, E. (荀恩东), Rao, G. (饶高琦), Xiao, X. (肖晓悦), & Zang, JJ (臧娇娇). (2016). Developing the BCC Corpus in a big data environment (大数据背景下BCC语料库的研制). *Corpus Linguistics* (语料库语言学), *3*(1), 93–109.
Zhang, Z. (2017). *Dimensions of variation in written Chinese*. New York: Routledge.
Zipf, G. (1935). *The psycho-biology of language*. Boston: Houghton Mifflin Company.
Zou, J. (邹嘉彦) & You, R., (游汝杰). (2010). *A Global Chinese Neologisms Dictionary* (《全球华语新词语词典》). Beijing: Commercial Press.

Pedagogical Applications of Chinese Parallel Corpora

Brody Bluemel

Abstract Parallel corpora are a unique resource in language acquisition that enables learners to conceptualize a target language through the established schemas of their first language by providing parallel representations of text in two or more languages. Parallel corpora are defined as specialized translation corpora that consist of source texts in one language that are aligned with translation texts in one or more additional languages. The following chapter thoroughly explores the pedagogical application of parallel corpora in general, before taking an in-depth look at how English L1 beginning-level learners of Mandarin Chinese applied a Chinese–English parallel corpus. In addition to elucidating the specific observed outcomes of parallel corpora in this unique learning context, numerous parallel corpus resources are detailed with suggestions for pedagogical application, and an extensive review of potential further applications based on continued research in the field is enumerated and analyzed.

1 Parallel and Translation Corpora

Corpora have long been valuable technology resources both in linguistic research and in language pedagogy, and as with all technologies, corpora continue to evolve and be adapted in new and innovative ways. Many specialized corpora have been developed to address a specific niche or need in research or learning, only to later be adapted differently to address a wider range of questions or problems. Parallel corpora are one such categorization of specialized corpora that have both been developed to address specific research and/or pedagogical needs, and also later innovatively adapted to assist in the acquisition of language and content. As parallel corpora have great potential for adaption in L2 curriculum and instruction, it is beneficial to fully explore and understand what parallel corpora are and the diverse ways they are constructed and used. Parallel corpora belong to a subcategory of corpora known as translation corpora. As the name implies, translation corpora are composed

B. Bluemel (✉)
Delaware State University, Dover, USA
e-mail: bbluemel@desu.edu

X. Lu and B. Chen (eds.), *Computational and Corpus Approaches to Chinese Language Learning*, Chinese Language Learning Sciences,
https://doi.org/10.1007/978-981-13-3570-9_5

of text material in more than one language. There are several types of translation corpora including comparable corpora, parallel corpora, and equivalent corpora (which combines collections of both comparable and parallel corpus materials). These iterations of translation corpora differ based on the construct of the source material, and their differences also direct how they can be applied in research and learning. It is imperative to understand how they are designed, created, and structured in order to appreciate the full extent to which they can be applied in teaching and learning the language.

Comparable corpora are created by compiling two or more monolingual subcorpora using the same sampling frame. The content in these corpora do not include direct translations of material from one language to another, but rather include representations of a specific discourse or sampling unit in multiple languages. Laviosa (2002) provides an illustration of comparable corpora as she developed an English news subcorpus that equated the news subcorpora of the Translational English Corpus (TEC), which includes news content in German, Italian, and other languages. The collections of texts are all comparable news texts but written independently in the respective languages. In contrast, parallel corpora are compilations of source texts in one language aligned with their direct translations in one (bilingual) or more (multilingual) additional languages. The source texts compiled into parallel corpora can be unidirectional, bidirectional, or multidirectional (McEnery and Xiao 2008: 20). Unidirectional indicates that source texts are from one language, and translations the other (e.g., English source texts/Chinese translations *or* Chinese source texts/English translations). Bidirectional denotes a balance of source texts from both languages and their translations (e.g., both English source texts/Chinese translations *and* Chinese source/English translations). Last, multidirectional refers to compilations of the same text in numerous languages (e.g., the same article in Chinese, English, and German).

A further design element of parallel corpora to address is alignment. Parallel corpora align the source texts and translations using phrasal alignment, sentential alignment, context-based alignment, or a combination of these approaches (Biçici 2008). Phrasal alignment links set constructs in the source text with the corresponding construct in the translated text; this can include phrases, clauses, set expressions, or even individual words. Sentential alignment links the different language texts in sentence segments. Context-based alignment is perhaps the most complex, as it requires multiple phases of machine processing to determine corresponding contextual phrases before linking the corpora together based upon the concept or idea being expressed (Biçici 2008: 435). As the different modes of alignment provide varied capacities for interaction with the texts, it is essential to distinguish what alignment method(s) are used in order to understand how a parallel corpus can be applied.

Identifying the type of translation corpus and the design characteristics such as direction of translation and alignment enable the user to select the right source for a particular application and to fully realize how to adapt the chosen source for optimal outcomes. For example, a comparable corpus aligned at the phrasal level may best suit a crosslinguistic exercise examining discourse markers and politeness. The phrasal-level alignment would allow for the easier comparison of specific discourse markers, and the source texts would include very similar representations of naturally occurring language production in each respective language. A parallel corpus, by contrast, provides translated representations of a source text in one or more target languages. Frankenberg-Garcia (2004: 225) points out "that the language of translation is not the same as language which is not constrained by source texts from another language" (see also Baker 1996). The language of translation, or "translationese" (see Salkie 1999) is, therefore, a representation of meaning expressed in the source language and not the direct equivalent. This inherent characteristic of translation, and parallel corpora provides a valuable pedagogical aid for learners in developing conceptual knowledge of a language as the translated texts exemplify how a language expert (translator) chose to represent the meaning and use of a source text in his/her translation.

Accordingly, parallel corpora present learners with a model of a translator's conceptual knowledge of a language and enable learners to take advantage of this knowledge in developing their own language skill and conceptual understanding. Aijmer (2008: 98) observes, "Translation is one of the very few cases where speakers evaluate meaning relations between expression not as part of some kind of metalinguistic, philosophical or theoretical reflection, but as a normal kind of linguistic activity". Tufiş (2007: 103) adds "the linguistic decisions made by the human translators in order to faithfully convey the meaning of the source text can be traced and used as evidence on linguistic facts which, in a monolingual context, might be unavailable to (or overlooked by) a computer program". These arguments conclude that parallel corpora provide users with a sampling of language that more accurately represents the meaning and use of a source text that can be accomplished through a computer program, dictionary, or other more typical resources for language learning. Essentially, the aligned parallel representations of content in the native and target language(s) allows users to conceptualize content in the target language(s) through the established schemas of their first language (L1). Consequently, the unique features of parallel corpora have extensive potential for informing foreign language education, translation, and pedagogical practices.

2 Pedagogical Applications of Parallel Corpora

Parallel corpora were initially envisioned and designed to address research questions in comparative linguistics and translation studies (Aijmer and Altenberg 1996; Aston 1997; Johansson 1999). The transition from linguistic research to language learning has occurred more recently and is an area that is still continuing to develop. The pedagogical studies that have been completed have returned promising results and led scholars to continue to call for further development of new parallel corpora and additional applications of existing technology (Fan and Xu 2002; Johansson 2009; Wang 2001). As the number of pedagogical studies using parallel corpora is still somewhat limited, the following review first draws upon examples from varied language pairs before examining in detail examples of Chinese/English parallel corpus applications.

Several initial applications of parallel corpora in language learning pedagogy used the technology for the development of materials that aided learners in addressing specific challenges unique to a particular language. For example, King (2003) details how parallel concordances were used to develop materials for the teaching usage of the French "*dont*" (whose), the differences between "*schlimm*" (bad) and "*schlecht*" (bad) in German as they both translate into English as *bad*, and for exploring the range of the many collocates of *carry out* in English (p. 162). Further, he developed a Greek–English parallel concordance to teach the difference between the modals *should* and *would* versus *will* and *must.* Though there are direct translations of these four modals in both languages, their functions are quite different. King's study demonstrates that by using parallel concordances students were able to learn "the extent to which natural Greek was produced by translating *would* as πρέπει (*must*), and by logical extension, how natural English in certain circumstances uses *would* to achieve the same pragmatic effect as Greek *must*" (ibid.: 162). The use of parallel concordances to create learning materials in these instances provided learners with tangible examples and illustrations of how the modals are conceptualized and function in the two different languages. Laviosa (2002) also used parallel concordances to create comprehension and production exercises for a group of English/Italian learners to use in exploring the difference between imperfect, the simple past, and the present perfect tenses in the two languages. Similar to Laviosa, McEnery and Wilson (2001) used the Chemnitz English/German parallel corpus to provide German L1 learners of English with a functional understanding of how aspect is communicated in the two respective languages.

Frankenberg-Garcia (2005) also provides additional insight into how parallel corpora can be adapted into the classroom. In addition to using parallel corpora to teach obscure lexical items, she analyzed the efficacy of the use of parallel corpora in comparison to monolingual corpora and language dictionaries, and she asserts that parallel corpora are the most effective resource for students to use when asking the questions, "How do you say ______ in L2?" and "Is it okay to say ______ in L2" (ibid.: 191–192). The parallel corpus allows learners to not just see how something is said, but to evaluate which term is contextually appropriate both in their L1 and target language. St. John (2001) further demonstrates this in teaching English L1 students of German to decipher the meaning of new vocabulary and formulate grammatical understanding independently with the use of a German/English parallel corpus. She noted that parallel corpora not only enable students to understand confusing vocabulary and concepts but also help them develop an ability to *learn how to learn*. Her observations strengthen the claims made by Frankenberg-Garcia and demonstrate an effective use of parallel corpora at the very beginning stages of foreign language learning.

Looking now to the application of Chinese/English parallel corpora, Wang (2002) demonstrates how this technology can be used to analyze the specific usage of "*xiànzài*" [现在] compared with its English translation "*now*". This application enabled the researchers to provide learners with a more complete depiction of how the term functions in Chinese and to illustrate the structural differences between the two languages when expressing this concept. Specifically, they reported that Chinese typically follows a "subject + *xiànzài*" structure, whereas the English had a "subject + be + *now*" structure, but also noted instances where "*xiànzài*" [现在] appeared in the Chinese text, but "*now*" was not present in the corresponding English translation. The detailed findings for this specific construct illustrate how parallel corpora can be used to more articulately present structural and contextual elements of word function in the two languages to enable learners to develop a more complete conceptual framework in both their target language and their L1.

The perceived ability of parallel corpora to aid learners in their conceptual development is substantiated in Fan and Xu's (2002) research using a Chinese/English legal parallel corpus. The focus of their research was on how students chose to use the parallel corpus and whether it was a preferred resource in learning. Their research was conducted among L1 Chinese students in Hong Kong where most coursework was completed in English. The legal parallel corpus was adapted to aid students in developing legal vocabulary and better understanding of legal concepts in both languages. Evaluation of student application of the corpus informs both how students used it and what they found most beneficial. One key finding of the research was that even though all students referenced material in their L1 (Chinese) first, the overwhelming majority (85%) found that using both the Chinese and English texts (thus the parallel concordances) was the most useful approach for comprehension (ibid.: 55). While the statistical analysis is based on student opinion, and would undoubtedly vary based on individuals and level of language experience, what is noteworthy in this study is that students overwhelmingly preferred the option of using the parallel corpus and immediately recognized the value in aiding their development and understanding. The authors conclude that the use of parallel corpora enhanced students' level of comprehension and learning experience. This avers that parallel corpora not only aid students in developing conceptual knowledge, but they are potentially more efficient than other methods—as students demonstrate a preference in using them.

A further study by Tsai and Choi (2005) of lexical development among Chinese language learners observes that parallel corpora aid students in comprehending terms with complex meanings more effectively than traditional instructional methods. They provided English L1 students of Chinese with nine lexical items that were divided into three categories based on the number of English equivalents that each Chinese lexical item had: (1) one or two equivalents, (2) more than two equivalents, and (3) no exact equivalent. The list of terms was given to both a control and an experimental group. Before being assessed with a common test, the control group used traditional methods (dictionaries, textbooks, etc.) to learn the vocabulary, while the experimental group used the Babel Chinese–English parallel corpus. The assessment results indicated that the experimental group participants performed significantly better in categories two and three where the Chinese term had either multiple equivalents or no direct equivalent in English and that both groups performed relatively similar in category one with the simpler Chinese terms that had only one or two direct equivalents in English. Further, it was noted that the control group only recalled the one meaning depicted in their textbook for terms in category two that had multiple meanings, whereas the experimental group remembered more possible meanings. Additionally, the control group tended to "use a direct translation of their L1 to compose a sentence," while the experimental group did not (Tsai and Choi 2005: 6). Collectively, these results indicate that students in the experimental group developed schemas for the lexical items, whereas the control group was limited to direct translations.

One final example illustrates the extent to which parallel corpora can be creatively adapted to meet the needs of specific populations and language learning challenges. Xu and Kawecki's (2005) adapted a trilingual parallel corpus for a group of French (L3) language learners who were all native Chinese speakers (L1) with advanced proficiency in English (L2). The authors reported that the parallel corpus was particularly helpful in aiding students in comprehending linguistic concepts that are often pragmatically and semantically challenging. As there are greater similarities between English and French than Chinese and French, the authors observed that the trilingual presentation of the texts enabled the students to compare challenging concepts to ideas they had already mastered and learned in English. The unique structure of this corpus and classroom allowed students to make use of their implicit L1 knowledge as well as their explicit L2 knowledge in developing concepts in their L3.

3 Applying Parallel Corpora in Chinese Reading and Writing Acquisition

Building on the applications of parallel corpora in Chinese language pedagogy, the author created and adapted a parallel corpus specific for addressing challenges of reading and writing acquisition faced by beginning-level Chinese language learners.

The Chinese orthographic system presents learners with several unique challenges. For instance, learners must be able to recognize between 3000 and 4000 characters in order to navigate a basic newspaper text (Norman 1988). Accordingly, beginning-level learners of the language are typically not able to traverse authentic language materials in their learning until a certain number of characters have been mastered. This differs greatly from languages with an alphabet where learners can sound out words after learning both the alphabet and phonology of the language and benefit from aural recognition and context.

Word parsing presents learners with a further challenge in recognizing words and phrases within a given text. Words in Chinese texts are not separated by spaces and the reader must parse units of meaning. Given that words may be composed of one, two, or more characters, and many characters have multiple meanings, identifying terms in text can be particularly challenging for language learners. As a basic example, the character "*diàn*" [电] by itself refers to *electricity*, but when combined with a second character it takes on a separate meaning such as "*diànnǎo*" [电脑] (*computer*) or "*diànhuà*" [电话] (*telephone*). This challenges learners as they are faced with learning multiple meanings and functions of the already numerous number of characters in order just begin parsing written meaning.

These particular challenges of written Chinese are here identified, as the unique features of parallel corpus technology are suited to aid learners in overcoming them. The Chinese/English parallel corpus created for this project, the Parallel Corpus Teaching Tool (PCTT), was designed to make it possible for beginning-level learners to navigate authentic Chinese texts and not be restricted by the many characters they have yet to learn. As has been established, corpora in general, and parallel or translation corpora in specific, aid learners in addressing challenges of polysemy and homonymy, and in conceptualizing multiple functions of words or phrases. Parallel corpora make it possible for learners to access schemas in their L1 to comprehend complex L2 concepts and the corpus tool designed for this project sought to capitalize on these unique features in order to more effectively assist language learners in the development of reading, writing, and lexical acquisition in their target language.

The PCTT was designed for both research and pedagogical application, but with a primary focus on creating a resource that provides more practical and fluid methods for effective and efficient written language acquisition. The typical format of parallel corpora enables the user to search a word in either language (in this case either Chinese or English), and the concordance query results display all sentences that contain that word—as well as all of the corresponding translations in the second language. This approach to language analysis and study allows learners to see how a word or phrase is used in a target language, and also to identify how that same expression is articulated in the corresponding or parallel language. The PCTT offers additional features beyond the typical platform, by allowing users to view the aligned texts not just in Chinese and English, but also in two additional formats: Chinese characters with tone marks and Romanized pinyin. This unique approach makes writings more accessible to language learners by providing texts in a format they are able to read (as the pinyin format aids them in identifying characters unknown to them). In practice, this made it possible for students to navigate complete authentic texts and to have minimal mediation in the process.

The pedagogical application of this corpus took place in two beginning-level high school Chinese classrooms in the United States over a 3-month period. During the first month of the study, participants learning experience remained unaltered. The parallel corpus was not introduced until the second month of the study, at which time students were instructed on its use and applications and encouraged to apply it. During the final month of the study use of the parallel corpus was required in order to complete several tasks. The students had access to the corpus tool both in class and outside of class to study and to complete a series of assignments and learning activities. The study followed their progression and analyzed performance and reported experience over this 3-month period.

In application, the parallel corpus functioned as a mediational tool that made reading Chinese texts less intimidating, more accessible, and interaction with both the characters and texts was more organic. The pedagogical study of this tool analyzed learner achievement, pedagogical application, and learner attitude/perception. The results demonstrated that integration of the parallel corpus led to substantial learner achievement and development when the participants adapted the parallel corpus as directed by the instructor. Students were able to comprehend complete texts, learn complex constructs, and later produce language using those constructs.

One example observed in the study followed a student in learning to use the term "*shíhòu*" [时候] (*time/time period*). This term had been encountered by students in supplementary texts, but not yet explicitly covered in the class. In evaluated screen recordings, this student is observed searching the term in the parallel corpus and then reviewing the 12 results returned from the query, presumably analyzing the meaning and use of the term (Fig. 1). The presumption is later confirmed in his exam essay when he writes, "Wǒ qùnián shèngdànjié de shíhòu xiǎng shì hùshì. Wǒ xiànzài xiǎng shì yīshēng." [我去年圣诞节的时候想是护士。我现在想是医生。] (*Last year at Christmas I wanted to be a nurse. Now I want to be a doctor.*)". This "*shíhòu*" 时候 (*time/time period*) construct functions differently in Chinese than in English and a more direct translation of the student's first sentence might read *I last year Christmas at that time wanted to be a nurse*. The student managed to use it correctly, but the reliance on the parallel corpus suggests the need for further mediation to review and correctly use the term in composing the sentence.

Several students were observed applying the PCTT similarly in searching terms and phrases to then evaluate meaning and usage. In this regard, the parallel corpus was successfully applied as a mediational tool that gave learners access to authentic language use that they could evaluate and fully comprehend through the L1 translation text.

Further, it was also observed that pedagogical implementation is integral to the successful adaptation of parallel corpora. The way an individual chose to apply the parallel corpus greatly influenced their learning experience and level of development. Analysis of the learners who did not evidence observable improvement by using the tool revealed that they chose to use the parallel corpus differently than directed

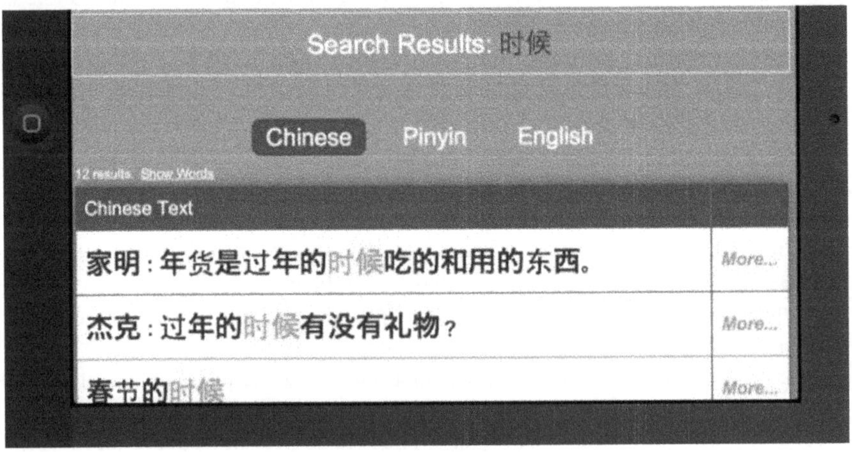

Fig. 1 Student search of "*shíhòu*" [时候] using PCTT

to simply search out answers and not to analyze the meaning and function of the language and specific constructs. Thus, while instructor mediation and guidance in using the tool is essential, ultimately learners must also actively choose to use the tool as a mediational artifact in order for it to benefit their learning.

Consideration of learner attitude/perception revealed that regardless of how students chose to adapt the tool they understood how it could aid learning. One student reported that while bilingual dictionaries "helped [her] find what new vocab items meant, [the] parallel corpus helped [her] figure out how to use them". Though there were many varied applications of the PCTT in the study, the resounding learner attitude reported was very positive. The observations of this study suggest not only the actual value and potential of implementing parallel corpora in the classroom but also the perceived value among learners. This attitude is also mirrored in the analysis of the instructor's perception, as he notes the overall positive learning experience throughout the study and his motivation to use the parallel corpus to make challenging learning objectives more accessible to the participants.

The varied applications of parallel corpora observed in the literature and the study outlined above demonstrate multiple methods that can be taken to aid students both generally in language learning and specifically in acquiring challenging constructs or concepts in the target language. The diverse potential approaches that can currently be applied in using this technology are diverse, and only stand to increase as current and future resources are developed and refined. In what follows, many existing Chinese/English parallel corpora and other resources based in this technology are identified with recommendations for immediate pedagogical application. The subsequent section then considers the future possibilities for continued development of parallel corpora for language learning.

4 Tools and Resources

It is essential to consider the design features of the available Chinese/English parallel corpora and associated resources in order to explore the possibilities for adapting them in the classroom. A compilation of available resources, organized into three subcategories, is provided below with suggestions for adaptation in the classroom. The first subcategory includes four Chinese/English parallel corpora that are accessible online. These corpora were all initially designed for the purpose of linguistic research and development. As such, the design of these resources did not provide extensive consideration to their potential pedagogical application. Nevertheless, these resources still readily lend themselves to classroom language learning. The second subcategory includes three resources that were designed intentionally for pedagogical application. Though each source is unique in design and features, all were created with the intent of language learners accessing and using them in their language learning studies. The final subcategory details three additional resources that were created as general learning resources that adapt features of translation corpora in their design.

4.1 Parallel Corpus Resources Designed for Research

Although there are still relatively few Chinese/English parallel corpora readily available, many of those that do exist are well-developed and excellent resources. Three examples include the Babel Chinese–English Parallel Corpus, the PKU Chinese–English Parallel Corpus, and the UM-Corpus. As these three corpora are easily accessible and freely available, they are explored in greater detail below. In addition to these, other resources such as the Hong Kong Bilingual Corpus of Legal and Documentary Texts and the Social Media Machine Translation Toolkit[1] also exist. These corpora have a somewhat steeper learning curve for adaptation as a parallel concordancer such as ParaConc[2] is necessary for fully employing the features of these resources. ParaConc itself is also a helpful additional resource as it is a bilingual or multilingual concordancer designed specifically for navigating translated corpus materials. ParaConc as a resource provides an excellent entry point for those with interest in pursuing more advanced parallel corpus applications and/or creating their own parallel corpora.

The Babel Chinese–English Parallel Corpus[3] serves as the first example of a readily accessible resource for application. This corpus was initially designed for a contrastive research study of Chinese and English. This unidirectional parallel corpus includes source texts in English with their translated representations in Mandarin Chinese. 327 English texts and their Chinese translations were extracted from the *World of English* and *Time*. Both English and Chinese texts were all tagged for part of speech and were aligned at the sentence level. This corpus can be downloaded from the Lancaster University website where it is housed, and then be adapted in a variety of ways. It is also directly accessible via the website interface set up by Beijing Foreign Studies University.[4] Through the website interface, users are able to search the corpus using a wide range of query restrictions including word lookup using wild-cards or selecting part of speech, conducting keyword analysis, or evaluating frequency lists. Essentially, the Babel Chinese–English Parallel Corpus provides users with an experience that is consistent with most corpus research tools. As such, it is a great resource for creating materials and gathering data for pedagogical application. Most language learners would not be prepared to use the corpus themselves in their language learning but would benefit greatly from the materials and samples compiled for them by an instructor.

The PKU Chinese–English Parallel Corpus[5] is comparable to the Babel corpus in terms of accessibility and usability. It is also hosted and available through Lancaster University's website. The texts in this corpus are also tagged for part of speech in both languages and aligned at the sentence level. The corpus is composed of over 200,000 aligned sentence pairs extracted from a wide range of source texts

[1]http://www.cs.cmu.edu/~lingwang/microtopia/#translation.

[2]http://www.athel.com/para.html.

[3]http://www.lancaster.ac.uk/fass/projects/corpus/babel/babel.htm.

[4]http://111.200.194.212/cqp/.

[5]http://www.lancaster.ac.uk/fass/projects/corpus/863parallel/default.htm.

including official documents, news texts, speech scripts, literary texts, academic propose, economics, and business. As the text samples only include sentence pairs, the language use context is apparently not as salient as other resources. However, a distinct pedagogical application of this resource would be in providing authentic language examples of a wide variety of language use, enabling users to compare and become cognizant of the differences of language use dependent upon genre, subject, and/or domain.

A final Chinese/English parallel research corpus example is the UM-Corpus.[6] This corpus varies significantly from the previous two as it is much larger and was created with a different purpose in mind. This corpus was created especially for statistical machine translation in order to *train* software created for computerized translation. Despite this intended use, it still serves a potentially useful resource for language pedagogy. The corpus itself includes approximately 15 million aligned English–Chinese sentences in eight different domains including education, laws, microblogs, news, science, spoken, subtitles, and thesis. Several of these eight domains are further categorized into topics. For example, the news domain is further demarcated for topics such as politics, economy, technology, and society. The extensive list of topics and domains in addition to the large size of the corpus make it a resource worth mentioning and considering. Due to the extensive processing required in aligning and creating parallel corpora, most resources are limited in size and scope. This corpus moves beyond this limitation and provides an exceptional resource for application. However, unlike the two previous parallel corpora outlined, the UM-Corpus does not currently have a web interface. It is freely available for download, but those looking to use this resource would need to have the necessary software and technical ability to actually make use of it. For those both motivated and able, though, this is an exceptional resource with limitless potential applications in research and pedagogy.

As pointed out, these research parallel corpora do have a somewhat steeper learning curve than the other resources discussed below, but the rich linguistic features that can be identified within these corpora make them very worthwhile. One of the most readily accessible adaptations of these resources is in the creation of learning material to present to learners. These corpora are particularly helpful when addressing challenging concepts or nuances in language. For example, when teaching the usage of the terms "néng" [能], "huì" [会], and "kěyǐ" [可以], all of which can be translated directly as *can*, though they have differentiated application, aligned parallel concordances can be presented to learners that allow individuals to not just learn the rule but to recognized the context and meaning associated with the term.

4.2 Parallel Corpus Resources Designed for Pedagogy

The second subcategory includes three resources that were designed intentionally for pedagogical application. The first two were created and identified as parallel corpora for pedagogy, whereas the third resource was designed and is identified as a Chinese

[6]http://nlp2ct.cis.umac.mo/um-corpus/.

language reading resource but uses parallel concordances and aligned translation texts. As all these resources were designed with pedagogy in mind, they are far more classroom ready than the other corpora considered, and all can be used independently by language learners and instructors.

The first resource closely resembles a research corpus but is simplified and more accessible to a wider range of users. The E-C Concord English–Chinese Parallel Concordancer[7] includes a collection of bidirectional texts aligned at the sentence level. While the sampling size is limited (1.8 million English words, 3.1 million Chinese characters), the texts do include several domains including novels, essays, fairy tales, and even an academic article and legal document. A clear advantage of this resource for pedagogy is its user-friendly interface that lets users search in Chinese or English, and also presents concordance results in several formats in including English–Chinese (traditional), English–Chinese (simplified), and English–Pinyin. Consequently, by conducting the same search with different output formats, users can have parallel concordance results displayed in English, Chinese characters, and pinyin. This resource has been used in the classroom to explore contextual samples of new constructs. For example, the concordance can be used to introduce a term such as "*dōu*" [都] (all/both), which functions differently in Chinese and English. After introducing the term, students explore concordances to develop a conceptual understanding of how it functions and how it is represented in both languages. Further, the text samples also make it possible to introduce full articles or books to students and allow them to reference their L1 as needed to fully comprehend the content of the material.

The second resource, the Parallel Corpus Teaching Tool (PCTT) includes the features of E-C Concord, while also adding additional functions to make it both more user-friendly and diverse in application (Bluemel 2013). It was created as an interactive web-based tool formatted for both computer and tablet access and was designed so that texts could continually be added or removed from the interface. As such, instructors can manage and control the texts that students have access to and also upload specific texts that are relevant to the content being addressed in the classroom. All texts in the tool are included in four language formats: Chinese characters, Chinese characters + tone marks, pinyin, and English. Adding the two additional formats (Chinese characters + tone marks and pinyin) was done specifically for language learner benefit. While the objective is for learners to be able to navigate Chinese texts, these two formats further mediate learner comprehension by providing additional resources as needed without having to default to the English (L1) text. The character + tone mark format was a new approach adapted in this technology as it is recognized that many Chinese language learners acquire the pinyin pronunciation of a character without simultaneously learning the tone, and therefore require further mediation in mastering appropriate tone.

The PCTT was designed to be used in one of two ways: first, either querying specific words or phrases or second, accessing complete texts in the aligned language formats. As the objective of the technology as a language learning resource is to

[7]http://ec-concord.ied.edu.hk/paraconc/index.htm.

aid students in written language acquisition, the goal is for students to use the least amount of mediation as possible. As such, regardless of how the resource is queried, it initially returns results in just Chinese and English. Users must select to have the additional language formats made available by either clicking to view the additional column or clicking on individual Chinese terms to have them displayed either with tone mark or as pinyin (see Bluemel 2014 for more detail). As was discussed previously under Sect. 5.3, this resource was used to assist learners in Chinese reading and writing acquisition. Learners were able to access and digest complete texts, even at the beginning-level, they were able to identify and develop conceptual understanding of new grammatical constructs, and they were able to learn multiple meanings of characters and words that have various applications. This was used readily in the classroom to facilitate students conceptual access to texts. Documents and readings regularly scheduled in the curriculum were made available through the PCCT in the parallel corpus format to provide them access to the concepts through their L1 as needed for navigating challenging concepts.

One final resource created using aligned parallel corpora is the *ReadChinese!*[8] e-learning tool created by the National Foreign Language Center at the University of Maryland. As the name transparently implies, this tool was designed specifically to aid learners reading comprehension and development and has materials created both for beginning and intermediate learners. *ReadChinese!* includes many features beyond the spectrum of a parallel corpus including topic-specific learning activities, glossary, dictionary, and comprehension exercises. All texts in each of the exercises, however, are formatted as aligned parallel texts and can be accessed in multiple formats including Chinese, Chinese with pinyin, Chinese audio, and English translation. This resource is a ready-made tool that applies parallel corpus technology and is created as a series of lessons and exercises. *ReadChinese!* can be adapted to any classroom with minimal or no further manipulation required by the instructor. This resource is set up as a classroom learning resource with comprehension activities.

4.3 Additional Resources that Incorporate Parallel Corpus Technology

The final subcategory of resources for applying parallel corpora in language learning include widely available tools that many language educators already use. Further exploring these resources, and recognizing how they employ parallel corpora, serves to enhance both how they are used and provide a launching point for further adaptations of them in the future. The first resource mentioned is TED talks. Many language educators have incorporated TED talks in the classroom as they are published online in many accessible formats on diverse topics of interest to students. Many of these talks are now readily available in parallel corpus formats as is discussed below. Additionally, the websites linguee.com and tatoeba.org are explored. These both are

[8]http://readchinese.nflc.org/.

marketed as online dictionaries, and query results return parallel concordances of the term appearing in authentic language materials. The final resource mentioned is the Bing Chinese–English dictionary. This resource uses Microsoft's Bing search engine as a dictionary that returns web results aligned in Chinese and English.

TED talks[9] have been an exceptional resource in academia and language learning for some time now. The speeches given by experts and innovators from numerous disciplines are both educational and inspiring. As a language learning resource, they are rich in content and are provided in a format readily accessible to learners as video, audio, and text (transcripts). As such, TED talks are frequently used for speaking/listening exercises in language learning. A further resource they have to offer, though, is the multiple language formats that they are made available in. Many speeches have been translated into 20+ languages and English and Chinese are two of the top languages that resources are made available in. The transcripts, which are segmented according to the presentation time, for almost any speech can be accessed in both Chinese and English and provide parallel texts that are rich both in content and in linguistic diversity. Beyond this basic application, The Beijing Foreign Studies University has also created a parallel concordance interface[10] of a select compilation of TED talks in both Chinese and English. The TED talk materials made available through this interface allow users to query the texts for specific word or phrases, search using wild-cards or by selecting part of speech, conduct a keyword analysis, or evaluate frequency lists. This makes the already rich resources provide by TED a lot more diverse and extensive in terms of their potential for application in teaching set constructs or ideas in the Chinese language classroom.

Two additional websites, linguee.com and tatoeba.org, function similarly to one another both as language dictionaries and as large repositories of translated language texts. Both websites offer many language pairings, including Chinese–English. Users can search a word or phrase and then have both a dictionary entry and parallel concordances returned as results. An ever-present challenge among language learners is the ability to use a bilingual dictionary effectively in identifying the proper term, or usage of a term when multiple translation equivalents are given. Linguee and Tatoeba are great pedagogical resources in this area as they return the simple dictionary results, but then also offer extensive lists of parallel concordances using the term in both Chinese and English. In this way, a user can identify the term they search in the target language and then see it in context to make sure that it is used to convey the meaning they are intending to express. Beyond term search, these websites can also be used by instructors to compile parallel concordances on a wide range of topics and/or using specific language constructs that are to be addressed in class.

Finally, The Bing Chinese–English dictionary[11] also provides an exceptional resource established using parallel corpus technology. Similar to both Linguee and Tatoeba, the Bing Chinese–English dictionary is both a dictionary and a parallel concordancer. It functions much the same as these two resources but with a couple

[9]http://www.ted.com.

[10]http://111.200.194.212/cqp/.

[11]http://cn.bing.com/dict/.

variances. First, it functions using Microsoft's Bing search engine and the results returned include extensive results available in both Chinese and English through a regular Internet search. Second, many of the concordance results also have audio and/or video as well. While many of these audio and video links are computerized generated, they do still provide a good pronunciation example for learners to emulate.

An apparent drawback of Bing's Chinese–English dictionary as well as Linguee and Tatoeba, is that they are crowd-sourced to an extent and as with any resource on the Internet, there is always the risk of misinformation, or in this case, mistranslations being displayed in the search results. Further, the alignment of texts in Linguee is not always clear and can sometimes return results that may be too challenging for a beginning or even intermediate-level language learner to navigate. With these caveats in mind, though, all of these resources can be used to improve pedagogical practices and increase learner development as they seek to not just learn language but to understand it in context of authentic language use.

All of the resources described herein use parallel corpus technology to make language more accessible to learners. There are multiple potential applications of each of these technologies, but noted limitations with each. In preparing to use any of these tools it is imperative that the instructor be mindful of how different resources are best suited for teaching specific language skills ad varying levels of language proficiency. For example, *ReadChinese!* could be adapted in a beginning-level class for reading comprehension and vocabulary building exercises but would be too remedial for advanced learners. Likewise, *Linguee* would be a challenging resource for a novice learner to navigate without mediation. Understanding these limitations, and also how these resources could be applied complementary to one another, would improve the learning experience and ensure the effective implementation of the technologies in the classroom.

5 Future Applications and Conclusion

The future of parallel corpus research is expanding as an open field of experimentation and growth in both linguistics research and pedagogical application. As Johansson (2009) optimistically states, parallel corpora "have only been in use for some 10–15 years, but have already proved to be of great value… It is likely that we are only at the beginning of an exciting development. Much remains to be done" (p. 315). His optimism is not unique as many others (Frankenberg-Garcia 2005; Wang 2002; Xu and Kawecki 2005) share this enthusiastic outlook for the future of parallel corpus research. The potential applications of parallel corpus research extend far beyond the approaches that have been tackled in the literature, and the future of this field will undoubtedly reveal many innovative and practical methods to aid learners in the acquisition of language.

Current findings suggest that future pedagogical applications of this technology should look beyond simply adapting extant corpora and seek to further develop the technology to better suit language learner needs. The current study demonstrated how presenting Chinese language learners with text in additional formats (pinyin and characters with tone marks) led to improved outcomes and interactions with the parallel corpus. Similarly, Xu and Kawecki (2005) illustrated how using a Chinese/English/French trilingual corpus benefited their unique population of learners who were native Chinese speakers with advanced English proficiency learning French. What both cases illustrate is how looking beyond the standard design of parallel corpora, and incorporating additional languages, formats, or other features specific to a population of learners can better serve that population. As each language is unique and presents learners with different obstacles, the design of each parallel corpus could also address these unique features.

Beyond addressing unique learning obstacles in various language pairings, a clear direction for further development of parallel corpora is in adapting multimedia content. Several participants in the current study suggested that the parallel corpus could be improved by adding audio features and video clips. Adding these and other multimedia features such as images and animations would likely improve learner experience by making the learning process more multimodal. From the perspective of the current study, the purpose in integrating the parallel corpus was to improve learners' acquisition of written Chinese and development of conceptual knowledge through the language. Providing learners with the ability to draw on parallel schemas from their L1 allowed them to more readily conceptualize content through in the target language. Going one step further to integrate audio, video, imagery, and any other multimedia form that aided this process of development would likely lead to improved outcomes and is a viable path for future exploration.

Finally, exploring new adaptations of existing parallel corpora, or technology such as linguee.com that are premised on parallel corpus design, holds great potential for improved language learning and instruction. As demonstrated, Linguee allows users to search parallel concordances in multiple language pairings and is composed using large data sets. While linguee.com provides far more content, its design is still limited in its capacity to mediate learner experience. Creating a resource, or adapting a tool that helps bridge this gap between resources with specific design features to aid instruction, would undoubtedly enhance either tool and ultimately provide a greater number of learners with an improved resource in their language learning journey. Further, continued consideration of learner and educator experience and perception in adapting and using this technology will provide an invaluable narrative and understanding of its resourcefulness. Parallel corpora are a valuable resource in language learning as they scaffold learner understanding and allow users to conceptualize language use in the target language through established L1 schemas. Parallel corpora have already been proven as exceptional resources for linguistic research and pedagogy, and as they continue to develop and be applied innovatively their value in language pedagogy will only continue to increase.

References

Aijmer, K. (2008). Translating discourse particles: A case of complex translation. In J. Anderman & M. Rogers (Eds.), *Incorporating corpora: The linguist and the translator* (pp. 95–116). New York: Multilingual Matters.

Aijmer, K., & Altenberg, B. (1996). Introduction. In K. Aijmer, B. Altenberg, & M. Johansson (Eds.), *Languages in contrast, papers from a symposium on text-based cross-linguistic studies* (pp. 11–16). Lund: Lund University Press.

Aston, G. (1997). Enriching the learning environment: Corpora in ELT. In A. Wichmann, et al. (Eds.), *Teaching and language corpora* (pp. 51–64). London/New York: Addison Wesley Longman Inc.

Baker, M. (1996). Corpus-based translation studies: The challenges that lie ahead. In H. Somers (Ed.), *Terminology, LSP and translation* (pp. 175–187). Amsterdam: John Benjamins.

Biçici, E. (2008). Context-based sentence alignment in parallel corpora. In A. Gelbukh (Ed.), *Lecture notes in computer science* (Vol. 4919, pp. 434–444). Heidelberg: Springer-Verlag.

Bluemel, B. (2013). Chinese/English parallel corpus & learning tool. State College. Pennsylvania: The Pennsylvania State University. Available at http://www.parallelcorpus.com.

Bluemel, B. (2014). Learning in parallel: Using parallel corpora to enhance written language acquisition at the beginning level. *Dimension, 1,* 31–48.

Fan, M., & Xu, X. (2002). An evaluation of an online bilingual corpus for self-learning of legal English. *System, 30,* 47–63.

Frankenberg-Garcia, A. (2004). Lost in parallel concordances. In G. Aston, S. Bernardini, & D. Stewart (Eds.), *Corpora and language learners* (pp. 213–229). Amsterdam/ Philadelphia: John Benjamins.

Frankenberg-Garcia, A. (2005). Pedagogical uses of monolingual and parallel concordances. *ELT Journal, 59*(3), 189–198.

Johansson, S. (1999). Towards a multilingual corpus for contrastive analysis and translation studies. In L. Borin (Ed.), *Parallel corpora, parallel worlds* (pp. 47–59). Amsterdam/New York: Rodopi.

Johansson, S. (2009). Some thoughts on corpora and second-language acquisition. In K. Aijmer (Ed.), *Corpora and language teaching* (pp. 33–46). Amsterdam/Philadelphia: John Benjamins.

King, P. (2003). Parallel concordancing and its applications. In S. Granger, J. Lerot, & S. Petch-Tyson (Eds.), *Corpus based approaches to contrastive linguistics and translation studies* (pp. 157–167). Amsterdam/New York: Rodopi.

Laviosa, S. (2002). *Corpus-based translation studies: Theory, findings, applications*. Amsterdam/New York: Rodopi.

McEnery, T., & Wilson, A. (2001). *Corpus linguistics*. Edinburgh: Edinburgh University Press.

McEnery, T., & Xiao, R. (2008). Parallel and comparable corpora: What is happening? In G. Anderman & M. Rogers (Eds.), *Incorporating corpora: The linguist and the translator* (pp. 18–31). New York: Multilingual Matters.

Norman, J. (1988). *Chinese*. New York: Cambridge University Press.

Salkie, R. (1999). How can linguists profit from parallel corpora? In L. Borin (Ed.), *Parallel corpora, parallel worlds* (pp. 93–109). Amsterdam/New York: Rodopi.

St. John, E. (2001). A case for using a parallel corpus and concordance for beginners of a foreign language. *Language Learning & Technology, 5*(3), 185–203.

Tsai, C., & Choi, H. (2005). Parallel corpus and lexical acquisition in Chinese learning. In *Proceedings of Fourth International Conference on Internet Chinese Education* (pp. 206–213). Taipei, Taiwan.

Tufiş, D. (2007). Exploiting aligned parallel corpora in multilingual studies and applications. In T. Ishida, S. R. Fussell, & P. T. J. M. Vossen (Eds.), *Lecture notes in computer science* (Vol. 4568, pp. 103–117). Berlin/Heidelberg: Springer-Verlag.

Wang, L. (2001). Exploring parallel concordancing in English and Chinese. *Language Learning & Technology, 5*(3), 174–184.

Wang, L. (2002). Parallel Concordancing in English and Chinese and Its Pedagogic Application. Edgbaston, UK: English for International Students Unit, University of Birmingham. http://home.ied.edu.hk/~lixun/Chinese/keyanketi.html. Accessed August 1, 2017.

Xu, X., & Kawecki, R. (2005). Trilingual corpus and its use for the teaching of reading comprehension in French. In G. Varnbrook, P. Danielsson, & M. Mahlberg (Eds.), *Meaningful texts: The extraction of semantic information from monolingual and multilingual corpora* (pp. 222–228). New York: Continuum.

Data-Driven Adapting for Fine-Tuning Chinese Teaching Materials: Using Corpora as Benchmarks

Wei Bo, Jing Chen, Kai Guo and Tan Jin

Abstract While there have been a considerable number of corpus-based studies informing the content of teaching materials, direct explorations of corpora by teachers to adapt source texts (i.e., data-driven adapting) for classroom teaching remain a largely unexplored area. This chapter examines how teachers adapt new texts in a more comprehensible manner for L2 Chinese learners using an online system, *Chi-Editor*. *Chi-Editor* was developed to automatically assess text complexity and tag Chinese words and sentences for text simplification purposes. The evaluation of a text in terms of its level of difficulty and annotation of difficult words and long sentences in the text are produced based on the data mining of linguistic features from a corpus of roughly 350 widely-used textbooks, selected from an anthology of L2 Chinese teaching materials and packages produced by over 1000 publishers around the world. To investigate both the process and outcome of data-driven adapting using *Chi-Editor*, a case study was conducted, involving a team of teachers working on the adaptation of texts. Results are discussed in terms of the effectiveness of the data-driven adapting practices by teachers in a classroom setting. Overall, the results contribute strong evidence that teachers can learn and benefit from data-driven adapting and support the notion that corpus data, including linguistic features, can be employed to facilitate the text simplification process. Implications are also given for integrating the data-driven adapting process into regular teacher-prepared L2 Chinese materials for classroom teaching.

W. Bo
Dali University, Dali, China
e-mail: bowei_2010@163.com

J. Chen · T. Jin (✉)
Sun Yat-sen University, Guangzhou, China
e-mail: jintan6@mail.sysu.edu.cn

J. Chen
e-mail: chenjing@mail.sysu.edu.cn

K. Guo
Shanghai Jiao Tong University, Shanghai, China
e-mail: dearmrk@163.com

X. Lu and B. Chen (eds.), *Computational and Corpus Approaches to Chinese Language Learning*, Chinese Language Learning Sciences,
https://doi.org/10.1007/978-981-13-3570-9_6

1 Introduction

In second language teaching and learning, text adaptation is often employed to ensure comprehensibility of the reading texts by L2 learners (Yano et al. 1994). In the L2 classroom, it is especially common for adapted texts (Young 1999) to be used. Previous studies on the process of text adaptation and its outcome have examined the use of both teacher intuition and automatic tools in text adaptation, with a common goal to find objective, consistent criteria that could be used to efficiently evaluate and improve the readability of texts by L2 learners. Research on the intuitive approach has examined how texts are perceived and adapted by teachers (e.g., Green and Hawkey 2011). In the absence of corpus data, teachers usually rely on their own intuitive judgments, sometimes in combination with guidance provided in a textbook, to adapt texts. Compared to the intuitive approach, the use of computational tools has the unique potential of being both more efficient and consistent. Recent research has also shown that data-driven computational tools have the added benefit of enhancing the accuracy of text adaption, by highlighting and annotating candidate words and sentences that contribute to the complexity of a text (Jin and Lu 2018).

The purpose of this chapter is to show how the use of a data-driven approach for adapting texts for L2 Chinese classrooms is more effective than solely relying on teacher intuition. To this end, we investigate the process and outcome when teachers adapt texts using the online tool, *Chi-Editor* (see Sects. 3.1–3.3), designed with corpus data for benchmarking. We focus in particular on how texts adapted using this tool differ from those adapted based on teacher intuition, and whether L2 Chinese teachers perceive it as a useful facilitative tool for text adaptation. In doing so, the authors hope to showcase how data-driven text adaption may be effectively integrated into regular teacher-prepared L2 Chinese materials for classroom teaching.

2 Literature Review

Since the late 1990s, there has been a tendency to advocate the use of either authentic or simplified texts as input to L2 learning, especially for L2 learners at the beginning and intermediate levels (e.g., Johnson 1981; Tomlinson et al. 2001). However, little empirical evidence has been provided to validate the effects of using either simplified or authentic texts on L2 development (e.g., Cummins 1981; Goodman 1986; Krashen 1981, 1985), and a more realistic question is whether the use of simplified or authentic texts leads to different learning outcomes. In an effort to investigate the extent of such differences and their implications for L2 learning, Crossley et al. (2007) measured linguistic features—including the lexical, syntactical, and discourse differences—that characterize authentic and simplified texts, respectively. To compare the linguistic features of authentic and simplified texts, over 250 linguistic and cohesion features were employed to configure the computational tool *Coh-Metrix*, developed to assess the coherence and cohesion of reading texts (Graesser et al.

2004). Crossley et al. analyzed a corpus of 81 simplified texts with 21,117 words and one of 24 authentic texts with 15,640 words using this tool. Subsequent statistical analysis revealed significant differences between simplified and authentic texts in syntactic complexity, word information and cohesion. These differences have useful implications for selecting texts as input to L2 learning. For instance, the simplified texts showed greater cohesion than did the authentic texts, indicating that adapted texts may be more appropriate for beginner and intermediate level L2 learners.

Research has shown that text adaptation is necessary in preparing teaching materials for L2 learners of certain levels in reading, but it remains opaque as to how text adaptation should be conducted in practice. Adaptation is regarded as a creative art (Wesman 1971), often improvised or carried out in intuitive ways in practice. In other words, it needs to be revealed how the process of text adaptation proceeds and whether there exist identifiable patterns of adaptation. To this end, Green and Hawkey (2011) conducted a case study of item writer practices based on qualitative analyses to standardize the rules for text adaptation. Four trained item writers working on the International English Language Testing System (IELTS) were selected as the subjects to be observed. Stimulated recall interviews and the subjects' writing reflections revealed common strategies such as text deletion, consolidation, expansion, substitution, and insertion. Results showed that during the item writers' adaptation process, they increased the proportion of frequent word types and decreased that of less frequent words. Item writers also reflected on their practices of reducing redundancy and technical language, changing styles, deciding on potentially sensitive issues and relationships between texts and test items when they adapted texts in order to make them appropriate for the proficiency levels of the L2 test takers.

It seems that in Green and Hawkey's study, item writers used a defined set of strategies for writing tests and that these strategies were deployed exclusively in isolation from feedback by the reader, that is, there is no direct feedback mechanism from the L2 learners on the effects of adaptation on the linguistic features of texts. To reveal the impact of different levels of text adaptation on reading comprehension, Crossley et al. (2012) used *Coh-Metrix* to quantitatively establish a link between the comprehension of adapted texts and proficiency levels. Three hundred news texts were simplified into three different levels, i.e., beginner, intermediate, and advanced. Fourteen indices were employed to measure linguistic features related to cohesion, linguistic sophistication, and surface-level variables, such as word frequency, lexical diversity, spatial cohesion, temporal cohesion, and syntactic complexity. The results showed that beginner-level texts are generally less lexically and syntactically sophisticated than the advanced-level ones and that the former contains more cohesive features than the latter. This quantitative study indicates that lexical, syntactic, and cohesive features are generally the best indices for classifying different levels of L2 texts.

Chinese Mandarin, a language in the Sino-Tibetan family, has linguistic features that differ significantly from English. The English language is based on clearly identifiable word units (which are of one or more syllables in length), whereas Chinese characters can be either a word or part of a word. For example, in English the word "computer" is one string of letters, whereas in Chinese, 电脑 (*dian nao*) is two separate characters, each of which has its own meaning: "电 (*dian* means electric)" and "脑 (*nao* means brain)". Thus, when processing a text, in English, "computer" would be a single word; whereas "电脑 (*dian nao*)" could be analyzed as either one or two words (i.e., either two characters combined or two separate characters). We, therefore, have two distinct ways to process text in Chinese: at the level of the character (i.e., character-based) or at the level of the 'word' (i.e., word-based). At the level of the word, processing text in English and in Chinese is operationally very similar. For example, in both languages, word-count, part-of-speech diversity, and frequency can be treated with very similar processes. However, at the level of the character, there is no equivalent in English. Therefore, in contrast to English, such features as the complexity of character strokes and usage-based frequency of characters are commonly applied to measure character complexity. Such criteria have been widely employed for developing teaching materials for both elementary native speakers and L2 learners. As a national standard, *the Graded Chinese Syllables, Characters and Words for the Application of Teaching Chinese to the Speakers of Other Languages* (Ministry of Education and State Language Commission, the People's Republic of China 2010, *GCSCW* hereafter) has been developed for the purpose of proficiency testing and has become integral to the L2 Chinese evaluation system (Liu and Ma 2010). Corpus techniques are central in *GCSCW* research in order to rank and design the characters and words by frequency. In addition, other natural language processing technologies are also applied in *GCSCW* research, such as automatic processing of word-segmentation and word-frequency statistics. The most notable feature of *GCSCW* research identifies three levels (beginner, intermediate, and advanced) by combining both character-based and word-based approaches and this combination approach has now become established as the standard to develop L2 Chinese teaching materials.

These multilevel linguistic features were also applied to level the readability of L2 Chinese texts by Sung et al. (2015), who used thirty linguistic features of L2 Chinese as well as 1578 classified texts to evaluate the accuracy of text leveling for instructional purposes—specifically, for teaching materials. Sung et al. produced a text that defines the levels comparable to the Common European Framework of Reference (CEFR) according to L2 Chinese experts; a readability assessment system was later created using the 30 linguistic features developed from previous studies. The F-score selection method was used to evaluate the relative importance of linguistic features. In the final system for L2 Chinese leveling, words and characters receive equal weight, and multiple features are used for both, such as the average of vocabulary levels, high-level words, mean square of vocabulary levels, two-character words, and intermediate stroke-count characters. Leveling, i.e., assigning a "level" to a given text, helps teachers, and learners select proper texts to enhance learning at an appropriate proficiency level. Another application suggested by this study is that the authors or editors also benefited from the leveling system when examining the linguistic features of L2 teaching materials they are editing.

In sum, previous studies have revealed two particularly important insights regarding text adaptation for L2 teaching materials: on the one hand, there is qualitative evidence showing that teachers employ adaptation strategies (e.g., text deletion, consolidation, expansion, substitution, and insertion) with certain patterns rather than treating adaptation as a purely "improvised art" (e.g., Green and Hawkey 2011); on the other hand, quantitative research has revealed a link between text adaptation and reading comprehension, and the key linguistic features (such as word frequency and spatial cohesion) at play in this link (e.g., Crossley et al. 2012). Such strategies used in text adaptation in previous studies are termed "teacher intuition" in this chapter. In the evaluation of L2 Chinese proficiency levels, a national standard for Chinese characters and words is being actively promoted by the *GCSCW* (Ministry of Education and State Language Commission, the People's Republic of China 2010). A more detailed empirical examination of this *GCSCW* standard was undertaken by Sung and his colleagues (Sung et al. 2015) using both the character-based and word-based approach to analyze a set of widely-used L2 Chinese teaching materials. The *GCSCW* and Sung et al.'s findings together demonstrate the following two aspects: first, the standard promoted by the *GCSCW* facilitates sound guidelines for editing L2 Chinese teaching materials and adapting learning texts; second, the relative importance of words and characters varied according to proficiency level (Sung et al. 2015). Therefore, the term "leveling" both in Sung et al. and in this chapter refers to evaluating the difficulty of linguistic features consistent with the L2 Chinese teaching syllabus. However, the relationship between the linguistic features and the result of text adaptation still has not been addressed by any empirical research. In other words, under the guidance of linguistic features in *GCSCW*, how L2 Chinese texts are adapted for pedagogical purposes (i.e., leveling of text difficulty, finding of linguistic features, etc.) remains unknown. The current study, therefore, attempts to fill this gap.

3 Introduction to the Online Tool *Chi-Editor*

To provide data-driven support for teachers in adapting new texts in a more comprehensible manner for L2 Chinese students, the online system, *Chi-Editor*, has been developed to automatically level texts in terms of linguistic complexity, to tag Chinese words and sentences as well as to report profiles of Chinese characters and words (Jin and Li 2016). The function of leveling and tagging in *Chi-Editor* are based on the data mining of linguistic features from a corpus compiled from roughly 350 widely-used textbooks, which were selected from an anthology of L2 Chinese teaching materials and packages produced by over one thousand publishers around the world (Base for International Chinese Teaching Materials Developing and Teacher Training 2017); the reporting function generates the lists of Chinese characters and words provided by *GCSCW*, which established a standard combining both character-based and word-based approaches.

We take a text as an example to illustrate the three main functions—leveling, tagging, and reporting—provided by *Chi-Editor* as follows. The text is extracted from the Level 3 book *I Want to Be a Lawyer* in a graded Chinese reader series titled *Friends* (Confucius Institute Headquarters 2014). The Preface of the textbook series

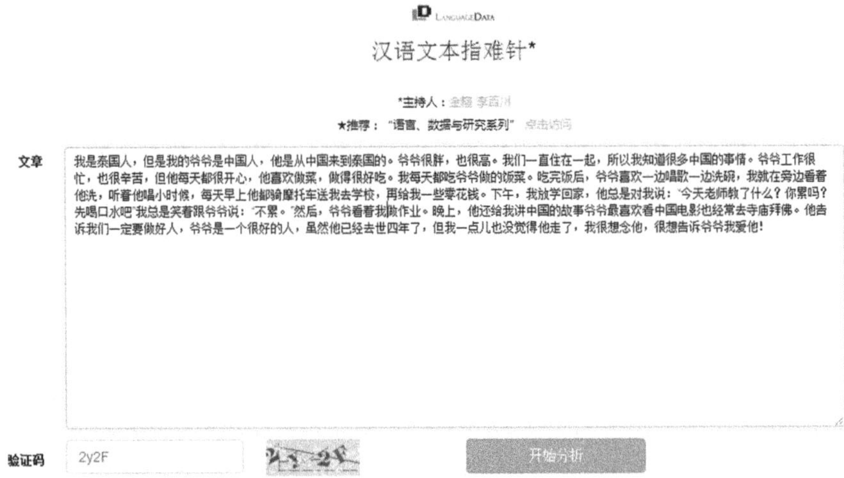

Fig. 1 Interface of text typing/pasting

states that Level 3 in all six levels uses 600 words in accordance with the new HSK (an abbreviation of *Hanyu Shuiping Kaoshi*, the Chinese Proficiency Test). Level 3 of HSK requires that students can read basic Chinese materials related to daily life and find specific information from paragraphs of familiar content according to the *International Curriculum for Chinese Language Education* (Confucius Institute Headquarters 2015). After typing or pasting the text into *Chi-Editor*, the resulting analysis can be accessed online (see Fig. 1, retrieved from http://www.languagedata.net/editor/) but the text length must fall within the limits of 100–5000 characters.

3.1 Leveling in Chi-Editor

After inputting a verification code and pressing "Start Analysis" (see Fig. 1), the user will see the results in a coordinate graph indicating the level of the text (see Fig. 2). The upper section of Fig. 2 summarizes the leveling result for the original text using several indices, namely, the overall level of difficulty (hereafter LD), CEFR level, L2 Chinese syllabus level, mean length of sentence, length of the longest sentence and length of the text. The lower section provides guidance on how the LD value is to be interpreted. The horizontal axis represents the LD, which corresponds to six levels in CEFR with real values ranging from 1.0 to 4.0; the accuracy of these values in judging text difficulty reaches over 90% as supported by empirical research (Lin 2016). The vertical axis represents L2 Chinese syllabus levels according to the *International Curriculum for Chinese Language Education* (Confucius Institute Headquarters 2015).

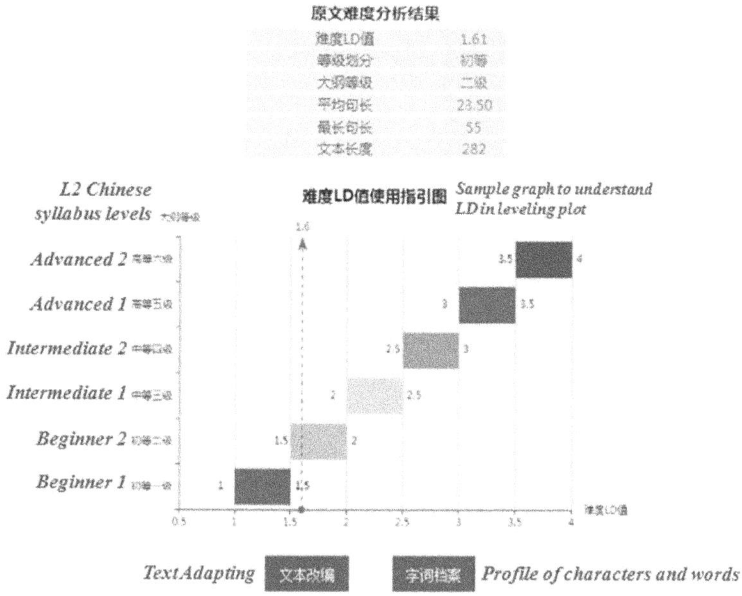

Fig. 2 Interface of leveling plot [English translation given in purple italics]

3.2 *Tagging in Chi-Editor*

More detailed information on the functions of the adapting interface can be found when users click the blue button *Text Adapting* as shown at the bottom of Fig. 2. Figure 3 shows the tagged elements that may help teachers or learners adapt. To operate this tagging interface, it is important to aware of the following procedures. First, the interface provides tagged words and sentences throughout the text adaptation process. Words can be tagged based on (1) word level and (2) word frequency or usage-based examples. Different colors are used to distinguish different word levels: beginner, intermediate, advanced, higher advanced, words beyond vocabulary (i.e., words that are beyond the vocabulary of the specific level; hereafter WBV), and proper nouns (PN). In the example, in Fig. 3, red words such as "摩托车 (motorcycle)" and "拜佛 (worship the Buddha)" are in the WBV level, green words like "胖 (fat)" and 辛苦 (laborious)" belong to the intermediate level. As for word frequency and usage-based examples, links are provided to allow users to explore examples of how a word is used in the corpus of. Further, all words at the WBV level are tagged with word frequency information to help teachers or learners judge their level. For example, the word "摩托车" (motorcycle) is marked as "22" to its upper right to indicate its word frequency, while the word "拜佛" (worship the Buddha) is marked as "2". Thus, users can easily identify the vocabulary levels of these words by comparing those numbers. Sentence tagging focuses on the longest sentence in the text and underlines it to draw user attention to it since the length of the longest

Fig. 3 Tagging for adapting

sentence is an important contributor to text complexity. Second, for the adapting function, *Chi-Editor* provides a Microsoft Word-like window where one can adapt the colored words through addition, deletion, or substitution. Finally, *Chi-Editor* can reanalyze results and reassess subsequent attempts. Using this text, as an example again, users could first separate the longest sentence into three and four short sentences before the reassessment automatically changes the LD value from 1.61 to 1.60 in three sentences and from 1.61 to 1.59 in four sentences. Moreover, the LD value changes from 1.61 to 1.49 and the syllabus level from grade 2 to grade 1 when researchers substitute such words “辛苦,饭菜,总是,想念” with “累,菜,常常,想”.

3.3 Reporting in Chi-Editor

Referring back to Fig. 2, users can click the blue button on the bottom right of the coordinate graph called *Lexical Profiling* during or after reassessment. The third main function—reporting, which is based on lists of Chinese characters and words by *GCSCW*—is illustrated in Fig. 4. The upper table presents information about characters, while the lower table presents information about words in the same text. Both reports include the number of types and tokens of characters or words at different levels, as well as coverage of those characters or words. These statistics are useful to be aware of as users try to generalize the level of the text. One more detailed report can be displayed by clicking the links known as *txt 1* and *txt 2* as shown in Fig. 5, in which the left portion represents the profile of characters, and right portion represents the profile of the words. In short, a *Chi-Editor* report allows teachers and learners to generalize the difficulty of texts by presenting information graphically.

汉语文本指难针

字词档案结果报告

表1：汉字档案

字表	字数	字种数	分布（%）	累积分布（%）
初级	273	130	96.81	96.81
中级	6	6	2.13	98.94
高级	3	2	1.06	100.00
更高级	0	0	0.00	100.00
超纲字	0	0	0.00	100
总计	282	138	100	100

表2：词语档案

词表	词数	词种数	分布（%）	累积分布（%）
初级	180	97	89.11	89.11
中级	7	4	3.47	92.57
高级	3	3	1.49	94.06
更高级	0	0	0.00	94.06
专有名词	2	1	0.99	95.05
超纲词	10	7	4.95	100
总计	202	112	100	100

txt 1: 汉字列表

txt 2: 词语列表

Fig. 4 Reporting for adapting

序号	字	字频	等级	比例	累计比例
1	爷	20	初级	7.09%	7.09%
2	我	17	初级	6.03%	13.12%
3	他	13	初级	4.61%	17.73%
4	很	10	初级	3.55%	21.28%
5	一	8	初级	2.84%	24.11%
6	是	7	初级	2.48%	26.60%
7	国	7	初级	2.48%	29.08%
8	的	6	初级	2.13%	31.21%
9	中	5	初级	1.77%	32.98%
10	做	5	初级	1.77%	34.75%
11	人	4	初级	1.42%	36.17%
12	也	4	初级	1.42%	37.59%
13	天	4	初级	1.42%	39.01%
14	看	4	初级	1.42%	40.43%
15	但	3	初级	1.06%	41.49%
16	每	3	初级	1.06%	42.55%
17	都	3	初级	1.06%	43.62%
18	喜	3	初级	1.06%	44.68%
19	欢	3	初级	1.06%	45.74%
20	好	3	初级	1.06%	46.81%

txt 1

序号	词	词频	等级	比例	累计比例
1	我	15	初级	7.43%	7.43%
2	他	13	初级	6.44%	13.86%
3	爷爷	10	初级	4.95%	18.81%
4	很	9	初级	4.46%	23.27%
5	的	6	初级	2.97%	26.24%
6	中国	5	初级	2.48%	28.71%
7	做	5	初级	2.48%	31.19%
8	是	4	初级	1.98%	33.17%
9	也	4	初级	1.98%	35.15%
10	看	4	中级	1.98%	37.13%
11	人	3	初级	1.49%	38.61%
12	每天	3	超纲词	1.49%	40.10%
13	都	3	初级	1.49%	41.58%
14	喜欢	3	初级	1.49%	43.07%
15	看	3	初级	1.49%	44.55%
16	了	3	初级	1.49%	46.04%
17	泰国	2	专有名词	0.99%	47.03%
18	我们	2	初级	0.99%	48.02%
19	在	2	初级	0.99%	49.01%
20	但	2	初级	0.99%	50.00%

txt 2

Fig. 5 Profiles in reporting

4 Research Questions

As discussed above, text adapting in L2 Chinese teaching is pragmatic, but the effect of the use of online tools on the text adaptation process and its outcome remains vague. It is unknown whether there are patterns in using the online tool for text adaption and whether such adapting contributes to improvements in teaching practice. The current study aims to compare teachers' perceptions of adapting by teacher intuition and adapting by using *Chi-Editor*. The specific research questions addressed are: (1) How does *Chi-Editor* affect teachers' adapting process, and (2) compared to adapting by teacher intuition, does adapting with *Chi-Editor* bring about different outcomes with its leveling, tagging and reporting functions?

Table 1 Teacher profiles

Teacher	Gender	Educational background	Relevant experience (years)	Pedagogical adapting
A	Female	Ph.D.	3.5	Experienced
B	Male	Ph.D.	>6	Experienced
C	Female	M.A.	>6	Experienced
D	Male	Ph.D.	>6	Experienced

5 Methodology

5.1 Interview Subjects

Four experienced L2 Chinese teachers participated voluntarily in this study. These four teachers had been selected based on three criteria: (1) educational background with postgraduate degrees and/or doctorate degrees in applied linguistics, (2) relevant practical experience including teaching and researching L2 Chinese, and (3) pedagogical attempts on text adapting for the relevant teaching level (see Table 1 for a profile of the four teachers).

5.2 Procedures

The four teachers followed four adapting procedures: (1) Training: the researchers briefed these teachers about adapting methods; all four teachers used two text samples to get familiar with *Chi-Editor* and reported to the researchers on how they used *Chi-Editor* to adapt the sample texts. (2) Familiarization: the four teachers became familiar with the graded L2 texts. Teachers then practiced using *Chi-Editor* with three graded L2 Chinese texts (beginner, intermediate, advanced). At this point, they made judgments independently without receiving any feedback or help from the researchers. They were allowed to judge text levels intuitively and focused on familiarizing themselves with different text features. (3) Pilot Adapting: the four teachers adapted these three graded texts again for pilot adapting, and subsequently received feedback from the researchers. This would help the four teachers see clearly what linguistic features had been adapted and how a text's level had been modified by *Chi-Editor*. (4) Adapting: the four teachers were required to accomplish independently the following two adapting tasks: (a) adapting one upper-intermediate text to a lower-intermediate level first using teacher intuition (followed by an interview), then using *Chi-Editor* (also followed by an interview); and (b) adapting a different text, of lower-intermediate level, to cater to L2 Chinese learners at beginner level. Tasks (a) and (b) are illustrated in Fig. 6.

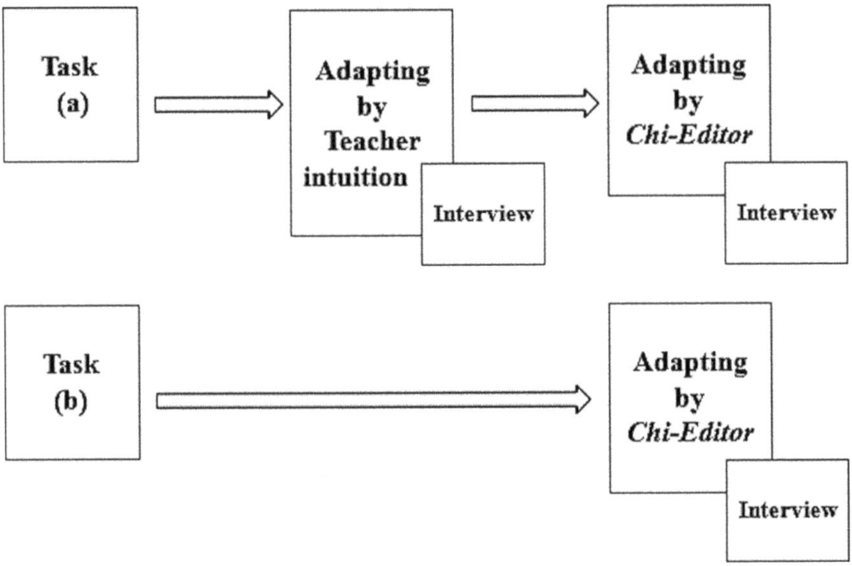

Fig. 6 Task procedure of adapting

5.3 Texts

For the abovementioned two assignments, we selected two passages, one of upper-intermediate level and the other of intermediate level, for two reasons. On the one hand, significantly different linguistic features exist between the beginning and the advanced levels (see Crossley et al. 2012), so we focused on adapting from upper-intermediate level to basic-intermediate level in task (a). On the other hand, pedagogical adapting requires more simplified texts for beginner level (or for basic-intermediate at most), so we asked interviewees to adapt to the beginner and the basic-intermediate levels in tasks (b) and (a), respectively. Therefore, we selected two passages in the series book of graded Chinese readers published by the Confucius Institute Headquarters (2014): the text in task (a) comes from Level 3 entitled *My Grandfather*, and the text in task (b) comes from Level 5 and is entitled *How the Internet Changed Our Lives*.

After the four teachers completed the whole set of adapting activities, qualitative interviews were carried out by the researchers to provide insights into the adapting process and outcomes of using *Chi-Editor*. The interviews were semi-structured, and three topics were designed according to the functions of *Chi-Editor* to investigate both the process and outcomes of data-driven adapting: (1) leveling, (2) tagging, and (3) reporting. An interview frame encompassing the three topics was first developed for guiding the interview, and it was then sent out for expert review before the formal interviews were conducted (see Fig. 7).

INTERVIEW FRAME

Topic 1 Leveling
Questions:
(1) When using traditional teaching methods, how did you assign a level to the teaching materials extract?
(2) When using *Chi-Editor*, how did you assign a level to the teaching materials extract?
(3) Did you notice any differences between the two results in assigning a level to the teaching materials extract?
(4) What did you learn, if anything, when using the *Chi-Editor* leveling function?

Topic 2 Tagging
Questions:
(1) When using traditional teaching methods, what text features did you identify in your adapting process?
(2) When using *Chi-Editor*, did you use the tagging function and if so what text features did you use and how?
(3) Did you notice any differences between text features identified when not using *Chi-Editor* compared to those identified by the *Chi-Editor* tagging function?
(4) What did you learn, if anything, when using the *Chi-Editor* tagging function?

Topic 3 Reporting
Questions:
(1) When using your teacher intuition and experience, how would you describe the process you used to adapt the teaching materials extract provided?
(2) When using *Chi-Editor* how did you use the report it generated to adapt the teaching materials extract provided?
(3) Did you notice any differences in your adapting process between using *Chi-Editor*, with its reporting function, and not using it?
(4) What did you learn, if anything, when using the report generated by *Chi-Editor*?

Fig. 7 Interview frame

The interviews were conducted in Chinese, which is the native language of all four teachers. All four interviews were recorded, resulting in a total of four hours of recorded audio, excluding another two hours for adapting by teacher intuition in task (a), which included reading, thinking, and analyzing by each interviewer. The audio files were transcribed into a total of 9023 Chinese characters by the researchers, including quotation marks.

During the qualitative analysis phase of this research, analytical categories emerged when the researchers were listening to the audio files and transcribing the interview. Based on the analytical categories, a coding scheme was made by two of the researchers, which was later sent for expert review and finalized.

6 Findings

After the interviews were transcribed, interviewees' comments were categorized to describe their usage of *Chi-Editor*. Among all dimensions provided by *Chi-Editor,* tagging (with 56% comment percentage) was the most frequent topic mentioned by the interviewees, followed by leveling (32%) and reporting (12%). The following presents the four interviewees' comments on the topics of leveling, tagging, and reporting.

6.1 Interview: Leveling

Leveling was the first fundamental step interviewee were asked to review in their adapting assignments, and information about language proficiency of the interviewee was noted. Procedurally, interviewees first examined text adapting in the traditional teaching setting; second, they provided reflections of their experiences using *Chi-Editor*. As for the indices used during the leveling process, the four interviewees observed similarities between the traditional teaching setting and using *Chi-Editor*, both of which focused on both words and sentences. The statements given below, by Interviewee B, are commonly found in the interviewees' description of such similarities.

Extract 1 (Interviewee B, #T1-B2)
I judged the text level mainly by the level of words, especially the words on intermediate and advanced levels of HSK word lists.

Commonly, the four interviewees focused on the word levels to discussing the similarities between the two different ways of leveling. In addition, language points—such as collocations, chunks, and complements in Chinese Mandarin—also attracted their attention. For example, Extract 2 was again excerpted from Interviewee B's comments on the traditional teaching setting.

Extract 2 (Interviewee B, #T1-B3)
…they (referring to "多得多" and "多多了," both of which mean "much more than") are complements in the sentences "网上的资料比学校图书馆的多得多 (There is more information on the Internet than in school libraries)" and "网上的电视剧比电视上多多了 (There are more TV shows on the Internet than on television)"; although their meanings are similar, their linguistic structures are completely different, especially after combining comparable structures (it refers to the "bi" structure in Mandarin Chinese).

While *Chi-Editor* made use of the character list in text leveling, the four interviewees did not seem to utilize either level or frequency information of characters. This indicates that many L2 Chinese teachers default to word-based teaching approaches instead of character-based teaching approaches, as illustrated in Extract 3 by Interviewee C:

Extract 3 (Interviewee C, #T1-C2)
It is hard to say attention toward characters is useless when a kind of approach conducts leveling for the purpose of text adapting. But as a L2 Chinese teacher, I would usually pay more attention to characters only if the learners are early beginners. According to your requirements (referring to requirements from the interviewer/researcher), I assumed it to be the level of basic-intermediate rather than a true beginner level. So it does not work if I pay any attention to the characters. In other words, I feel it is tough to determine which character affects the text level and which does not.

In this claim, Interviewee C expresses a presumption that learners' levels result from two different teaching approaches. Namely, the beginner level requires a more character-based teaching approach, and after that, a word-based teaching approach should serve as the backbone under the communication approach. Interviewee A voiced an opinion on a different aspect regarding the character-based approach: "*In my opinion, character-based teaching materials are really boring, and learners can benefit nothing from them when communicating in spoken Chinese*" (Interviewee A, #T1-A4).

It is apparent that the L2 Chinese teachers regard the word-based teaching approach as the more effective alternative; the four interviewees reported similar sentiments regarding Topic 1. Specifically, we find that teacher intuition, in identifying word levels and linguistic features, exactly matches the criteria used by *Chi-Editor*. Nevertheless, *Chi-Editor* as an online system can provide more detailed quantitative data for text leveling in terms of linguistic features, such as mean length of utterance (MLU; Ellis 1999), the LD value, the total number of words and characters, etc. It seems possible that interviewees are often also referring to external frameworks, such as the HSK test or other established teaching syllabi, to refine their teacher intuition. Moreover, the preference for using a word-based approach is also based on teacher intuition rather than any particular theoretical basis.

6.2 Interview: Tagging

Tagging is typically implicit when one is learning to adapt texts, but it is explicit in *Chi-Editor* processing due to its data-driven design. In commenting on the tagging function of *Chi-Editor*, interviewees showed great interest in the explicit tagging interface, which, as introduced in Sect. 3.2, includes such functions as underlining the longest sentence, marking word frequency, and citing examples linked to teaching materials. Interviewee A first noticed how she leveled the text using the implicit tags in her mind.

Extract 4 (Interviewee A, #T2-A1)
(By teacher intuition) I basically leveled the text with marks derived from difficult words and grammar already in mind, and these marks made me more confident in

text leveling. However, I would not write them down or list them in a quantitative way. I memorized these marks, and they permeated a part of my judging instinct.

As for the helpfulness of explicit tags offered by *Chi-Editor*, all interviewees commented on the positive effect on teaching practice because the tagging results could help interviewees rethink a specific word or grammar level. Interviewee B described *Chi-Editor* as a "flexible friend" in that teachers could find more information with data sources rather than merely concludes the word frequency and word difficulty by color and number on the interface.

Extract 5 (Interviewee B, #T2-B6)
During the process of using *Chi-Editor*, I found it to be a helpful friend who could tell you the places where we should pay attention to in the text. For example, when I was processing the text with *Chi-Editor*, it marked "摩托车 (the motorcycle)" as a WBV; Meanwhile, it was also marked with a relatively high word frequency and a link to data sources. At first glance, you might assume this word falls under WBV, but because of its high frequency (the frequency rank was 22), you would need to link it to teaching materials as a data source. After checking the data source, it showed this word's frequency was 9 in beginning materials, 9 in intermediate materials, and 4 in advanced materials. Your judgment was clear that this word should not be categorized as WBV in the teaching syllabus. On the contrary, the data source showed a frequency of 9 in intermediate materials, so this word instead became a new lexical point in your teaching syllabus for the beginner level. In another example, in the same text processing, the program marked "泰国 (Thailand)" as a PN, without any hint about word frequency aside from the blue color indication. However, after you linked it to the data source, you would find the word frequency was 114, a relatively high frequency. According to my intuition from teaching Chinese, you could keep and teach this word if you met a Thai student, or you could delete or change this word if you do not want to teach it. The *Chi-Editor* just marked this word in blue in case you might deal with this scenario. Another word, "拜佛 (worship the Buddha)," which was a WBV word for non-Thai students but an all-level-fitted word for Thai students, was only 2 according to the data source despite the word frequency.

While teachers found the tagging of the longest sentences provided *Chi-Editor* to be useful, they indicate that they paid attention to other long sentences or complex components of certain sentences as well. Interviewee D, for example, stated:

Extract 6 (Interviewee D, #T2-D3)
The online available *Chi-Editor* provides the tag of the longest sentence, and it truly reminds me to pay more attention to this sentence. However, according to your requirement of adapting the text from upper-intermediate level to lower-intermediate level, I might look carefully for something other than the longest sentence tagged by *Chi-Editor.* For example, the attribute "住在中国的 (who lives in China)" is difficult because the attribute is similar to the relative clause in English, and it probably lifts the difficulty of the full sentence "我可以跟我住在中国的朋友发电子邮件 (I can email my friend who lives in China)". In that case, although this sentence is not the

longest one according to the online system, this sentence should be noticed due to the attribute part in it. As for an adapting solution in this example, I think it is better to separate the sentence into two, or to substitute the attribute with a simple one, such as "中国的 (Chinese)".

Tagging not only demonstrates the analytical result of *Chi-Editor* but also immediately computes text difficulty levels. Interviewee C provides the operational details and discusses the longest sentence as follows:

Extract 7 (Interviewee C, #T2-C11)
I have noticed the longer sentences when I am asked to level the text, and I just kept thinking about how the situation would change if I shorten the sentences. *Chi-Editor* underlined the longest sentence in the text, which confirmed my original judgment (the sentence was "吃完饭后，爷爷喜欢一边唱歌一边洗碗，我就在旁边看着他洗，听着他唱小时候的歌，每天早上他都骑摩托车送我去学校，再给我一些零花钱。"). The difference is, I could easily shorten or separate this sentence, and I tried calculating this again and again using *Chi-Editor* to make sure the difficulty could be reduced. In the longest sentence, for example, the LD value before my adaptation was 1.61, and the length was 57 characters. The LD value then changed to 1.60 (length = 32 characters) and 1.59 (length = 32 characters) when I tried to separate the sentence into three single sentences and four single sentences, respectively. In that case, you could select the proper LD value after adapting.

6.3 *Interview: Reporting*

Reporting in *Chi-Editor* summarizes information about the characters and words used in the text in a list format. Most comments on the reporting function touched upon teachers' perceptions of how the resulting word/character lists could be properly used. Interviewee B expressed this viewpoint as follows:

Extract 8 (Interviewee B, #T3-B1)
I typically focused on the WBV and PN after adapting a text, even if the text was not a typical long passage. I assumed that the WBV and PN would be just as effective in this small passage. So, I focused on their word frequency and word percentage. However, I wasn't guessing the level when I encountered a WBV or PN unless the word/character list was reported in *Chi-Editor*. For example, the program shows the word "总是 (always)" as a WBV, but you do not need to worry about it because the word frequency was 2 and the word percentage was 0.98%. Most importantly, *Chi-Editor* will tell you the result, and you don't need to do the calculations by yourself. You can imagine the effect numbers have on word frequency and word percentage in a long text.

Interviewee D agreed that using the reporting function was helpful in adapting a long text. She went a step further, stating that "…if I need to edit or revise my textbook on passages, I'm certain that numbers and calculations in the reporting could help where I need to change the word or the character in a lesson". The following provides more details:

Extract 9 (Interviewee D, #T3-D2)
The word list told me that some word frequencies were really high, but it might make the whole text seem redundant, at least to a native speaker. For example, the word "爷爷 (grandfather)" has been used in this text 11 times according to the word frequency in reporting. Because the word is a noun, I feel that the number is too high due to Chinese being a topic-dominant language. Subsequently, I read the text again more closely. The adapting of this word is supposed to allow discourse cohesion, and this word could usually be replaced or substituted by a pronoun "他 (he/him)".

In relation to the reporting function, interviewees agreed that character/word lists were less effective in a short text, but agreed that these lists would be very useful in highlighting the distribution of words and characters by word frequency, word percentage and word percentage within a certain range in a long text.

7 Discussion and Conclusion

This study generated qualitative data to assess teachers' perceptions of the differences between the intuitive approach and data-driven approach (using *Chi-Editor*) to text adaptation. Our findings indicate that teachers can be trained to use *Chi-Editor* and to take advantage of its benefits.

First, despite the different syllabi referred to by Chinese teachers and *Chi-Editor*, the interviewees noted similarities in leveling by intuition or with *Chi-Editor*, particularly with reference to the consideration of word difficulty and sentence length. The major difference between the two lied in the use of character information by *Chi-Editor* and the disregard of such information by teachers when leveling by intuition. However, studies on Chinese information processing show that Chinese characters contribute useful information to text leveling. These differences bring to light the question of how much weight character level should carry in text leveling by teacher intuition.

Second, interviewees benefited from the analysis and tagging provided by *Chi-Editor* during text adaptation process. It is interesting to note that a high percentage of comments made by the interviewees were on tagging. In general, they agreed that the tagged elements offered directly useful information for their consideration that is not necessarily available to them intuitively. For example, Interviewee C in Extract 7 mentioned said that she could "shorten or separate a sentence without hesitation" when using *Chi-Editor's* longest sentence tagging function, and that she no longer needed to keep "thinking about the situation if [she] shortened the wrong sentence" as she would have done when using teacher intuition. Interviewee A in Extract 4 indicated that when not using *Chi-Editor*, she relied on her own instinct and "impressions," whereas she became more "confident" when using the tagging function in *Chi-Editor*.

Third, regarding the reporting function of *Chi-Editor*, the interviewees reported that the word list provided by *Chi-Editor* could help them better understand the levels of the words. They did not, however, seem to attach much value to the character list reported, mostly due to their preferences for the word-based approach to teaching. Additional comments indicated that the reporting function may be more practically useful with longer texts and that the reported word frequency and coverage information could be useful when editing or revising a text.

Overall, these findings show that *Chi-Editor* facilitates a text adaptation process that is in some ways similar to one that relies on teacher intuition, such as the use of word difficulty information for leveling and the focus on reducing difficult words and long sentences in adaptation. Meanwhile, it is critical to note that the data-driven approach and the intuitive approach should best be integrated in complementary ways. *Chi-Editor* is developed on the basis of the *GCSCW*, which was rooted in pedagogical practices in the first place. Utilizing data-driven technology, it provides rich, detailed information that can inform teachers' text adaptation process. At the same time, many other dimensions of text complexity are not yet captured by *Chi-Editor*, and teachers' expertise would certainly be necessary to complement *Chi-Editor* in considering those dimensions in text adaptation.

Acknowledgements This research was supported by the Fundamental Research Funds for the Central Universities (16wkpy09). We are indebted to Dr. Xiaofei Lu, Dr. Baichuan Li, and Dr. Le Wang for their suggestions and feedback on earlier drafts of the chapter.

References

Base for International Chinese Teaching Materials Developing and Teacher Training. (2017). https://www.cntexts.com/. Accessed July 9, 2017.

Confucius Institute Headquarters (Hanban). (2014). *I want to be a lawyer* (Level 3). Beijing: Beijing Language and Culture University Press.

Confucius Institute Headquarters (Hanban). (2015). *International curriculum for Chinese language education*. Beijing: Beijing Language and Culture University Press.

Crossley, S. A., Louwerse, M. M., McCarthy, P. M., & McNamara, D. S. (2007). A linguistic analysis of simplified and authentic texts. *The Modern Language Journal, 91*(1), 15–30.

Crossley, S. A., Allen, D., & McNamara, D. S. (2012). Text simplification and comprehensible input: A case for an intuitive approach. *Language Teaching Research, 16*(1), 89–108.

Cummins, J. (1981). The role of primary language development in promoting educational success for language minority students. *California State Department of Education Office of Bilingual Education, Schooling and Language Minority Students: A theoretical framework*. Sacramento, CA: Author.

Ellis, R. (1999). *Understanding second language acquisition*. Shanghai: Shanghai Foreign Language Education Press.

Goodman, K. (1986). *What's whole in whole language*. Portsmouth, NH: Heinemann Educational Books.

Graesser, A., McNamara, D., Louwerse, M., & Cai, Z. (2004). Coh-Metrix: Analysis of text on cohesion and language. *Behavioral Research Methods, Instruments, and Computers, 36*(2), 193–202.

Green, A., & Hawkey, R. (2011). Re-fitting for a different purpose: A case study of item writer practices in adapting source texts for a test of academic reading. *Language Testing, 29*(1), 109–129.

Jin, T., & Li, B. (2016). *Chi-Editor: A data-driven tool for Chinese text adaptation*. Guangzhou: LanguageData. Retrieved from www.languagedata.net/editor.

Jin, T., & Lu, X. (2018). A data-driven approach to text adaptation in teaching material preparation: Design, implementation and teacher professional development. *TESOL Quarterly, 52*(2), 457–467.

Johnson, P. (1981). Effects on reading comprehension of language complexity and cultural background of a text. *TESOL Quarterly, 15*(2), 169–181.

Krashen, S. (1981). *Second language acquisition and second language learning*. Oxford: Oxford University Press.

Krashen, S. (1985). *The input hypothesis: Issues and implications*. London: Longman.

Lin, X. (2016). *The design and realization of an online tool for assessing text complexity of L2 Chinese reading materials*. (Unpublished undergraduate dissertation). Sun Yat-sen University, Guangzhou, China.

Liu, Y. L., & Ma, J. F. (2010). The development of the graded Chinese syllables, characters and words: Exploring the new perspective of global Chinese education. *Chinese Teaching in the World, 24*, 82–92.

Ministry of Education & State Language Commission, the People's Republic of China. (2010). *The graded Chinese syllables, characters and words for the application of teaching Chinese to the speakers of other languages*. Beijing: Language and Literature Press.

Sung, Y. T., Dyson, S. B., Chen, Y. C., Lin, W. C., & Chang, K. E. (2015). Leveling L2 texts through readability: Combining multilevel linguistic features with the CEFR. *The Modern Language Journal, 99*(2), 371–391.

Tomlinson, B., Dat, B., Masuhara, H., & Rubdy, R. (2001). EFL courses for adults. *ELT Journal, 55*(1), 80–101.

Wesman, A. G. (1971). Writing the test item. In R. L. Thorndike (Ed.), *Educational measurement* (pp. 99–111). Washington, DC: American Council on Education.

Yano, Y., Long, M., & Ross, S. (1994). Effects of simplified and elaborated texts on foreign language reading comprehension. *Language Learning, 44*(2), 189–219.

Young, D. J. (1999). Linguistic simplification of second language reading material: Effective instructional practice? *The Modern Language Journal, 83*(3), 350–366.

Part III
Specific Applications

Context Analysis for Computer-Assisted Near-Synonym Learning

Liang-Chih Yu, Wei-Nan Chien and Kai-Hsiang Hsu

Abstract Despite their similar meanings, near-synonyms may have different usages in different contexts. For second-language learners, such differences are not easily grasped in practical use. This chapter introduces several context analysis techniques such as pointwise mutual information (PMI), *n*-gram language model, latent semantic analysis (LSA), and independent component analysis (ICA) to verify whether near-synonyms do match the given contexts. Applications can benefit from such techniques to provide useful contextual information for learners, making it easier for them to understand different usages of various near-synonyms. Based on these context analysis techniques, we build a prototype computer-assisted near-synonym learning system. In experiments, we evaluate the context analysis methods on both Chinese and English sentences, and compared its performance to several previously proposed supervised and unsupervised methods. Experimental results show that training on the independent components that contain useful contextual features with minimized term dependence can improve the classifiers' ability to discriminate among near-synonyms, thus yielding better performance.

1 Introduction

Near-synonym sets represent groups of words with similar meanings, which can be derived from the existing lexical ontologies such as WordNet (Fellbaum 1998), EuroWordNet (Rodríguez et al. 1998), and Chinese WordNet (Huang et al. 2008). These are useful knowledge resources for computer-assisted language learning

L.-C. Yu (✉) · W.-N. Chien
Yuan Ze University, Taoyuan, Taiwan
e-mail: lcyu@saturn.yzu.edu.tw

W.-N. Chien
e-mail: s986223@mail.yzu.edu.tw

K.-H. Hsu
Yuanze University, Taoyuan, Taiwan
e-mail: s986220@mail.yzu.edu.tw

X. Lu and B. Chen (eds.), *Computational and Corpus Approaches to Chinese Language Learning*, Chinese Language Learning Sciences,
https://doi.org/10.1007/978-981-13-3570-9_7

(CALL) (Cheng 2004; Inkpen and Hirst 2006; Inkpen 2007; Ouyang et al. 2009; Wu et al. 2010) and natural language processing (NLP) applications such as information retrieval (IR) (Moldovan and Mihalcea 2000; Navigli and Velardi 2003; Shlrl and Revle 2006; Bhogal et al. 2007; Yu et al. 2009) and (near-)duplicate detection for text summarization (Vanderwende et al. 2007). For example, in composing a text, near-synonyms can be used to automatically suggest alternatives to avoid repeating the same word in a text when suitable alternatives are available in the near-synonym set (Inkpen and Hirst 2006). In information retrieval, systems can perform query expansion to improve the recall rate, for example, through recognizing that the weapon sense of "arm" corresponds to the weapon sense of "weapon" and of "arsenal".

Although the words in a near-synonym set have similar meanings, they are not necessarily interchangeable in practical use due to their specific usage and collocational constraints (Wible et al. 2003). Consider the following examples.

(E1) {strong, powerful} coffee
(E2) ghastly {error, mistake}
(E3) {bridge, overpass, tunnel} under the bay.

Examples (E1) and (E2) both present an example of collocational constraints for the given contexts. In (E1), the word "strong" in the near-synonym set {strong, powerful} is more suitable than "powerful" to fit the given context "coffee," since "powerful coffee" is an anti-collocation (Pearce 2001). Similarly, in (E2), "mistake" is more suitable than "error" because "ghastly mistake" is a collocation and "ghastly error" is an anti-collocation (Inkpen 2007). In (E3), the near-synonym set {bridge, overpass, tunnel} represents the meaning of a physical structure that connects separate places by traversing an obstacle. Suppose that the original word is "tunnel" in the context "under the bay". The word "tunnel" cannot be substituted by the other words in the same set because all the substitutions are semantically implausible (Yu et al. 2010). The above examples indicate that near-synonyms may have different usages in different contexts, and such differences are not easily captured by second-language learners. Therefore, we develop a computer-assisted near-synonym learning system to assist Chinese English-as-a-Second-Language (ESL) learners to better understand different usages of various English near-synonyms and use them appropriately in different contexts.

This chapter introduces the use of NLP techniques such as automatic near-synonym choice (Edmonds 1997; Gardiner and Dras 2007; Inkpen 2007; Islam and Inkpen 2010; Wang and Hirst 2010; Yu et al. 2010; Yu and Chien 2013; Yu et al. 2016) to verify whether near-synonyms match the given contexts. The problem of automatic near-synonym choice has been formulated as a "fill-in-the-blank" (FITB) task, as shown in Fig. 1. Given a near-synonym set and a sentence containing one of the near-synonyms, the near-synonym is first removed from the sentence to form a lexical gap. The goal is to predict an answer (best near-synonym) that can fill the gap from the given near-synonym set (including the original word). The systems can then be evaluated by examining their ability to restore the original word with the best near-synonym.

English Sentence:	This will make the __ message easier to interpret.
Original word:	error
Near-synonym set:	{error, mistake, oversight}

Fig. 1 Example of FITB evaluation for automatic near-synonym choice

2 Automatic Near-Synonym Choice

Among many approaches to automatic near-synonym choice, Edmonds' pioneering study used a lexical co-occurrence network to determine the near-synonym that is most typical or expected in a given context (Edmonds 1997). Other proposed methods can generally be categorized as unsupervised (Gardiner and Dras 2007; Inkpen 2007; Islam and Inkpen 2010; Yu et al. 2010) and supervised methods (Wang and Hirst 2010; Yu and Chien 2013; Yu et al. 2016).

2.1 Unsupervised Methods

In the unsupervised methods, the pointwise mutual information (PMI) (Gardiner and Dras 2007; Inkpen 2007) and *n*-gram-based methods (Islam and Inkpen 2010; Yu et al. 2010) are the two major methods.

2.1.1 PMI-Based Method

The PMI is used to measure the strength of co-occurrence between a near-synonym and each individual word appearing in its context. A higher mutual information score indicates that the near-synonym fits well in the given context, and thus is more likely to be the correct answer. The pointwise mutual information (Church and Hanks 1990) between two words x and y is defined as

$$\mathrm{PMI}(x, y) = \log_2 \frac{P(x, y)}{P(x)P(y)}, \tag{1}$$

where $P(x, y) = C(x, y)/N$ denotes the probability that x and y co-occur; $C(x, y)$ is the number of times x and y co-occur in the corpus; and N is the total number of words in the corpus. Similarly, $P(x) = C(x)/N$, where $C(x)$ is the number of times x occurs in the corpus, and $P(y) = C(y)/N$, where $C(y)$ is the number of times y occurs in the corpus. Therefore, Eq. 1 can be rewritten as

$$\mathrm{PMI}(x, y) = \log_2 \frac{C(x, y) \cdot N}{C(x) \cdot C(y)}. \tag{2}$$

The frequency counts $C(\cdot)$ presented in Eq. 2 can be retrieved from a large corpus such as the Waterloo terabyte corpus used in (Inkpen 2007), and the Web 1T 5-gram corpus used in (Gardiner and Dras 2007).

Given a sentence s with a gap, $s = \ldots w_1 \ldots w_\ell \ldots w_{\ell+1} \ldots w_{2\ell} \ldots$, the PMI score for a near-synonym NS_j to fill the gap is computed from the words around the gap, defined as

$$\mathrm{PMI}(NS_j, s) = \sum_{i=1}^{2\ell} \mathrm{PMI}(NS_j, w_i). \tag{3}$$

where ℓ is a window size representing ℓ words to the left and right of the gap. Finally, the near-synonym with the highest score is considered to be the answer.

2.1.2 5-Gram Language Model

N-grams can capture contiguous word associations within given contexts. Assume a sentence $s = \ldots w_{i-4}w_{i-3}w_{i-2}w_{i-1}w_iw_{i+1}w_{i+2}w_{i+3}w_{i+4} \ldots$, where w_i represents a near-synonym in a set. In computing the 5-gram scores for each near-synonym, only the five product items $P(w_i|w_{i-4}^{i-1})$, $P(w_{i+1}|w_{i-3}^{i})$, $P(w_{i+2}|w_{i-2}^{i+1})$, $P(w_{i+3}|w_{i-1}^{i+2})$, and $P(w_{i+4}|w_{i}^{i+3})$ are considered (Islam and Inkpen 2010). The other items are excluded because they do not contain the near-synonym and thus will have the same values. Accordingly, the 5-gram language model ($n = 5$) with a smoothing method can be defined as

$$\begin{aligned} P(s) &= \prod_{i=1}^{5} P(w_i|w_{i-n+1}^{i-1}) \\ &= \prod_{i=1}^{5} \frac{C(w_{i-n+1}^{i}) + (1 + \alpha_n)M(w_{i-n+1}^{i-1})P(w_i|w_{i-n+2}^{i-1})}{C(w_{i-n+1}^{i-1}) + \alpha_n M(w_{i-n+1}^{i-1})} \end{aligned} \tag{4}$$

where $M(w_{i-n+1}^{i-1})$ denotes a missing count used in the smoothing method, defined as

$$M(w_{i-n+1}^{i-1}) = C(w_{i-n+1}^{i-1}) - \sum_{w_i} C(w_{i-n+1}^{i}) \tag{5}$$

where $C(\cdot)$ denotes an n-gram frequency, which can be retrieved from a large corpus such as the Web 1T 5-gram corpus used in (Islam and Inkpen 2010). The 5-gram language model is implemented as a back-off model. That is, if the frequency of a higher order n-gram is zero, then its lower order n-grams will be considered. Conversely, if the frequency of a higher order n-gram is not zero, then the lower order n-grams will not be included in the computation. Similar to the PMI-based method, the near-synonym with the highest score is considered to be the answer.

2.2 Supervised Methods

Supervised methods usually approach near-synonym choice tasks as classification tasks in which each near-synonym in a near-synonym set represents a class, and the features used for classification are the words which occur in the contexts of the near-synonyms. The near-synonyms and their context words are represented by vector-based representation which is frequently used in distributional models of lexical semantics (Harris 1954; Lin 1998; Roussinov and Zhao 2003; Weeds et al. 2004). Based on this representation, a co-occurrence matrix of the near-synonyms and their context words can be built from the training data, i.e., a collection of sentences containing the near-synonyms. Each entry in the matrix represents a co-occurrence frequency of a context word and a near-synonym. Different context analysis techniques such as latent semantic analysis (LSA) and independent component analysis (ICA) can then be applied to the context matrix to identify useful context features that contribute to the classification task (Wang and Hirst 2010; Yu and Chien 2013).

2.2.1 Latent Semantic Analysis (LSA)

LSA is a technique for analyzing the relationships between words and documents and has been widely used in many application domains such as information retrieval (Landauer et al. 1998), latent topic discovery (Cribbin 2011), and document clustering (Wei et al. 2008). For automatic near-synonym choice, LSA is used as a context analysis technique to identify useful latent context features for the near-synonyms through indirect associations between words and sentences.

The first step in LSA is to build a word-by-document matrix for near-synonyms and their context words (Wang and Hirst 2010). In addition to documents, for our task, other text units such as sentences or 5-grams could also be used to build the matrix because these text units also contain contextual information for near-synonyms. Figure 2 shows a sample matrix $\mathbf{X}$ built using the sentence as the unit. The columns in $\mathbf{X}_{v\times d}$ represent d sentences containing the near-synonyms in a near-synonym set and the rows represent v distinct words occurring in the near-synonyms' contexts in the corpus. Singular value decomposition (SVD) (Golub and Van Loan 1996) is then used to decompose the matrix $\mathbf{X}_{v\times d}$ into three matrices as follows:

$$\mathbf{X}_{v\times d} = \mathbf{U}_{v\times n} \sum_{n\times n} \mathbf{V}^{T}_{n\times d}, \tag{6}$$

where $\mathbf{U}$ and $\mathbf{V}$, respectively, consist of a set of latent vectors of words and sentences, $\sum$ is a diagonal matrix of singular values, and $n = \min(v, d)$ denotes the dimensionality of the latent semantic space. Additionally, each element in $\mathbf{U}$ represents the weight of a context word, and the higher weighted words are the useful context features for the near-synonyms. By selecting the largest k_1 ($\leq n$) singular values together with the first k_1 columns of $\mathbf{U}$ and $\mathbf{V}$, the near-synonyms and their context words

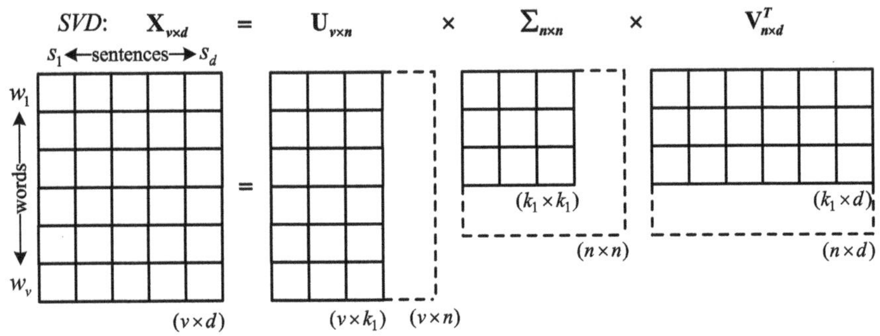

Fig. 2 Illustrative example of singular value decomposition for latent semantic analysis

can be represented in a low-dimensional latent semantic space. The original matrix can also be reconstructed with the reduced dimensions, as shown in Eq. 7

$$\widehat{\mathbf{X}}_{v\times d} = \mathbf{U}_{v\times k_1} \sum_{k_1\times k_1} \mathbf{V}^T_{k_1\times d}, \tag{7}$$

where $\widehat{\mathbf{X}}$ represents the reconstructed matrix.

In SVM training and testing, each input sentence with a lexical gap is first transformed into the latent semantic representation as follows:

$$\hat{\mathbf{t}}_{k_1\times 1} = \sum_{k_1\times k_1}^{-1} \mathbf{U}^T_{k_1\times v}\mathbf{t}_{v\times 1}, \tag{8}$$

where $\mathbf{t}_{v\times 1}$ denotes the vector representation of an input sentence and $\hat{\mathbf{t}}_{k_1\times 1}$ denotes the transformed vector in the latent semantic space. Each transformed training vector is then appended by the correct answer (the near-synonym removed from the sentence) to form a $(k_1 + 1)$-dimensional vector for SVM training.

The strength of LSA lies in discovering the latent context features for near-synonyms using SVD. Consider the example shown in Fig. 3. The original matrix, as shown in Fig. 3a, is built using five training sentences containing two different near-synonyms NS_i and NS_j. Suppose that the words w_1, w_2 are the useful features for NS_i, and w_3, w_4 are useful for NS_j, but w_4 is a latent feature because it does not frequently occur in the context of NS_j. After applying SVD, the latent features can be identified by replacing the zero entries in the original matrix with nonzero real values through the indirect associations between words and sentences. For instance, w_4 originally does not occur in s_3 and s_4, but it does co-occur with w_3 in the matrix (e.g., in s_5), which means that w_4 might also occur in the sentences where w_3 occurs (e.g., s_3 and s_4). Therefore, the zero entries (w_4, s_3) and (w_4, s_4) are replaced with a nonzero value through the indirect associations between of w_3 and w_4 in s_5, as shown in Fig. 3b. This helps identify a useful latent feature w_4 for NS_j. However, identi-

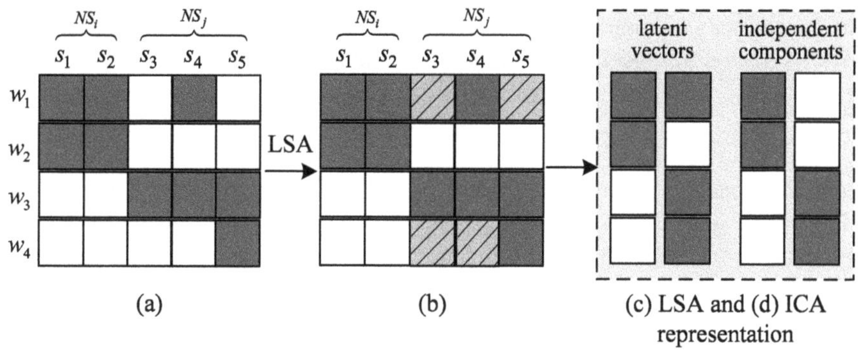

Fig. 3 Comparison of LSA and ICA for feature representation

fying latent features through the indirect associations cannot avoid feature overlap when different near-synonyms share common words in their contexts. This might be possible because near-synonyms usually have similar contexts. For instance, in Fig. 3a, w_1, which is useful for NS_i, still occurs in the context of NS_j (e.g., s_4). Through the indirect associations between of w_1 and w_3 in s_4, the frequency of w_1 increases in the context of NS_j because it may also occur in the sentences where w_3 occurs (e.g., s_3 and s_5), as shown in Fig. 3b. Therefore, when all word features are to be accommodated in a low-dimensional space reduced by SVD, term overlap may occur between the latent vectors. As indicated in Fig. 3c, the two sample latent vectors which contribute to two different near-synonyms share a common feature w_1. Classifiers trained on such latent vectors with term overlap may decrease their ability to distinguish among near-synonyms.

2.2.2 Independent Component Analysis (ICA)

ICA is a technique for extracting independent components from a mixture of signals and has been successfully applied to solve the blind source separation problem (Hyvärinen et al. 2001; Lee 1998). Recent studies have shown that ICA can also be applied to other application domains such as text processing (Kolenda and Hansen 2000; Rapp 2004; Sevillano et al. 2004). In contrast to LSA, ICA extracts independent components by minimizing the term dependence of the context matrix. Therefore, LSA and ICA can be considered complementary methods where LSA can be used to discover latent features that do not frequently occur in the context of near-synonyms, and ICA can be used to further minimize the dependence of the latent features such that overlapped features can be removed, as presented in Fig. 3d. Based on this complementariness, the ICA-based framework can be used to analyze the LSA output to discover more useful latent features for different near-synonyms, and the dependence between them can also be minimized. The discriminant power of classifiers can thus be improved by training them on the independent components with minimized term overlap. The ICA model can be formally described as

$$\mathbf{X} = \mathbf{AS}, \tag{9}$$

where $\mathbf{X}$ denotes the observed mixture signals, $\mathbf{A}$ denotes a mixing matrix, and $\mathbf{S}$ denotes the independent components. The goal of ICA is to estimate both $\mathbf{A}$ and $\mathbf{S}$. Once the mixing matrix $\mathbf{A}$ is estimated, the demixing matrix can be obtained by $\mathbf{W} = \mathbf{A}^{-1}$, and Eq. 9 can be rewritten as

$$\mathbf{S} = \mathbf{WX}, \tag{10}$$

That is, the observed mixture signals can be separated into independent components using the demixing matrix.

For our problem, the context matrix can be considered as a mixture of signals because it consists of the contexts of different near-synonyms. Therefore, ICA used, herein is to estimate the demixing matrix so that it can separate the mixed contexts to derive the independent components for each near-synonym. Figure 4 shows the ICA-based framework combining LSA and ICA.

LSA decomposition and reconstruction In the training phase, the original context matrix $\mathbf{X}_{v\times d}$ is first decomposed by SVD using Eq. 6, and then reconstructed with reduced dimensions using Eq. 7. Useful latent features that do not frequently occur in the original matrix can thus be discovered in this step.

ICA decomposition and demixing To further minimize term dependence in deriving the independent components, the reconstructed matrix $\widehat{\mathbf{X}}_{v\times d}$ is passed to ICA to estimate the demixing matrix. ICA accomplishes this by decomposing $\widehat{\mathbf{X}}_{v\times d}$ using Eq. 11. Figure 5 shows an example of the decomposition.

$$\widehat{\mathbf{X}}_{v\times d} = \mathbf{A}_{v\times k_2}\mathbf{S}_{k_2\times d}. \tag{11}$$

Based on this decomposition, the demixing matrix can be obtained by $\mathbf{W}_{k_2\times v} = \mathbf{A}^{-1}_{v\times k_2}$, where k_2 ($\leq n$) is the number of independent components. Similar to the matrix $\mathbf{U}$ in LSA, each element in $\mathbf{W}$ also represents the weight of a context word, and the higher weighted words are useful context features for the near-synonyms. Therefore, the demixing matrix contains useful context features with minimized term dependence for different near-synonyms.

Once estimated, the demixing matrix is used to separate $\widehat{\mathbf{X}}_{v\times d}$ to derive the independent components as follows:

$$\mathbf{S}_{k_2\times d} = \mathbf{W}_{k_2\times v}\widehat{\mathbf{X}}_{v\times d}, \tag{12}$$

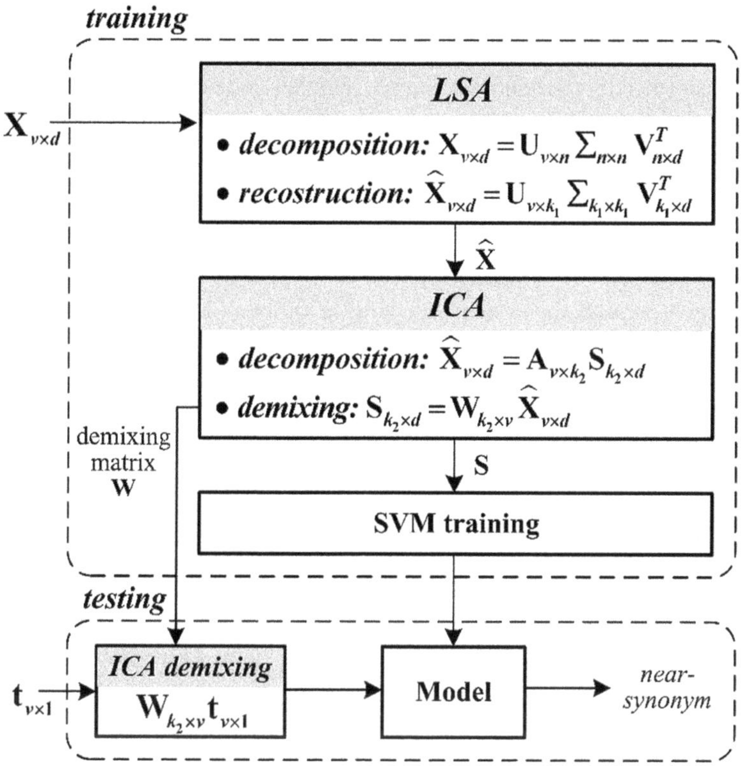

Fig. 4 ICA-based framework for near-synonym choice

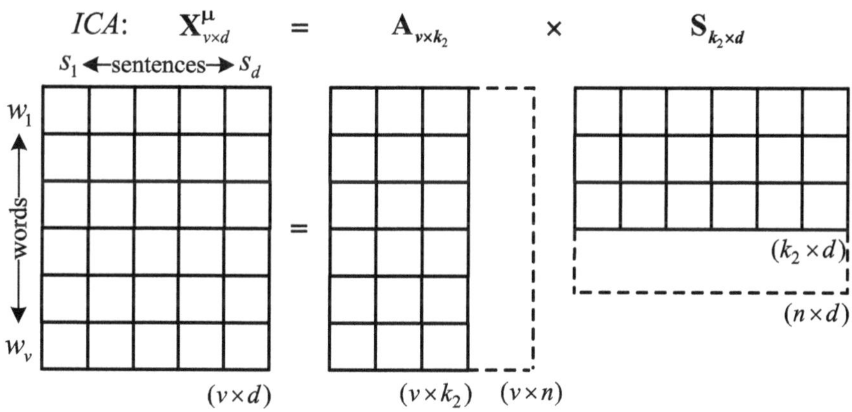

Fig. 5 Illustrative example of ICA decomposition

Each column vector in $\mathbf{S}_{k_2 \times d}$ is then appended by the correct answer for SVM training. Similarly, as shown in Fig. 4, each test instance $\mathbf{t}_{v \times 1}$ in the testing phase is also transformed by the demixing matrix, and then predicted with the trained SVM model.

3 Experimental Results

This section presents the evaluation results of different methods for near-synonym choice. Section 3.1 describes the experiment setup, including experimental data, implementation details of methods used, and the evaluation metric. Section 3.2 investigates the selection of optimal parameters for LSA and ICA-based methods. Section 3.3 compares the results obtained by the various methods. Section 3.4 presents a detailed analysis to examine the effect of term overlap on classification performance.

3.1 Experiment Setup

3.1.1 Data

As shown in Table 1, seven English and Chinese near-synonym sets was used for evaluation. For Chinese near-synonym choice evaluation, two test corpora were used: the Chinese News Corpus (CNC) and the Sinica Corpus (SC), both released by the Association for Computational Linguistics and Chinese Language Processing (ACLCLP). The test examples were collected from the two corpora by selecting sentences containing the near-synonyms in the seven Chinese near-synonym sets. A total of 36,427 (CNC) and 26,504 (SC) sentences were collected, where 20% of sentences from each corpus were randomly selected as a development set for parameter tuning of LSA and ICA-based methods, and the remaining 80% were used as the test set for performance evaluation. In addition, the classifiers (described in the next section) were built from the Chinese Web 5-gram corpus released by the Linguistic Data Consortium (LDC). For English near-synonym choice evaluation, the Web 1T 5-gram corpus released by LDC was used for both classifier training and evaluation using the cross-validation method.

3.1.2 Classifiers

The classifiers involved in this experiment included PMI, the 5-gram language model, cosine measure, LSA, and ICA-based methods (including stand-alone ICA and a combination of LSA and ICA). The implementation details for each classifier are as follows:

Table 1 English and Chinese near-synonym sets

No.	Near-synonym sets
1	Difficult, hard, tough 困難的, 艱難的, 艱苦的, 難懂的
2	Error, mistake, oversight 錯誤, 錯, 過失, 失察
3	Job, task, duty 工作, 任務, 義務
4	Responsibility, burden, obligation, commitment 責任, 職責, 職務, 約定
5	Material, stuff, substance 物質, 材料, 質料
6	Give, provide, offer 給, 給予, 給與, 供應, 供給
7	Settle, resolve 決定, 確定, 定奪, 終結

The English and Chinese near-synonyms in each set corresponds to the same sense

PMI: Given a near-synonym set and a test example with a gap, the PMI scores for each near-synonym were calculated using Eq. 3, where the size of the context window ℓ was set to 2. The frequency counts were retrieved from the Web 1T 5-gram corpus and Chinese Web 5-gram corpus, respectively, for English and Chinese near-synonym choice evaluation.

5 GRAM: The 5-gram scores for each near-synonym in a test example were calculated using Eq. 4. The frequency counts for *n*-grams were retrieved by querying Google (as in Yu et al. 2010) for English near-synonym choice evaluation, and from the Chinese Web 5-gram corpus for Chinese evaluation.

COS: Given a near-synonym set, all 5-grams containing the near-synonyms in the set were first extracted from the training data (i.e., from the Web 1T 5-gram corpus for English near-synonyms and from the Chinese Web 5-gram corpus for Chinese near-synonyms). The 5-grams with the near-synonyms are removed and were then used to build a word-by-class matrix for the near-synonym set. The best near-synonym for each test example was then predicted by comparing the cosine similarity of the test example and the near-synonyms in the matrix.

LSA: COS used all 5-grams to build the context matrix but, due to the efficiency consideration, we randomly selected only 20,000 5-grams to build the word-by-document (5-gram) matrix for each English and Chinese near-synonym set. The number of the 5-grams for each near-synonym in the matrix was selected according to their proportions in the corpus. Once the matrix was built, each training instance (i.e., each column vector of the matrix) was transformed into the latent space using Eq. 8. The correct answer (the near-synonym removed from the training instance) was then appended to the corresponding transformed vector to form a $(k_1 + 1)$-dimensional vector for SVM training.

ICA: Stand-alone ICA was implemented using Eqs. 9 and 10. The input matrix was the same as that of LSA, and the demixing matrix was estimated using the FastICA package (Hyvärinen 1999). An SVM classifier was then trained using the independent components obtained using Eq. 10 with the correct answers appended.

LSA + ICA: The combination of LSA and ICA was implemented by taking the LSA result as input to estimate the demixing matrix in ICA, as shown in Eq. 11. An SVM classifier was then trained using the independent components obtained from Eq. 12 with the correct answers appended. For LSA, ICA, and LSA + ICA, the best near-synonym for each test example was predicted using the trained SVM models.

3.1.3 Evaluation Metric

In testing, this experiment followed the FITB evaluation procedure (Fig. 1) to remove the near-synonyms from the test samples. The answers proposed by each classifier are the near-synonyms with the highest score. The correct answers are the near-synonyms originally in the gap of the test samples. Performance is determined by accuracy, which is defined as the number of correct answers made by each classifier, divided by the total number of test examples.

3.2 Evaluation of LSA and ICA-Based Methods

Experiments were conducted to compare the performance of LSA, ICA, and LSA + ICA using different settings for the parameters k_1 and k_2, which, respectively represent the dimensionality of the latent semantic space and the number of independent components. The optimal settings of the two parameters were tuned by maximizing the classification accuracy on the development set. Figure 6 shows the classification accuracy of LSA, ICA, and LSA + ICA with different settings of dimensionality (k_1 or k_2). The accuracies were obtained by averaging the seven Chinese near-synonym sets. For LSA, the x-axis represents different values of k_1, with performance increasing with k_1 up to 2000. For ICA, the x-axis represents different values of k_2, with an optimal performance at $k_2 = 500$. For LSA + ICA, the performance was tuned by varying both k_1 and k_2. Due to the large number of combinations of k_1 and k_2, for LSA + ICA, Fig. 7 only plots the optimal accuracy for each value of k_1 on the x-axis, and the optimal accuracy for each value of k_1 (e.g., 500) was determined by increasing k_2 by increments of 100 to select the highest accuracy among the different settings of k_2. For instance, the accuracy of LSA + ICA at $k_1 = 500$ was selected from the highest achieved at $k_2 = 500$, and this accuracy (i.e., that reached at $k_1 = 500$ and $k_2 = 500$) was also the optimal performance of LSA + ICA.

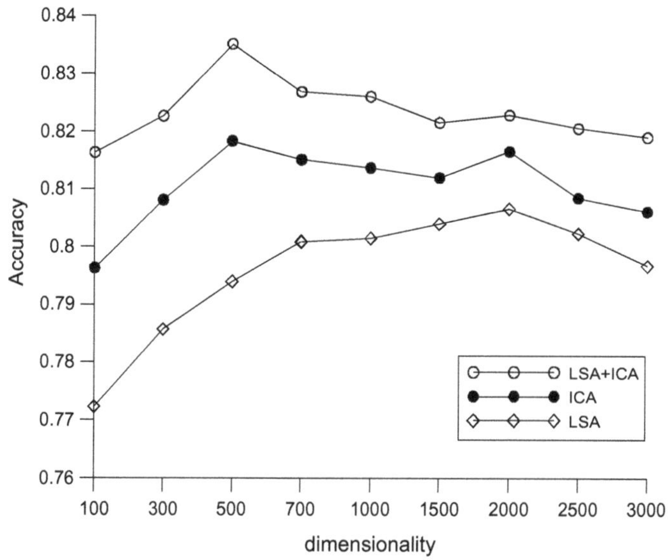

Fig. 6 Classification accuracy of LSA, ICA, and LSA + ICA on the development set, as a function of dimensionality

The results presented in Fig. 6 show that LSA + ICA improved the performance of LSA for all dimensionalities because the degree of term overlap in LSA was reduced by ICA. In addition, the performance difference between LSA + ICA and LSA was greater when the dimensionality was smaller, indicating that ICA was more effective in reducing the degree of term overlap in a low-dimensional space. More detailed analysis of the relationship between the term overlap and the classification performance is discussed in Sect. 3.4. The best settings of the parameters were used in the following experiments.

3.3 Comparative Results

This section reports the classification accuracy of supervised and unsupervised methods including PMI, 5GRAM, COS, LSA, ICA, and LSA + ICA. Table 2 shows the comparative results for the Chinese corpora including Chinese News Corpus (CNC), Sinica Corpus (SC), and both (ALL). The *binomial exact test* (Howell 2007) was used to determine whether the performance difference was statistically significant.

For the two unsupervised methods, 5GRAM outperformed PMI on both test corpora. One possible reason is that the 5-gram language model can capture contiguous word associations in a given context, whereas in PMI, words are considered independently within the given context. In addition, all supervised methods (i.e., COS, LSA, ICA, and LSA + ICA) achieved better performance than the two unsupervised

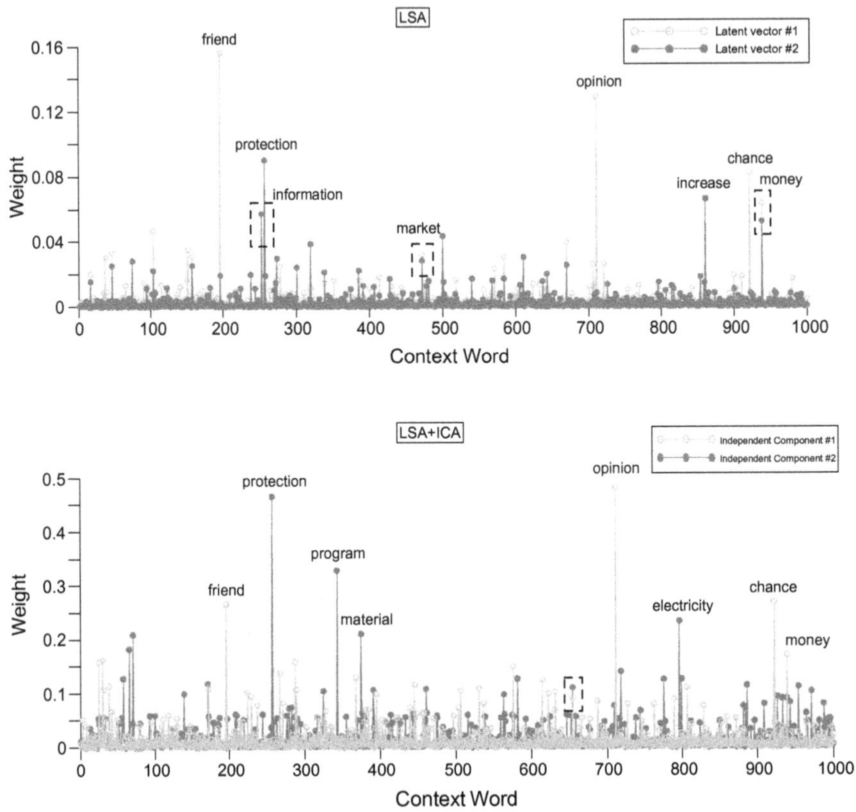

Fig. 7 Examples of latent vectors, selected from $\mathbf{U}_{v \times k}$, and independent components, selected from $\mathbf{W}_{v \times k}^{T}$, for the near-synonyms "give" and "provide". The weights shown in this figure are the absolute values of the weights in the latent vectors and independent components

methods on both test corpora. In the supervised methods, COS provided the baseline results since it did not use any technique for context analysis. As indicated in Table 2, COS yielded higher average accuracy than the best unsupervised method (i.e., 5GRAM) by 2.55 and 7.83% on CNC and SC, respectively, and by 4.79% on ALL. Once context analysis techniques were employed, LSA, ICA, and LSA + ICA significantly improved COS, indicating that context analysis is a useful technique for near-synonym choice. For LSA, it improved the average accuracy of COS by 7.52, 4.29, and 6.16%, respectively, on CNC, SC, and ALL. The improvement mainly came from the discovery of useful latent features from the contexts of the near-synonyms. ICA also outperformed COS, with the improvement mainly coming from the discovery of independent components by minimizing the feature dependence among near-synonyms. After combining LSA and ICA, the performance of both LSA and ICA was further improved because LSA + ICA cannot only discover useful latent features for different near-synonyms but also can minimize the dependence between them, thus improving the discriminant power of classifiers to distinguish between near-synonyms.

For the evaluation of English near-synonym choice, 20,000 5-grams for each English near-synonym set were randomly selected from the Web 1T 5-gram corpus (Web 1T), and the near-synonyms in the 5-grams were removed for the purpose of FITB evaluation. Ten-fold cross-validation was then used to determine the classification accuracy of the methods used, with a *t-test* to determine statistical significance. In addition, for PMI, frequency counts were retrieved from the whole Web 1T 5-gram corpus, and those for 5GRAM were retrieved by querying Google (as in Yu et al. 2010). Table 3 shows the comparative results of the various methods, showing that LSA + ICA improved the performance of both stand-alone LSA and ICA.

3.4 Term Overlap Analysis

This section investigates the effect of term overlap on classification performance. Term overlap in LSA and the ICA-based methods can be estimated from their respective corresponding matrices $\mathbf{U}_{v \times k}$ and $\mathbf{W}^T_{v \times k}$. Each column of $\mathbf{U}_{v \times k}$ and $\mathbf{W}^T_{v \times k}$ represents a latent vector/independent component of v words, and each element in the vector are a word weight representing its relevance to the corresponding latent vector/independent component. Therefore, the meaning of each latent vector/independent component can be characterized by its higher weighted words. Figure 7 shows two sample latent vectors for LSA and two independent components for LSA + ICA.

The upper part of Fig. 7 shows parts of the context words and their weights in the two latent vectors, where latent vector #1 can be characterized by *friend*, *opinion*, and *chance*, which are the useful features for identifying the near-synonym "give," and latent vector #2 can be characterized by *protection*, *information*, and *increase*, which are useful for identifying the near-synonym "provide". Although the two latent vectors contained useful context features for the respective different near-synonyms, these features still had some overlap between the latent vectors, as marked by the dashed rectangles. The overlapped features, especially those with higher weights, may reduce the classifier's ability to distinguish between the near-synonyms. The lower part of Fig. 7 also shows two independent components for the near-synonyms "give" and "provide". As indicated, the term overlap between the two independent components was relatively low.

To formally compare the degree of term overlap of LSA and the ICA-based methods, we used a measure, *overlap@n*, to calculate the degree of overlap of the top n ranked words among the latent vectors in $\mathbf{U}_{v \times k}$ and independent components in $\mathbf{W}^T_{v \times k}$. First, the words in each latent vector (or independent component) were ranked according to the descending order of their weights. The top n words were then selected to form a word set. Let s^n_i and s^n_j be the two word sets of the top n words for any two latent vectors (or independent components). The degree of term overlap between them was calculated by the number of intersections between their corresponding

Table 2 Classification accuracy for Chinese corpora

CNC	Accuracy					
	PMI	5GRAM	COS	LSA	ICA	LSA + ICA
1	72.72	71.33	67.47	71.49	72.81	76.55
2	59.70	53.70	65.05	65.97	68.65	69.36
3	67.90	70.68	81.40	87.02	88.38	89.38
4	56.35	56.87	59.90	69.62	70.53	72.63
5	75.85	64.39	78.96	83.77	83.69	86.32
6	51.85	57.71	57.67	65.98	66.35	67.99
7	60.81	72.27	63.69	73.53	79.98	82.03
Average	61.49	66.41	68.96	76.48	79.02*	80.58†
Data size	29,141		28,694			
SC	Accuracy					
	PMI	5GRAM	COS	LSA	ICA	LSA + ICA
1	68.84	70.66	69.35	68.08	72.37	73.31
2	67.51	52.47	76.12	77.40	79.02	80.11
3	64.67	76.72	84.96	90.01	90.71	92.06
4	50.14	68.58	68.86	75.70	77.51	79.10
5	73.29	59.52	76.13	72.13	75.96	78.63
6	69.85	65.68	76.72	81.52	82.66	84.57
7	61.58	71.98	70.17	74.88	76.79	78.75
Average	65.26	70.11	77.94	82.23	83.60*	85.28†
Data size	21,192		21,098			
ALL	Accuracy					
	PMI	5GRAM	COS	LSA	ICA	LSA + ICA
1	70.35	70.92	68.63	69.35	72.54	74.55
2	63.48	53.11	70.41	71.51	73.67	74.57
3	66.52	73.25	82.92	88.30	89.38	90.53
4	54.17	60.98	63.06	71.76	72.99	74.91
5	74.26	61.37	77.20	76.53	78.88	81.54
6	60.81	61.68	67.25	73.80	74.55	76.33
7	61.05	72.18	65.72	73.95	78.98	81.00
Average	63.07	67.97	72.76	78.92	80.96*	82.57†
Data size	50,333		49,792			

All figures are in %

*ICA versus LSA significantly different ($p < 0.05$)

†LSA + ICA versus ICA significantly different ($p < 0.05$)

Table 3 Classification accuracy for the English corpus

Web 1T	Accuracy					
	PMI	5GRAM	COS	LSA	ICA	LSA + ICA
1	60.36	61.36	60.88	62.68	63.57	65.29
2	76.62	72.67	76.39	79.16	79.85	82.05
3	70.67	71.33	76.17	78.95	80.30	80.97
4	68.75	70.25	67.25	68.50	72.21	73.50
5	70.58	70.35	71.53	74.79	77.25	79.50
6	65.93	61.98	66.25	72.53	73.22	75.08
7	71.29	68.50	76.56	77.89	79.06	81.06
Average	69.17	68.06	70.72	73.50	75.07*	76.78†

All figures are in %
*ICA versus LSA significantly different ($p < 0.05$)
†LSA + ICA versus ICA significantly different ($p < 0.05$)

Fig. 8 Example of computing the degree of term overlap

k=1		k=2		k=3	
A	0.4381	F	0.3678	F	0.2218
B	0.2708	A	0.2342	H	0.1582
C	0.2532	G	0.2095	E	0.1416
D	0.2342	H	0.1972	I	0.1332
E	0.2104	I	0.1895	C	0.1276

word sets divided by n, i.e., $\left|s_i^n \cap s_j^n\right| / n$. Therefore, the degree of term overlap for a whole matrix, namely $overlap_{\mathbf{U}_{v\times k}}$ (or $overlap_{\mathbf{W}^T_{v\times k}}$), can be calculated by the average of the degrees of term overlap between all latent vectors (or independent components) in $\mathbf{U}_{v\times k}$ (or $\mathbf{W}^T_{v\times k}$). That is,

$$overlap_{\mathbf{U}_{v\times k}}@n = \frac{1}{C_2^k}\sum_{i=1}^{k}\sum_{j=i+1}^{k}\frac{\left|s_i^n \cap s_j^n\right|}{n}, \tag{13}$$

where C_2^k denotes the number of combinations of any two vectors in $\mathbf{U}_{v\times k}$ (or $\mathbf{W}^T_{v\times k}$). Figure 8 presents a sample matrix for computing the degree of term overlap, consisting of three vectors of the top five terms. The respective *overlap@5* between the vectors (1, 2), (1, 3), and (2, 3), was 1/5, 2/5, and 3/5, yielding an average 2/5 as the *overlap@5* for the matrix.

By averaging the degree of term overlap over the matrices corresponding to the near-synonym sets, we can obtain the degree of term overlap of LSA, ICA, and LSA + ICA, respectively, defined as $overlap_{LSA}@n$, $overlap_{ICA}@n$, and $overlap_{LSA+ICA}@n$. Figure 9 shows the degree of term overlap for LSA, ICA, and LSA + ICA averaged over the seven Chinese near-synonym sets against various dimensionality values.

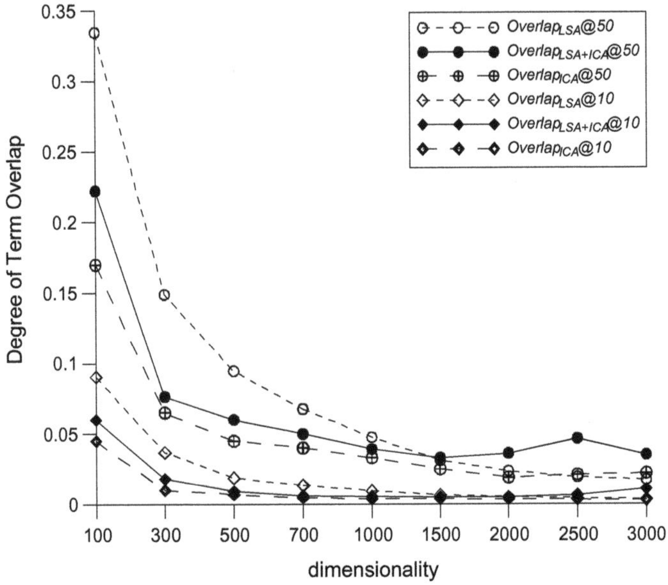

Fig. 9 Degree of term overlap of LSA, ICA, and LSA + ICA, as a function of dimensionality

The results show that ICA achieved the lowest degree of term overlap for both *overlap@10* and *overlap@50*. In addition, combining LSA and ICA reduced the degree of term overlap of using LSA alone, especially for a smaller dimensionality. As indicated in Fig. 9, the difference between both $overlap_{LSA+ICA}@10$ and $overlap_{LSA}@10$ and $overlap_{LSA+ICA}@50$ and $overlap_{LSA}@50$ increased with smaller dimensionality, mainly due to the fact that the features discovered by LSA were not easily separable in a lower dimensional space. In this circumstance, incorporating ICA can more effectively reduce the degree of term overlap. As the dimensionality increased, the difference between LSA and LSA + ICA gradually decreased, mainly because the increase in dimensionality decreased the degree of term overlap in LSA, thus ICA only produces a limited reduction of term overlap in LSA. As indicated, both $overlap_{LSA+ICA}@10$ and $overlap_{LSA+ICA}@50$ yielded a small decrease or increase of overlap when the dimensionality exceeded 1000.

To further analyze the relationship between term overlap and classification performance, Fig. 10 compares the classification accuracy of LSA, ICA, and LSA + ICA from Fig. 6 and $overlap_{LSA}@50$, $overlap_{ICA}@50$, and $overlap_{LSA+ICA}@50$ from Fig. 9. Comparing the degree of term overlap and classification performance of LSA + ICA and LSA found that reducing the degree of term overlap improved classification performance. Given a small dimensionality, the performance of LSA was low due to the high degree of term overlap. Combining LSA and ICA in this stage yielded a greater performance improvement because LSA + ICA effectively reduced the degree of term overlap in LSA such that useful context features could be separated into different independent components according to their contribution to dif-

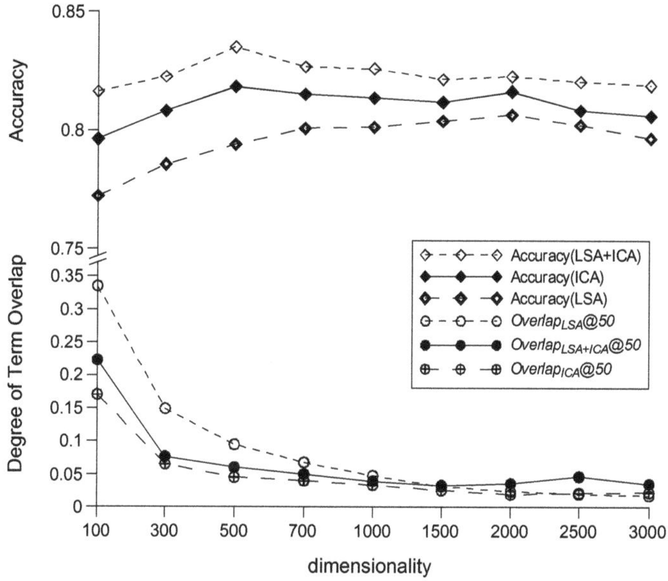

Fig. 10 Comparison of the classification accuracy and the degree of term overlap of LSA, ICA, and LSA + ICA, as a function of dimensionality

ferent near-synonyms. An increase in the dimensionality improves the performance of LSA due to the reduced degree of term overlap. Meanwhile, the performance of LSA + ICA was not similarly improved due to the small reduction of the degree of term overlap, resulting in a gradual decrease in the performance difference between LSA + ICA and LSA. Another observation is that LSA + ICA also outperformed ICA, despite ICA having a lower degree of term overlap than LSA + ICA. This is mainly due to the fact that LSA + ICA can discover more useful context features than ICA, and also minimizes feature dependence.

4 Applications

Based on the contextual information provided by the PMI and n-gram, we implement a prototype system with two functions: contextual statistics and near-synonym choice, both of which interact with learners.

4.1 Contextual Statistics

This function provides the contextual information retrieved by PMI and n-gram. This prototype system features a total of 21 English near-synonyms grouped into seven near-synonym sets, as shown in Table 1. Figure 11 shows a screenshot of the interface for contextual information lookup. Once a near-synonym set is selected, the 100 top-ranked context words and *n*-grams are retrieved for each near-synonym in the set. For PMI, both proportion-based PMI scores and co-occurrence frequencies between near-synonyms and their context words are presented. For n-gram, the 100 top-ranked *n*-grams with their frequencies are presented. Through this function, learners learn to determine the most frequently co-occurring and discriminative words and *n*-grams for different near-synonyms.

4.2 Near-Synonym Choice

This function assists learners in determining suitable near-synonyms when they are not familiar with the various usages of the near-synonyms in a given context. Learners can specify a near-synonym set and then input a sentence with "*" to represent any near-synonym in the set. The system will replace "*" with each near-synonym, and

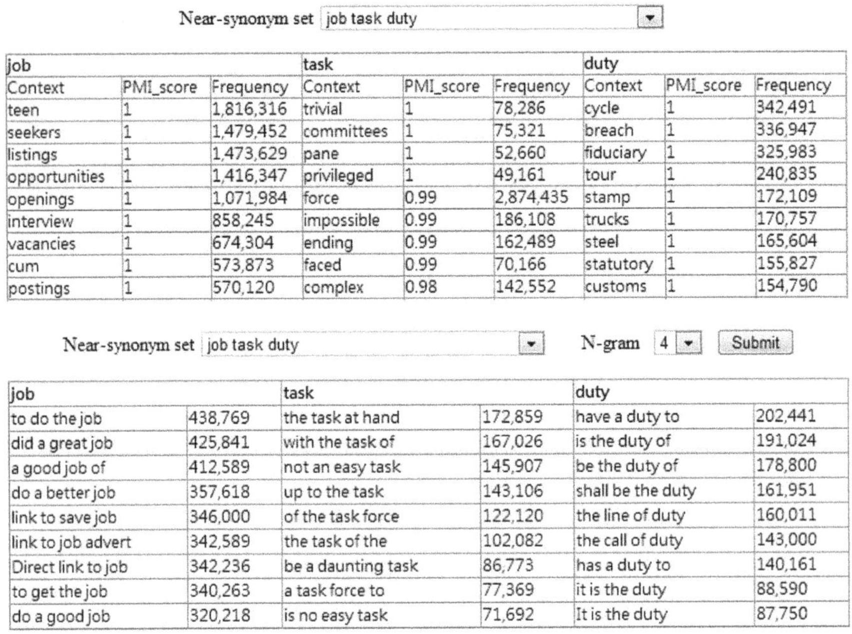

Near-synonym set: job task duty

job			task			duty		
Context	PMI_score	Frequency	Context	PMI_score	Frequency	Context	PMI_score	Frequency
teen	1	1,816,316	trivial	1	78,286	cycle	1	342,491
seekers	1	1,479,452	committees	1	75,321	breach	1	336,947
listings	1	1,473,629	pane	1	52,660	fiduciary	1	325,983
opportunities	1	1,416,347	privileged	1	49,161	tour	1	240,835
openings	1	1,071,984	force	0.99	2,874,435	stamp	1	172,109
interview	1	858,245	impossible	0.99	186,108	trucks	1	170,757
vacancies	1	674,304	ending	0.99	162,489	steel	1	165,604
cum	1	573,873	faced	0.99	70,166	statutory	1	155,827
postings	1	570,120	complex	0.98	142,552	customs	1	154,790

Near-synonym set: job task duty N-gram: 4 Submit

job		task		duty	
to do the job	438,769	the task at hand	172,859	have a duty to	202,441
did a great job	425,841	with the task of	167,026	is the duty of	191,024
a good job of	412,589	not an easy task	145,907	be the duty of	178,800
do a better job	357,618	up to the task	143,106	shall be the duty	161,951
link to save job	346,000	of the task force	122,120	the line of duty	160,011
link to job advert	342,589	the task of the	102,082	the call of duty	143,000
Direct link to job	342,236	be a daunting task	86,773	has a duty to	140,161
to get the job	340,263	a task force to	77,369	it is the duty	88,590
do a good job	320,218	is no easy task	71,692	It is the duty	87,750

Fig. 11 Screenshot of contextual statistics

Near-Synonym set: material stuff substance

It was found that the * of the matter and not only mere theory was to be regarded [submit]

Window size: 3

PMI	material	stuff	substance
found	0.35	0.34	0.31
that	0.24	0.49	0.28
the	0.31	0.27	0.42
of	0.28	0.28	0.44
the	0.31	0.27	0.42
matter	0.15	0.08	0.77
	1.64	1.73	2.64

Bi-gram	the material	7,488,173	the stuff	2,581,457	the substance	1,319,583
	material of	817,776	stuff of	392,805	substance of	848,188
Tri-gram	that the material	237,330	that the stuff	25,305	that the substance	52,803
	the material of	129,580	the stuff of	254,931	the substance of	545,206
	material of the	179,643	stuff of the	31,130	substance of the	341,962
4-gram	found that the material	1,706	found that the stuff	211	found that the substance	623
	that the material of	3,082	that the stuff of	910	that the substance of	15,240
	the material of the	48,148	the stuff of the	9,307	the substance of the	242,832
	material of the matter	0	stuff of the matter	0	substance of the matter	6,205
5-gram	found that the material of	0	found that the stuff of	0	found that the substance of	110
	that the material of the	1,229	that the stuff of the	150	that the substance of the	7,898
	the material of the matter	0	the stuff of the matter	0	the substance of the matter	5,427

Fig. 12 Screenshot of near-synonym choice

then retrieve the contextual information around "*" using PMI and n-gram. Figure 12 shows a sample sentence (the original word *substance* has been replaced with *) along with its contextual information retrieved by the system. For PMI, at most five context words (window size) before and after "*" are included to compute proportion-based PMI scores for each near-synonym. In addition, the sum of all PMI scores for each near-synonym is also presented to facilitate learner decisions. For n-gram, the frequencies of the *n*-grams (2–5) containing each near-synonym are retrieved. In the example shown in Fig. 12, learners can learn useful word pairs such as (substance, matter) and *n*-grams such as "substance of the matter," thus learning to discriminate between *substance*, *material*, and *stuff*.

5 Conclusion

A framework that incorporates LSA and ICA for near-synonym choice is presented. Both LSA and ICA are used to analyze the contexts of near-synonyms. LSA is used to discover useful latent contextual features, while ICA is used to estimate the independent components with minimal dependence between the features. Experiments compared several supervised and unsupervised methods on both Chinese and English corpora. Results show that the ICA-based methods can reduce the degree of term overlap to improve the classifiers' ability to distinguish among near-synonyms, thus yielding higher classification accuracy.

Future work will focus on improving classification performance by combining multiple features such as predicate-argument structure and named entities occurring in the context of near-synonyms. In addition, current near-synonym choice evaluation is carried out on several preselected near-synonym sets. To make the near-synonym choice task more practical (similar to all-words word sense disambiguation), all-words near-synonym choice evaluation could also be designed and implemented to verify whether every word in a text fits the context well.

References

Bhogal, J., Macfarlane, A., & Smith, P. (2007). A review of ontology based query expansion. *Information Processing and Management, 43*(4), 866–886.

Cheng, C.-C. (2004). Word-focused extensive reading with guidance. In *Proceedings of the 13th International Symposium on English Teaching* (pp. 24–32).

Church, K., & Hanks, P. (1990). Word association norms, mutual information and lexicography. *Computational Linguistics, 16*(1), 22–29.

Cribbin, T. (2011). Discovering latent topical structure by second-order similarity analysis. *Journal of the American Society for Information Science and Technology, 62*(6), 1188–1207.

Edmonds, P. (1997). Choosing the word most typical in context using a lexical co-occurrence network. In *Proceedings of the 35th Annual Meeting of the Association for Computational Linguistics* (pp. 507–509).

Fellbaum, C. (1998). *WordNet: An electronic lexical database*. Cambridge, MA: MIT Press.

Gardiner, M., & Dras, M. (2007). Exploring approaches to discriminating among near-synonyms. In *Proceedings of the Australasian Language Technology Workshop* (pp. 31–39).

Golub, G. H., & Van Loan, C. F. (1996). *Matrix computations* (3rd ed.). Baltimore, MD: Johns Hopkins University Press.

Harris, Z. (1954). Distributional structure. *Word, 10*(2–3), 146–162.

Howell, D. C. (2007). *Statistical methods for psychology* (6th ed.). Belmont, CA: Thomson.

Huang, C.-R., Hsieh, S.-K., Hong, J.-F., Chen, Y.-Z., Su, I.-L., Chen, Y.-X., & Huang, S.-W. (2008). Chinese Wordnet: Design, implementation, and application of an infrastructure for cross-lingual knowledge processing. In *Proceedings of the 9th Chinese Lexical Semantics Workshop*.

Hyvärinen, A. (1999). Fast and robust fixed-point algorithms for independent component analysis. *IEEE Transactions on Neural Networks, 10*(3), 626–634.

Hyvärinen, A., Karhunen, J., & Oja, E. (2001). *Independent component analysis*. New York: Wiley.

Inkpen, D. (2007). A statistical model of near-synonym choice. *ACM Transactions on Speech and Language Processing, 4*(1), 1–17.

Inkpen, D., & Hirst, G. (2006). Building and using a lexical knowledge-base of near-synonym differences. *Computational Linguistics, 32*(2), 1–39.

Islam, A., & Inkpen, D. (2010). Near-synonym choice using a 5-gram language model. *Research in Computing Science, 46,* 41–52.

Kolenda, T., & Hansen, L. K. (2000). Independent components in text. *Advances in Neural Information Processing Systems, 13,* 235–256.

Landauer, T. K., Foltz, P. W., & Laham, D. (1998). An introduction to latent semantic analysis. *Discourse Processes, 25*(2–3), 259–284.

Lee, T. W. (1998). *Independent component analysis—Theory and applications*. Norwell, MA: Kluwer.

Lin, D. (1998). Automatic retrieval and clustering of similar words. In *Proceedings of the 35th Annual Meeting of the Association for Computational Linguistics* (pp. 768–774).

Moldovan, D., & Mihalcea, R. (2000). Using Wordnet and lexical operators to improve internet searches. *IEEE Internet Computing, 4*(1), 34–43.

Navigli, R., & Velardi, P. (2003). An analysis of ontology-based query expansion strategies. In *Proceedings of the Workshop on Adaptive Text Extraction and Mining*.

Ouyang, S., Gao, H.-H., & Koh, S.-N. (2009). Developing a computer-facilitated tool for acquiring near-synonyms in Chinese and English. In *Proceedings of the 8th International Conference on Computational Semantics* (pp. 316–319).

Pearce, D. (2001). Synonymy in collocation extraction. In *Proceedings of the Workshop on WordNet and Other Lexical Resources*.

Rapp, R. (2004). Mining text for word senses using independent component analysis. In *Proceedings of the 4th SIAM International Conference on Data Mining* (pp. 422–426).

Rodríguez, H., Climent, S., Vossen, P., Bloksma, L., Peters, W., Alonge, A., et al. (1998). The top-down strategy for building EuroWordNet: vocabulary coverage, base concepts and top ontology. *Computers and the Humanities, 32*, 117–159.

Roussinov, D., & Zhao, J. L. (2003). Automatic discovery of similarity relationships through Web mining. *Decision Support Systems, 35*(1), 149–166.

Sevillano, X., Alías, F., & Socoró, J. C. (2004). Reliability in ICA-based text classification. In *Proceedings of the 5th International Conference on Independent Component Analysis and Blind Signal Separation* (pp. 1213–1220).

Shlrl, A., & Revle, C. (2006). Query expansion behavior within a thesaurus-enhanced search environment: A user-centered evaluation. *Journal of the American Society for Information Science and Technology, 57*(4), 462–478.

Vanderwende, L., Suzuki, H., Brockett, C., & Nenkova, A. (2007). Beyond SumBasic: Task-focused summarization with sentence simplification and lexical expansion. *Information Processing and Management, 43*(6), 1606–1618.

Wang, T., & Hirst, G. (2010). Near-synonym lexical choice in latent semantic space. In *Proceedings of the 23rd International Conference on Computational Linguistics* (pp. 1182–1190).

Weeds, J., Weir, D., & McCarthy, D. (2004). Characterising measures of lexical distributional similarity. In *Proceedings of the 20th International Conference on Computational Linguistics* (pp. 1015–1021).

Wei, C. P., Yang, C. C., & Lin, C. M. (2008). A Latent semantic indexing-based approach to multilingual document clustering. *Decision Support Systems, 45*(3), 606–620.

Wible, D., Kuo, C.-H., Tsao, N.-L., Liu, A., & Lin, H.-L. (2003). Bootstrapping in a language learning environment. *Journal of Computer Assisted learning, 19*(1), 90–102.

Wu, C.-H. Liu, C.-H., Matthew, H., & Yu, L.-C. (2010). Sentence correction incorporating relative position and parse template language models. *IEEE Transactions* on *Audio, Speech and Language Processing, 18*(6), 1170–1181.

Yu, L.-C., & Chien, W.-N. (2013). Independent component analysis for near-synonym choice. *Decision Support Systems, 55*(1), 146–155.

Yu, L.-C., Lee, L.-H., Yeh, J.-F., Shih, H.-M., & Lai, Y.-L. (2016). Near-synonym substitution using a discriminative vector space model. *Knowledge-Based Systems, 106*, 74–84.

Yu, L.-C., Wu, C.-H., Chang, R.-Y., Liu, C.-H., & Hovy, E. H. (2010). Annotation and verification of sense pools in OntoNotes. *Information Processing and Management, 46*(4), 436–447.

Yu, L.-C., Wu, C.-H., & Jang, F.-L. (2009). Psychiatric document retrieval using a discourse-aware model. *Artificial Intelligence, 173*(7–8), 817–829.

Visualizing Stylistic Differences in Chinese Synonyms

Zheng-Sheng Zhang

Abstract Synonyms and near-synonyms are a major source of difficulty in the acquisition of Chinese vocabulary, possibly due to the formal similarities between them. It is also difficult to describe their stylistic differences in a clear and objective manner. The observations found in reference works such as dictionaries can be vague, equivocal, and limited in explanatory power. The present paper demonstrates how the corpus-based, multi-feature, multi-dimensional framework for studying register variation (Biber in Variation across speech and writing. Cambridge University Press, New York, 1988) and Correspondence Analysis, a particular implementation of factor analysis, can be used to show stylistic differences in (near) synonyms by way of two-dimensional bi-plots ("stylistic maps" in a sense). After presenting a two-dimensional analysis for Chinese, five sets of synonyms will be used to demonstrate the approach, together with comparisons with previous observations. Not only can the present approach provide a clearer and more nuanced picture than what introspection allows, it also enables us to go beyond the spoken versus written dichotomy and gain a broader perspective on stylistic variation.

1 Background

With its predominance of compound words, which often share component morphemes, the Chinese lexicon is particularly rich in synonyms and near-synonyms. Perhaps due to the minimal difference in form, they seem to be particularly prone to misuse. Even native speakers are often caught using the wrong word, as evidenced by their self-repairs. Yet, efforts to explain the differences between synonyms have not been particularly illuminating. Clearer elucidation will contribute to better understanding and possibly more successful acquisition.

Z.-S. Zhang (✉)
San Diego State University, San Diego, USA
e-mail: zzhang@sdsu.edu

X. Lu and B. Chen (eds.), *Computational and Corpus Approaches to Chinese Language Learning*, Chinese Language Learning Sciences,
https://doi.org/10.1007/978-981-13-3570-9_8

1.1 What Are (Near) Synonyms?

In the literature, there has been no shortage of disagreement over the definition of synonymy (see Chi 1999 for a critical summary). One basic issue of contention is whether the intension (sense) or extension (reference) should be the basis for deciding if words have the same meaning. For identifying synonyms, different heuristic criteria such as substitutability, compositional similarity, and distributional equivalence have been proposed. There is also disagreement about the scope of inclusion and whether synonyms and near-synonyms belong together or should be dealt with separately. A related issue is whether synonyms need to be of the same parts of speech. Given the multifaceted nature of meaning, such disagreement is all but expected.

Since our purpose is to offer a clearer way to show the differences between words, we will not be contributing to the theoretical discussion on synonymy. But as we are more interested in differences than similarities, we will take as axiomatic Bolinger's (1977) famous dictum "if two ways of saying something differ in their words or their arrangement they will also differ in meaning".

1.2 How Can Synonyms Differ?

With a more inclusive conception of synonymy, there can be several ways in which (near) synonyms can differ. Some are different in lexical meanings, such as 批评 versus 批判 "criticize", where the former is not as severe as the latter. Some can differ in grammatical properties, for example, 帮 versus 帮助 versus 帮忙 "help", where only 帮 and 帮助 can be transitive verbs but only 帮助 and 帮忙 can be nouns. Some are different in connotation, such as 成果 "achievement" versus 结果 "result" versus 后果 "aftermath", which are positive, neutral, and negative, respectively. Still others differ in collocation, such as 维护 "maintain" versus 保护 "protect", which collocate with 权威 "authority" and 环境 "environment" respectively, and 交换 versus 交流 "exchange", which combine with 礼物/意见 "gift/opinion" and 思想/经验 "thought/experience" respectively.

1.3 Stylistic Differences

Still other synonyms may be identical in lexical meaning and grammatical, collocative, and connotative properties but differ in their stylistic nuances. To focus on the stylistic differences, we will, therefore, select words that are minimally different in other aspects of meaning. They tend to have shared component morphemes and similarity in how they are rendered in English, as exemplified by the following sets of examples:

做, 作 "do/make"

仍旧, 仍然 “still”
人民, 人们, 人 “people/person”
男人, 男子, 男士, 男性 “male people/person”
女人, 女子, 女士, 女性, 妇女 “female people/person”
如果, 倘若, 要是, 的话, 假如 “if”.

2 Problems in Common Discourse on Style

2.1 Terminological/Conceptual Fuzziness

Some textbooks and dictionaries include stylistic information for vocabulary or dictionary entries. Quite a few terms have been used to refer to the “written” style, such as 书面语 (“written”), 文言 (“literary”), and 正式 (“formal”) but it is not clear whether they are identical in meaning. For example, Teng (1996) uses the terms “literary”, “formal”, “colloquial”, “informal”, and “casual”. But it is not clear if there is any difference between “literary” and “formal”; nor is it clear whether labeling a word as both “literary” and “colloquial” (as 严肃 “solemn”, 严厉 “severe”, 严格 “strict”, 责备 “scold”, 指责 “accuse”, and 争论 “dispute” are so labeled) means the word is neutral with respect to these two stylistic values or that the two styles are compatible with each other. Similarly, it is not explicitly explained how “colloquial” is different from “casual,” as 谈判 “negotiate” is marked as colloquial but not casual while 商谈 “negotiate/discuss” is marked as casual but not colloquial. One is inclined to conclude that the fuzziness in terminology reflects a certain degree of conceptual confusion.

2.2 Lack of Agreement

Reference works also do not agree with each other. For example, while both Lü (1980) and Yang and Jia (2005) note that 仍旧 “still” and 仍然 “still” are written in style, Wang (2005) maintains that 仍然 is more written than 仍旧.

2.3 Impressionistic

The fuzziness and lack of agreement referred to above can both be traced to a basic problem with previous discussions about stylistic matters in general, which is that they are largely based on subjective introspection. While introspection is useful for eliciting grammaticality judgements about syntax, it may not be as dependable with respect to stylistic matters. Introspection can be misleading. One example is the common idea associating the written style with classical Chinese elements. While there is definite association between classical Chinese elements and the written style, it may not be true that classical elements are exclusively used for the written style, nor is it necessary for the written style to be expressed exclusively through classical elements. Expressions such as 无所谓 "of no consequence", 之所以 "the reason why", 之+adj. (e.g., 之大 "so big"), 无非 "be no more than", 何止 "be more than", and 非亲非故 "neither kin or acquaintance", all containing classical Chinese elements, are very often found in speech, if not exclusively so.

Introspection can also be quite limiting. As shown in Biber et al. (1999), even syntactic categories like nouns and verbs, and morphological processes such as nominalization can have different stylistic profiles. Such information is hard to obtain without resorting to corpus and quantitative methods.

In contrast, using empirical evidence furnished by corpus data can be advantageous in more than one way. To start with, corpus evidence can be used to verify the veracity of intuition. For example, the intuitively felt stylistic difference between 帮助 and 帮忙 "help" can be clearly confirmed with the help of corpus data, as seen in their dramatically different distribution patterns in the *BCC* corpus (Beijing Language and Culture University Corpus, http://bcc.blcu.edu.cn/). As seen in Figs. 1 and 2, the two words are exactly complementary in distribution, with 帮助 occurring more frequently in 报刊 and 科技 while 帮忙 more frequently in 文学 and 微博.

What is perhaps of greater value of the corpus alternative is that it can overcome the inherent limitation of introspection in providing concrete and quantifiable evidence and uncovering hidden patterns that are not accessible to introspection, as will be seen later.

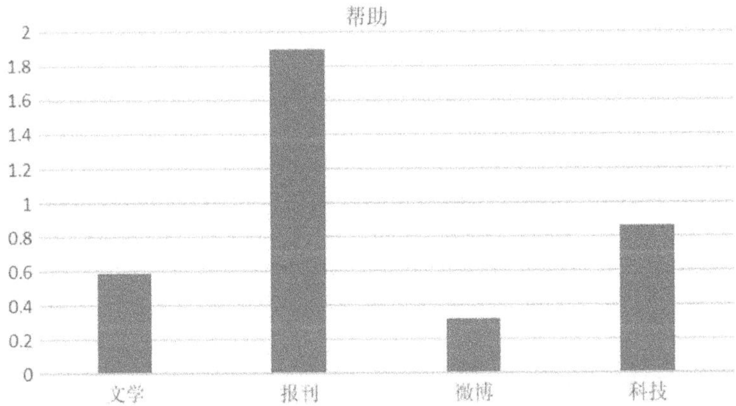

Fig. 1 Distribution of 帮助 in *BCC* (N = per 10 k) (The four text types are: 文学 (literature), 报刊 (press), 微博 (tweets) and 科技 (science/technology). As the four types are of different sizes, the raw frequency figures need to be normalized to ensure comparability. The formula used is: N = # of tokens of target word / total # of tokens of the text type * 10000)

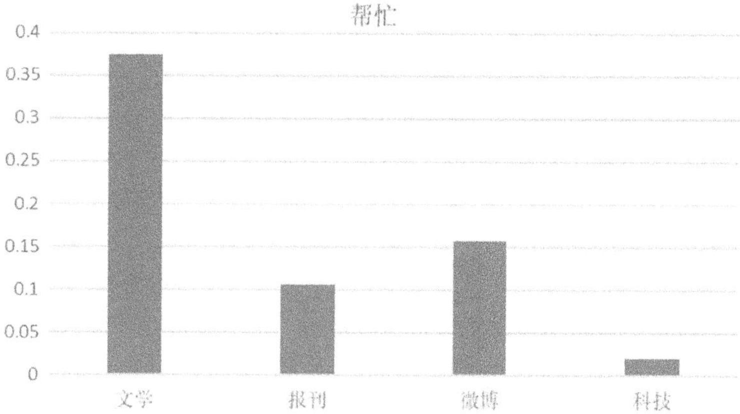

Fig. 2 Distribution of 帮忙 in *BCC* (N = per 10 k)

2.4 *Simplistic Dichotomy*

Most previous discussion on style tends to be overly simplistic and assumes a dichotomous distinction, i.e., 书面 "written" versus 口语 "spoken". In addition to obscuring the possible internal differences within the two categories, having a dichotomous distinction implies a hierarchical structure which is not conducive to sharing cross-categorical similarities. Although one synonym dictionary (Zhang 2010) seems to entertain the gradient nature of style by having four values (*1 = vulgar, 1 = informal/colloquial, 2 = neutral, and 3 = formal/written) and even allowing in-between values such as 2 to 1 (between 2 and 1), 1 to *1(between 1 and *1), the scale is still based on categorical distinction.

3 Multi-dimensional Approach to Stylistic Variation

The multifaceted nature of style (register[1]) was rather well conveyed by Halliday and Hasan's (1985) tri-partite division: "field", the content, "tenor", the participants, and "mode", the channel of communication. The multiplicity of the existing terminology used to describe style may have arisen out of this complexity. For example, the distinction between "formal" and "casual" seems to be different from "literary" and "colloquial", in that the former relates to the nonlinguistic situation and the latter linguistic diction. This may be why Teng (1996) marks 谈判 "negotiate" as colloquial but not casual, but 商谈 "negotiate/discuss" the other way around.

[1]For the purpose of this paper, the terms 'style' and 'register' will be used interchangeably.

3.1 Multi-dimension/Multi-feature Framework

It was precisely in reaction to the common assumption of the dichotomous distinction between spoken and written styles that the Multi-dimension/Multi-feature (MM) framework for investigating register variation came into being. Biber (1988) is widely credited as being the most influential in developing this research paradigm. MM-style research is different in the following ways:

(a) it is corpus-based and quantitative
(b) multiple features are examined simultaneously
(c) multiple dimensions are entertained

The MM paradigm has afforded great power in capturing the complexity of register variation. Since Biber's initial study on English, MM-style studies of register variation have been carried out for other languages, including one on Min Chinese (Jang 1998) and a series of studies on Mandarin Chinese by the present author (Zhang 2012, 2013, 2017).

Biber's dimensions for English number as many as six: "Informational vs. Involved production", "Narrative vs. Non-narrative", "Explicit vs. Situation dependent reference", "Overt expression of persuasion", "Abstract/non-specific", and "On-line informational elaboration". It is important to point out that different researchers using different corpora and methods, may achieve different results. But regardless of the number of dimensions, an important point to be underscored is that no one single distinction is sufficient to capture the complexity of register variation.

3.2 Factor Analysis and Correspondence Analysis

In MM-style studies, Factor Analysis has been used for the extraction of dimensions. But for the present study, Correspondence Analysis (CA), a variant form of Factor Analysis, is used instead (for details of this method, see Greenacre 1984).

Originally developed in France (Benzérci 1973), CA has been used extensively in market research, such as on brand preference by different demographic groups. In literary studies, it has also been used to study stylistic patterns, such as a writer's preference in lexical choice (Tabata 2002, 2007). In semantics, it has been used in the study of near-synonyms and semantic structure (McGillivray et al. 2008). But according to Gries (2015), CA is only occasionally used in corpus work. And as far as the author is aware, it has not been adopted for MM-styled studies.

CAs greatest appeal lies in its use of the intuitive visualization of dimensions, which can help to detect relationships among variables and the interpretation of the dimensions. "Categories that are similar to each other appear close to each other in the plots. In this way, it is easy to see which categories of a variable are similar to each other or which categories of the two variables are related." (SPSS Help).

The decision to use CA for the present project was also dictated by the structure of the data. CA is highly flexible with data requirements, the only requirement being a rectangular data matrix with columns (features) and rows (registers) with no negative entries. According to Tabata (2007), which also employs CA instead of principal component and factor analysis, "one advantage CA has over PCA and FA is that PCA and FA cannot be computed on a rectangular matrix where the number of columns exceeds the number of rows". As the number of features is many times the number of registers in the present study, the data do not readily lend themselves to factor analysis. Finally, CA is easier to use than FA. There is no need to deal with the choice of rotation methods to seek "simple structure" for more interpretable results.

3.3 Feature Selection

The considerations going into the selection of features include stylistic relevance, ease of search, and potential number of hits, which depends on the size of corpus. Features can be either lexical or structural/functional, which includes parts of speech and particles/construction markers. While it may be harder to see, structural features are in fact stylistically relevant, as shown by their varying distributions across genres in English (Biber et al. 1999). While they require the corpus to be tagged, they do have high frequencies of occurrence, which makes the use of smaller corpora like *LCMC* possible. In contrast, easily searchable lexical features, especially less frequent ones, necessitate the use of larger corpora such as *BCC* to ensure adequate number of hits.

As the present study is mainly for the proof of concept, the selection of features may neither be systematic nor exhaustive, due to the limitation of space. For example, the class of question particles is exemplified only by 吗 "ma" and 呢 "ne"; similarly, syntactic classes such as classifiers are not included. Executions with greater number of features and more complete coverage can be found in the author's recently published monograph (Zhang 2017).

4 Two Dimensions in Written Chinese

In this section, we will show that there are two dimensions in written Chinese. In addition to the primary dimension of literate-ness, there is a secondary dimension for the choice of diction. The results are quite robust, as replications have been done with corpora of different scale and structure (Zhang 2017). In Sec. 5, independent support will be presented, first from Feng (2010) and then a crosslinguistic comparison with English (Zhang 2017).

The two dimensions will be motivated first with the *Lancaster Corpus of Mandarin Chinese* (henceforth, *LCMC*, McEnery and Xiao 2004). A replication with the much larger *BCC* corpus will then be presented. The replication also serves as an extension into the lexical domain, as the much larger corpus makes the study of lexical items more feasible.

Table 1 *LCMC* registers and their abbreviated labels

Register	Label
News reportage	NewsRep
News editorials	NewsEd
News reviews	NewsRev
Religion	Religion
Skills, trades, and hobbies	Hobbies
Popular lore	PopLore
Essays and biographies	Biography
Reports and official documents	Official
Science (academic prose)	Academic
General fiction	FicGen
Mystery and detective fiction	FicDec
Science fiction	FicSci
Adventure and martial arts fiction	FicMart
Romantic fiction	FicRom
Humor	Humor

4.1 The Two Dimensions a la LCMC

Although small by today's standard,[2] *LCMC* is eminently suited for investigating register variation, as it includes as many as 15 finely differentiated (sub) registers. It will, therefore, be used first to motivate the 2 dimensions. Given in Table 1 is the list of the 15 registers with their abbreviated labels to be used in later figures.

Only 50 features, mostly grammatical markers and function words, are selected, as only these high-frequency items can yield sufficient number of tokens from a small corpus such as *LCMC* (a list of these features is given in Appendix A). From the frequency data of these features in the 15 registers, the Correspondence Analysis procedure in SPSS can automatically extract 14 dimensions (=15 registers–1). However, only the first 2 dimensions seem interpretable. Although small in number, the 2 dimensions can account for as much as 79% of the total variation. It is a happy coincidence that the number of dimensions is most suitable for the bi-plot visualization.

4.2 The First (Horizontal) Dimension

On the bi-plot where the 50 features are scattered, clear distribution patterns can be observed. There is clear clustering of interactive/narrative features on the left of the horizontal dimension, as marked by the larger circle in Fig. 3. Personal and espe-

[2]The total number of tokens is one million.

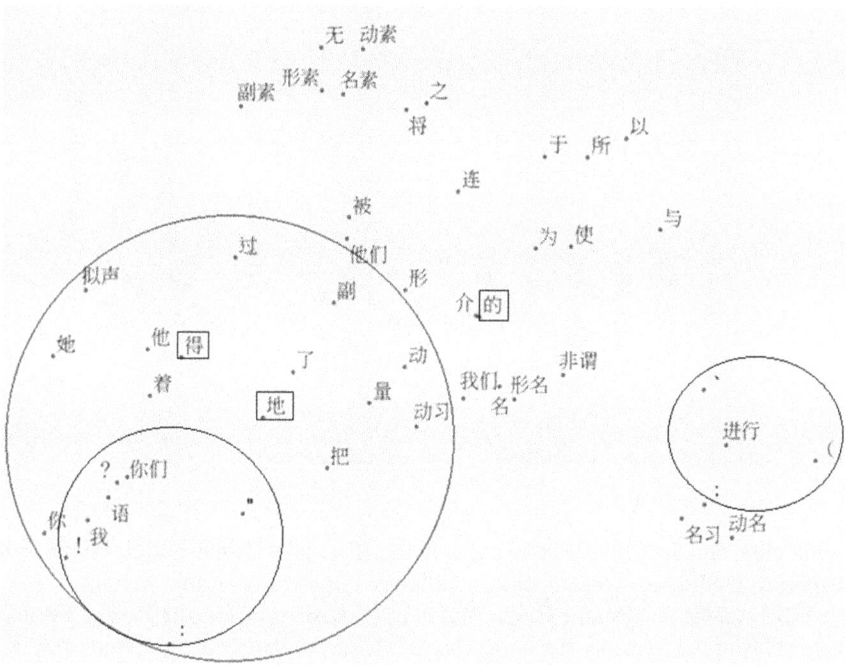

Fig. 3 Notable features on Dimension 1 (horizontal)

cially, singular pronouns (我 "I", 你 "you", 他 "he", 她 "she", and 你们 "you (pl.)"; conspicuously different are the plural 我们/他们 "we/they"), aspectual markers (了 "le", 着 "zhe", and 过 "guo"), measure/classifier (量), modal particles (语), and onomatopoeia words (拟声).

There is also clear difference between verbal and nominal features, which may reflect the difference between nominal and verbal styles (Wells 1960). Closer to the left are verbs (动) and associated features, such as adverbs (副) and verbal idioms (动习); closer to the right are nouns (名) and associated features, such as nominalized verbs (动名), nominalized adjectives (形名), and nominal idioms (名习). Related to the verbal versus nominal distinction are the three homophonous structural markers "DE" 的, 地 and 得 (enclosed in squares). It is clear the nominal 的 is much further to the right than the verbal 地 and 得, which are closer to each other as well.

Within a large category, there are also differences between the subcategories. Light verbs such as 进行 "carry out" are much further to the right than the centrally located verbs in general (动). There is also a contrast between general adjective (形) and attributive adjectives (非谓). Attributive adjectives, which are associated with noun phrases, are further to the right than adjectives in general.

Equally significant is the difference between the two sets of punctuation marks, enclosed in the two smaller circles in Fig. 3. Question, exclamation, colon, and quotation marks are all enclosed in the small circle on the left, whereas parenthesis,

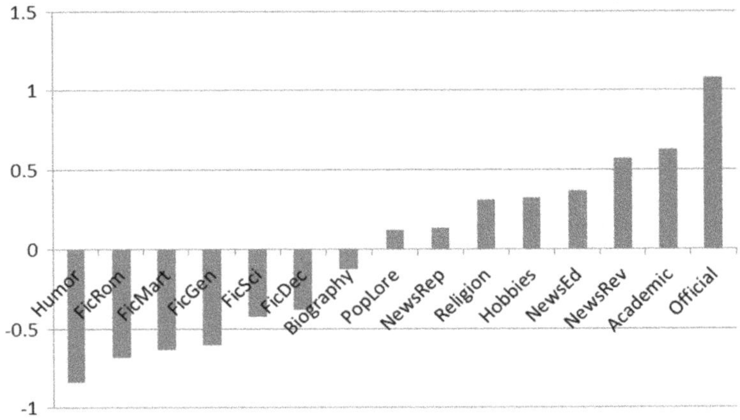

Fig. 4 Ranking of registers on Dimension 1 (N = dimension score)

semicolon, and the Chinese style pause mark (,) are all within the circle on the right. Especially telling is the semicolon, a hallmark of carefully crafted writing.

What can the distributional patterns tell us? A basic principle that will be assumed here is "Birds of a feather flock together". Whatever features are in greater physical proximity are also closer in stylistic values. Based on the observed contrasts, we therefore interpret Dimension 1 as the "Literate" dimension, fully aware that the overly simplistic term is but a convenient label for this complex dimension.

Dimension 1 is indeed a very complex dimension. Functional considerations (interactive and narrative), structural characteristics (nominal vs. verbal), and production circumstances (the amount of careful editing) all seem to contribute to it. Possibly due to its complexity, Dimension 1 is a very strong dimension, accounting for as much as 66.4% of the total variation. Although the common spoken versus written distinction seems to be related to this dimension, not all the contrasts observed here seem to have received equal attention.

Along with bi-plots, dimension scores are also generated by Correspondence Analysis. The ranking of registers by the dimension scores is given in Fig. 4. The ranking and grouping of the registers are strikingly consistent with intuition, which lends credence to the procedure. Humor, all the fiction subtypes, and biography are on left, while academic prose and official documents are on the right, with journalistic and other popular registers in between. The fact that all the subtypes of fiction are adjacent to each other seems to further confirm the soundness of the procedure.

4.3 *The Second (Vertical) Dimension*

On Dimension 2, one immediately notices the clear clustering of classical elements (circled) on the upper half of the bi-plot, as seen in Fig. 5.

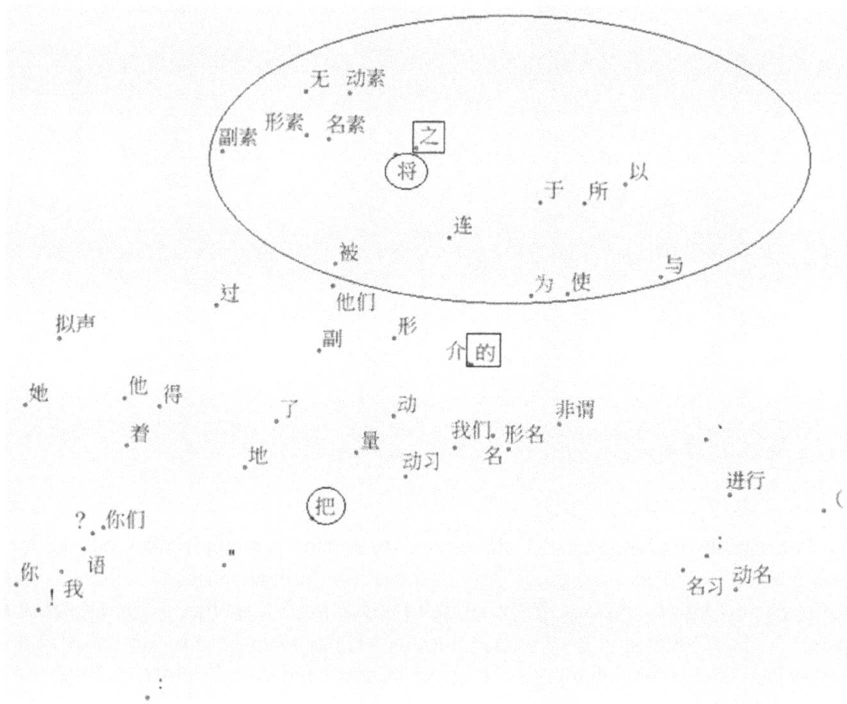

Fig. 5 Notable features on Dimension 2 (vertical)

These classical elements include both individual lexical items (为 "be", 以 "with", 所 "object marker", 与 "and", 于 "at", 之 "classical counterpart to DE", 将 "classical counterpart to BA", 无 "not have", and 使 "cause") and classes of bound morphemes of classical origin (名素 "nominal morpheme", 动素 "verbal morpheme", 形素 "adjectival morpheme", and 副素 "adverbial morpheme"; for details see Zhang 2017). The contrast between classical and nonclassical counterparts can be seen in the distribution of the two minimal pairs 将 versus 把 "BA" (enclosed in smaller circles) and 之 versus 的 (enclosed in squares). The classical 将 and 之 is both north of the nonclassical 把 and 的.

The ranking of registers by dimension scores is given in Fig. 6. Given the saliency of classical elements on this dimension, it is perhaps not too surprising that Religion ranks the highest; nor is it surprising that Humor ranks the lowest. The fact that Martial arts fiction also ranks high on this dimension is not too surprising. This kind of fiction is conventionally written in a pseudo-classical style, which fits the typical settings of this genre. That Hobbies is very high on the scale may be initially surprising, but this seems to make sense upon further reflection. Recipes, which belong to this category, are indeed peppered with short phrases written in semiclassical diction. This is consistent with Tao's (1999) observation that the classical-sounding 将 "classical counterpart to BA" occurs more frequently in recipes than in political commentaries.

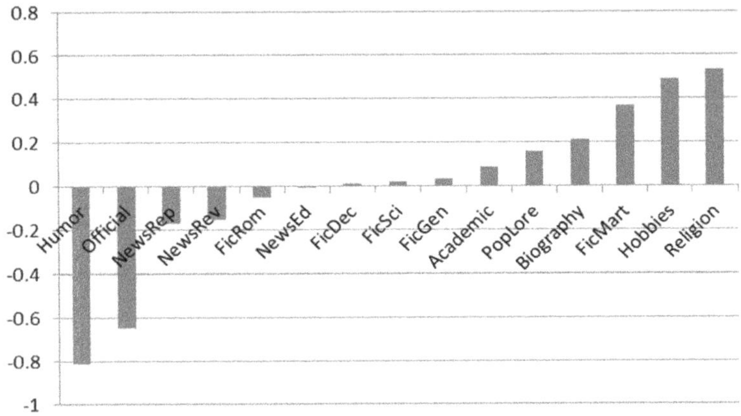

Fig. 6 Ranking of registers on Dimension 2 (N = dimension score)

Compared with Dimension 1, the second dimension is much weaker and accounts for only 12.1% of the variation. This may well be indicative of the relative importance of the two dimensions. Even though Dimension 2 is neither as complex nor as prominent as Dimension 1, its interpretation does not seem as straightforward. One's initial hypothesis may change when larger corpora and crosslinguistic comparisons are brought into play.

As most notable on this dimension is the clustering of classical elements at the top, one may straightforwardly interpret it as the "classical" dimension (Zhang 2012, 2013, 2017). There certainly are justifications for doing so. The association of a whole dimension with classical elements is consistent with our strong awareness of these elements. But doing so is not without problems. It will be shown with the larger *BCC* corpus later that different kinds of nonclassical elements such as dialectal words and innovative neologisms also share similar distribution as classical elements.

Instead of "classical", one could use "literary" to accommodate the nonclassical elements. But there are also problems with this choice. First, doing so runs the risk of terminological confusion. The term "literary" has been used in quite a few different ways. It can mean "written", as opposed to "spoken". This broader sense of the term seems synonymous with "literate" or 书面语 and therefore would be identical to the interpretation of Dimension 1. The narrower usage specifically refers to classical Chinese, also known as 文言文. The third usage refers to the quality associated with literary works such as creative fiction. This is different from classical Chinese, because the language of literature can be considered literary, even though most modern literature is not written in classical Chinese. The use of "literary" will also be problematic with the afore-mentioned nonstandard elements.

A more inclusive and for the moment somewhat open-ended interpretation of the second dimension is "alternative diction", which seems to be related to the "ornamental vs. plain" distinction of Carroll (1960). In Sec. 5, where independent support of the two-dimensional analysis is presented, the concepts of "diction" and "alternative diction" will also find independent support.

4.4 A Two-Dimensional Space for LCMC Registers

The distributional space of the *LCMC* registers can also be two-dimensional, as shown in Fig. 7. Having two dimensions makes it possible for registers to relate to each other differently on the two dimensions. For example, Official documents (官方) and Humor (幽默), which are very close on Dimension 2, in fact, occur at the opposite ends of Dimension 1. Martial art fiction (武打), which is sandwiched between General (小说) and Romantic fiction (言情) on Dimension 1, is quite far from the other fiction subtypes on Dimension 2. Registers can rank differently on the two dimensions too. Official documents rank the highest on Dimension 1 but almost the lowest on Dimension 2; Hobbies and skills (技能) and Martial art fiction which rank high on the second dimension, do not rank high at all on the first dimension.

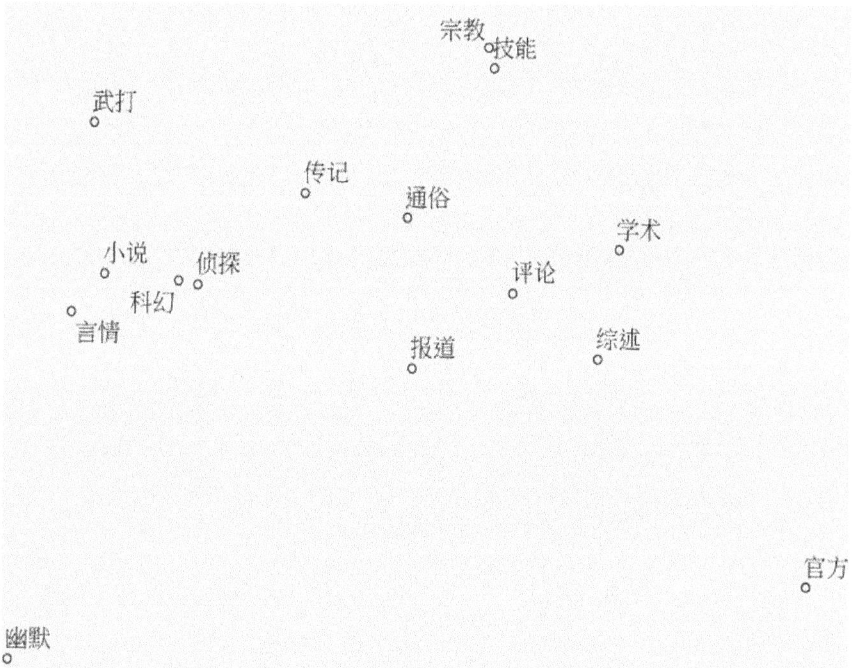

Fig. 7 Distribution of *LCMC* registers on Dimension 1 and 2

4.5 Replication and Extension with BCC

The *BCC* corpus from Beijing Language and Cultural University is 10,000 times the size of *LCMC*.[3] It also has a different structure, with only 4 text types: 文学 (literature), 报刊 (press), 微博 (tweets), and 科技 (science/technology). The selection of this much larger corpus serves 2 purposes. It can be used to replicate the study and thereby remedy any possible artifact with the smaller *LCMC* corpus. As it is much larger, it also allows the selection of lexical items that are not high in frequency of occurrence, making it possible to extend the approach into the realm of lexical stylistics. The fewer and broader types of *BCC* can also provide us with a different perspective.

A total of 95 features (with many lexical ones) were selected for the replication (the list is given in Appendix B). As with *LCMC*, 2 dimensions are extracted that are interpretable. Figure 8 shows the distribution of 95 features. Although the dimensions are flipped in orientation, the basic distributional patterns that we saw with *LCMC* are again observed.

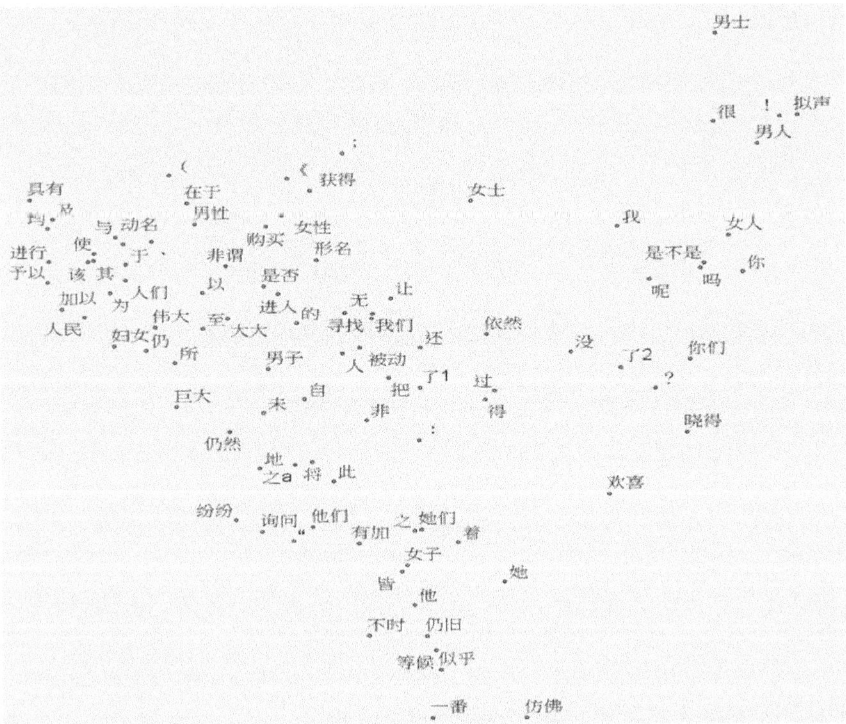

Fig. 8 Distribution of 95 features in *BCC*

---

[3]The total number of tokens is over 10 billion.

On the first (horizontal) dimension, features like personal pronouns and question particles, onomatopoeia words (拟声) are on the right, whereas attributive adjectives (非谓), nominalized verbs (动名), and light verbs (进行, 予以, 加以) are on the left. The grammatical pattern 是不是 "be not be" contrasts sharply with the synonymous 是否, being located at opposite sides. So is the contrast between 把 "BA construction marker" versus 将 "classical counterpart to BA". Punctuation marks are again split into two groups, located at opposite sides of the plot. Therefore, the same interpretation of "literate-ness" can be given to this dimension, as in the case of *LCMC*.

On the second (vertical) dimension, we find the clustering of words such as 似乎 "as if", 仿佛 "as if", 不时 "occasionally",—番 "(do) quite a bit of/a kind of", 仍旧 "still", and V./Adj. +有加 "highly" (e.g., 称赞有加 "highly praise") at the bottom, all of which seem to have a special affinity with literary writings. Some dialectal words such as 晓得 "know" and 欢喜 "like" (alternatives to 知道 and 喜欢) are also leaning in this direction.

Unlike *LCMC*, however, the distribution of classical elements is not as uniform. Although a few classical words and patterns such as 皆 "all", 此 "this", 将 "classical counterpart to BA", 之 "classical counterpart to DE", and 之+adj. (e.g., 之好, 之大, "very good, very big") are found in the bottom half of Dimension 2, more of the classical words, such as 为 "be", 其 "his/her/its/their", 该 "this", 与 "and", 于 "at", 以 "with", and 至 "to", are found on the left on Dimension 1, which is interpreted as "literate". This in fact agrees with our intuition about the association of classical elements with the written style. It also lends support to our proposal that the second dimension is not "classical", but is "alternative diction".

The distribution of the four text types, as seen in Fig. 9, lends further credence to the hypothesis. While 科技 (science/technology) and 微博 (tweets) occupy the two polar extremes of the horizontal dimension, 文学 (literature) is at the extreme bottom of the vertical dimension. Literature, which values creativity, would have natural affinity to alternative diction.

Fig. 9 Distribution of four text types in *BCC*

5 Independent Support

Independent support from Chinese and English can be found for both the two-dimensional analysis and the interpretation of the second dimension as one of the "alternative diction".

5.1 Feng (2010)

Interestingly, the present two-dimensional analysis achieved through corpus and statistical means largely dovetails with the proposal independently arrived at by Feng (2010). Feng also rejects the singular "spoken vs. written" dichotomy and the common practice of equating the formal/written style with classical elements. In addition to the distinction between 正式 "formal" and 随便 "casual", he posits a separate opposition between 通俗 "common" (associated with 白话 "vernacular") and 庄典 "dignified and elegant" (associated with 古代词语 "classical diction").

The consequence of the separation of formality from diction is that genres with more classical diction are not necessarily more formal. Feng uses two examples to show the disassociation of the classical and the formal, i.e., 黄帝祭文 "Yellow Emperor Epitaph" and 西厢记 "Romance of the West Chamber". Although the Epitaph is both formal and classical, the classically worded but erotic 西厢记 is not formal at all. This is reminiscent of Tao's (1999) observation that recipes, by no means a formal genre, tend to use classical diction such as 将 "classical counterpart to BA" liberally as well. If classical diction is not what contributes to the formal written style, then what is? According to Feng, an important contributor to the formal style in modern written Chinese is the disyllabic rhythmic pattern.

Sharing the similarity of more than one opposition, the present study nonetheless differs from Feng (2010) in some ways. The present work benefits from its quantitative method, which shows the vertical dimension of diction to be secondary, accounting for much less variation than the horizontal one. Second, the interpretation of the dimensions is also somewhat different. His oppositions are given more specific attributes such as formality and classical diction than the present study. As was argued earlier, the literate dimension is rather complex, incorporating a range of factors including structural, situational variables and those arising from production circumstances. It may not be possible to subsume all this under "formality", which is primarily situational. Similarly, as evidence from the larger *BCC* corpus shows, we may not want to associate the second dimension solely with classical diction, thus leaving open the possibility of other nonclassical alternative forms of expression.

5.2 Crosslinguistic Comparison

Crosslinguistic comparison also lends support to our interpretation of the second dimension as "alternative diction". In Zhang (2017), a two-dimensional analysis was given for English based on the *COCA* corpus.[4] The first dimension seems to be a close parallel to the one in Chinese and can also be interpreted as one of "literate-ness". On the second dimension, a cluster of features, known to be literary flavored, all congregate at the top of the bi-plot, as seen in Fig. 10. They include lexical items such as *thou*, *hereby*, and constructions such as *what a N.* (e.g., *what a wonderful morning*), *many a + N.* (e.g., *many a thing you know you'd like to tell her*), and *none too Adj.* (e.g., *none too pleased about the prospects of meeting the family*).

Of special interest are the constructions with inverted word order that are conventionally associated with literary usages (Green 1982). They include *were I* (alternative to *if I were*), *had I* (alternative to *if I had*), *in came* (alternative to *came in*), and

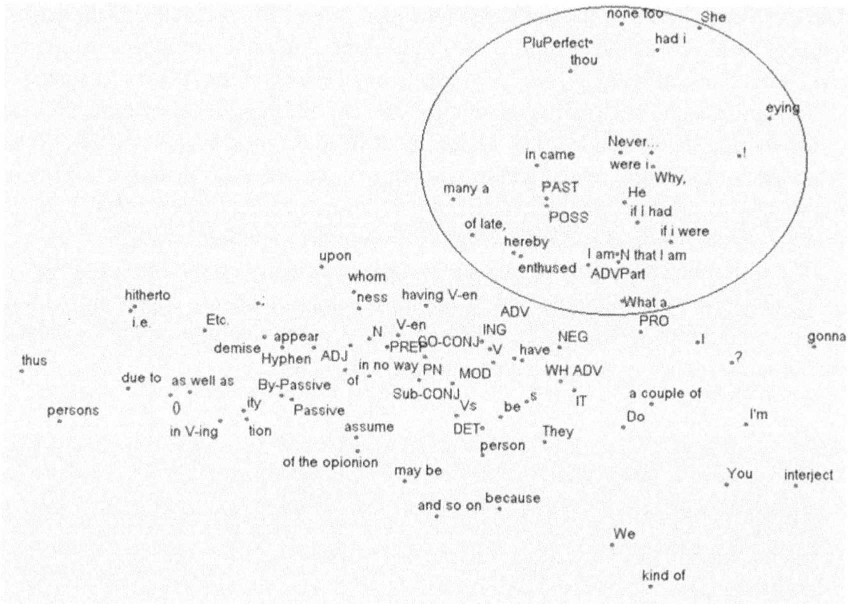

Fig. 10 Clustering of alternative diction/patterns in *COCA*

[4]Corpus of Contemporary American English at https://corpus.byu.edu/coca/.

never + inverted clause (e.g., never have I been so insulted!). The interpretation of this dimension as "alternative diction/pattern" would provide a functionally motivated, crosslinguistic parallel.

6 Five Groups of (Near) Synonyms

In this section, the *BCC* corpus and the two-dimensional framework will be used to examine the differences in five groups of synonyms. Comparisons will also be made between this approach and that based on a narrower conception of stylistic variation assuming a single distinction between spoken and written styles.

6.1 作 Versus 做

The difference between the homophonous pair 作 and 做 "do/make" is the bane of Chinese teachers, as they seem to mean the same thing and are indeed sometimes used interchangeably. Although Lü (1980), Teng (1996), Wang (2005), Yang and Jia (2005) and Zhang (2010) all agree that the two are different in collocation, 作 being more abstract (better rendered as "doing") but 做 more specific and concrete (better rendered as "making"), their stylistic assessments are not quite as uniform. Teng has nothing to say about the stylistic difference between the two. Lü considers 作 to have more classical flavor. But Zhang assigns 2 (=neutral) to both 做 and 作.

The difference between the two shows up quite clearly on the bi-plot in Fig. 11, as 作 lies at the more literate end of the horizontal dimension, consistent with the fact that it is more abstract than 做. As can be seen, the distributional pattern based on corpus evidence is much clearer and less equivocal.

Fig. 11 Partial bi-plot contrasting 作 and 做 in *BCC*

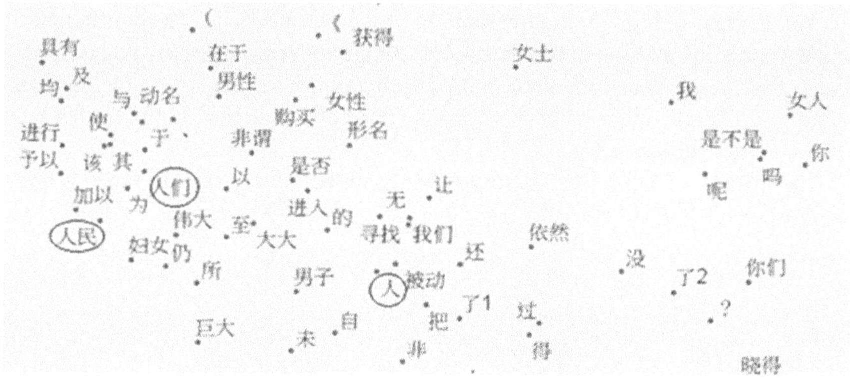

Fig. 12 Partial bi-plot for 人民, 人们, 人

6.2 人民, 人们, 人

The triplet 人民, 人们, and 人, all translatable as “people”, nonetheless differ appreciably, stylistically as well as in collocation. Between 人民 and 人们, Zhang (2010) considers 人民 to be more formal/written than 人们, their values being 3–2 and 2, respectively. As Zhang did not include 人 in the comparison, it is not clear what value she would assign to it and whether she would consider it to be less formal/written than 人们.

While it may be true that 人们 is less formal/written than 人民, its neutral stylistic designation is quite surprising, given its collocation requirement that seems as stringent as 人民. It also seems to be at odds with the distributional evidence, as shown in Fig. 12. Both 人们 and 人民 are quite close to the left end of the horizontal dimension, while 人 is near the center. Therefore, it seems that 人们 should be closer to 人民 in stylistic value and 人 is more likely to be neutral instead of 人们. That 人民 and 人们 are closer together than either is to 人 seems to be consistent with the fact that both 人民 and 人们 refer to collective entities whereas 人 is countable and takes measure words. One’s intuition may thus be at odds with the distributional evidence, which is well worth paying further attention to.

6.3 仍旧 Versus 仍然

仍旧 and 仍然 both mean “still” and their difference seems extremely nebulous to describe verbally. Of the three reference works that include this pair, only Wang (2005) tries to distinguish the two and considers 仍然 to be more written than 仍旧; neither Lü (1980) nor Yang and Jia (2005) distinguish the two and both consider the pair to be similarly written in style.

Yet, as seen in Fig. 13, the distribution of the two words is clearly different. Lü (1980) and Yang and Jia (2005) thus seem to have under-differentiated them. On one hand, 仍然 is, as Wang observed, more literate, being further left on the horizontal dimension. On the other hand, 仍旧 is also different in diction, being further south on the vertical dimension.

The affinity of 仍旧 with literary writing can be clearly seen in Fig. 14, which contrasts with 仍然 in Fig. 15.

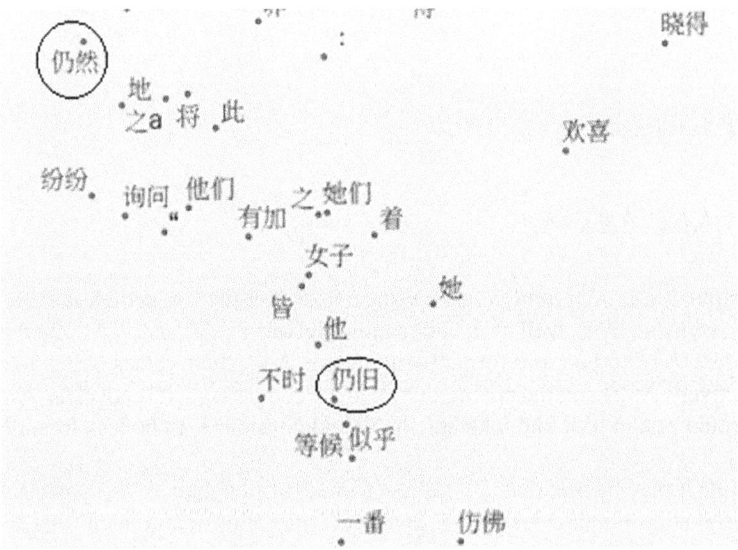

Fig. 13 Partial bi-plot contrasting 仍然 and 仍旧

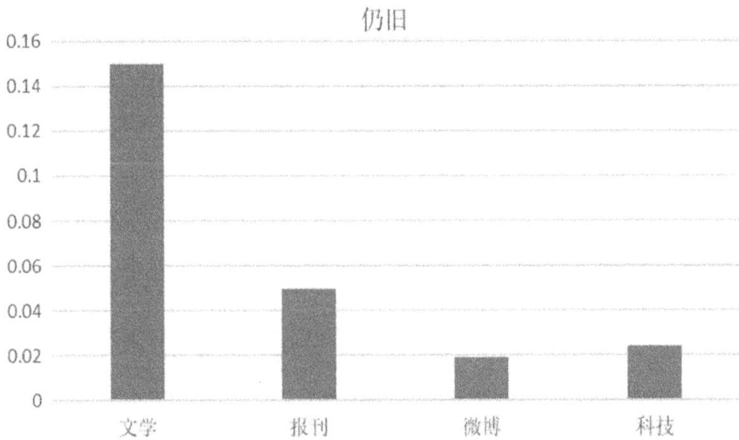

Fig. 14 Distribution of 仍旧 in *BCC* (*N* = per 10 k)

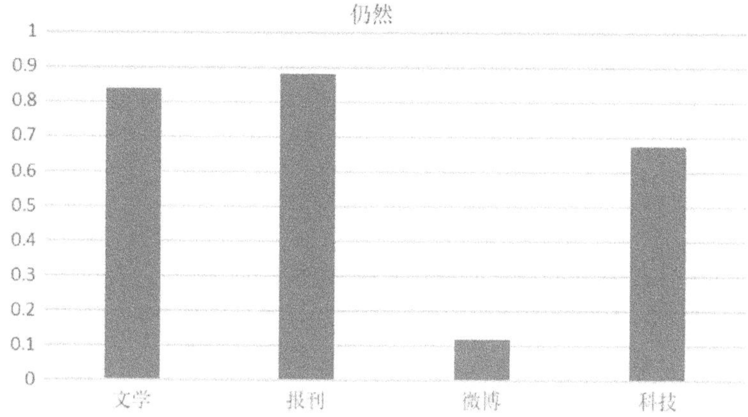

Fig. 15 Distribution of 仍然 in *BCC* (*N* = per 10 k)

While 仍然 is more evenly distributed in written genres, except in the nonliterate tweets, 仍旧 clearly is skewed in favor of literary writings, which among other things are marked by alternative diction.

6.4 妇女, 女性, 女子, 女士, 女人, and 男士, 男性, 男子, 男人

Even though the words for "women" and "men" seem to be as good an exemplar of stylistic differences as any, only one of the dictionaries consulted includes them. Zhang (2010) notes that 妇女 is generic, 女士 is polite, and 女子 is often used for sports events. For stylistic values, she assigns 3 (=formal/written) to both 女士 and 女性, and 3–2 (=formal/written-neutral) to both 妇女 and 女子, and 2 (=neutral) to 女人. The same is said about the four words for "men", with both 男士 and 男性 as 3 (=formal/written), 男子 as 3–2 (=formal/written-neutral) and 男人 as 2 (=neutral).

In contrast, the bi-plot shows a much finer distribution pattern, as seen in Fig. 16. The group of words for women is astonishingly widely dispersed along the horizontal dimension, from the most literate 妇女 on the left to the least literate 女人 on the right. Even though their ranking on the horizontal dimension may be obscured by their different heights on the vertical dimension, the ranking from the most literate to the least literate seems to be: 妇女 → 女性 → 女子 → 女士 → 女人. In a less drastic fashion, the four words for "men" rank on the horizontal dimension thusly: 男性 → 男子 → 男士 → 男人. The parallel between the two series is nothing less than astounding. So is the fineness of distinctions. Even though we may have an intuition about words at the extreme ends, such as 妇女 versus 女人 and 男性 versus 男人, we would be hard-pressed to have definite intuition about the whole lineups. G. Zhang, for example, seems to face exactly this problem when she assigns the in-between values.

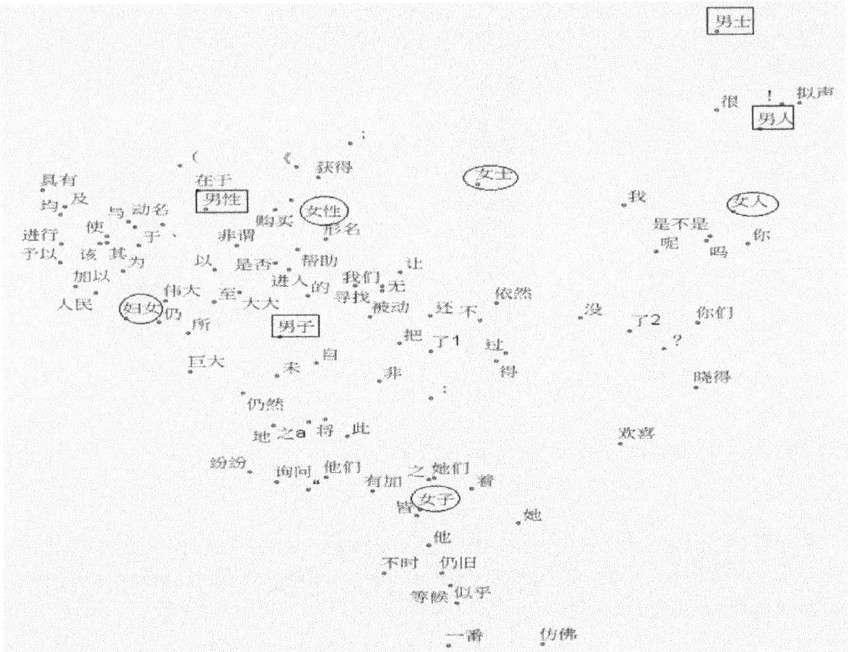

Fig. 16 妇女, 女性, 女子, 女士, 女人 and 男性, 男子, 男士, 男人

What cannot escape notice is the exceptional behavior of 女子, which veers southward on the vertical dimension. Less dramatically, 男子 also pulls away in the same direction. According to our interpretation of the second dimension, 女子 and 男子should be considered as having alternative diction. This is borne out by the distribution of 女子 in the four genres, as seen in Fig. 17, which shows that 女子 occurs most frequently in literature.

This in fact largely agrees with our intuition, as 子 does evoke a literary flavor and may well be at home in pseudo-classical genres such as martial art fiction.

6.5 如果, 要是, 假如, 的话, 倘若

Even though their frequencies of occurrence differ, the set of words meaning "if" seem to be truly synonymous and their differences seem largely a matter of style. Not all the dictionaries consulted, however, include the whole set in their comparisons. No one includes 的话. Wang (2005) only compares 如果 and 若, noting that the latter is more written in style. Between 如果 and 要是, Yang and Jia (2005) unsurprisingly consider the latter to be more spoken. For 要是, 如果, and 假如, Zhang's (2010) stylistic assignments are 要是 = 1 (colloquial), 如果 = 2 (neutral), and 假如 = 3

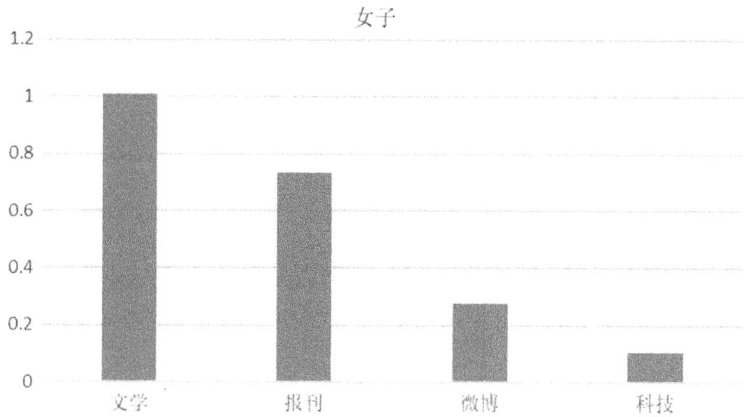

Fig. 17 Distribution of 女子 in *BCC* (N = per 10 k)

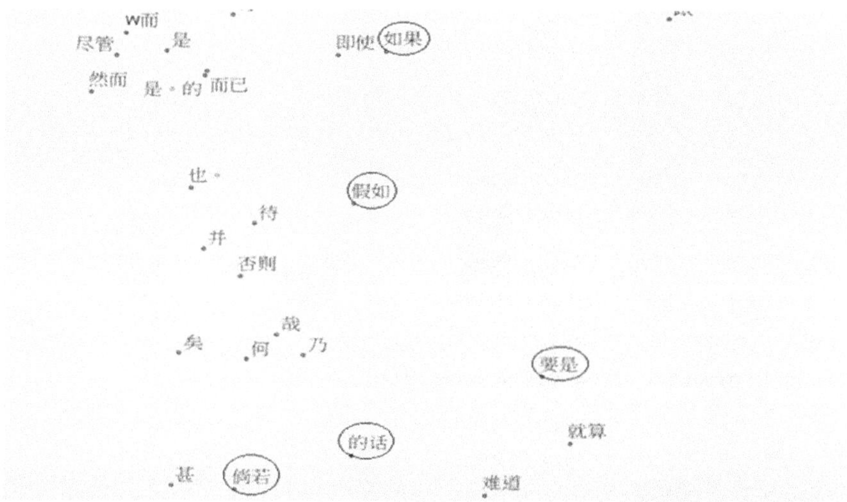

Fig. 18 Partial bi-plot for 如果 versus 假如 versus 要是 versus 的话 versus 倘若

(formal/written). Lü (1980) is alone in including 倘若 and it is also the only one equating two of the words as stylistically identical. It considers both 假如 and 倘若 to be written.

The bi-plot of Fig. 18 both confirms some of the dictionaries' observations and at the same time reveals some surprising patterns. On one hand, it confirms that 要是 is indeed the least literate, being further toward the right on the horizontal dimension. Lü's observation that 假如 and 倘若 are both written is also reasonable, as they are not too far from each other, both leaning left. The degree of literate-ness is thus ranked: 倘若 → 假如/的话 → 如果 → 要是, with 假如/的话 apparently identical in value.

What is surprising, however, is that the words are much more dispersed on the vertical dimension. 倘若 and 假如, which Lü considers similar stylistically, are in fact quite distant from each other on this dimension. 倘若, 的话 and 要是 are also far from 如果. The ranking on the vertical dimension is 倘若 → 的话 → 要是 → 假如 → 如果.

According to our interpretation of the second dimension, 倘若, 的话, and 要是 should all be considered high on alternative diction. This receives some support from their similarly high frequency in literary writings, as seen in Figs. 19, 20, and 21.

The similarity in distribution between 倘若, 的话, and 要是 on the second dimension may be surprising from the point of view of a one-dimensional conception of stylistic variation, which would most likely consider 倘若 as diametrically opposed

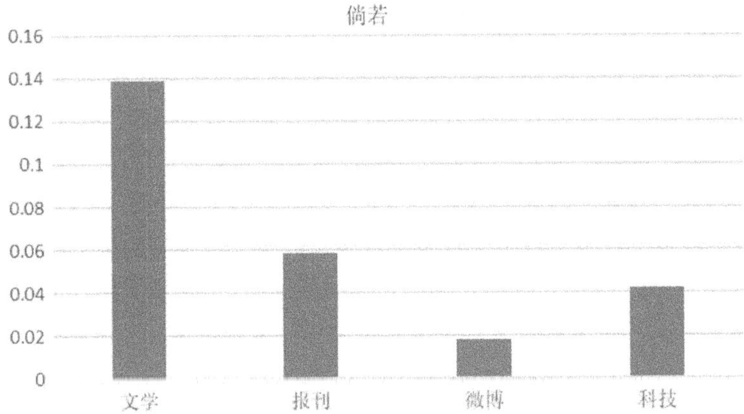

Fig. 19 Distribution of 倘若 in *BCC* (*N* = per 10 k)

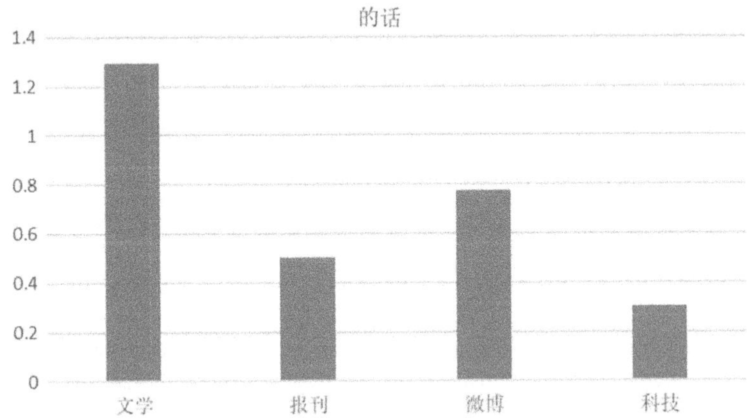

Fig. 20 Distribution of 的话 in *BCC* (*N* = per 10 k)

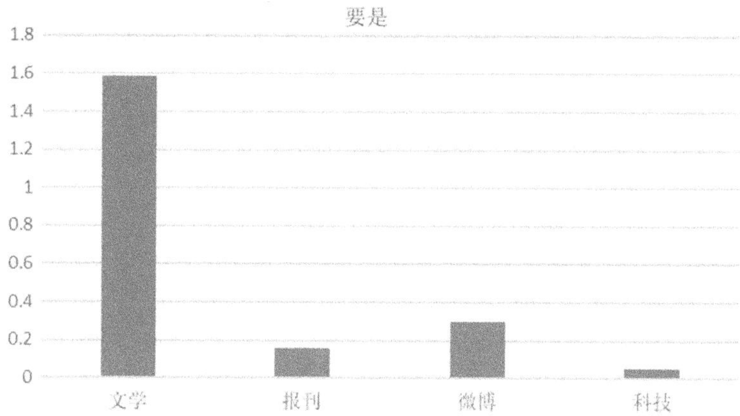

Fig. 21 Distribution of 要是 in *BCC* (*N* = per 10 k)

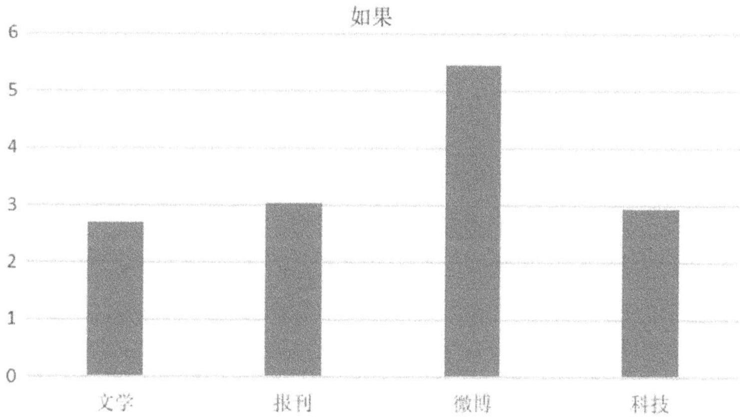

Fig. 22 Distribution of 如果 in *BCC* (*N* = per 10 k)

to 的话 and 要是 in the written versus spoken dichotomy. In a two-dimensional framework, however, their similarity lies in their common opposition to 如果 and 假如, which represent more conventional diction. The distribution of 如果 is shown in Fig. 22.

7 Concluding Remarks

In this paper, the problem of how to clarify the stylistic differences between (near) synonyms has been approached anew by using the corpus-based, two-dimensional framework for stylistic variation. The five groups of synonyms examined exemplify several advantages of the current approach. First, distributional evidence based on corpus data can challenge some of our long-held beliefs based on intuition. Second, stylistic variation is no longer only conceptualized along the single dimension of formality or written-ness. Third, finer differentiation is possible than using introspection. Finally, the differences between (near) synonyms can be more intuitively visualized. The addition of a second dimension has opened new avenues for further research.

Lacking an understanding of the pervasive stylistic variation in Chinese has been one of the obstacles to achieving superior proficiency. Students otherwise proficient in the spoken language may not have sufficient sensitivity to style and are apt to produce language that is totally inappropriate stylistically. Teachers may have only a vague notion of the distinction between spoken versus written Chinese, knowing even less about the internal variation in written registers. Very few textbooks address the issue of stylistics. Those that do are also mostly based on the dichotomous distinction of non-written versus written styles, heuristically useful it may be. Therefore, the present approach has clear pedagogical implications. Visualization of stylistic differences on stylistic "maps" (bi-plots) can perhaps help sharpen stylistic awareness by providing a fuller, more nuanced picture of stylistic variation in Chinese. The crosslinguistic comparison with English may also be of help to learners with English language background, potentially enhancing stylistic awareness in both languages.

Appendix A: 50 Features for the *LCMC* Study

我, 我们, 你, 你们, 他, 她, 他们, 了, 着, 过, 被, 使, 名, 动, 形
副, 地, 得, 的, 量, 名习, 介, 动习, 进行, 拟声, 将, 把, 之, 为, 所
于, 以, 与, 无, 名素, 动素, 形素, 副素, 连, 语, 形名, 非谓, 动名
“?”, “!”, “:”, ““”, “;”, “,”, “(”

Appendix B: 95 Features for the *BCC* Study

“!”, “?”, “:”, ““”, “(”, “《”, “;”, 吗, 呢,
了1, 了2, 着, 过, 动名, 形名, 拟声, 的, 得, 地, 把, 将, 非谓,
被动, 使, 让, 我, 你, 他, 她, 我们, 你们, 他们, 她们, 购买, 具有
在于, 寻找, 获得, 巨大, 询问, 进入, 进行, 加以, 予以, 所, 以,
于, 与, 之, 之a, 为, 无, 未, 其, 非, 此, 该, 均, 皆, 自, 至, 及,
人, 人们, 人民, 没, 很, 是不是, 是否, 还, 仍, 仍然, 仍旧, 等候,
依然, 大大, 纷纷, 有加, 似乎, 仿佛, 不时, 一番, 女人, 女士, 女性,
女子, 妇女, 男人, 男子, 男士, 男性, 伟大, 欢喜, 晓得

References

Benzérci, J. P. (1973). *Analyse des donnees*. Paris: Dunod.

Biber, D. (1988). *Variation across speech and writing*. New York: Cambridge University Press.

Biber, D., Johansson, S., Leech, G., Conrad, S., & Finegan, E. (1999). *Longman grammar of spoken and written English*. Harlow: Pearson Education.

Bolinger, D. (1977). *Meaning and form*. London/New York: Longman.

Carroll, J. B. (1960). Vectors of prose style. In T. A. Sebeok (Ed.), *Style in language* (pp. 283–292). Cambridge, MA: MIT Press.

Chi, C. H. (池昌海) (1999). 对汉语同义词研究重要分歧的再认识. 《浙江大学学报：人文社科版》1999 年第 01 期 第 77–84 页

Feng, S. (冯胜利) (2010). On the mechanism of style and its grammatical properties (论语体的机制及其语法属性). *Zhongguo Yuwen* (《中国语文》), *5*, 400–412.

Green, G. (1982). Colloquial and literary uses of inversions. In D. Tannen (Ed.), *Spoken and written language: Exploring orality and literacy*. Norwood, NJ: ABLEX Publishing Corporation.

Greenacre, M. (1984). *Theory and applications of correspondence analysis*. London: Academic Press.

Gries, S. T. (2015). Quantitative designs and statistical techniques. In D. Biber & R. Reppen (Eds.), *The Cambridge handbook of English corpus linguistics* (pp. 50–71). Cambridge: Cambridge University Press.

Halliday, M. A. K., & Hasan, R. (1985). *Language, context, and text: Aspects of language in a social-semiotic perspective*. Geelong: Deakin University Press.

Jang, S. (1998). *Dimensions of spoken and written Taiwanese: A corpus-based register study*. Unpublished doctoral dissertation. University of Hawaii, Manoa.

Lü, S. (吕叔湘) (1980). *Eight hundred words in contemporary Chinese* (现代汉语八百词). Beijing: Commercial Press (商务印书馆).

McEnery, A., & Xiao, Z. (2004). The Lancaster corpus of Mandarin Chinese: A corpus for monolingual and contrastive language study. In *Proceedings of the Fourth International Conference on Language Resources and Evaluation* (pp. 1175–1178). Lisbon, Portugal.

McGillivray, B., Johansson, C., & Apollon, D. (2008). Semantic structure from correspondence analysis. In *Proceedings of the third text graphs workshop on graph-based algorithms in natural language processing* (pp. 49–52). Manchester, UK.

Tabata, T. (2002). Investigating stylistic variation in Dickens through correspondence analysis of word-class distribution. In T. Saito, J. Nakamura, & S. Yamazaki (Eds.), *English corpus linguistics in Japan* (pp. 165–182). Amsterdam/New York: Rodopi.

Tabata, T. (2007). *A statistical study of superlatives in Dickens and Smollett: A case study in corpus stylistics*. Paper Presented at the Digital Humanities 2007 Conference. Urbana-Champaign, IL.

Tao, H. (陶红印) (1999). On the grammatical significance of register distinctions (试论语体分类的语法学意义). *Contemporary Linguistics* (《当代语言学》), *3*, 15–24.

Teng, S.-H. (鄧守信) (1996) *Chinese synonyms usage dictionary* (汉英汉语常用近义词用法词典). Beijing: Beijing Language Institute Press (北京语言学院出版社).

Wang, H. (王还) (2005). *A dictionary of Chinese synonyms* (汉语近义词典). Beijing: Beijing Language and Culture University Press (北京语言大学出版社).

Wells, R. (1960). Nominal and verbal style. In T. A. Sebeok (Ed.), *Style in language* (pp. 213–220). Cambridge, MA: MIT Press.

Yang, J. (杨寄洲), & Jia Y. (贾永芬) (2005). *1700 groups of frequently used Chinese synonyms* (1700对近义词语用法对比). Beijing: Beijing Language and Culture University Press (北京语言大学出版社).

Zhang, G. Q. (2010). *Using Chinese synonyms*. Cambridge: Cambridge University Press.

Zhang, Z.-S. (2012). A corpus study of variation in written Chinese. *Corpus Linguistics and Linguistic Theory, 8*(1), 209–240.

Zhang, Z.-S. (2013) The classical elements in written Chinese: A multidimensional quantitative study, *Chinese Language and Discourse, 4*(2),157–180.
Zhang, Z.-S. (2017). *Dimensions of variation in written Chinese*. London/New York: Routledge.

Using Corpus-Based Analysis of Neologisms on China's New Media for Teaching Chinese as a Second or Foreign Language

Wengao Gong and Huaqing Hong

Abstract As a mirror of present-day China, Chinese neologisms on new media are useful not only for linguistic analysis but also for teaching advanced learners of Chinese as a foreign language. Through analysing the word-formation mechanisms or strategies of Chinese neologisms on new media, learners can not only reinforce their understanding about the unique linguistic features of the Chinese language that they acquired before but also obtain a better understanding of the social and cultural soil that nurtures and shapes the Chinese language and its development. Using a small corpus that consists of authentic usage samples of 50 neologisms originated from Chinese new media, we attempt to explain how information about neologism formation strategies can be utilized in teaching Chinese as a second or foreign language.

1 Introduction

Neologism is a natural phenomenon in language development. According to *Cambridge Dictionary*, neologism is "a new word or expression, or a new meaning for an existing word". Algeo (1993: 2) defines it as "a form or use of a form not recorded in general dictionaries". Kerremans (2015) defines neologisms as lexical units that are "no longer nonce-formations" but "have not yet occurred frequently and are not widespread enough in a given period to have become part and parcel of the lexicon of the speech community and the majority of its members" (pp. 30–31). Kerremans' definition touches upon the membership fluidity of neologisms in the lexicon of a particular language. This fluidity not only causes headaches to lexicographers but

W. Gong (✉)
Chinese University of Hong Kong (Shenzhen), Shenzhen, China
e-mail: gongwengao@cuhk.edu.cn

H. Hong
Nanyang Technological University, Singapore, Singapore
e-mail: Huaqing.hong@ntu.edu.sg

X. Lu and B. Chen (eds.), *Computational and Corpus Approaches to Chinese Language Learning*, Chinese Language Learning Sciences,
https://doi.org/10.1007/978-981-13-3570-9_9

also makes it difficult for language teachers to decide whether neologisms should be taught to foreign language learners.

To better understand the value of neologisms, we may need to borrow a metaphor that Burridge (2004, 2005) uses in discussing the lexical changes in the English language. She compares the English vocabulary to a garden of words and neologisms to weeds in this garden. Depending on the ecosystem of the garden and sometimes the will of the gardener(s), some weeds may be accepted as regular members whereas others may be ignored or eradicated. In fact, weeds are part and parcel of the garden ecosystem: they may make the garden look untidy, but their very presence demonstrates diversity, uniqueness, and harmony. By studying the weeds, we can get a better understanding of the genes of the non-regular species, the soil, the ecological environment, the climate change, and the aesthetic perspectives of the gardener(s), etc.

With the proliferation of Internet-based smart devices and various social media, the wall that used to be standing between ordinary language users and the imperial garden where only approved species will be planted is now being removed. As a consequence, the weeds in the garden seem to have acquired the power of mutation and changed their behaviour patterns. They germinate fast, grow rapidly, propagate widely, and then fade quickly into the dark corner of the garden. As Hargraves (2007) writes, the Internet "not only spawns and propagates a huge number of neologisms, but also serves as one of the main vehicles by which we find them, track them, and document their distribution, frequency, and forms" (p. 139). This is also true for the Chinese language. According to China Internet Network Information Center (2017), China's Internet users reached 731 million by December 2016, among which mobile Internet users amounted to 695 million. One direct impact of this development is that social media (e.g. Sina Weibo, Zhihu, WeChat, and so on) has become an indispensable tool for information sharing and interpersonal communication in Chinese people's daily life. Social media empowers ordinary language users to demonstrate their linguistic talents, which in turn leads to the booming of neologisms on the Internet.

The booming of Chinese neologisms on social media has created a dilemma for teachers of Chinese as a foreign language. On the one hand, social media acts as the prime medium of linguistic innovation and supplies abundant interesting examples for foreign learners to appreciate the innovativeness, creativity, and vigour of the Chinese language. On the other hand, the diversity of neologisms makes it difficult for language teachers to decide which ones to teach. This chapter discusses how the newly grown weeds in the garden can be utilized in teaching Chinese as a foreign language (TCFL) to advanced learners.

2 Literature Review

As exotic plants or flowers are more likely to catch people's attention even if they are just weeds, neologisms in a language seldom escape the eyes of observant users. This is even more the case for neologisms on social media, because many of them became popular overnight and went viral on the Internet. Chinese neologisms on social media have attracted the attention of many researchers and language teachers over the past 15 years. From the studies that we are able to access, we see two main strands: linguistic studies and applied linguistic ones. The former focus on documenting the new words created by Chinese netizens at various stages and offering explanations to the motivation and the mechanism behind the creation of such new vocabulary from various perspectives. The latter focus on the pedagogical value of neologisms and how they can be utilized in TCFL.

One major theme in the linguistic studies regarding Chinese neologisms on social media is the polysyllabification and word-formation strategies. You (2012) investigated the newly emerged Chinese words and expressions from 2006 to 2009 and identified an obvious trend of trisyllabification in newly coined words. According to her observation, despite the dominance of two-character (disyllabic) words in the Chinese language, the neologisms predominantly took the forms of three and four characters. The methods of neologism construction include borrowing, transferring, equivocation, amplification and narrowing. Hou (2015) studied the 359 neologisms of the year 2008 and found that three-character neologisms reached 48% and four-character neologisms covered about 28%. Among all the neologisms of the year, 66 were collected from the Internet (approximately 19%). This trend lasted from 2006 all the way to 2012, according to the Language Situation Reports published by the China Ministry of Education (MOE 2006–2012). Shei (2014) studied the Chinese neologisms on Sina Weibo in great detail and reported that Chinese netizens mainly adopted strategies such as homophones and near homophones, derivational process, local accents Romanization, media catchphrases, abbreviations, and orthographical play in creating new words. Tong (2015) adopted the conceptual blending theory (Coulson and Fauconnier 1999) in studying meaning construction of four-character (quadrisyllabic) neologisms on the Internet, and found that blending is one of the main methods for Chinese netizens to create new words.

The rapid increase of neologisms both in mainstream media and on Internet-mediated new media has also attracted the attention of CFL teachers. In fact, the discussion about whether neologisms should be officially included in the curriculum of TCFL started more than a decade ago. Xia and Hua (2007) proposed that neologisms be included in TCFL to advanced learners as a supplement to the standard wordlist (or words in prescribed textbooks). As neologisms tend to capture the latest development of the Chinese society, they believe that understanding such social developments is a crucial goal for international students to learn the Chinese language. Having said that, the authors discouraged the teaching of certain types of neologisms: words only used in particular communities; words with negative connotations; words that foreign students should not know; and words that are not widely acknowledged. It is not very clear why certain words cannot be taught to foreign students, but the idea is that there should be criteria for selecting what to teach. Bai and Zhang (2008) proposed a similar approach, emphasizing the necessity of teaching neologisms to foreign learners of Chinese. According to them, one way to teach neologisms to foreign students is through word-formation analysis and subsequent explanations. They found that teaching neologisms to foreign students can be a useful way to help them understand the drastic social and cultural changes that China is experiencing. In a similar vein, Huang (2011) proposed three criteria for selecting new words in TCFL: they should be widely used, semantically stable and productive. According to her, neologisms are both opportunities and challenges in TCFL. On the one hand, neologisms may look appealing to foreign learners owing to their novelty. On the other hand, they can be difficult, because these words may come from various sources and touch upon very different aspects of Chinese people's life. Also, many of those words could not be found in any dictionaries. As such, they may become one of the obstacles for international students learning Chinese. Thus, giving more attention to teaching neologisms is necessary. Ge (2012) held a positive view about teaching neologisms from social media to foreign students but recommended that only words with high level of recognition, high usefulness in daily communication, and very clear and stabilized meaning should be taught. The number of words to be taught should be controlled so that they do not overshadow the teaching of basic vocabulary and general words. He held the same view as Xia and Hua (2007) that vulgar words and words with negative connotations should not be taught.

The studies reviewed above suggest a general consensus that Chinese neologisms originated from social media are a rich source that should be tapped in TCFL, especially to advanced students, but they should be handled with care when it comes to neologisms with sensitive or negative connotations. It makes great sense to focus on "good" words (so to speak) in TCFL, but it does not mean "bad" words (offensive words and words with negative connotations) are worthless. The idea that even bad language can be utilized as teaching resources is not new. Mercury (1995) discussed the benefits of teaching "bad" language to adult English learners 20 years ago. This idea is echoed by Horan (2013) who holds that "cursing and swearing are a linguistically, communicatively and culturally significant topic that should be addressed sensitively and knowledgeably in the FL classroom" (p. 296). Finn (2017) expresses a similar view that there are positive reasons for teachers to include swearing as a part of ESL courses for educational purposes. We feel that the "bad" members in Chinese neologisms can also be used for educational purposes in TCFL, especially for advanced learners. To use the weeds and garden analogy again, certain weeds may be poisonous. In tropical areas, wild plants (i.e. weeds) which are extremely appealing are probably the most deadly. However, we cannot just pretend that they do not exist. Studying the weeds and teaching students to identify the potentially harmful ones should also be an important part of TCFL for advanced learners.

Apart from the high relevance of neologisms to vocabulary teaching, some scholars believe that neologisms on social media have other pedagogical values in foreign language teaching as well. For instance, Thorne and Reinhardt (2008) argued for including "new media vernaculars" and new media literacies in teaching a foreign language to advanced learners. They advocated the use of a teacher-mediated language awareness framework, student-supplied texts, contrastive analysis, corpus-informed analyses, and qualitative discourse analysis methodologies. Their ultimate goal was to improve students' understanding of both conventional and digital text genres, raise their awareness of genre specificity and context-appropriate language use, build their metalinguistic, meta-communicative, and analytic skills that enable lifelong learning, and a bridge toward relevance to their communicative lives in the real world. The Chinese neologisms on social media can also be used to achieve similar goals.

One theme that is of extremely high relevance to what is being discussed in this chapter is the concept of advancedness. As we are targeting advanced CFL learners, we should define the term "advanced" first, because it has pedagogical implications. Unfortunately, the concept of "advancedness" in foreign language learning is fluid and difficult to define. According to Ortega and Byrnes (2009), advancedness can be approached from four different (yet overlapping) perspectives: "institutional status", "characterizations gleaned from standardized tests", "late-acquired language features", and "sophisticated language use in context" (p. 7). The last one is what they favour most. According to them, "advancedness" should be linked to "aspects of literacy, to diverse manifestations of cultural competence, choice among registers and multiple speech community repertoires, voice, and identity in cross-cultural communicative settings" (p. 8). Greatly influenced by M. A. K. Halliday's teaching, Matthiessen (2006) holds that learning a foreign language consists of three fundamental aspects: learning the language, learning through the language and learning about the language. The more advanced learners become, the more these three aspects will influence one another. According to him, "learning a language can increasingly be helped by learning about this language—not only passively, but also actively by *investigating* it and by developing one's own resources for learning" (Matthiessen 2006: 33, italics added). By encouraging students to investigate the target language itself, we are actually developing their awareness. "Fostering advanced L2 abilities requires learners to be highly aware language users, with regard to language as a culturally embedded system for making meanings and with regard to diverse approaches toward language learning" (Byrnes 2012: 515). Such meta-awareness will itself need to be created in instruction. Indeed, it is considered to be at the heart of continuing development toward very advanced literacies, often a life-long project.

3 Constructing the Corpus

We constructed a small teaching corpus by starting with a list of neologisms that we collected from the Internet and then using Google to search for real instances of how these neologisms are used on popular Chinese social media. As this chapter focuses more on demonstrating how to explore the pedagogical values of neologisms in TCFL rather than what neologisms to teach, the primary criteria for selecting sample neologisms include the number of syllables, the relevance of entries to unique Chinese linguistic and sociocultural features, and their popularity. Eventually, we selected 50 entries of neologisms that have been very popular on social media over the past year. Table 1 shows 10 examples: for each syllable pattern, two examples were given with each representing a different word-formation strategy.

Table 1 List of sample neologism entries

Entry	Chinese Pinyin	English translation	Category (syllables)	Remarks
槑	Mei2	Very stupid	Monosyllabic	Orthographic play; old Chinese
怼	Dui2	Abhor	Monosyllabic	Chinese dialect traceable to ancient times
水军	Shui3jun1	Paid reviewers or commenters	Disyllabic	New meaning of an old form
围观	Wei2guan1	Watching	Disyllabic	Extension of meaning
背锅侠	Bei1guo1xia2	Scapegoats	Trisyllabic	New compounds formed via analogy
搞事情	Gao3shi4qing2	Make trouble	Trisyllabic	Colloquial phrase from dialects
一脸懵逼	Yi1lian3 meng1bi1	Totally confused	Quadrisyllabic	Analogy
细思极恐	Xi4si1ji2kong2	Feel horrified at hindsight	Quadrisyllabic	Abbreviations following the structure of idioms
全都是套路	Quan3dou1shi4 tao4lu4	It's all by design. It's a trap.	Polysyllabic	Phrase
厉害了，word哥	Li4hai4le, wo3de4ge1	Wow, how/absolutely amazing!	Polysyllabic	Phrase

Our list of neologisms was based on the information that we synthesized from the following sources and our own observations:

1. Wikipedia[1]
2. Baidu Baike[2]
3. ChinaSmack[3]

For each neologism, we only collected the first 10 pages of the Google search results. The texts included in the corpus are just what the Google search engine displayed on each individual page. In other words, we did not expand the hyperlinks listed on the search results to get the full text of each entry. Although we could have expanded the hyperlinks to obtain the full texts where the target neologisms appeared and constructed the corpus based on the full texts retrieved, we did not take

[1]https://zh.wikipedia.org/wiki/.

[2]https://baike.baidu.com/item/%E7%BD%91%E7%BB%9C%E6%96%B0%E8%AF%8D.

[3]https://www.chinasmack.com/glossary.

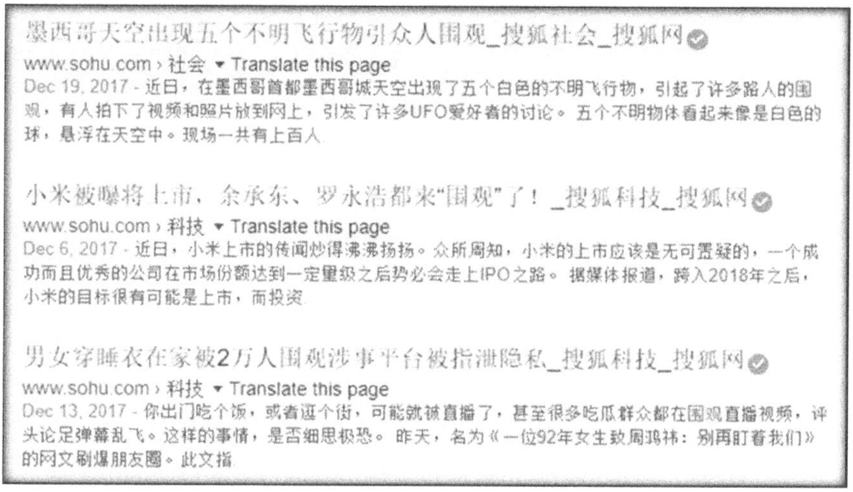
墨西哥天空出现五个不明飞行物引众人围观_搜狐社会_搜狐网
www.sohu.com › 社会 ▾ Translate this page
Dec 19, 2017 - 近日，在墨西哥首都墨西哥城天空出现了五个白色的不明飞行物，引起了许多路人的围观，有人拍下了视频和照片放到网上，引发了许多UFO爱好者的讨论。五个不明物体看起来像是白色的球，悬浮在天空中。现场一共有上百人

小米被曝将上市，余承东、罗永浩都来"围观"了！_搜狐科技_搜狐网
www.sohu.com › 科技 ▾ Translate this page
Dec 6, 2017 - 近日，小米上市的传闻炒得沸沸扬扬。众所周知，小米的上市应该是无可置疑的，一个成功而且优秀的公司在市场份额达到一定量级之后势必会走上IPO之路。据媒体报道，跨入2018年之后，小米的目标很有可能是上市，而投资

男女穿睡衣在家被2万人围观涉事平台被指泄隐私_搜狐科技_搜狐网
www.sohu.com › 科技 ▾ Translate this page
Dec 13, 2017 - 你出门吃个饭，或者逛个街，可能就被直播了，甚至很多吃瓜群众都在围观直播视频，评头论足弹幕乱飞。这样的事情，是否细思极恐。昨天，名为《一位92年女生致周鸿祎：别再盯着我们》的网文刷爆朋友圈。此文指

Fig. 1 Sample Google search results

that approach due to limited manpower and time. Besides, the complete discourse may not be relevant all the time since what has been displayed in the search results offers enough information for vocabulary teaching (see Fig. 1).

In order to make sure that all cases of neologisms in the corpus are real usage ones, we took the approach that Kerremans (2015) adopted in dealing with metalinguistic discourse. According to Kerremans, "metalinguistic discourse involves readers or writers, speakers or hearers commenting on the coinage, existence, emergence or formal shape of a neologism or providing explanations and definitions" (p. 20). To be more accurate, the metalinguistic discourse referred to here is something similar to dictionary definitions of new terms. In that sense, the pages containing metalinguistic discourse about the target neologisms were not real usage cases and were thus excluded. All the hyperlinks were also removed, although they can provide more information about where the original texts can be located if the need arises. We manually removed all duplicated cases. As the focus of this chapter is on exploring the pedagogical value of neologisms, rather than identifying them from a large sample of authentic language data, the size of the corpus is not a key issue. As long as the corpus can provide sufficient information to illustrate how and in what contexts these neologisms are used, and there are enough lines to show collocational patterns if any, it can serve its purposes well.

Following the principles mentioned above, we constructed a small corpus of about 700,000 Chinese characters, mainly based on the Google research results of the 50 neologism entries. The corpus went through Chinese segmentation using the tool developed by Chang et al. (2008). Human intervention was conducted when the tool failed to segment new words correctly. As our corpus is small, running through the wordlist generated can easily tell whether the targeted neologisms were properly segmented. The incorrect segmentations can be easily corrected using the "search and replace" function of any text editor. We used EditPlus Text Editor 4.0 (ES-Computing 2017) in our corpus construction and editing. The software we used for wordlist generation, concordances, collocation identification is WordSmith Tools (version 6) developed by Mike Scott (2015).

4 Using Neologisms from Social Media for Teaching

The novelty of neologisms is one of the factors that make them a valuable teaching resource in TCFL. Very often, the newness (in form/meaning/usage) does not come from nowhere. Popular neologisms became popular for a reason. Exploring this newness and the reasons for the propagation is of natural attraction to both language teachers and learners. This exploration allows students to learn more about how the Chinese language is used in Internet-mediated texts. For advanced CFL learners, being able to understand the social indexical value of neologisms and use them properly on social media or in daily communication is a good indicator of the advancedness of their Chinese proficiency. Apart from that, studying neologisms can also open a window for the students to see the linguistic and socio-cultural factors behind the scene which have shaped the formation of these new words and expressions.

In this chapter, we propose a corpus-supported three-stage approach to teaching neologisms from social media. At stage one, we focus on the form, meaning and usage, just like what we usually do with teaching any new words. Despite the popularity of neologisms, it might be a challenge to find out how exactly they are used, because they may scatter over various corners of the Internet. With a corpus like what we built for this chapter, we will be able to show how a particular neologism is used in real-life situations. For instance, using the concordance lines of a particular neologism, we can obtain information about its collocation, colligation and sometimes even the semantic prosody. This cannot be easily achieved if we only show them one or two examples. That is on top of the analysis about the morphological and phonological features. At stage two, we divert students' attention to understanding the motivation and mechanism of the formation of neologisms and help them to see the linguistic, sociolinguistic, cultural and technical factors at play in the formation of these neologisms. At stage three, we ask them to use these neologisms in their speaking and writing. Basically, we focus on two of the three fundamental aspects of foreign language learning proposed by Matthiessen (2006): learning the language and learning about the language. We will demonstrate how this can be done, using some sample neologisms we obtained from the Internet. For the convenience of explanation, we will organize our discussion according to the word-formation strategies.

4.1 Old Junks and Orthographic Play

As mentioned earlier, neologisms are often featured by their novelty which may come with a new form or an old form with a new meaning. One observation that can be made from the monosyllabic Chinese neologisms originated from social media is that netizens tend to make use of old junks to express new meanings. As Aitchison (2001: 180) remarks, [language] "always contains some useless thingummyjigs from the past. Sometimes, these relics just fade away. At other times, the human mind thinks up a use for them". One typical example is "槑" (mei2). According to *Kangxi Dictionary*, "槑" is the old form of "梅" (mei2), meaning "plum". It was a word with positive connotation. The character "槑" can be divided into two characters "呆" and "呆" (dai1, meaning "stupid"). As this word is very rarely used and not many people know how to read it, when netizens started to use it to refer to "stupid people" or "people who look very confused", the wisdom and humour would be immediately recognized. This new meaning is further reinforced by a phrase in a Chinese dialect (Guanzhong dialect) spoken in some parts of Shaanxi and Henan provinces. There is a phrase in this dialect for people who are cowardly and not very smart: 槑怂 (mu4song2). In this phrase, 槑 is pronounced "mu4" rather than "mei2, but the Chinese character remains the same. The character itself also looks like two people standing side by side. It is not very clear whether that has contributed anything to the new meaning of the word. To a large extent, this is an orthographic play, which reveals something unique about the Chinese writing system: many Chinese characters can be broken down into parts that are also stand-alone characters, e.g. 人 (a person), 从 (cong2, meaning one person is following another person), and 众 (zhong4, a large crowd, three people staying together). The formation of these characters suggests that the repetition of the character helps increase the number or quantity.

To demonstrate how to teach neologisms created out of orthographic play, we designed the following task:

Task 1. Find a partner to work with (or work in groups of four), read the concordance lines in Fig. 2, discuss with your partner(s) what the phrase "又双叒叕 (you4shuang1ruo4zhuo2)" may mean, why these four characters are put together, in what kind of circumstances people are more likely to use this phrase, and report to the class your discussion results. Consult a dictionary when necessary.

For advanced CFL learners, it will not take them long to figure out the meaning of this phrase, although they may have problems recognizing "叒" (ruo4) and "叕" (zhuo2). After hearing students' reports, the teacher can ask students to come up with Chinese characters with similar orthographic pattern and explain the mechanism (old junk plus orthographic play) behind the formation of this phrase. After that, the teacher can draw students' attention to the semantic prosody of this phrase if they did not manage to notice that. A follow-up activity would be to ask students to make new sentences with this phrase to describe the repeated occurrences of unpleasant or undesirable experience in their daily life.

The explanation can go as follows. Just like the word "槑", "叒" (ruo4) and "叕" (zhuo2) are rarely used in modern Chinese. In ancient Chinese, "叒" has the same

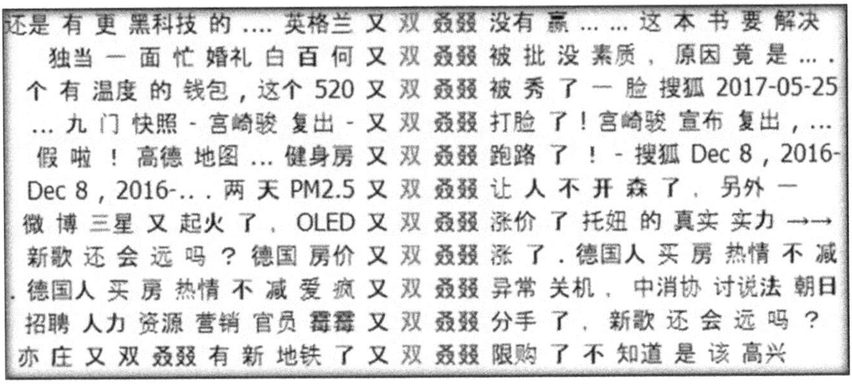
还是 有 更 黑科技 的 .... 英格兰 又 双 叒叕 没有 赢 ... ... 这 本 书 要 解决
独当 一 面 忙 婚礼 白 百 何 又 双 叒叕 被 批 没 素质 , 原因 竟 是 ... .
个 有 温度 的 钱包 , 这个 520 又 双 叒叕 被 秀 了 一 脸 搜狐 2017-05-25
... 九 门 快照 - 宫崎骏 复出 - 又 双 叒叕 打脸 了 ! 宫崎骏 宣布 复出 , ...
假 啦 ! 高德 地图 ... 健身房 又 双 叒叕 跑路 了 ! - 搜狐 Dec 8 , 2016-
Dec 8 , 2016-.. . 两 天 PM2.5 又 双 叒叕 让 人 不 开 森 了 . 另外 一
微 博 三星 又 起火 了 . OLED 又 双 叒叕 涨价 了 托妞 的 真实 实力 →→
新歌 还 会 远 吗 ? 德国 房价 又 双 叒叕 涨 了 . 德国人 买 房 热情 不 减
. 德国人 买 房 热情 不 减 爱 疯 又 双 叒叕 异常 关机 . 中消协 讨说法 朝日
招聘 人力 资源 营销 官员 霜霜 又 双 叒叕 分手 了 . 新歌 还 会 远 吗 ?
亦 庄 又 双 叒叕 有 新 地铁 了 又 双 叒叕 限购 了 不 知道 是 该 高兴

Fig. 2 Concordance lines of 叒叕

pronunciation as "若" (ruo4, meaning "obey or follow" or "a kind of legendary tree"). The character "叕" has four different pronunciations: zhuo2 (meaning "short"), yi1 (meaning "a net"), li4 (meaning "stop or end"), and jue2 (meaning "fast" or "speed"). All four characters in this new phrase "又双叒叕" have nothing in common except that they all consist of the base character "又" (you4, meaning "again"). In fact, the character "又" is repeated ten times in this phrase. The meaning of this phrase is quite obvious to native Chinese speakers and its English equivalence is "again" (repeated ten times). From the concordance lines, we can easily read the kind of negativity that this phrase is associated with and the sentiment of frustration over something that people did not really want to see just happened again. For instance, the first line simply means "Unbelievable, England lost the game AGAIN!" The second line means something like "Bai Baihe (a famous movie star in a scandal) was criticized AGAIN for not being well-educated". The sixth line means "Yesterday's PM2.5 (an index for measuring air pollution) reading made me unhappy AGAIN!" (People were complaining about the bad air pollution). In other words, this phrase is often associated with a negative semantic prosody. The teacher should remind students of this feature.

Another example of monosyllabic neologism formed from what Aitchison (2001) called "making use of the old junk" is "怼" (dui4). Again, this word was rarely used before it became popular on social media. It is a very formal word, meaning "to resent or hate". Since being re-discovered by Chinese netizens, it has picked up a new meaning of "to criticize" and typically collocates with "怒" (nu4, meaning "angrily"). In other words, "怒怼 (nu4dui4)" has become a rather fixed usage, as can be observed from the concordance lines in Fig. 3.

A similar task can be designed for "怼" (dui4). By doing all this, we are offering a very rich learning experience for our learners. To expand the learning experience even further, we can ask them to think about whether they can find similar cases in their own languages and tell them to explain why this is the case.

有的 " 怒怼 " ... 俄 常 驻 联合国 代表 怒怼 英 代表 ： 看 着 我 的 眼睛 侮辱
我们 不 能 总是 依赖于 派出所 的 " 怒怼 " 来 怒 对 奇葩 证明 。 再 者 ，
不利 最终 遗憾 中盘 败北 。 老师 发文 怒怼 王者 荣耀 ！ 学生 哭诉 ： " 我
： 美国 队长 就 是 一 宣传 工具 怒怼 美式 超级 英雄 电影 称 对 其
观察 ， 上 周 美国 和 朝鲜 两 国 " 怒怼 " ， 双方 均 展示 出 强硬 立场
情 ， 疑似 再次 回应 被 诈捐 行为 ， 怒怼 网友 喷子 。 为 生活费 怒怼
又 见 奇葩 证明 ！ 根治 不 能 只 靠 怒怼 --- 我们 不 能 总是 依赖于
将 通报 银行 单位 的 纪检 ... 遭 柯洁 怒怼 媒体 道歉 网友 再怼 ： 用 中文
坐 公交 不 给 钱 还 耍 无赖 ， 男童 怒怼 全 车 人 点 赞- 铁血网 没 想到
都 少 得 多 。 法国 总统 遭 农展 农民 怒怼 ： 你 或许 关心 农业 可 你 要
行为 ， 怒怼 网友 喷子 。 为 生活费 怒怼 母亲 ， 将 索取 视为 理所当然 -
我们 10 人 也 能 赢 。 " 苏宁携 天天 怒怼 京东 ， 你们 可 想 过 上帝 的
有 一 打 小品 会 活 到 带妆 ... 网友 怒怼 云南 旅游 官员 ： 蛋 裂缝 还

Fig. 3 Concordance lines of 怼

4.2 Semantic Extension

Semantic extension is another strategy that is commonly employed in creating new words. One interesting example would be the extension of meaning for a very common character "枚 (mei2)". This monosyllabic word is a numeral classifier for small objects such as a coin, a button, or a ring most of the time, although it can also be used for enormous objects such as a missile, a rocket and a satellite. Regardless of the size, this classifier is supposed to modify objects (inanimate things). Since some netizens used it to refer to people or animals on social media, this word has acquired some new meanings and its usage has also undergone interesting changes. We designed the following task to demonstrate how neologisms created out of semantic extension can be used in TCFL classes.

> **Task 2**. Form groups of four. Write the Chinese character 枚 on the board. Ask students to look for items that can be talked about using the numeral classier (e.g. 一枚硬币) and ask one representative from each group to tell the whole class what objects they have collected and how many. If students do not have any real objects with them, they can talk about anything they know that can be classified by the word 枚. The teacher (or a student designated by the teacher) can write down the names of the items on the board. After that, ask students to analyse the item names on the board and share their observations with the class. After that, the teacher shows Fig. 4 to the whole class and ask them to analyse the concordance lines in groups. Ask them to compare their observations about the list on the board and the list of concordance lines and report the differences to whole class. [Follow-up activities can be arranged for them to learn to use this phrase.]

Among the 13 concordance lines, 7 lines were the new usage of "枚" referring to people. For instance, on the first line, it is used to refer to a "newbie front end web developer" (前端小白, qian2duan1xiao3bai2). The word "小白" (xiao3bai2) itself is a neologism originated from social media, meaning a green hand or newbie. On the second line, it is used to refer to a first-time microwave oven user. Line 5 refers

下来 小武 ... 笔者 是 前端 小 白	一 枚	， 在 往 前端 页面 重构 方向 学习
师 ， 关注 移动 互联网 . 烤箱 新手	一 枚	， 肉食 动物 .. 这 不 是 一 枚
新手 一 枚 ， 肉食 动物 .. 这 不 是	一 枚	赤裸裸 的 口头 offer 么 ！ 第一
：好帅 的 回答 ， 楼 主送 上 香 吻	一 枚	， 以 表 诚挚 谢意 ！ 文科生 一
一 枚 ， 以 表 诚挚 谢意 ！ 文科生	一 枚	在 看《 切尔诺贝利 回忆 》这 本
幅 画 开启 的 世界 》日文 原著《	一 枚	の絵から 》- 陈 丹青 在《 看 理想
的《 局部 》... .... .python 小 白	一 枚	， 秉持 着 在 代码 中 学习 中 的
硬币 ， 一个 纸夹 ， 一 枚 纽扣 ，	一 枚	珠子 ， 一个 小玩具 ， 一 颗 骰子
， 一 颗 骰子 等等 。 立志 做	一 枚	小 透明 。 偶尔 把 这 当成 树洞 。
， 在 里面 藏 一些 小 东西 ， 比如	一 枚	硬币 ， 一个 纸夹 ， 一 枚 纽扣 ，
， 比如 一 枚 硬币 ， 一个 纸夹 ，	一 枚	纽扣 ， 一 枚 珠子 ， 一个 小玩具
利 鹏 EN ：CharlieI AMC++ 码 农	一 枚	， 热爱 并 专注于 C++ 相关 技术
的 一些 东西 ， 主要 是 ... 现在 是	一 枚	Android 攻 城 师 ， 关注 移动

Fig. 4 Concordance lines of 枚

to a liberal art student. Line 7, a newbie of Python. Line 9, a transparent person. The last line but one refers to a programmer whereas the last line refers to an Android engineer. By blending the semantic association of small objects with human roles, the users have created a mental image of someone without much experience yet very cute. This new shade of meaning applies to young people more often.

Of course, semantic extension does not only apply to monosyllabic words. This is also very common in disyllabic and even trisyllabic words. For instance, the disyllabic word "备胎" (bei4tai1) used to refer to a "backup tyre" but now its meaning has been extended to refer to "backup boyfriend or girlfriend". The word "主播" (zhu3bo1) that used to refer to an anchor-man (host) or anchor-woman (hostess) of a TV news program, but now it has been extended to include hosts and hostesses in the webcasting industry, a newly emerged sector in entertainment. Another example to show semantic extension of ordinary Chinese words is "翻墙 (fan1qiang2)". The original meaning of this word was "climbing a wall", but now it has been extended to mean circumventing the Chinese government's Internet control (the Great Fire Wall). This is not a very new word, but the new meaning has been increasingly reinforced in recent years due to the increasingly tightening of Internet control. By asking students to study neologisms like the ones cited above and asking them to explore the changes of meaning, we are not only asking them to learn the language but also offering them good opportunities to gain a deeper understanding of the Chinese society: its developments and its problems.

4.3 Analogy

Another way for creating neologisms on social media is through analogy: forming new words modelling on existing word-building patterns. For instance, "用心 (yong4xin1)" is a very common word in Chinese, meaning "being focused on doing something". The literal meaning of these two Chinese characters is "using heart". In ancient Chinese philosophy, the heart is regarded as the thinking and reasoning organ which unifies human will, desire, emotion, intuition, reason and thought (Yu 2008). In north China, people will use "上心" (shang4xin1, literal meaning: putting something in your heart) to replace 用心. For instance, people may say "那小孩学习不上心" (That boy was not interested in studying or that boy didn't study very hard). Here "上心" and "用心" are interchangeable. Following the same pattern of "Verb +心", a new word "走心" (zou3xin, literal meaning "going through the heart") has been generated on social media. Apart from governing our thinking, the heart is also believed to control some of our emotions. We have "伤心" (shang1xin1, literal meaning: break heart), meaning "feeling sad or heart-broken". Probably influenced by the association of the organ "heart" with mind and emotion, the new word "走心" has now been used to refer to "putting lots of thoughts on doing something" or "carefully designed", or "taking something really serious", all implying the appeal to considerateness and careful planning. The examples extracted from our corpus offer a glimpse of how this word is used on social media (or the Internet).

From Fig. 5, we can see "走心广告" (carefully designed advertisements), "走心礼物" (a well-designed gift), and "走心设计" (a well-conceived design). When this word is used to describe a romantic relationship between a male and a female, it picks up the new meaning of "real love (using one's heart to love someone)". The opposite of this is "走肾" (zou3shen4, literal meaning: going through the kidneys), love driven by sexual drive. Kidneys are believed to be the source of sexual drive by Chinese people. If someone (particularly a man) is described as "走肾" in a love relationship, this person is actually accused of being interested in the partner's beauty or any other bodily attraction. The formation of the word itself has followed the same pattern as that of "走心". Figure 6 shows some examples of how this new word is used.

To demonstrate how neologisms such as "走心" and "走肾" can be used in teaching advanced CFL learners, we designed the following tasks:

Task 3A. Show students Figs. 5 and 6. Ask them to work in pairs (or groups) to figure out what these two phrases ("走心" and "走肾") mean and why they think so. Ask them to report their findings to the whole class afterwards.

Task 3B. Work in pairs and make a list of words and expressions that involve different parts of human body in Chinese and share the list with the whole class. After class, write a report on the differences between Chinese and your native language in using human body parts to express emotions.

By asking students to connect the dots between "用心", "上心", "走心", and "走肾", we can help them see the trajectory or pathway of "走肾" acquiring its new meaning and how useful analogy can be as a strategy of formation new words. More

APP 一 份 没有 标准 答案 的 十 大 " 走心 " 广告 榜单【 案例 精选 】- 数
正在 全 党 开展 。在 全体 党员 ... 走心 的 微生物（ 七 ）人类 正在
Segway 童 车 首 发 ， 给 孩子 的 走心 礼物 . 2017-04 - 24. Segway 童
」. 臺灣 人聽 了 很 刺耳 因 為臺灣 的 走心 是 分心 不 專心 的 意思 大陸
。这 一 年 ， 站 在 技术 时代 的 ..." 走心 " 方 能 留住心 - 重庆市 烟草
走心 是 分心 不 專心 的 意思 大陸 的 走心 是 用心 專心 走 進心裡 的 意思
他 继承 了 家族 ... 海口 看 我 的 ！ 走心 的 设计 送给 高 要求 的 你 ！ -
的 恋爱 互相 喜欢 ， 还 能 赚 钱 的 走心 的 社交 APP 一 份 没有 标准
... Segway 童 车 首 发 ， 给 孩子 的 走心 礼物 - 纳 恩博 Segway 童 车 首
... 讲 好 故事 ， 改革 教育课 动情 走心 - 解放 军报 - 中国 军网 Mar 21
中部 战区 空军 改革 实施 ... 简单 而 走心 ： 是 什么 让 家 充满 想象力 ？
部分 基层 党 组织 在 网 上 发起 ... # 走心 经营 客户 # 你 必须 知道 的 三
出售 给 一 家 ... 父亲节 给 他 一 份 走心 的 礼物 -Land Rover 小时候 ，
灯光 重 又 亮 了 ... 90 后 , 做 个 " 走心 少年 " 可 好 ？ _ 手机 新浪网

Fig. 5 Concordance lines of 走心

恋爱 中 的 这些 星座 ， 不 走 肾 只 走心 ！ - 在 线 观看 - 热点 -
你 把 我 心都 偷走 了 ， 还 怪 我 走 肾 不 走 心 。再 爱 也 不过 自己 ，
5 , 2014-《 前任 攻略 》： 上半场 走 肾 ， 下半场 走心 一 个 人 要 经历
《 前任 攻略 》： 上半场 走 肾 ， 下半场 走心（ 前任 攻略 ）影评
不 走 肾 只 走心 ！ , 现在 恋爱 ， 走 肾 的 人 越来越 多 了 ， 还 有 人

Fig. 6 Concordance lines of 走肾

importantly, by asking them to explore the use of body parts in the Chinese language, we are offering students opportunities to understand Chinese culture. Meanwhile, we are also raising their awareness about cultural differences. A good reference book for conducting Task 3B would be *Culture, Body, and Language: Conceptualizations of Internal Body Organs across Cultures and Languages* edited by Sharifian et al. (2008).

Analogy is also a very important strategy for generating trisyllabic neologisms on social media. Due to the huge success of two famous Hollywood movies "Batman" and "Spiderman", the Chinese translation of the movie titles has become very well-known almost to the whole Chinese population: "蝙蝠侠" (Batman) and "蜘蛛侠" (Spiderman). Even a more recent TV series *Arrow* has been translated into "绿箭侠" (lv4jian4xia2, literal meaning: "green arrow man"). The heroes in the movies or TV series are all figures with special power and are able to punish evil people and get injustice done when the government or the legal system fails to function due to corruption. The Chinese translation adds a strong heroic flavour to the three original English titles. The word "侠" (xia2) originally refers to established Kungfu (martial arts) masters well known for their integrity, high moral standards and their determination to get justice done. It is very similar to the concept of knighthood in Western culture. Basically, it is a word with a strong positive connotation. The neologisms following the pattern of "X+侠", however, have developed some negative sense with a

的 怎么 渣 了 ， 哪个 男 的 受得了 当 接盘侠 ， 多 恶 心人 她 认为 ， 中共
产业 基金 的 猜想 ， 赚 吆喝 还 是 当 接盘侠 ? 北 中午 下 了 2017 年 的
也 没有 人 想 在 房地产 市场 中 当 " 接盘侠 " 吧 ， 如果 你 的 朋友 中 有
光 总裁 因 健康 原因 离职 : 谁 来 当 接盘侠 ? 北京 时间 1 月 5 日 午间
乐视 危局 、 令 人 叹为观止 。 易 到 " 接盘侠 " 揭开 神秘 面纱 : 韬 蕴 资本
中国 的 接盘侠 。 . 法国 终于 等 到 " 接盘侠 " ， 当然 是 十万 个 愿意 了
， 土豪 有 钱 才 能 任性 。 易 到 " 接盘侠 " 称 广泛 布局 旅游业 旅游
卓尔 和 丰盛 的 ..... 其实 相当 多 的 接盘侠 对 此 心知肚明 ， 只是 由于
严重 过剩 的 房产 转 到 万民 构成 的 接盘侠 手里 ... 为 国 接盘 侠 ... 我
" 卖身 " 传闻 ， 只不过 这 次 的 " 接盘侠 " 变成 了 快递 企业 顺丰 。
没有 选择 他 ， 日后 还 可以 当 她 的 接盘侠 。 但 我 对 他 说 ， 关键 是

Fig. 7 Concordance lines of 接盘侠

shade of humour. The first new word is "接盘侠 (jie1pan2xia2)". "接盘" (jie1pan2) is a technical term used in stock trading, meaning "buying the stocks what other people are selling". It does not have much negative connotation. However, when this word is followed by "侠" (xie2), the neutral or technical nature of the original term becomes undermined. In its place comes a sentiment of either a heroic or quixotic deed. Being able to take what other people do not want to keep in business requires either great wisdom or a huge amount of capital or both. It still carries some elements of the knight spirit of being daring to do what other people will not do. Depending on the context, this new word has another meaning, which is not so positive. If this word is used to refer to the relationship between men and women, the negative sense becomes more prominent. Here "接盘侠" (jie1pan2xia2) becomes someone who takes a girl dumped by someone else as a girlfriend or a guy who marries a lady who got pregnant with another man (Shenzhen Daily 2015). Figure 7 reveals how this new word is used on social media. Except for the first line and the last line where 接盘侠 is used to refer to romantic relationship, all the rest are cases about investment and business operations.

Another neologism following the same pattern is "背锅侠" (bei1guo1xia2, literal meaning: one who carries a wok), meaning someone who is always blamed for things he has never done. It is very similar to the English word "scapegoat". In fact, there is a play on the sound happening here. "背锅" (bei1guo1, carrying a wok) sounds very much like "背过" (bei1guo4, being blamed) and in Chinese there is a very commonly used phrase called "背黑锅" (bei1hei1guo1, carrying a black wok), meaning being wrongly blamed. "背锅" (bei1guo1) is actually the short form of "背黑锅" (bei1hei1guo1). Just like in the previous example, adding the word "侠" (xia2) to "背锅" (bei1guo1) also creates a sentiment of bearing the blame owing to having a strong heart or very bad luck. Overall, the meaning of this word is between neutral and positive. It carries a strong sense of humour. Figure 8 shows some examples extracted from the corpus.

Not every word carrying the character "侠" has a good connotation. The new word "键盘侠" (jian4pan2xia2, literal meaning: keyboard man/warrior) is one with neg-

也 没 变 。在 热火 时 ， 经常 成为 “ 背锅侠 ” 的 是 波什 ， 与 詹姆斯
变成 了 小 ... 林 更新 出演 楚乔传成 背锅侠 ， 一言不合 就 背锅 - 娱乐 -
新浪网 本泽马之前 他 是 足坛 最 大 背锅侠 37 岁 仍 在 拼杀 .
在 一派 ... 本泽马之前 他 才 是 最 大 背锅侠 _ 手机 新浪网 本泽马之前 他
到 中国 的 ATL 电池 ... 解码 恒 大 背锅侠 马T内斯 ： 他 是 无解 的
人 想到 冤 大 头 . . . 萧何 ， 一 代 背锅侠 ， 是 汉 初 最 能 为 刘邦 背
齐普丘 脚 下 ， 罗霍 硬 着 ... 历 代 背锅侠 盘点 谁 将 接过 背锅侠 的
而且 总是 背 黑锅 ， 终于 成 了 一 代 背锅侠 。“ 背锅侠 ” 李达康 书记
人 想到 冤 大 头 . . . 萧何 ， 一 代 背锅侠 ， 是 汉 初 最 能 为 刘邦 背

Fig. 8 Concordance lines of 背锅侠

前 ... 宁泽涛 破 亚洲 纪录 ， 打脸 键盘侠 什么 水平 ？ - 步行街 主干道
热辣 新 车 ， 不 用 隔 着 荧屏 当 键盘侠 ， 这 一 次 ， 用 最 真实 最
是 外骚型 ， 不 喜欢宅 在 家 里 当 键盘侠 ， 总 有 一 股 “ 就 是 想 出来
要命 ， 上网 立刻 化身 正义 伙伴 的 键盘侠 以及 大 喷子 （ 这 两 个 网络
主动 呼吁 “ 不 要 做 不 负 责任 的 键盘侠 ， 不 要 动不动 抡起 道德
days ago - 这么 回复 就 是 典型 的 键盘侠 ， 不 考虑 后果 反正 不 是
的 喷子 大多 是 心智 不 太 成熟 的 键盘侠 ， 或者 甚至 就 是 赌狗 ，
， 总是 比 躲 在 暗处 、 道德 无敌 的 键盘侠 要 值得 尊重 的 。NBA 首 页
那些 说 站 在 什么 仁义道德 位置 的 键盘侠 的话 的 我 无话可说 。我 又

Fig. 9 Concordance lines of 键盘侠

ative connotation. A keyboard man or warrior is someone who is calling for justice to be done but will never do anything to help the process. What they would do is just typing (talking): they just post messages on social media. A closer examination of the concordance lines reveals that this new word builds a negative semantic prosody around it. The words associated with 键盘侠 include: “不用隔着荧屏当键盘侠” (no need to stay behind the screen and be a keyboard man); “不用宅在家里当键盘侠” (no need to stay at home, being a keyboard man); “化身键盘侠以及大喷子” (disguise oneself as a keyboard man and an angry complainer); “不负责任的键盘侠” (an irresponsible keyboard man); “不考虑后果的” (a typical keyboard man who cares nothing about the consequences of what they say); “心智不太成熟的键盘侠” (an intellectually immature keyboard man); “躲在暗处的键盘侠” (a keyboard man always hiding in a dark corner), and so on. None of these collocates are positive. By examining the concordance lines (see Fig. 9), students can understand the meaning of this word better and learn to use it in the right context.

Moreover, neologisms like those cited above can provide Chinese teachers with a good opportunity to compare the concept of “侠” in Chinese culture and the “knight spirit” in western culture to see whether these concepts have exerted other influence on respective languages. Again, this will open another window for students to see the cultural differences between China and the world.

4.4 Applying the Principle of Economy

Many Chinese neologisms originated from social media demonstrate the application of the principle of economy. To save time, Chinese netizens often use different strategies to make long phrases (sometimes full sentences) short and put them into the typical phonological or morphological framework of the Chinese language. Studying these unconventional short forms may give advanced learners of Chinese opportunities to think about the general linguistic features of the Chinese language (be it phonological, prosodic, or morphological). To achieve this goal, we designed the following task:

> **Task 4**. Work in pairs (or groups of four). Examine Figs. 10, 11 and 12, focus on the keywords in the middle, and try to figure out the original phrases (the ones before abbreviation). Report your results to the class. If you have problems getting the original phrases, that is fine. Focus on the number of characters left after abbreviation for each phrase and think about whether other possibilities are possible.

Figure 10 shows the concordance of a disyllabic word called "躺枪" (tang3qiang1, literal meaning: "lie gun"). The meaning of this new word is almost opaque. It is not easy to figure out what it means exactly by reading the two characters involved. In fact, this is the short form of a much longer phrase "躺着也中枪" (meaning "got shot even when lying on the ground). This is a phrase to express a kind of frustrating experience where irrelevant people were dragged into a scandal.

Figure 11 shows the concordance of another neologism "然并卵" (ran2bing4luan2, meaning "but in vain" or "seemingly useful but actually useless"). There are many well-known neologisms created through abbreviations, for instance, "白富美" (bai2fu4mei3, meaning "white-rich-pretty"), "高富帅" (gao1fu4shuai4, meaning "tall-rich-handsome"), and "高大上" (gao1da4shang4, meaning "fancy" or "high-end"). Very often, the meanings of these words are transparent. But the

白 百 何 约 会 男模 事件 中 莫名	躺枪	的 明星 _ 一 床 情 书 _ 新浪
穿 日本 军服 在 车站 作秀 快手 莫名	躺枪	- 站长 之 家 - 随着 各 种 直播
特朗普 抨击 欧洲 难民 政策 ， 瑞典 "	躺枪	" - 纽约 时报 国际 生活 北京
恤 在 … 法国 游客 减少 ， 瑞士 手表	躺枪	- SWI swissinfo.ch Sep 27 ,
， 有的 为 … 白 百 何 出轨 王珞丹	躺枪	！ 微博遭卓伟 观光团 攻陷 _
印度 炮制 " 洞朗 事件 " ， 不丹 为何	躺枪	？ - 前沿网 距离 印度 边防 部队
" 尼古拉斯 赵四13 " ， 所以 也 无辜	躺枪	， 新加坡 球迷 举横幅 促 下课 ·
理工 大学 的 男生 李炳鑫 无辜 "	躺枪	" ， 被 网友 … 默克尔 一语令
， 被 网友 … 默克尔 一语令 美元 无辜	躺枪	黄金 多头 再 下 一 城 - 黄金
， 先 是 名叫 李炳鑫 的 小伙 无辜 "	躺枪	" ， 被 误认 成 猥亵 事件 的 男
球员 ， 现任 国脚 国脚 赵明 剑 无辜	躺枪	， 他 在 社交 媒体 自嘲 ， 先 替
女孩 不 足 10 岁 … 哈 理工 小伙 "	躺枪	" 成 " 猥亵 男 " 李炳鑫 发声 ：
男子 被 抓 网民 " 人肉 " 让 无辜 小伙	躺枪	_ 社会 新闻 _…- 南京 南站
大牌 。 中 印 边境 对峙 俄罗斯 意外	躺枪	！ 有 人 不安 好心 又 想 给 中

Fig. 10 Concordance lines of 躺枪

排位 . 3D touch 和 曲面屏 ， 哪 个 更 然并卵 ？ - 步行街 主干道 - 虎扑
的 ！ 售后 让 自己 双 清 ， 结果 还是 然并卵 ， 现 . . . 售后换 摄像头 ---
055 期 · 我 用 10 万 装 了 小 三 居 ： 然并卵 ，在 装修 这 条 路 上 ，真的
五 名 球员 全部 收缩 到 了 篮下 ， 然并卵 ！ 2 、 流畅 的 左手 运球 ，
双生 海妖 —— 科幻 战舰 为何 沦为 然并卵 的 鸡肋 ？ 多 体 船 是 代表
.. 双生 海妖 —— 科幻 战舰 为何 沦为 然并卵 的 鸡肋 ？ | 界面 新闻 ·
在 球场 内 发呆 。 当 我们 喊 着 努力 然并卵 时 ， 他们 却 让 努力 成为
USNews 套路 深 ， 想 留学 只 看 排名 然并卵 - 智课网 同学们 在 选校 的
，就 连 ... 3.15 国际 消费者 权益日 ， 然并卵 ... ... 不 信 你 看 ！ - 德国
自己 的 副 教授 ，不过 ，结果 好像 是 然并卵 。不 知道 张鸣 现在 还 有
是 可以 在 一 方面 直接 反映 学校 ... 然并卵 ： 本 以为 停牌 躲过 一 劫
ago - 于是 ， 一 路 跌 ， 一路撸 ， 然并卵 ， 最后 除了 几 个 翻白眼 的
呢 ？ 还 有 哪些 科技 ... 对 中国 然并卵 的 巴拿马 文件 | 博谈网 Apr

Fig. 11 Concordance lines of 然并卵

加拿大 华人 女生 泳池 自 拍 ， 拍 到 细思极恐 的 东西 ，奇闻 .... . 温哥华
小心 拍 到 了 细思 极 恐 的 东西 ... 细思极恐 —— 谁 最 害怕 " 加息 " ？
大学 毕业 以后 我 就 在 ...【 独家 】细思极恐！花都 的 儿女 快 问问 爸妈
宏观 外汇 " ， 授权 华尔街 见闻 发表 细思极恐 ！ 孔令辉 被 爆涉赌 竟 是
想起 ， 被 细细 体味 ， 脊背 发凉 ， 细思极恐 。西班牙 重 口味 漫画家 的
股 难以 形容 的 洪荒 之 力 。18 个 细思极恐 的 推理 小 故事 ： 看后
的 像 是 小学生 的 小孩子们 。几 个 细思极恐 的 故事 ， 看懂 的 瞬间 给
软件 的 ...《 人民 的 名义 》中 10 个 细思极恐 的 细节 你 注意 到 几 个 _
的 恐惧感 ... 多 玩 图库 提供 几 个 细思极恐 的 故事 ， 看懂 的 瞬间 给
的 画面 感和 深深 的 恐惧感 几 个 细思极恐 的 故事 ， 看懂 的 瞬间 给
。因为 这 次 大选 ， 从 开始 就 ... 细思极恐 ！ 我们 真正 的 麻烦 来 了
: . 两 台 智能 机器人 突然 摆脱 了 ... 细思极恐 ！ 男子 买 一 盒 避孕套
了 上海 房价 暴 涨 背后 的 逻辑 - 细思极恐 ！ 细思极恐 的 美国 大选 (

Fig. 12 Concordance lines of 细思极恐

meaning of "然并卵" is almost opaque. It is the short form of "然而并没有卵用" (but it is useless). The newly formed word is sometimes used simply as the short form of the original phrase and sometimes used as an adjective. When it is used as an adjective, it simply means "useless". What is of interest here is why it was put into a trisyllabic framework. This is the kind of question we can ask advanced CFL students to explore. Encouraging them to think about the sound patterns of Chinese words can open a new window for them to look back at the development process of the Chinese language in terms of word formation.

Figure 12 shows the concordance of "细思极恐" (xi4si1ji2kong3) or "细思恐极" (xi4si1kong3ji2), meaning "feel horrified at hindsight" or "feel horrified after thinking about it very carefully". This is a quadrisyllabic word created through abbreviation. It is often used to refer to an experience which may not appear to be dangerous until you start to think about it. It is the short form of "仔细想想, 觉得恐怖至极 or

仔细想想，觉得极度恐怖". It is more often used as an adjective, meaning "horrible". The meaning of the newly formed word is transparent because it can be easily understood. A question for the students is: why four words?

Students may find Task 4 very challenging, but that does not matter, because the main purpose of this task is to set them thinking about why neologisms also follow disyllabic, trisyllabic, and quadrisyllabic patterns in modern Chinese. To help students understand more about the sound patterns of Chinese words, the teacher can organize a lecture and explain the process of polysyllabification, using the information presented in the following section.

4.5 *The Sound Patterns of Chinese Words*

Abbreviations are often constrained by the inherent sound patterns of a particular language. The examples presented in the previous section have been chosen to illustrate a very important point about the Chinese language. Modern Chinese words can be typically put into four major categories in terms of the number of syllables each word contains: one syllable, two syllables, three syllables and four syllables. Ancient Chinese was dominated by monosyllabic words. Over the past 2500 years, Chinese has gone through a long process of polysyllabification. After the disyllabification process starting in the Eastern Han dynasty, many originally monosyllabic words were replaced by disyllabic ones. As a result, disyllabic words constitute the majority in the lexicon of Modern Mandarin (Dong 2012). As the basic patterns of Chinese lexicon are monosyllabic and disyllabic, a natural lexical generation approach would be to combine the two, which naturally generates two more new patterns: trisyllabic and quadrisyllabic words (Wu 1986).

The surge of trisyllabic words took place in Yuan Dynasty (A.D. 1271–1368) where Yuan Plays became very popular. This trend was further enhanced in Ming and Qing dynasties with the popularity of novels (Sheng 2015). The use of trisyllabic words in Yuan Plays may have to do with the phonological or prosodic requirements of the plays (Zhai 2006), but it does show that popularity of literary works may have contributed to the polysyllabification of the Chinese words. Yang (2014) investigated the trisyllabic words in the *Journey to the West* and identified 452 trisyllabic words. It may not be a coincidence to see the increase of incidences of trisyllabic words in very popular classic literary texts that were written in a colloquial style rather than the typical scholastic style that had been dominating ancient written Chinese. The influence of classics such as the "Three Character Classic" (Chau 2009; Zheng 2016) and Di Zi Gui (Students' Rules) (Li 1989) may have played an important role as well. Both texts were written in three-character sentences and easy to memorize and recite. Even now, these two texts are still very popular.

Chinese people's love for quadrisyllabic words may come from two major sources: one is the idioms which are typically of four characters and the other may be the "Thousand Character Classic" which was written in four-character sentences. The long-time popularity of these texts may have shaped our perceptions about word length, which in turn may have reinforced our preference for the syllabic patterns. If we can associate the syllabic patterns of neologisms from social media with the classic texts written in similar patterns, we will be offering advanced CFL learners an opportunity to better understand the Chinese language.

5 Conclusion

In this chapter, we have presented a brief analysis of some of the neologisms originated from the Chinese new media. By adopting a corpus-supported approach, we are able to show how those neologisms are used in authentic communication settings. The analysis of the word-formation strategies can help advanced CFL learners develop awareness of the linguistic features of the language. This analysis also provides an interface for advanced CFL learners to explore the social, linguistic and cultural factors that are at play in the formation of new Chinese words on social media. We have also attempted to illustrate how neologisms can be used in classroom teaching. Chinese neologisms on social media are just like the weeds in the garden of the Chinese lexicon. Some of them may be eventually accepted whereas the majority of them may wither and die, but their existence itself helps reveal the defining features of the Chinese language, the Chinese culture, the socio-economic development of China over the past two decades, and the linguistic creativity of Chinese netizens. All this should be an important part of teaching Chinese as a foreign language.

References

Aitchison, J. (2001). *Language change: Progress or decay?* (3rd ed.). Cambridge: Cambridge University Press.

Algeo, J. (1993). *Fifty years among the new words: A dictionary of neologisms 1941-1991*. Cambridge: Cambridge University Press.

Bai, D., & Zhang, L. (2008). Teaching neologisms to students of Chinese as a foreign language. *China Education Innovation Herald, 2008*(9), 140–141.

Burridge, K. (2004). *Blooming English: Observations on the roots, cultivation and hybrids of the English language*. Cambridge: Cambridge University Press.

Burridge, K. (2005). *Weeds in the garden of words: Further observations on the tangled history of the English language*. Cambridge: Cambridge University Press.

Byrnes, H. (2012). Advanced language proficiency. In S. M. Gass & A. Mackey (Eds.), *The Routledge handbook of second language acquisition* (pp. 506–521). London: Routledge.

Chang, P.-C., Tseng, H., & Andrew, G. (2008). *Stanford Chinese segmenter*. Stanford, CA: The Stanford Natural Language Processing Group.

Chau, Y.-W. (2009). An introduction to four English translations of "Three Character Classic" and imitative works by Western missionaries in late Qing Dynasty. *Library Tribune, 29*(2), 158, 177–178.

CINIC. (2017). *39th Statistical Report on Internet Development in China*. https://cnnic.com.cn/IDR/ReportDownloads/201706/P020170608523740585924.pdf. Accessed August 1, 2017.

Coulson, S., & Fauconnier, G. (1999). Fake guns and stone lions: Conceptual blending and privative adjectives. In B. Fox, D. Jurafsky, & L. Michaelis (Eds.), *Cognition and function in language* (pp. 143–158). Palo Alto, CA: Center for the Study of Language and Information.
Dong, X. (2012). Lexicalization in the history of the Chinese language. In J. Z. Xing (Ed.), *Newest trends in the study of grammaticalization and lexicalization in Chinese* (pp. 235–274). Berlin/Boston: De Gruyter.
ES-Computing. (2017). EditPlus Text Editor (Version 4.3). http://www.editplus.com. Accessed August 1, 2017.
Finn, E. (2017). Swearing: The good, the bad & the ugly. *ORTESOL (Oregon Teachers of English To Speakers of Other Languages) Journal, 34*, 17–26.
Ge, J. (2012). *Popular netspeak and teaching Chinese as a foreign language*. Unpublished Master's thesis. Guangzhou University, Guangzhou, China.
Hargraves, O. (2007). Taming the Wild Beast. *Dictionaries: Journal of the Dictionary Society of North America,* 28, 139–141.
Horan, G. (2013). 'You taught me language; and my profit on't/Is, I know how to curse': Cursing and swearing in foreign language learning. *Language and Intercultural Communication, 13*(3), 283–297.
Hou, M. (2015). Chinese neologisms of the year (2007–2008). In W. Li (Ed.), *The language situation in China* (Vol. 2, pp. 263–266). Boston/Beijing: De Gruyter Mouton & The Commercial Press.
Huang, C. (2011). *The teaching of new words and new meanings and teaching of Chinese as a foreign language*. Unpublished Master's thesis. Heilongjiang University, Harbin, China.
Kerremans, D. (2015). *A web of new words: A corpus-based study of the conventionalization process of English neologisms*. Bern: Peter Lang.
Li, Y. (1989). *Di Zi Gui (Students' Rules)* (X.-M. Feng Trans.).
Matthiessen, C. M. I. M. (2006). Educating for advanced foreign language capacities: Exploring the meaning-making resources of languages systemic-functionally. In H. Brynes (Ed.), *Advanced Language Learning: The Contributin of Halliday and Vygotsky* (pp. 31–57). New York, NY: Continuum.
Mercury, R.-E. (1995). Swearing: A "bad" part of language; a good part of language learning. *TESL Canada Journal, 13*(1), 28–36.
Ortega, L., & Byrnes, H. (2009). The longitudinal study of advanced L2 capacities: An introduction. In L. Ortega & H. Byrnes (Eds.), *The longitudinal study of advanced L2 capacities* (pp. 3–20). New York: Taylor & Francis.
Scott, M. (2015). WordSmith Tools (Version 6.0).
Sharifian, F., Dirven, R., Yu, N., & Niemeier, S. (2008). *Culture, body, and language: Conceptualizations of internal body organs across cultures and languages*. Berlin/New York: De Gruyter Mouton.
Shei, C. (2014). *Understanding the Chinese Language: A comprehensive linguistic introduction*. London/New York: Taylor & Francis.
Sheng, K. (2015). The historical evolution of Chinese multisyllable words. *Journal of Heilongjiang College of Education, 34*(4), 123–126.
Shenzhen Daily. (2015). Jiepan Xia. http://www.szdaily.com/content/2015-04/14/content_11452026.htm. Accessed August 1, 2017.
Thorne, S. L., & Reinhardt, J. (2008). "Bridging activities", new media literacies, and advanced foreign language proficiency. *CALICO Journal, 25*(3), 558–572.
Tong, Y. (2015). *A cognitive study of Chinese four-syllable netspeak neologisms from the perspective of conceptual blending theory*. Unpublished Master's thesis. Hunan Normal University, China.
Wu, W. (1986). A study on the formation of trisyllabic words in modern Chinese. *Chinese Learning, 5,* 1–2.
Xia, Q., & Hua, Y. (2007). Neologisms and teaching Chinese as a foreign language. *Language Teaching and Learning Research, 2007*(3), 102–103.
Yang, Y. (2014). *An investigation into the trisyllabic words in the Journey to the West*. Unpublished Master's thesis. Yangzhou University, China.

You, Y. (2012). *Characteristics of neologism and its cognitive motivations: A study of Chinese neologisms from 2006 to 2009*. Unpublished doctoral dissertation. Shanghai International Studies University, Shanghai, China.

Yu, N. (2008). The Chinese heart as the central faculty of cognition. In F. Sharifian, R. Dirven, N. Yu, & S. Niemeier (Eds.), *Culture, body, and language: Conceptualizations of internal body organs across cultures and languages* (pp. 131–168). Berlin/New York: Mouton de Gruyter.

Zhai, Y. (2006). On the surge of trisyllabic Chinese words with the patter of ABB in Yuan Dynasty. *Qilu Journal, 2006*(2), 85–87.

Zheng, Z. (2016). Two hundred years of translating the "Three Character Classic": From 1812 to 2015. *Forum on Chinese Culture, 2016*(10), 126–133.

Part IV
Learner Language Analysis and Assessment

Acquisition of the Chinese Particle *le* by L2 Learners: A Corpus-Based Approach

Hai Xu, Xiaofei Lu and Vaclav Brezina

Abstract The Chinese particle *le* (了) has proven to be challenging for L2 learners to acquire, both because it may function as either a perfective aspect marker or a sentence-final modal particle and because its usage is subject to various semantic, syntactic, prosodic, and discourse constraints. Previous research into the development of knowledge of the uses of *le* and the order of acquisition of its functions and meanings has yielded inconsistent results. Furthermore, due to the limited data available, previous studies have usually employed written corpus data produced by a small number of learners from a specific L1 background. Utilizing the spoken subcorpus of the large-scale Guangwai-Lancaster Chinese Learner Corpus, this study closely examines the uses of *le* by learners of Chinese from diverse L1 backgrounds as well as the developmental pattern of their acquisition of this particle. Results demonstrate that learners generally use *le* in speech with a low frequency and a high degree of accuracy. Significant increase in frequency of use is observed between beginner and intermediate learners, while that in accuracy is observed between intermediate and advanced learners. Evidence from the current study does not support a specific acquisition order for the basic functions of *le*. Learner errors primarily involve overuse of the particle in conjunction with statives and may be largely attributed to learners' deficient knowledge of the constraints of its usage. Findings of our investigation have useful implications for the instruction of the particle *le*.

H. Xu
Guangdong University of Foreign Studies, Guangzhou, China
e-mail: xuhai1101@gdufs.edu.cn

X. Lu (✉)
The Pennsylvania State University, University Park, USA
e-mail: xxl13@psu.edu

V. Brezina
Lancaster University, Lancaster, UK
e-mail: v.brezina@lancaster.ac.uk

X. Lu and B. Chen (eds.), *Computational and Corpus Approaches to Chinese Language Learning*, Chinese Language Learning Sciences,
https://doi.org/10.1007/978-981-13-3570-9_10

1 Introduction

The Chinese particle (PART) *le* (了), which is used frequently in both spoken and written production in Mandarin Chinese, is notoriously difficult for Chinese as a Second Language (CSL) learners to acquire. Generally, *le* has two main functions: as a perfective aspect marker and as a sentence-final modal particle (Chao 1968; Li and Thompson 1981; Lü 1999), as illustrated in the examples in (1) and (2), respectively. The former expresses perfectivity (PFV) of a bounded event, and the latter signals a "Currently Relevant State" (CRS) (Li and Thompson 1981: 240). The time schemata implied by *le* can be past, present or future (Li and Thompson 1981: 290). It has been found that CSL learners are prone to equate *le* with the past tense marker (Duff and Li 2002; Huang et al. 2000; Sun 1993; Wen 1995; Zhao 1997), which is absent in Chinese. The usage of *le* is further affected by such confounding factors as lexical aspect, syntactic structure, prosody, and the discourse in which it occurs (Ding 1990; Yang 2016; Yang et al. 1999).

(1)	我们	总共	去	看	了	四个	景点。
	Wǒmen	zǒnggòng	qù	kàn	le	sìgè	jǐngdiǎn.
	we	altogether	go	see	PART_PFV	four	scenic-spots

'We visited four scenic spots altogether.'

(2)	呃，	差不多	两年	了。
	È,	chàbùduō	liǎngnián	le.
	er	almost	two-years	PART_CRS

'Er, it's been almost two years.'

Previous studies have investigated whether CSL learners tend to overuse or underuse *le* and which basic function of *le* learners acquire first. While some studies find that CSL learners are likely to overuse *le* (Yang et al. 1999; Zhao 1997), others report that learners may underuse it (Chen 2010; Peng and Zhou 2015). Results pertaining to the acquisition order of the two basic functions of *le* are inconsistent in the literature. Sun (1993) and Teng (1999) argue that the acquisition of the sentence-final *le* precedes that of the perfective aspect marker, whereas Wen (1995), Chen (2010), and Wang and Peng (2013) claim that learners acquire the perfective *le* first.

A growing body of research has also examined how the acquisition of *le* is affected by variables such as proficiency level, lexical aspect, and syntactic structure. With respect to the effect of proficiency level, while some studies have reported significantly better performance by intermediate and/or advanced learners than by beginner learners (Chen 2010; Wen 1995), several other studies indicate that there is no significant difference in the accuracy of usage of *le* across different proficiency levels (Wen 1997; Yang et al. 1999).

Lexical aspect, also called situation aspect, refers to the "characteristics inherent in the lexical items which describe the situation" (Shirai and Andersen 1995: 744). Verbs (more precisely, verbal predicates) can be roughly categorized into four event types (Vendler 1967: 97–121): state [−dynamic, −telic, −punctual], activity [+dynamic, −telic, −punctual], accomplishment [+dynamic, +telic, −punctual], and achievement [+dynamic, +telic, +punctual]. As a perfective marker, *le* often encodes an event with an endpoint. It has been found that the accuracy of use of *le* by CSL learners is generally higher when it follows an accomplishment/achievement verb than when it co-occurs with some state and activity terms (Chen 2010; Duff and Li 2002; Huang et al. 2000; Sun 2000; Yang 2016). This finding appears to support one tenet of the Primacy of Aspect Hypothesis: "Learners will initially restrict past or perfective marking to achievement and accomplishment verbs (those with an inherent end point) and later gradually extend the marking to activities and then states, with states being the last category to be marked consistently" (Andersen and Shirai 1996: 559). However, Peng and Zhou (2015) reported that Vietnamese learners' error rate of *le* with accomplishment verbs is as high as that with state and activity verbs.

Several studies have discussed how the acquisition of *le* is conditioned by the syntactic structures it appears in, such as the negative structure, the serial verb structure, the duplicative verb structure, and the "verb + direct/indirect speech" structure, among others (Chen 2010; Ding 1990; Han 2003; Liu and Chen 2012; Yang et al. 2015). A few studies have shown that the use of *le* is subject to prosodic and discourse constraints as well (Huang et al. 2000; Yang et al. 2015; Yang 2016; Zhao 1997).

The inconsistencies in the results reported on various issues surrounding the use and acquisition of *le* clearly call for further research in this area. In addition, many previous studies are based on small and/or single-sourced datasets. Data produced by one or two participants (Sun 1993; Zhao 1997) or elicited from small groups with fewer than 10 subjects (Duff and Li 2002; Wen 1995 1997; Yang and Wu 2014) are more revealing of individual differences than general tendencies of acquisition. While the number of corpus-based studies on the acquisition of *le* (Liu and Ding 2015; Wang 2011; Yang 2016; Yang et al. 1999) is growing, such studies have so far largely relied on written corpus data. Given that *le* is used more often in spontaneous speech than in written production (Li and Thompson 1981: 290), an analysis of CFL learners' use of *le* in spontaneous spoken corpus data will likely offer additional insights into CFL learners' acquisition of this particle. Previous studies have also tended to focus on learners from singular L1 backgrounds, such as English-speaking learners (Ma 2006; Sun 1993; Wen 1995 1997; Yang et al. 1999), Korean learners (Han 2003; Wang 2015; Yang et al. 2015), Vietnamese learners (Chen 2011; Liu and Ding 2015; Peng and Zhou 2015), Thai learners (Chen 2004; Liu and Chen 2012) and Russian learners (Wang 2011), while learners from many other L1 backgrounds have been underrepresented. An analysis of balanced corpus data produced by learners with more diverse L1 backgrounds will help paint a more representative picture of CFL learners' acquisition of the particle *le*.

By exploiting the spoken part of a large-scale balanced Chinese interlanguage corpus, this study aims to address the following research questions:

(1) How frequently is *le* used in CSL learners' speech?
(2) Do CSL learners at three different proficiency levels find it difficult to use *le* in their oral production? Which basic function of *le* do learners across different proficiency levels have lower confidence in using: the perfective *le* or the sentence-final *le*?
(3) Are learners across different proficiency levels more likely to overuse, underuse, misform or misorder *le* when it functions as the perfective aspect marker and the sentence-final particle, respectively?
(4) What lexical aspects does *le* most commonly co-occur with when it is incorrectly used by CFL learners?
(5) What other sources of error exist for CFL learners' use of the particle *le*?

2 The Present Study

2.1 Corpus Data

The Guangwai-Lancaster Chinese Learner Corpus (GLCLC),[1] which our study is based on, represents a major new addition to corpora of L2 Chinese. GLCLC contains 1,294,714 words, balanced with both a written component (652,329 tokens, 50.38%) and a spoken component (642,385 tokens, 49.62%). Data in the corpus were produced by 1492 study-abroad Chinese learners from 107 countries at three proficiency levels,[2] covering a variety of task types and topics. The corpus contains rich metadata and is fully error tagged.

The spoken component of GLCLC (GLCLC_S) distinguishes the corpus from other Chinese interlanguage corpora. This component draws spoken data from L2 learners in four task types: (1) oral tests administered by a native Chinese instructor to 1–3 test-takers (379,839 tokens), (2) interviews conducted by a native Chinese speaker with individual advanced learners (119,982 tokens), (3) free talks (monologues) on the topic "My Hometown" or "A Memorable Trip" (81,630 tokens), and (4) tutorials given by a native speaker to individual learners (60,934 tokens). In contrast, the Monitor Corpus of HSK Essays,[3] which is widely used in Chinese interlanguage studies, contains solely written essays by HSK test-takers. Table 1 summarizes the

[1]GLCLC is a result of the collaboration between Guangdong University of Foreign Studies and Lancaster University under the British Academy Scheme (Grant No. 120462). It is freely accessible at: https://www.sketchengine.eu/guangwai-lancaster-chinese-learner-corpus/.

[2]Learners in this corpus are categorized as beginner, intermediate, and advanced learners based on their proficiency test (e.g., HSK) scores.

[3]HSK is short for *Hànyǔ Shuǐpíng Kǎoshì* (the Chinese Proficiency Test), an official test similar to TOEFL or IELTS in English. This corpus is freely accessible at: http://bcc.blcu.edu.cn/hsk.

Table 1 Distribution of GLCLC_S data across proficiency levels and tasks

	Oral tests	Interviews	Free talks	Tutorials	Total
Beginner	**116,470**	/	**3505**	**14,990**	134,965
Intermediate	**102,083**	/	**68,617**	**16,885**	187,585
Advanced	**35,250**	**69,892**	**8646**	**7374**	121,162
Total	253,803	69,892	80,768	39,249	443,712

distribution of GLCLC_S data across the three proficiency levels and four tasks.[4] As the spoken data in GLCLC_S are produced online, they can reveal learners' implicit grammatical knowledge that is not always detectable in written corpus data.

2.2 Method

We retrieved all the occurrences of *le* (了) from GLCLC_S[5] and saved them in three separate datasets according to the proficiency level of the learners who produced them. The Sketch Engine platform, which hosts the corpus, has performed word segmentation on the corpus automatically. Thus, occurrences of the Chinese character 了 as part of a word can be easily filtered, such as 好了 (*hǎole*, all right), 为了 (*wèile*, for the sake of), 不了 (*bùliǎo*, without end, unable to finish), 了解 (*liǎojiě*, understand), 了不得 (*liǎobùdé*, terrific), and 了不起 (*liǎobùqǐ*, amazing).

Instances of incorrect use of *le* in the datasets can be easily identified, as the data in GLCLC have been fully error tagged. Adopting the surface strategy taxonomy proposed by Dulay et al. (1982), GLCLC classifies errors into four broad types: (1) omission (i.e., underuse), (2) incorrect inclusion (i.e., overuse), (3) incorrect form (i.e., misformation), and (4) wrong order (i.e., misordering).[6] Instances that are irrelevant to the use of *le* were discarded manually. For example, in (4) and (5), the misformation error 发[7] and the misordering error 终于我们[8] are not related to the use of *le*.

[4]The data produced by L1 interlocutors were excluded.

[5]All the incidences of *le* produced by native Chinese speakers were excluded.

[6]Another type of error encoded in GLCLC involves incomplete or empty sentence meaning, as in (3). This type of error is excluded from the analysis as it has little to do with the use of *le*.

[7]It should be replaced by 发生 (*fāshēng*, happen).

(3) *我，呃，	学习	汉语，	因为	我	要，	呃，搬家	<了>。
Wǒ, è,	xuéxí	hànyǔ,	yīnwèi	wǒ	yào,	è, bānjiā	le.
I, er,	learn	Chinese,	for	I	will,	er, move	PART.

[8]The correct word order is 我们终于成功了 (*wǒmen zhōngyú chénggōngle*).

(4) *但是 那， 那 去 前 云南 发 <了> 那个
Dànshì nà, nà qù qián yúnnán fā < le > nàgè
but then then go before Yunnan happen PART that
地震……
dìzhèn…
earthquake
'But, well, before (we) travelled to Yunnan, an earthquake happened…'
[Korean advanced]

(5) *呃， 成功， 可是， 终于 我们 成功 <了>。
È, chénggōng, kěshì, zhōngyú women chénggōng < le >.
er succeed but finally we succeed PART
'Er, succeeded, but we finally succeeded.'
[French advanced]

The sentence-final *le* and the perfective *le* can be easily separated from each other according to their position in a sentence. The sentence-final *le* often precedes a punctuation mark, as illustrated in (2) above, or a sentence-final particle (SP), such as 吗 (ma), 吧 (ba), 啊 (a), 嘛 (ma), and 的 (de),[9] as illustrated in (7).

(7) 可能 习惯 了 吧。
Kěnéng xíguàn le ba.
maybe accustomed PART SP
'Maybe (I) get used to it.'
[Thai advanced]

For each instance of incorrect use of *le*, the lexical aspect of the verbal predicate was coded manually, as the same verb may have a different lexical aspect in different predicates. For example, though 跑 (*pǎo*, run) and 跑了十圈 (*pǎo le shí quān*, run 10 laps) have the same verb 跑 (*pǎo*), they were coded as activity and accomplishment, respectively. Finally, the bottom-up approach was taken to manually code the instances with respect to the semantic, syntactic, prosodic, or discourse constraints on the use of *le* as well.

---

[9] The Sketch Engine automatically extracted 83 instances of *le* + SP. The instance in (6) was excluded because it was clearly an instance of perfective *le*:

(6) 我 忘了 哪 [sic 那]， 哪个 [sic 那个] 名字。
Wǒ wangle nǎ, nǎge míngzì.
I forgot that, that name.

3 Results and Discussion

3.1 Frequency of Use of le Across Proficiency Levels

Table 2 shows that overall the particle *le* is not frequently used in learners' speech, with only 3958 hits out of 443,712 lexical units in GLCLC_S, or a normalized frequency of 8.92 per thousand words. This is in contrast to a normalized frequency of 18.11 and 14.94 per thousand words in the written component of GLCLC (GLCLC_W) and LCMC, respectively. Pairwise log-likelihood ratio tests reveal significant differences in the frequency of use of *le* between NNS speech and NNS writing (LL = 1648.42, $p < .05$), between NNS speech and NS writing (LL = 875.25, $p < .05$), and between NNS writing and NS writing (LL = 225.97, $p < .05$).

A Chi-square analysis indicates significant differences in the proportion of the particle *le* in learners' speech across the three proficiency levels ($\chi^2 = 36.445$, df = 2, $p < .05$). Pairwise Chi-square analyses further reveal significant differences between beginner and intermediate learners ($\chi^2 = 31.696$, df = 1, $p < .05$) and between beginner and advanced learners ($\chi^2 = 25.294$, df = 1, $p < .05$), but not between intermediate and advanced learners ($\chi^2 = .013$, df = 1, $p > .05$). In other words, *le* is used significantly more frequently by intermediate and advanced learners than by beginner learners (c.f. Chen 2010; Wen 1995).

Le has been claimed to be more prevalent in informal than in formal style (Li and Thompson 1981: 290), but why does it occur less frequently in learners' speech than in both learners' writing and native-speakers' writing? A likely reason for this imbalance of distribution could be that learners' writing resembled their speech in style but benefited from more production time than their speech. Due to the resource constraints in online production, learners may be more cautious about using lexical items that they are not certain of. This assumption is reinforced by the fact that beginner learners use *le* less frequently than the other two groups.

3.2 Accuracy of le Across Proficiency Levels

Table 3 summarizes the error rate of *le* across the three proficiency levels. On average, the error rate is 4.118%. A Chi-square analysis shows significant differences in the error rate of the particle *le* in learners' speech across the three proficiency levels

Table 2 Frequency of the particle *le* in GLCLC_S

	Beginner	Intermediate	Advanced	Total
Frequency of the particle *le*	1030	1782	1146	3958
Total tokens	134,965	187,585	121,162	443,712
Proportion of *le* (%)	.763	.950	.946	.892

Table 3 Error rates of *le* across the three proficiency levels of learners

	Beginner	Intermediate	Advanced	Total
Correct use of *le*	987	1677	1131	3795
Incorrect use of *le*	43	105	15	163
Total	1030	1782	1146	3958
Error rate (%)	4.175	5.892	1.309	4.118

Table 4 Error rates of *le* by function and by proficiency level

	Beginner	Intermediate	Advanced
Perfective le			
Number of errors	11	40	7
Total tokens	275	713	485
Error rate (%)	4.000	5.610	1.443
Sentence-final le			
Number of errors	32	65	8
Total tokens	755	1069	661
Error rate (%)	4.238	6.080	1.210
Log-likelihood ratio	.03	.16	.12

($\chi^2 = 37.117$, df = 2, $p < .05$). Advanced learners commit significantly fewer errors than both beginner ($\chi^2 = 17.173$, df = 1, $p < .05$) and intermediate learners ($\chi^2 = 37.278$, df = 1, $p < .05$), but the difference between beginner and intermediate learners is insignificant ($\chi^2 = 3.862$, df = 1, $p = .049$).

Table 4 summarizes the error rate of *le* by function (perfective vs. sentence-final) and by proficiency level. In general, there is no significant difference between the overall error rates for the two types of *le*, as confirmed by the results of both a Chi-square analysis ($\chi^2 = 2.970$, df = 2, $p > .05$) and log-likelihood ratio tests (see the last row in Table 4). However, significant differences in the error rate of the perfective *le* are found across the three proficiency levels ($\chi^2 = 13.253$, df = 2, $p < .05$). Pairwise Chi-square analyses further reveal significant differences between intermediate and advanced learners ($\chi^2 = 13.503$, df = 1, $p < .05$) and between beginner and advanced learners ($\chi^2 = 4.961$, df = 1, $p < .05$), but not between beginner and intermediate learners ($\chi^2 = 1.051$, df = 1, $p > .05$). Significant differences are also found in the error rate of the sentence-final *le* across the three proficiency levels ($\chi^2 = 23.939$, df = 2, $p < .05$). Advanced learners commit fewer errors of the sentence-final *le* than both beginner ($\chi^2 = 11.773$, df = 1, $p < .05$) and intermediate learners ($\chi^2 = 23.970$, df = 1, $p < .05$), but the difference between beginner and intermediate learners is insignificant ($\chi^2 = 2.982$, df = 1, $p > .05$).

The results on the accuracy of use of *le* in its different functions suggest a general pattern of acquisition by learners at different proficiency levels. While advanced learners demonstrate superior grammatical and pragmatic knowledge of *le* than both intermediate and beginner learners, intermediate learners do not yet show superior knowledge than beginner learners. One possible reason is that intermediate learners have reached the so-called plateau stage (Teng 1999: 58). They need more exposure to the correct usage of *le* before they can skillfully use it.

There is a discrepancy between the error rates of *le* observed in this study and the ones reported in the literature. While the highest error rate observed in this study is 6.08% (sentence-final *le*, intermediate learners), the error rates reported in previous studies range from 6.8% for the sentence-final *le* by Thai intermediate learners (Liu and Chen 2012) to 47.2% for the perfective *le* by Vietnamese beginner learners (Peng and Zhou 2015). The differences may be partially attributed to the size and register of the data, as previous studies have often used small-sized, written or elicited data, which do not represent learners' use of *le* in spontaneous speech.

Concerning the acquisition order of the perfective *le* and sentence-final *le*, our findings are incongruent with those reported by previous studies (Chen 2010; Sun 1993; Teng 1999; Wang and Peng 2013; Wen 1995). As discussed above, no significant difference is found between the error rates of the two types of *le* for any of the three proficiency levels. Our data, therefore, do not directly support any particular acquisition order for the two functions of the particle *le*.

3.3 *Types of Incorrect Use of le*

Table 5 summarizes the frequency and proportion of different types of errors of use of the perfective and the sentence-final *le*. Notably, no instance of underuse of *le* is found in GLCLC_S. Across all proficiency levels, the predominant error type is the overuse of *le* for both functions of the particle. Meanwhile, misordering appears to be more likely with the sentence-final *le* than with the perfective *le* (log-likelihood ratio = 4.24, $p < .05$).

We ran a series of Chi-square tests to examine the relationship between proficiency level and error type. In general, when the two functions of *le* are considered together, no significant difference is found in the distribution of error types across the three proficiency levels ($\chi^2 = 8.673$, df = 1, $p > .05$). For the perfective *le*, significant differences are found only in the rates of misformation between beginner and advanced learners ($\chi^2 = 5.657$, df = 1, $p < .05$) and between intermediate and advanced learners ($\chi^2 = 3.887$, df = 1, $p < .05$). For the sentence-final *le*, significant differences are only found in the rates of misformation between beginner and intermediate learners ($\chi^2 = 6.961$, df = 1, $p < .05$).

The results of this study corroborate the claim that CSL learners tend to overuse *le* (Yang et al. 1999; Zhao 1997). Without full command of the semantic, syntactic and other constraints on the use of *le*, learners are prone to use the particle improperly, as illustrated by (8) and (9).

Table 5 Types of incorrect use of *le*

	Beginner	Intermediate	Advanced	Total
Perfective le				
Overuse	10 (90.909%)[a]	33 (82.500%)	4 (57.143%)	47 (81.034%)
Underuse	0	0	0	0
Misformation	0	5 (12.500%)	3 (42.857%)	8 (13.793%)
Misordering	1 (9.091%)	2 (5.000%)	0	3 (5.172%)
Total errors	11	40	7	58
Total tokens	275	713	485	1473
Sentence-final le				
Overuse	23 (71.875%)	49 (75.385%)	7 (87.500%)	79 (75.238%)
Underuse	0	0	0	0
Misformation	6 (18.750%)	2 (3.077%)	1 (12.500%)	9 (8.571%)
Misordering	3 (9.375%)	14 (21.538%)	0	17 (16.190%)
Total errors	32	65	8	105
Total tokens	755	1069	661	2485

[a]The percentage indicates the proportion of a specific type of error at a certain proficiency level

(8)

*他	常	玩	〈了〉	四	个	小时	的	游，	游戏。
Tā	cháng	wán	le	sì	gè	xiǎoshí	de	yóu,	yóuxì.
he	often	play	PART	four	MEASURE	hours	of	ga-	game

'He often plays four hours' games.'

[Vietnamese beginner]

(9)

*然后	一	出去	〈了〉，	就	下雨	了。
Ránhòu	yī	chūqù	le,	jiù	xiàyǔ	le.
then	as-soon-as	go out	PART	immediately	rain	PART

'Then as soon as (you) go out, it starts raining.'

[Russian advanced]

The absence of instances of underuse of *le* deserves further research. Peng and Zhou (2015) argue that Vietnamese learners are more likely to underuse *le* than overuse it because tense-aspect markers are not obligatory in Vietnamese. Our results do not seem to support this claim, as no instance of underuse is found in the speech samples produced by Vietnamese learners in GLCLC_S (16,883 tokens in total; 151 tokens of *le*).

Another major error type of the sentence-final *le* is misordering, which is often found in intermediate learners' speech, as illustrated in (10). In this discourse context, it is more acceptable to place *le* immediately after the verb 到 (*dào*, arrive). Discourse constraints constitute a stumbling block to the acquisition of the sentence-final *le*. As advanced learners gain more awareness of such discourse constraints, their use of sentence-final *le* becomes free from misordering errors, as shown in Table 5.

(10)	*然后	我们	到	深圳	〈了〉，	然后	我们	不
	Ránhòu	women	dào	shēnzhèn	le,	ránhòu	women	bù
	Then	we	arrived	Shenzhen	PART	then	we	don't
	知道	做	什么。					
	zhīdào	zuò	shénme.					
	know	do	what					

'Then we arrived at Shenzhen, and we didn't know what to do.'

[Tajik intermediate]

Errors of misformation, while relatively rare in learners' oral production, tend to arise from learners' deficient knowledge of the semantic constraints. Consider (11), (12) and (13). In (11), the correct form should be 好吃极了 (*hǎo chī jí le*, extremely yummy), as *le* generally does not follow a stative predicate unless a morpheme such as 极 (*jí*, extremely) is used to indicate an extreme state. In the same vein, in (12), 发展成 (*fāzhǎn chéng*, develop into) instead of 发展 (*fāzhǎn*, develop) should be used to denote a bounded event. By contrast, in order to denote a state rather than a bounded event, the particle 的 (*de*, DEG) should replace *le* in (13).

(11)	*好	吃	〈了〉，	好	极	了。
	Hǎo	chī	le,	hǎo	jí	le.
	good	eating	PART,	good	extremely	PART

'Yummy, superb.'

[Spanish beginner]

(12)	*呃，	以前	是	一	个	农村，	但是	很
	È,	yǐqián	shì	yī	gè	nóngcūn,	dànshì	hěn
	er	formally	is	one	MEASURE	village	but	very
	快	发展	〈了〉	一	个	大	城市。	
	kuài	fāzhǎn	le	yī	gè	dà	chéngshì	
	quickly	develop	PART	a	MEASURE	big	city	

'Er, it had been a village, but soon it developed into a metropolis.'

[Korean intermediate]

(13) *呃，　呃，　我　第一　次　来　中国　的
È,　è,　wǒ　dìyī　cì　lái　zhōngguó　de
er　er　I　first-time　MEASURE　come　China　DEG
时候，　跟　我　的　爸爸　来　〈了〉。
shíhòu,　gēn　wǒ　de　bàba　lái　le
when　with　my　DEG　father　come　PART
'Er, er, when I visited China for the first time, I came with my father.'
[Russian intermediate]

3.4 Lexical Aspects in Relation to the Errors of *le*

When *le* is incorrectly used in GLCLC_S, what lexical aspects does it often co-occur with? Table 6 presents the proportions of different lexical aspects of the verbal predicates in relation to incorrect uses of *le*. Beginner learners have difficulties mostly with the lexical aspects of states and activities, intermediate learners with achievements and states, and advanced learners with states. However, a Chi-square analysis finds insignificant differences in the overall distribution of different lexical aspects associated with incorrect uses of *le* across the proficiency levels ($\chi^2 = 12.480$, df = 6, $p > .05$).

A series of pairwise Chi-square tests were run to examine whether learners of different proficiency levels differ significantly in their incorrect uses associated with each lexical aspect. For the aspect of states, significant differences exist between intermediate and advanced learners ($\chi^2 = 6.222$, df = 1, $p < .05$). For the aspect of activities, significant differences are found between beginner and advanced learners ($\chi^2 = 5.845$, df = 1, $p < .05$). No cross-proficiency variation exists for the aspect of accomplishments. For the aspect of achievements, intermediate learners are found to commit a higher proportion of errors of *le* than beginner learners ($\chi^2 = 4.912$, df = 1, $p < .05$).

Table 6 Lexical aspects in relation to the incorrect use of *le*

	Beginner	Intermediate	Advanced	Total
States	19 (44.186%)[a]	35 (33.333%)	10 (66.667%)	64 (39.264%)
Activities	13 (30.233%)	22 (20.952%)	0	35 (21.472%)
Accomplishments	2 (4.651%)	6 (5.714%)	1 (6.667%)	9 (5.521%)
Achievements	9 (20.930%)	42 (40.000%)	4 (26.667%)	55 (33.742%)
Total	43	105	15	163

[a]The percentage indicates the proportion of a specific type of lexical aspect at a certain proficiency level

The results are largely compatible with the Primacy of Aspect Hypothesis, according to which learners will initially limit perfective marking to achievements and accomplishments, and finally to states (Andersen and Shirai 1996; Shirai and Andersen 1995). That explains why in this study there are a larger number of errors of *le* with states than with other aspects. One of the rules governing the usage of *le* is that it generally does not follow a stative predicate unless it indicates a quantified, definite or specific event (Li and Thompson 1981: 185–195). Beginner learners who are clearly confused about this rule use *le* after such statives as 漂亮 (*piàoliang*, beautiful), 舒服 (*shūfú*, comfortable), 喜欢 (*xǐhuān*, like), 明白 (*míngbái*, understand), 想 (*xiǎng*, cherish the memory), 住 (*zhù*, live), 工作 (*gōngzuò*, work), 不可以 (*bù kěyǐ*, cannot) and 不知道 (*bù zhīdào*, don't know). The error rate with statives decreases slightly with intermediate learners. While advanced learners commit fewer errors overall, the largest proportion of errors they commit are still associated with statives. Consider the examples in (14) and (15). Apparently, some advanced learners "relied on local contextual cues" (Wen 1995: 57), such as 已经 (*yǐjīng*, already) and a past reference time 二零一三年四月的时候 (in April 2013), to decide on the marking of statives with *le*, but ignored the stative aspect of the sentences, conditioned by 都 (*dōu*, have been) and 在 (*zài*, progressive aspect marker), respectively. Hence, to reduce their errors, advanced learners need to develop a global meaning-based learning strategy (Wen 1995, 1997).

(14)	*差不多，	十八	岁，	我	都	已经	讨厌	〈了〉	下雪。
	Chàbùduō	shíbā	suì	wǒ	dōu	yǐjīng	tǎoyàn	le	xiàxuě.
	Almost	18	age	I	even	already	hate	PART	snow

'I was almost 18 years old, and I already hated snow.'

[Russian advanced]

(15)	*呃，	我	二零一三年	四月	的	时候，	在
	È,	wǒ	èrlíngyīsānnián	sìyuè	de	shíhòu,	zài
	er	I	2013	April	DEG	when,	PROGRESSIVE
	北京		留学，	留学		〈了〉。	
	běijīng		liúxué,	liúxué		le.	
	Beijing		study-abroad	study-abroad		PART	

'Er, in April 2013, I was studying abroad in Beijing.'

[Korean advanced]

Another notable observation is that the highest proportion of errors made by intermediate learners are in relation to achievements. A close scrutiny of the data reveals that some intermediate learners have not acquired the semantic, syntactic, prosodic and discourse constraints on the co-occurrence of *le* with achievements. In (16), (17) and (18), the incorrect use of *le* is attributed to semantic constraints. Although 去麦当劳 (*qù màidāngláo*, go to McDonald's), 出国 (*chūguó*, go abroad) and 搬出去 (*bān chūqù*, move out) are all achievement predicates, the time adverbs 经常 (*jīngcháng*, often) and 第一次 (*dì yī cì*, for the first time) as well as the modal 要 (*yào*, want) change the whole sentences from achievements into states.

(16) *我们 经常 去 〈了〉 麦当劳…
Wǒmen jīngcháng qù le màidāngláo…
We often go PART McDonald's
'We often went to McDonald's.'
[Angolan intermediate]

(17) *我 第一 次 出 〈了〉 国。
Wǒ dìyī cì chū le guó.
I first-time MEASURE go PART abroad
'I went abroad for the first time.'
[Kazakh intermediate]

(18) *我, 我 要 搬出去 〈了〉, 因为 学校 里 不安静…
Wǒ, wǒ yào bānchū qù le, yīnwéi xuéxiào lǐ bùānjìng…
I, I want move-out PART because campus in not-quiet
'I, I wanted to move out, because (the dorm) on campus is not quiet.'
[Malian intermediate]

The co-occurrence of *le* with achievements is also conditioned by syntax. The negative structure (i.e., 考不上 *kǎo bù shàng*, fail to be admitted to) in (19), the attributive clause (上次去澳门的旅行 *shàngcì qù àomén de lǚxíng*, the trip to Macau last time) in (20), the imperative (该… *gāi*…, it's time to…) in (21), and the serial verb structure (放弃学习 *fàngqì xuéxi*, abandon studying) in (22) all disallow the use of *le* with achievements.

(19) *他 本来 学习 也 不 太 好, 所以 就
Tā běnlái xuéxí yě bù tài hǎo, suǒyǐ jiù
he originally study too not very good so then
考不上 〈了〉 大学。
kǎobùshàng le dàxué.
test-not-pass PART college
'He also didn't do well in his studies, so was unable to be admitted to col-lege.'
[Thai intermediate]

(20) *我 最 难忘 的 旅行 是 上次 去 〈了〉
Wǒ zuì nánwàng de lǚxíng shì shàngcì qù le
My most unforgettable DEG trip be last-time go
PART
澳门 的 旅游…
àomén de lǚyóu…
Macau DEG trip
'My most unforgettable trip is my visit to Macau last time…'
[Korean intermediate]

(21) *该 忘记 〈了〉 习惯 的 生活。
Gāi wàngjì le xíguàn de shēnghuó.
It's-time forget PART accustomed DEG life
'It's time to forget the life (I) was used to.'
[Madagascan intermediate]

(22) *他 就 放弃 〈了〉 学习， 下定 决心 开始 做 了
Tā jiù fàngqì le xuéxí, xiàdìng juéxīn kāishǐ zuò le
he so abandon PART study make decision start do
PART
生意。
shēngyì.
business
'So he abandoned his study, and determined to start doing business.'
[Thai intermediate]

Prosody and discourse are two additional factors that may condition the co-occurrence of *le* with achievements. In (23), 进去 (*jìnqù*, go inside) and 进 (*jìn*, enter) share almost identical meanings, but *le* could only be used with a monosyllabic achievement verb (e.g., 进 *jìn*) instead of a disyllabic achievement verb (e.g., 进去 *jìnqù*) (Huang et al. 2000; Yang 2016). The example in (10) is a case in point for discourse constraints.

(23) *我， 进去 〈了〉 宿舍， 宿舍 我 不 喜欢…
Wǒ, jìnqù le sùshè, sùshè wǒ bù xǐhuān…
I enter PART dorm dorm I not like
'I went inside the dorm, which I disliked.'
[Kazakh intermediate]

3.5 Other Sources of Errors of *le*

Errors of *le* can arise from semantic, syntactic, prosodic and discourse factors. Table 7 summarizes the number of errors of *le* due to such factors. Notably, these factors account for over 60% of the errors of *le* (66/105) made by intermediate learners and over 20% of the errors made by beginner learners (12/43) and advanced learners (3/15). However, there are generally no significant differences in the distribution of these error source categories across the three proficiency levels ($\chi^2 = 12.569$, df = 12, $p > .05$). The only significant differences found were between beginner and advanced learners ($\chi^2 = 4.286$, df = 1, $p < .05$) and between intermediate and advanced learners ($\chi^2 = 4.355$, df = 1, $p < .05$) in the word class category (under syntax).

In the previous section, we discussed the interaction between lexical aspects and some of the semantic, syntactic, prosodic and discourse factors regarding incorrect uses of *le*. Table 7 further demonstrates that syntactic errors are the most prominent ones at all three proficiency levels. In addition to the attributive clause and the

Table 7 Semantic, syntactic, prosodic and discourse factors in relation to the errors of *le*

	Beginner	Intermediate	Advanced	Total
Semantics				
Time adverbs	3	7	0	10
Modals	3	16	0	19
Syntax				
Syntactic structures	3	19	2	24
Separable words	0	5	0	5
Word class	0	3	1	4
Prosody	1	2	0	3
Discourse	2	14	0	16
Subtotal	12	66	3	81
Total errors of *le*	43	105	15	163

imperative, some other errors in relation to syntactic structures include 是… (*shì*…, *be* structure), as illustrated in (24), …时候 (…*shíhòu*, *when* clause), as illustrated in (25), and 一…就… (*yī… jiù*…, *as soon as* clause), as illustrated in (9) above.

(24) *呃， 我 的 爱好 是 踢球 〈了〉。
È, wǒ de àihào shì tīqiú le.
er, my DEG hobby is kick-ball PART
'Er, my hobby is playing football.'

[Angolan beginner]

(25) *呃， 我， 他 来 <了> 上课 的 时候…
È, wǒ, tā lái le shàngkè de shíhòu…
er I he come PART classes DEG when
'Er, when I, he comes to classes…'

[Uzbek beginner]

The correct use of *le* is also undermined by separable words and word classes. As an "ionized form" (Chao 1968), it would sound more natural to insert *le* in between the two morphemes of a *liheci* (separable word) than to place *le* after the word, as in 逛(了)街 (*guàng (le) jiē,* go shopping), 聊(了)天 (*liáo (le) tiān*, have a chat), 散(了)步 (*sàn (le) bù*, take a walk) and 结(了)婚 (*jié (le) hūn*, get married). A typical case is (26), in which it is more acceptable to say 聊了很多天 (l*iáo le hěnduō tiān*, chat a lot).

(26)	*我们	在	那里	聊 了，	聊天	〈了〉	很多。
	Wǒmen	zài	nàlǐ	liáo le,	liáotiān	le	hěnduō.
	we	at	there	chat PART	chat	PART	much

'We chatted, chatted a lot there.'

[Korean intermediate]

Le is generally used to modify a verb or adjective predicate, but as Table 7 indicates, some intermediate and advanced learners mistakenly added *le* after an adverb (更加 *gèngjiā*, more), a preposition (对*duì*, towards), a conjunction (和*hé*, and), or an interrogative pronoun (什么*shénme*, what). Such errors may be a slip of tongue, as in (27),[10] but they may also be due to learners' inadequate knowledge of the word class that *le* can modify, as illustrated in (28).[11]

(27)	*那个	困难，	呃，	更加	〈了〉。
	Nàgè	kùnnán,	è,	gèngjiā	le.
	that	difficulty	er	more	

'That becomes more difficult.'

[Korean advanced]

(28)	*什，	什么	〈了〉?
	Shén,	shénme	le?
	wh-,	what	PART

'Wh-, what?'

[Thai intermediate]

4 Conclusion

This paper exhaustively analyzed the frequency and accuracy of the particle *le* in CSL learners' spoken production in GLCLC_S as well as the factors that affect their misuses of the particle. CSL learners use *le* much less frequently in their speech than in both their own writing and native-speakers' writing. Beginner learners use *le* less frequently than both intermediate and advanced learners, while the latter two groups use it with comparable frequency. The error rates of *le* in this study are much lower than those reported in previous studies. Advanced learners use *le* more accurately than both intermediate and beginner learners, while the latter two groups demonstrate comparable error rates. These results indicate that as learners reach the intermediate level, they are more willing to use the particle *le*, but it is not until after they reach the advanced level when their competence in using it correctly improves. Our results do not provide evidence in favor of any particular acquisition order of the perfective and the sentence-final *le*. The predominant type of errors committed by CSL learners is overuse of *le*, and no instance of underuse is found. As the Primacy of Aspect

[10] 更加大了 (*gèngjiā dà le*, much bigger) may have be intended here, with 大 (*dà*, big) missing.

[11] As a reviewer points out, an additional explanation for this error may be its aural similarity to the common expression 怎么了(*zěnmele*, what's wrong).

Hypothesis predicts, learners are more likely to use *le* incorrectly with statives than with other aspects. A large proportion of learner errors can be attributed to their deficient knowledge of the semantic, syntactic, prosodic and discourse constraints on the usage of *le*.

This study yields some inconsistent results with previous studies, including, for example, the lower incidence and higher accuracy of *le* in learners' speech, the indeterminate order of acquisition of the two basic functions of *le*, the absence of instances of underuse of *le*, misordering errors conditioned by discourse, and the undermining effects of separable words and word classes. These inconsistencies may have arisen from the difference in the size and register of the data that the studies are based on, and point to the need for additional research using large-scale, good-quality corpus data to further confirm our findings.

Our results suggest that in order to help CSL learners successfully acquire the particle *le*, it is important to not only help them understand the basic functions of the particle, but also its relationship to lexical aspects as well as the semantic, syntactic, prosodic, and discourse constraints on its usage. Certain types of errors, such as those associated with "**shì…le*" (be…) and "**yi…le, jiu…*" (as soon as…) structures, persist even in advanced learners' production. To entrench the correct usage of *le*, explicit instruction alone may not be sufficient, and learners need more exposure to different functions and uses of the particle and more opportunities to practice using it in diverse contexts.

Acknowledgements This study was supported by the National Social Science Fund of China (Grant No. 15BYY062), by the MOE Project of Key Research Institute of Humanities and Social Sciences at Universities in P. R. China (Project No. 17JJD740004), and by the Centre for Linguistics and Applied Linguistics, Guangdong University of Foreign Studies.

References

Andersen, R. W., & Shirai, Y. (1996). The primacy of aspect in first and second language acquisition: The pidgin-creole connection. In W. C. Ritchie & T. K. Bhatia (Eds.), *Handbook of second language acquisition* (pp. 527–570). San Diego: Academic Press.

Chao, Y. (1968). *A grammar of spoken Chinese*. Berkeley: University of California Press.

Chen, C. (2004). Taiguo Xuesheng Xuexi Xiandai Hanyu Xuci "le" de Tantao (Discussions on problems encountered by Thai students in learning "le": A structural word in modern Chinese). *Nanjing Shifan Daxue Wenxueyuan Xuebao (Journal of School of Chinese Language and Culture Nanjing Normal Universtiy), 2*, 173–175.

Chen, C. (2010). *Liuxuesheng Hanyu Ti Biaoji Xide de Shizheng Yanjiu (An Empirical study on overseas Students' acquisition of Chinese aspect marker "le")*. Unpublished Ph.D. Thesis, Minzu University of China, Beijing.

Chen, C. (2011). Yuenan Liuxuesheng Hanyu "Le" Xide Tedian ji Yuji Qianyi Xianxiang Yanjiu (Acquisition of the Chinese "Le" by overseas Vietnamese students and cross-language transfer phenomenon). *Guoji Hanyu Xuebao (Journal of International Chinese Studies), 2*(2), 35–45.

Ding, G. (1990). Guangyu Waiguo Ren Xuexi Hanyu Zhuci "le" de Jige Wenti (Several issues on the acquisition of Chinese Particle "le" by L2 Chinese Learners). *Hunan Shifan Daxue Shehui Kexue Xuebao (Journal of Social Science of Hunan Normal University), 19*(2), 99–103.

Duff, P., & Li, D. (2002). The acquisition and use of perfective aspect in Mandarin. In R. Salaberry & Y. Shirai (Eds.), *The L2 acquisition of tense—Aspect morphology* (pp. 417–454). Amsterdam/Philadelphia: John Benjamins.

Dulay, H., Burt, M., & Krashen, S. (1982). *Language two*. Oxford: Oxford University Press.

Han, Z.-J. (2003). Hanguo Xuesheng Xuexi Hanyu "le" de Changjian Pianwu Fenxi (Error analysis in learning Chinese "le" for Korean students). *Hanyu Xuexi (Chinese Language Learning), 4,* 67–71.

Huang, Y., Yang, S., & Cao, X. (2000). Hanyu Ti Biaoji Xide Guocheng Zhong de Biaoji Buzu Xianxiang (Underuse of aspect markers in acquisition of Chinese). *Journal of the Chinese Language Teachers Association, 35*(3), 87–115.

Li, C. N., & Thompson, S. A. (1981). *Mandarin Chinese: A functional reference Grammar*. Berkeley: University of California Press.

Liu, M., & Chen, C. (2012). Taiguo Liuxuesheng Hanyu "Le" de Xide Kaocha-Jiyu HSK Dongtai Yuliaoku de Yanjiu (The acquisition of Le-sentence by the Thailand students-based on the HSK dynamic corpus). *Haiwai Huawen Jiaoyu (Overseas Chinese Education), 3,* 302–310.

Liu, H., & Ding, C. (2015). Hanyu "Le" zai Yuenanyu Zhong de Duiying Xingshi ji Muyu Huanjing Xia Yuenan Chuji Hanyu Xuexizhe "Le" de Xide (The corresponding forms of Le in Vietnamese and the acquisition of elementary learners in native language environment). *Yuyan Jiaoxue Yu Yanjiu (Language Teaching and Linguistic Studies), 4,* 25–32.

Lü, S. (1999). *Xiandai Hanyu Babai Ci (Zengding Ben) (800 words in Modern Chinese (Revised Version))*. Beijing: Commercial Press.

Ma, L. (2006). *Acquisition of the perfective aspect marker le of Mandarin Chinese in discourse by American college learners.* University of Iowa.

Peng, Z., & Zhou, X. (2015). Yuenan Liuxuesheng Hanyu Ti Biaoji "le1" Xide Yanjiu-Jiyu Qingzhuang Leixing de Kaocha (The acquisition of the marker of aspect in Chinese le among Vietnamese students-based on the type of lexical aspect). *Guanxi Minzu Daxue Xuebao (Journal of Guangxi University for Nationalities), 37*(1), 168–172.

Shirai, Y., & Andersen, R. W. (1995). The acquisition of tense-aspect morphology: A prototype account. *Language, 71*(4), 743–762.

Sun, D. (1993). Waiguo Xuesheng Xiandai Hanyu "le" de Xide Guocheng Chubu Fenxi (Initial analysis of the acquisition process of Le by L2 Chinese students). *Yuyan Jiaoxue Yu Yanjiu (Language Teaching and Linguistic Studies), 2,* 65–75.

Sun, D. (2000). Waiguo Xuesheng Hanyu Ti Biaoji "le", "zhe", "guo" Xide Qingkuan de Kaocha (Acquisition of Chinese aspect markers "le", "zhe" and "guo" by foreign students). *Hanyu Xuebao (Chinese Linguistics), 2,* 232–243.

Teng, S.-H. (1999). The Acquisition of "了le" in L2 Chinese. *shijie Hanyu Jiaoxue (Chinese Teaching in the World)*, (1), 56–63.

Vendler, Z. (1967). *Philosophy in linguistics*. Ithaca/London: Cornell University Press.

Wang, H. (2011). Eluosi Liuxuesheng Shiyong "le" de Pianwu Fenxi (An error analysis on "Le" used by Russian students). *Hanyu Xuexi (Chinese Language Learning), 3,* 99–104.

Wang, Y. (2015). Hanguo Liuxuesheng de "Le" de Pianwu Diaocha Fenxi (An analysis on errors of "Le 了" by students from Korea). *Haiwai Huawen Jiaoyu (Overseas Chinese Education), 3,* 344–350.

Wang, Q., & Peng, J. (2013). Yingyu Wei Muyu Liuhua Xuesheng "Le1" he "Le2" de Xide Shunxu Yanjiu (On the different acquisition order of "Le (了$_1$)" and "Le (了$_2$)" for overseas students with English as mother language). *Journal of Hefei University, 30*(6), 89–93.

Wen, X. (1995). Second language acquisition of the Chinese particle Le. *International Journal of Applied Linguistics, 5*(1), 45–62.

Wen, X. (1997). Acquisition of Chinese aspect: An analysis of the interlanguage of learners of chinese as a foreign language. *ITL-International Journal of Applied Linguistics, 117*(1), 1–26.

Yang, S. (2016). "Ti Jiashe" ji le and zhe de Eryu Xide ("Aspect Hypothesis" and L2 acquisition of the aspect marking in Chinese *-le* and *-zhe*). *Shijie Hanyu Jiaoxue (Chinese Teaching in the World), 30*(1), 101–118.

Yang, B., & Wu, Q. (2014). Acquiring the perfective aspect marker *Le* in different learning contexts. In N. Jiang (Ed.), *Advances in Chinese as a second language: Acquisition and processing* (pp. 10–32). Newcastle: Cambridge Scholars Publishing.

Yang, S., Huang, Y., & Sun, D. (1999). Hanyu Zuowei Dier Yuyan de Ti Biaoji Xide (On the L2 acquisition of the Chinese aspect markers). *Journal of the Chinese Language Teachers Association, 34*(1), 31–54.

Yang, D., Gong, Y., & Yao, J. (2015). Hanguo Xuesheng Dongtai Zhuci "Le" de Pianwu Fazhan ji Chansheng Yuanyin Fenxi (On the development of the errors of "le" of South Korean students and analysis of the reasons for errors arising). *Haiwai Huawen Jiaoyu (Overseas Chinese Education), 4,* 501–510.

Zhao, L. (1997). Liuxuesheng "le" de Xide Guocheng Kaocha yu Fenxi (Investigation into and analysis of the acquisition process of "le" by CSL learners. *Yuyan Jiaoxue yu Yanjiu (Language Teaching and Linguistic Studies), 2,* 112–124.

Mandarin Chinese Mispronunciation Detection and Diagnosis Leveraging Deep Neural Network Based Acoustic Modeling and Training Techniques

Berlin Chen and Yao-Chi Hsu

Abstract Automatic mispronunciation detection and diagnosis are two critical and integral components of a computer-assisted pronunciation training (CAPT) system, collectively facilitating second-language (L2) learners to pinpoint erroneous pronunciations in a given utterance so as to improve their spoken proficiency. In this chapter, we will first briefly introduce the latest trends and developments in mispronunciation detection and diagnosis with state-of-the-art automatic speech recognition (ASR) methodologies, especially those using deep neural network based acoustic models. Afterward, we present an effective training approach that estimates the deep neural network based acoustic models involved in the mispronunciation detection process by optimizing an objective directly linked to the ultimate performance evaluation metric. We also investigate the extent to which the subsequent mispronunciation diagnosis process can benefit from the use of these specifically trained acoustic models. For this purpose, we recast mispronunciation diagnosis as a classification problem and a set of indicative features are derived. A series of experiments on a Mandarin Chinese mispronunciation detection and diagnosis task are conducted to evaluate the performance merits of such an approach.

1 Introduction

The acceleration of globalization has been calling for the demand of foreign language proficiency. In face of the shortage of professional teachers for foreign language learners, computer-assisted pronunciation training (CAPT) is emerging as an attractive surrogate or supplement to the instructions of human teachers. CAPT, in general, manages to pinpoint and diagnose erroneous pronunciations in the utter-

B. Chen (✉)
National Taiwan Normal University, Taipei, Taiwan
e-mail: berlin@ntnu.edu.tw

Y.-C. Hsu
Delta Research Center, Taipei, Taiwan
e-mail: joe.yc.hsu@deltaww.com

X. Lu and B. Chen (eds.), *Computational and Corpus Approaches to Chinese Language Learning*, Chinese Language Learning Sciences,
https://doi.org/10.1007/978-981-13-3570-9_11

ances of second-language (L2) learners in response to given text prompts, so as to improve their spoken proficiency in a self-directed manner. On a separate front, the recent significant progress being made in the field of automatic speech recognition (ASR) has led to its growing applications in CAPT. For example, a common practice for mispronunciation detection is to extract decision features (attributes) (Chen and Li 2016; Li et al. 2016, 2017) from the prediction output of phone-level acoustic models which normally are estimated based on certain criteria that maximize the ASR performance. Over the past two decades, hidden Markov models with Gaussian mixture models accounting for state emission probabilities (hereafter denoted by GMM–HMM) had been the predominant approach for building the acoustic models involved in the mispronunciation detection process (here, a state corresponds to a subphonetic unit, which is usually termed a senone in the ASR community) (Gales and Young 2007). However, a recent school of thought is to leverage various state-of-the-art deep neural network (DNN) architectures in place of GMM for modeling the state emission probabilities in HMM (hereafter denoted by DNN–HMM) (Hinton et al. 2012; Yu and Deng 2014; LeCun et al. 2015; Goodfellow et al. 2016), which shows excellent promise for improving empirical performance (Qian et al. 2012; Hu et al. 2013). In regard to decision feature extraction, log-likelihood, log-posterior probability, and segment-duration-based scores, among others, are frequently used in evaluating phone- (Kim et al. 1997) or word-level (Lo et al. 2010) pronunciation quality, while log-posterior probability based scores and its prominent extension, namely, the goodness of pronunciation (GOP) measure (Witt and Young 2000; Zhang et al. 2008), are the most prevalent and have been shown to correlate significantly with human assessments. At the same time, there are a wide array of studies that capitalize on various acoustic and prosodic cues, confidence measures, and speaking style information, to name just a few, for use in mispronunciation detection. Regarding mispronunciation diagnosis, one celebrated approach has been to build a phone-level extended recognition network (ERN) (Kim et al. 1997; Harrison et al. 2009), which augments the search space of an ASR system by common mispronunciation patterns of learners, apart from the canonical ones with respect to a given text prompt. By aligning the best decoded phone-level pattern sequence from ERN with the canonical counterpart for a learner's input utterance, it is easy to identify the location(s) and type(s) of phonetic differences, thereby facilitating mispronunciation diagnosis in addition to mispronunciation detection. The performance of ERN, however, hinges largely on whether high coverage of possible mispronunciation patterns can be achieved, which is often difficult to guarantee due to unanticipated patterns deduced from handcrafted rules or inferred by data-driven mechanisms. Interested readers may also refer to (Wei et al. 2009; Chen and Jang 2015; Hu et al. 2015a, b; Huang et al. 2015; Wang and Lee 2015; Chen and Li 2016; Li et al. 2016; Qian et al. 2016; Hsu et al. 2016) for comprehensive reviews and new insights into the characteristics of major state-of-the-art methods that have been successfully developed and applied to various mispronunciation detection tasks.

The rest of this chapter is organized as follows. We will first introduce mispronunciation detection and diagnosis building on top of the mathematical formulation of goodness of pronunciation (GOP). Afterward, we present an effective training approach that estimates the deep neural network based acoustic models involved in the process of mispronunciation detection by optimizing an objective directly linked to the ultimate performance evaluation metric. In addition to mispronunciation detection, we also investigate the extent to which the subsequent mispronunciation diagnosis process can benefit from the use of these specifically trained acoustic models. For this purpose, we recast mispronunciation diagnosis as a classification problem leveraging various kinds of commonly used classification methods.

2 Mispronunciation Detection and Diagnosis

2.1 *Goodness of Pronunciation (GOP)*

The general task of mispronunciation detection is to determine whether there exist mispronounced phone segments in the utterance of an L2 learner with regard to the canonical phone-level pronunciations indicated by a text prompt. Given an utterance u composed of N_u phone segments, the GOP score for a phone segment $\mathbf{O}_{u,n}$, aligned to a canonical (reference) phone label $q_{u,n}$, can be defined by (Witt and Young 2000; Zhang et al. 2008; Hu et al. 2015a, b; Hsu et al. 2016) as given below:

$$\mathrm{GOP}(q_{u,n}) = \frac{1}{T_{u,n}} \log P\left(q_{u,n} | \mathbf{O}_{u,n}\right), \tag{1}$$

where $T_{u,n}$ is the duration of $\mathbf{O}_{u,n}$ in terms of the number of speech frames. The equation in (1) is in fact the log probability of the phone label $q_{u,n}$ with respect to its corresponding phone segment $\mathbf{O}_{u,n}$, normalized by the duration of $\mathbf{O}_{u,n}$. By applying Bayes' rule and further assuming that all phones share the same prior probability, we can calculate the GOP score through the derivations in (2) as follows:

$$\begin{aligned} \mathrm{GOP}(q_{u,n}) &= \frac{1}{T_{u,n}} \log \frac{P(\mathbf{O}_{u,n} | q_{u,n})}{\sum_{\tilde{q} \in Q_{u,n}} P(\mathbf{O}_{u,n} | \tilde{q}) P(\tilde{q})} \\ &\approx \frac{1}{T_{u,n}} \log \frac{P(\mathbf{O}_{u,n} | q_{u,n})}{\sum_{\tilde{q} \in Q_{u,n}} P(\mathbf{O}_{u,n} | \tilde{q})} \end{aligned} \tag{2}$$

where $Q_{u,n}$ represents the set of acoustic models for all possible phone labels corresponding to $\mathbf{O}_{u,n}$; $P\left(\mathbf{o}_{u,n} | q_{u,n}\right)$ and $P\left(\mathbf{o}_{u,n} | \tilde{q}\right)$ are the probabilities of the phone segment $\mathbf{O}_{u,n}$ generated by acoustic models $q_{u,n}$ and $\tilde{q}$, respectively (see Sect. 2.2 for more details about the acoustic models); and $P(\tilde{q})$ is the prior probability of $\tilde{q}$. Alternatively, we may use the maximum operation (Witt and Young 2000; Hu et al. 2013) to approximate the summarization operation in (2) for the sake of computational simplicity, which leads to the formula in (3) as given below:

$$\mathrm{GOP}(q_{u,n}) \approx \frac{1}{T_{u,n}} \log \frac{P(\mathbf{O}_{u,n}|q_{u,n})}{\max_{\tilde{q}\in Q_{u,n}} P(\mathbf{O}_{u,n}|\tilde{q})} \tag{3}$$

The probabilities $P(\mathbf{O}_{u,n}|q_{u,n})$ and $P(\mathbf{O}_{u,n}|\tilde{q})$ involved in (2) and (3) can be calculated with either the GMM–HMM- or the DNN–HMM-based acoustic models; the latter, however, has demonstrated superior performance over the former in a wide range of ASR and mispronunciation detection tasks (Hinton et al. 2012; Qian et al. 2012; Hu et al. 2013; Yu and Deng 2014; Hsu et al. 2016).

2.2 Deep Neural Networks for Acoustic Modeling

Speech signals are locally or piecewise stationary sequences. As such, phone segments contained in a speech signal can be, respectively, hypothesized as a parametric random (stochastic) process which is, in turn, modeled by a specific acoustic model. The acoustic model corresponding to a phone segment had been commonly parameterized with a hidden Markov model with Gaussian mixture models (GMM–HMM) for use in the contexts of traditional ASR and mispronunciation detection over the past several decades. In more detail, a GMM–HMM-based acoustic model consists of a finite set of states and transitions between them (here, a state corresponds to a subphonetic unit and is usually termed a senone in the ASR community), where Gaussian mixture models are used to characterize the emission probabilities of frame-level speech feature vectors being generated by each state. More recently, with the successful development of deep neural networks (DNN) (i.e., neural networks with multiple hidden layers or more sophisticated network architectures), they have been employed in place of Gaussian mixture models for estimating the state emission probabilities in HMM leading to the so-called DNN–HMM-based acoustic models. DNN–HMM has demonstrated superior performance over GMM–HMM in a wide range of ASR tasks, as long as a large amount of speech data is provided for model training (Hinton et al. 2012; Qian et al. 2012; Hu et al. 2013; Yu and Deng 2014; Hsu et al., 2016). The main reasons for the superior performance of DNN–HMM over GMM–HMM may lie in that DNN–HMM removes the need of Gaussian assumption for the distributions of speech feature vectors and is capable of modeling long-span, high-dimensional, and strongly correlated speech feature vectors as its input (Qian et al. 2014). In this chapter, we will adopt both the GMM–HMM-based and DNN–HMM-based acoustic models to calculate the probabilities $\left(\mathbf{o}_{u,n}|q_{u,n}\right)$ and $P\left(\mathbf{o}_{u,n}|\tilde{q}\right)$ involved in (2) and (3), comparing their performance levels for the purpose of mispronunciation detection and diagnosis.

2.3 Mispronunciation Detection

The GOP-based score for an arbitrary phone segment $\mathbf{O}_{u,n}$, in turn, is taken as a decision feature and fed into a decision function, such as the logistic sigmoid function (Bishop 2006) as follows:

$$\mathrm{D}(q_{u,n}) = \frac{1}{1 + \exp[\alpha(\mathrm{GOP}(q_{u,n}) + \beta)]} \quad (4)$$

where α and β are tunable parameters controlling the shape of the decision function. The function in (4) has a domain of all real numbers, with its output value monotonically increasing from 0 to 1; the higher the value of the output, the more likely that the phone segment is mispronounced. As such, we can use the output value of the decision function in relation to a pre-established threshold to determine whether the phone segment is correctly pronounced or mispronounced.

Further, in an attempt to obtain a more fine-grained inspection of the pronunciation quality of a phone segment $\mathbf{O}_{u,n}$, we can align $\mathbf{O}_{u,n}$ into a sequence of senone segments $\mathbf{O}_{u,n,i}$ in accordance with its canonical phone label $q_{u,n}$, where each senone segment may consist of one to several consecutive speech frames that belong to the same senone identity. By doing so, we can calculate the GOP score $\mathrm{GOP}(u, n, i)$ and subsequently the senone-level decision score $\tilde{\mathrm{D}}(q_{u,n,i})$ for each senone segment $\mathbf{O}_{u,n,i}$ involved in $\mathbf{O}_{u,n}$, using formulas defined similarly to (1–4). After that, an ensemble of the output scores of all senone-level decision functions for $\mathbf{O}_{u,n}$ can be taken as a more elaborate measure to determine whether $\mathbf{O}_{u,n}$ is mispronounced or not, as shown in (5) as given below:

$$\mathrm{D}(q_{u,n}) = \frac{1}{S_{u,n}} \sum_{i=1}^{S_{u,n}} \tilde{\mathrm{D}}(q_{u,n,i}) \quad (5)$$

where $\mathrm{S}_{u,n}$ denotes the total number of senone segments corresponding to $\mathbf{O}_{u,n}$.

2.4 Mispronunciation Diagnosis

In addition to the ERN-based approach mentioned above, another mainstream approach to mispronunciation diagnosis is to recast it as a classification problem, leveraging commonly used methods, such as support vector machines (SVM), decision tree (DT), multilayer perceptron (MLP), and the like (Bishop 2006). To this end, a rich set of indicative features, mostly extracted from ASR or the mispronunciation detection process, can be used as the input to a classifier which outputs the most possible mispronunciation (impostor) pattern for a phone segment that has been identified beforehand by the mispronunciation detection process as an incorrect pronunciation. Given a mispronounced phone segment $\mathbf{O}_{u,n}$ (with the canonical pronunciation $q_{u,n}$), we can, for example, extract a set of indicative features for this segment, as represented in (6) (Hu et al. 2015a, b) as follows:

$$\mathbf{f}(q_{u,n}|\mathbf{o}_{u,n}) = \{\mathrm{GOP}(q_1), \mathrm{GOP}(q_2), \ldots, \mathrm{GOP}(q_M), \\ \mathrm{DGOP}(q_1|q_{u,n}), \mathrm{DGOP}(q_2|q_{u,n}), \ldots, \mathrm{DGOP}(q_M|q_{u,n})\} \quad (6)$$

where $q_1, \ldots, q_M$ are possible impostor phones, one of which is likely to be actually pronounced by a learner instead of the canonical phone $q_{u,n}$; DGOP(•) is the difference between the GOP scores of an impostor phone and the canonical phone $q_{u,n}$, which is defined in (7) as follows:

$$\mathrm{DGOP}(q_m|q_{u,n}) = \mathrm{GOP}(q_m) - \mathrm{GOP}(q_{u,n}) \quad (7)$$

The associated classifier (e.g., SVM, DT, and MLP) involved in the mispronunciation diagnosis process can be trained on a training set that contains utterances of L2 learners along with manually diagnosed mispronunciation annotations from human experts.

3 Maximum Evaluation Criterion Training (MECT)

3.1 Principle

In the conventional setting for GOP-based mispronunciation detection and diagnosis, the underlying acoustic models are normally trained with criteria that maximize the ASR performance, such as maximum likelihood (ML) estimation, minimum cross-entropy (MC) estimation (LeCun et al. 2015), and the state-level minimum Bayes risk (sMBR) estimation (Goel and Byrne 2000; Gibson and Hain 2006; Kingsbury 2009), to name just a few, while the parameters of the decision function are often determined empirically. A recent line of research is to learn the DNN–HMM-based acoustic models, as well as the decision function, with a discriminative objective that is directly linked to the ultimate evaluation metric of mispronunciation detection and/or mispronunciation diagnosis, referred to as the maximum evaluation criterion training (MECT) approach (Hsu et al. 2016). Here, we take the maximization of the F1 score for illustration, since it has been frequently adopted as the evaluation metric in previous work on mispronunciation detection (Lee et al. 2013; Luo et al. 2009; Huang et al. 2012). The F1 score is a harmonic mean of precision and recall, whose formulation will be described in more detail in Sect. 4.2. Further, the parameters of the decision function employed in the mispronunciation detection process can be set to be either phone or senone dependent when the phone-level [*cf.* (4)] or finer grained senone-level decision functions [*cf.* (5)], respectively, are used for mispronunciation detection.

More formally, in the context of mispronunciation detection, the objective function of the MECT approach, in terms of the F1 score, can be defined in (8) as follows:

$$\begin{aligned}\Xi(\boldsymbol{\theta}) &= \frac{2C_{\mathrm{D}\cap\mathrm{H}}}{C_{\mathrm{D}} + C_{\mathrm{H}}} \\ &= \frac{2 \cdot \sum_{u=1}^{U} \sum_{n=1}^{N_u} \mathrm{I}(\mathrm{D}(u,n)) \cdot \mathrm{H}(u,n)}{\left[\sum_{u=1}^{U} \sum_{n=1}^{N_u} \mathrm{I}(\mathrm{D}(u,n))\right] + C_{\mathrm{H}}}\end{aligned} \tag{8}$$

where $\boldsymbol{\theta}$ denotes the set of parameters involved in both the DNN–HMM-based acoustic models and the decision functions for mispronunciation detection, U is the total number of training utterances, N_u is the total number of phone segments in an utterance u, $\mathrm{C_D}$ is the total number of phone segments in the training set that are identified as being mispronounced by the current mispronunciation detection module, $\mathrm{C_H}$ is the total number of phone segments in the training set that are identified as being mispronounced by the majority vote of human assessors, $\mathrm{C_{D\cap H}}$ is the total number of phone segments in the training set that are identified as being mispronounced simultaneously by both the current mispronunciation detection module and the majority vote of human assessors, and the indicator function $\mathrm{I}(\mathrm{D}(u,n))$ can be further expressed in (9) as follows:

$$\mathrm{I}(\mathrm{D}(u,n)) = \begin{cases} 1 \text{ if } \mathrm{D}(u,n) \geq \tau \\ 0 \text{ otherwise} \end{cases} \tag{9}$$

where τ a prespecified threshold. As a matter of convenience, the training objective defined in Eq. (8) can be further approximated by Eq. (10) as given below:

$$\Xi(\boldsymbol{\theta}) \approx \frac{2 \cdot \sum_{u=1}^{U} \sum_{n=1}^{N_u} \mathrm{D}(u,n) \cdot \mathrm{H}(u,n)}{\left[\sum_{u=1}^{U} \sum_{n=1}^{N_u} \mathrm{D}(u,n)\right] + C_{\mathrm{H}}} \tag{10}$$

The training objective shown in (10) can be viewed as a soft version of the training objective defined in (8), which, in turn, can be optimized using a stochastic gradient ascent algorithm (Goodfellow et al. 2016), in conjunction with the chain rule for differentiation, to iteratively update the parameter set of both the DNN–HMM acoustic models and the decision function (Witt and Young 2000; Hsu et al. 2016).

3.2 Implementation Procedure

In the following, we briefly highlight the implementation procedure for the MECT approach (Hsu et al. 2016):

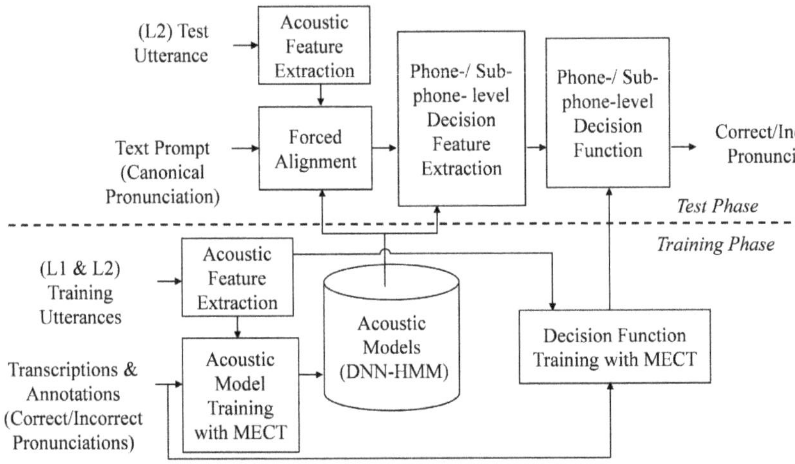

Fig. 1 A schematic depiction of the mispronunciation detection process with MECT

(1) Train the DNN–HMM-based acoustic models on the native-speaker (denoted by L1) portion of the training data with the minimum cross-entropy (MC) estimation (Yu and Deng 2014).
(2) On top of the DNN–HMM-based acoustic models estimated from Step 1, try to compute the decision scores of all phone segments of the training utterances (some of them contain mispronunciations) that belong to the L2 learners, where the decision function can be instantiated with either (4) or (5) and the parameters of the decision functions are empirically determined and set to be identical for all phones or senones.
(3) Use the training objective introduced in (10) to iteratively update the parameters of the DNN–HMM-based acoustic models and the parameters of the phone- [expressed by (4)] or senone-level [expressed by (5)] decision function, with the stochastic gradient ascent algorithm and the chain rule for differentiation (Goodfellow et al. 2016). Note here that the estimated parameters of the decision function can be either phone (or senone) independent or phone (or senone) dependent.

Figure 1 shows a schematic depiction of the mispronunciation detection process with MECT. We note in passing that the notion of leveraging evaluation metric-related training criteria for training the GMM–HMM-based acoustic models has recently attracted much attention in the CAPT research with some success (Qian et al. 2010; Huang et al. 2012, 2015). However, as far as we are aware, little work has been devoted to exploring this notion for jointly training the DMM–HMM-based acoustic models and decision functions (Hsu et al. 2016).

4 Experimental Setup

4.1 Corpus and Acoustic Modeling

The dataset employed in this study is a Mandarin annotated spoken (MAS) corpus compiled by the Center of Learning Technology for Chinese, National Taiwan Normal University, between 2012 and 2014 (Hsiung et al. 2014; Hsu et al. 2016). The corpus was split into three subsets: training set, development set, and test set. All three subsets are composed of speech utterances (containing one to several syllables) pronounced by native speakers (L1) and L2 learners. Each utterance of an L2 learner may contain mispronunciations, which were carefully annotated by at most four human assessors with a majority vote. Table 1 briefly summarizes the statistics of the speech corpus employed in this study.

The ASR system was built on top of the Kaldi toolkit (Povey et al. 2011). Each GMM–HMM-based acoustic model consists of three states, where each state has at least 16 Gaussian mixtures (Gales and Young 2007). In regard to speech feature extraction, a 48-dimensional feature vector was extracted for each speech frame, including 13 mel-frequency cepstral coefficient (MFCC) features, one energy feature, and three-pitch features, as well as their respective delta and delta–delta derivatives. The delta and delta–delta derivatives provide an estimation of the local temporal derivatives of the aforementioned features, while the speech frame length (window size) and frameshift were set to 32 and 10 ms, respectively.

In addition, different structures for building the DNN–HMM-based acoustic models are investigated, as shown in Table 2. For the DNN–HMM-based acoustic models, the activation function of the hidden layers in the DNN module is the sigmoid function, and the activation function of the output layer is the softmax function (Hinton et al. 2012; Yu and Deng 2014). The input feature vector to DNN–HMM is an augmented, 11-frame super vector, including five preceding speech frames, the current speech frame, and five succeeding speech frames. Each speech frame is composed of 40-dimensional mel-scale frequency spectral coefficient (MFSC) features and three-

Table 1 The statistical information of the speech corpus used in the mispronunciation detection experiments

		Duration (h)	# Speakers	# Phone tokens	# Errors
Training set	L1	6.68	44	73,074	NA
	L2	15.79	63	118,754	26,434
Development set	L1	1.40	10	14,216	NA
	L2	1.46	6	11,214	2699
Test set	L1	3.20	26	32,568	NA
	L2	7.49	44	55,190	14,247

Table 2 Different structures of the DNN module in DNN–HMM

	# Layers	# Neurons per layer
DNN(A)–HMM	4	1024
DNN(B)–HMM	4	2048
DNN(C)–HMM	6	1024

Table 3 ASR experimental results

	Syllable error rate (%)	Phone error rate (%)
GMM–HMM	50.9	34.3
DNN(A)–HMM	41.2	27.7
DNN(B)–HMM	40.1	27.0
DNN(C)–HMM	40.7	27.2
DNN(B)–HMM+sMBR	37.9	24.9

pitch features, as well as their respective delta and delta–delta derivatives (Povey et al. 2011).

The ASR (free-syllable decoding without language model constraints) results on the test set (only the L1-speaker portion), using either GMM–HMM or DNN–HMM, are shown in Table 3 in terms of syllable error rate (SER) and phone error rate (PER). Notice here that the SER and PER measures are widely adopted as the figure of merits for performance evaluation on an ASR system; for example, the PER measure is defined in (11) as follows:

$$\text{PER} = \frac{\text{Ins} + \text{Sub} + \text{Del}}{\text{Ref}} \tag{11}$$

which is the sum of the insertion (Ins), deletion (Del), and substitution (Sub) errors between the recognized and reference phone strings, divided by the total number of phones in the reference string (Ref). A similar formula is employed for the SER measure.

DNN(B)–HMM (with or without sMBR training) achieves the best performance, with a PER of 40.1% and a SER of 27.0% for DNN(B)–HMM, and a PER of 37.9% and a SER of 24.9% for DNN(B)–HMM+sMBR. As such, in the following experiments, the acoustic models are built on top of DNN(B)–HMM, unless otherwise stated.

4.2 Performance Evaluation

One of the commonly used evaluation metrics for mispronunciation detection is the F1 score, which is a harmonic mean of precision and recall, defined as

$$\text{F1 score} = \frac{2 \cdot \text{Precision} \cdot \text{Recall}}{\text{Precision} + \text{Recall}} \tag{12}$$

$$\text{Precision} = \frac{C_{\mathrm{D} \cap \mathrm{H}}}{C_{\mathrm{D}}} \tag{13}$$

$$\text{Recall} = \frac{C_{\mathrm{D} \cap \mathrm{H}}}{C_{\mathrm{H}}} \tag{14}$$

where C_{D}, C_{H}, and $C_{\mathrm{D} \cap \mathrm{H}}$ were previously introduced in Sect. 3, but are instead counted on the test set for performance evaluation here.

As for mispronunciation diagnosis on phone (i.e., Initial or Final for the Mandarin Chinese) and tonal segments, respectively, the diagnosis accuracy rate measure is adopted as the figure of merit for performance evaluation. For example, the accuracy rate of mispronunciation diagnosis on tone patterns is defined as the total number of correctly diagnosed tonal segments divided by the total number of mispronounced tonal segments for all L2 learners in the test set.

5 Experimental Results

5.1 Experiments on Mispronunciation Detection

In the first place, we report on the results obtained using either the phone-level decision functions [*cf.* (4)] or the senone-level decision functions [*cf.* (5)] for mispronunciation detection. The acoustic models used here are DNN(B)–HMM trained with the conventional minimum cross-entropy (MC) estimation, while the parameters of the decision functions are empirically tuned at optimum values based on the development set. As can be seen from the first two rows of Table 4, mispronunciation detection with the senone-level decision function offers slight improvement over that using the phone-level decision function in terms of the F1 score. In particular, the precision value is increased (from 0.537 to 0.545) by about 1.5% relative; this gain comes at the expense of a relatively lower recall value (a decrease from 0.681 to 0.675).

Table 4 Mispronunciation detection results achieved using either the phone- or senone-level decision function and with or without the MECT training criterion

	Recall	Precision	F1 score
Phone level	0.681	0.537	0.600
Senone level	0.675	0.545	0.603
+MECT (Both)	0.696	0.626	0.659
+MECT (AM)	0.697	0.621	0.657
+MECT (DF)	0.688	0.581	0.630

The acoustic models are DNN(B)–HMM

Table 5 Mispronunciation detection results achieved using either the phone- or senone-level decision function and with or without the MFC training criterion

	Recall	Precision	F1 score
Phone level	0.671	0.551	0.605
Senone level	0.652	0.555	0.599
+MECT (Both)	0.743	0.587	0.656
+MECT (AM)	0.738	0.586	0.653
+MECT (DF)	0.698	0.570	0.627

The acoustic models are DNN(B)–HMM+sMBR

Next, we turn our attention to evaluating the utility of exploiting the MECT training criterion in estimating the parameters of the acoustic models (MECT(AM)), the decision function (MECT(DF)), or both of them (MECT(Both)), taking the senone-level decision functions for illustration. Notice here that the acoustic models are pretrained with the MC estimation. The corresponding results are shown in the last three rows of Table 4, where two interesting observations can be drawn. First, all the three MFC training settings can significantly boost the mispronunciation detection performance with respect to the F1 score, as well as the recall and precision values. Especially, the F1 score is increased (from 0.603 to 0.659) by about 10% relative when using the MECT(Both) training setting, indicating the effectiveness of using the MECT-based discriminative training for the mispronunciation detection task. Second, using MECT to train the acoustic models alone (MECT(AM)) seems to deliver much more performance gains than using MECT to estimate the decision functions alone (MECT(DF)), corroborating the crucial role of acoustic modeling in mispronunciation detection.

In addition, we also investigate the performance levels of using the acoustic models estimated with the conventional discriminative training criterion for ASR (i.e., sMBR; denoted by DNN(B)–HMM+sMBR), as well as its combination with the MECT-based approach. The corresponding results are summarized in Table 5. Comparing the results shown in Tables 4 and 5, we can see that even though sMBR can considerably improve the ASR performance in terms of SER and PER (*cf.* Table 3), it does not provide any additional gain for mispronunciation detection that employs either the MC-estimated acoustic models or the acoustic models further trained with the MECT approach. The performance trends exhibited in Table 5 are quite in parallel with those shown in Table 4. In addition, Fig. 2 depicts the overall distribution of the F1 scores for GOP-based mispronunciation detection on different kinds of phone (i.e., Initial and Final) segments, in terms of the corresponding normalized segment count, based on either the conventional MC criterion (denoted by MC Training) or the MECT-based approach [denoted by MECT(Both)] for acoustic model training. We can observe from Fig. 2 that the distribution of the F1 scores for the MECT-based approach leans toward higher values compared to that for the MC training.

Going a step further, Figs. 3 and 4, respectively, depict the recall–precision curves and the receiver operating characteristic (ROC) curves for the aforementioned different training settings (all with the senone-level decision functions) illustrated in

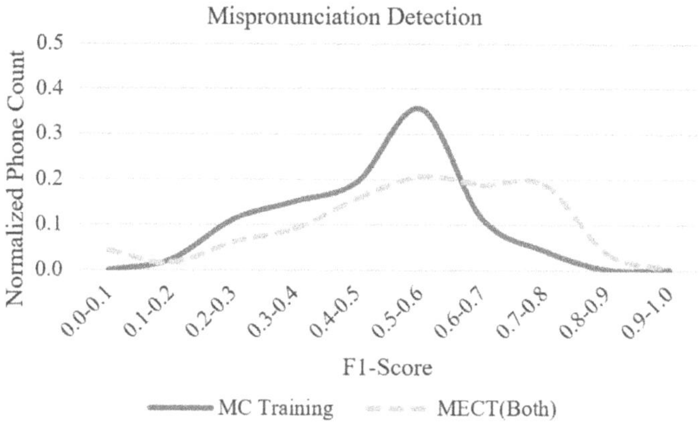

Fig. 2 The overall distribution of the F1 scores for GOP-based mispronunciation detection on different kinds of phone (i.e., Initial and Final) segments, based on either the conventional MC criterion or the MECT-based approach for acoustic model training

Fig. 3 Recall–precision curves for different training settings shown in Table 4 (with the senone-level decision functions)

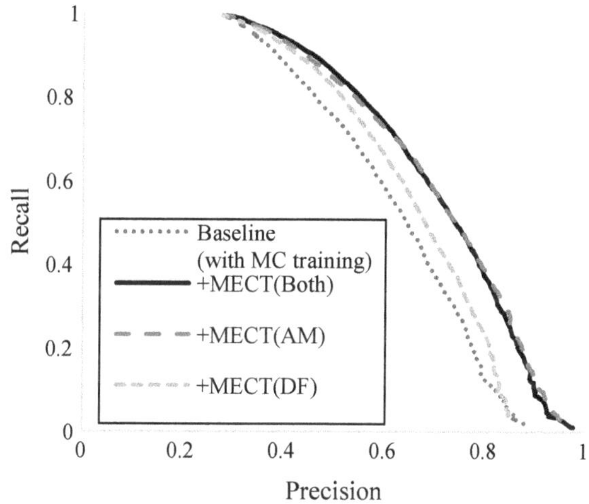

Table 4. Visual inspections of these two figures, again, confirm the obvious advantage of MECT. We also have observed similar trends when using some other popular metrics [e.g., the Rand index measure (Rand 1971)] for performance evaluation; however, we omit the details here.

5.2 *Experiments on Mispronunciation Diagnosis*

In this subsection, we explore the feasibility of adopting the classification-based approach for the purpose of mispronunciation diagnosis. At the outset, we com-

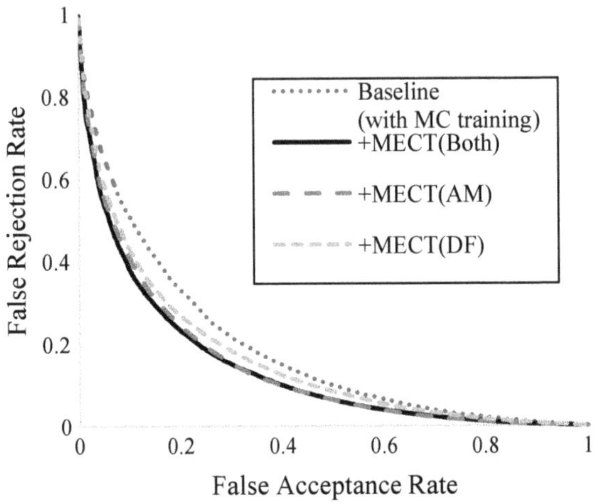

Fig. 4 ROC curves for different training settings shown in Table 4 (with the senone-level decision functions)

pare the performance levels of three state-of-the-art methods, namely, support vector machines (SVM), decision tree (DT), and multilayer perceptron (MLP) (Bishop 2006), each of which takes the set of indicative features mentioned above in Sect. 2.3 as the input. It should be mentioned here that these features can be extracted based on the DNN–HMM-based acoustic models either trained with the conventional MC criterion or the MECT-based discriminative training approach. The corresponding results of the three classifiers trained with either the conventional MC criterion or the MECT-based approach are shown in Tables 6 and 7, respectively, from which three noteworthy observations can be drawn. First, MLP stands out in performance in comparison to SVM and DT, while the latter two classifiers appear to keep abreast with each another. Second, the performance for mispronunciation diagnosis on tone patterns is considerably improved for all three classifiers when using the indicative features extracted on top of the DNN–HMM-based acoustic models trained with the MECT-based approach instead of the conventional MC criterion. Third, the MECT-based approach brings noticeable improvements to the performance of DT and MLP (except for SVM) for mispronunciation diagnosis on the Initial segments. On the other hand, these three classifiers obtain almost the same or even worse results for mispronunciation diagnosis on the Final segments when with the MECT approach. The reason for this, however, awaits further studies. It is anticipated that the training of acoustic models with the MECT-based approach which instead optimizes an objective pertaining to the accuracy rate measure for mispronunciation diagnosis would be a good remedy for this phenomenon.

As a final note, Fig. 5 depicts the overall distribution of the accuracy rates for the MLP-based classifier performing mispronunciation diagnosis on different kinds of phone (i.e., Initial and Final) segments, in terms of the corresponding normalized segment count, based on either the conventional MC criterion (denoted by MC Training) or the MECT-based approach [denoted by MECT(AM)] for acoustic model training. We can observe that there is a marked shift of the distribution to the direction

Table 6 Accuracy rate results of mispronunciation diagnosis achieved by three different classifiers using indicative features extracted based on the DNN–HMM acoustic models trained with the conventional MC criterion

	Initial (%)	Final (%)	Tone (%)
DT	43.7	32.8	61.8
SVM	47.1	31.3	61.5
MLP	51.6	45.4	70.9

Table 7 Accuracy rate results of mispronunciation diagnosis achieved by three different classifiers using indicative features extracted based on the DNN–HMM acoustic models trained with the MECT-based approach

	Initial (%)	Final (%)	Tone (%)
DT	47.0	32.6	66.4
SVM	47.0	27.3	67.6
MLP	54.8	44.1	75.2

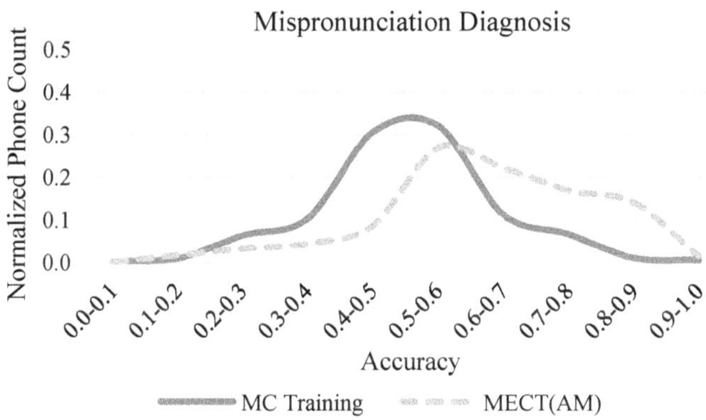

Fig. 5 The overall distribution of the accuracy rates for the MLP-based classifier performing mispronunciation diagnosis on different kinds of phone (i.e., Initial and Final) segments, based on either the conventional MC criterion or the MECT-based approach for acoustic model training

of higher accuracy rates when with the MECT approach in relation to the MC criterion, revealing again the practical utility of MECT for training DNN–HMM-based acoustic models.

6 Conclusion and Outlook

In this chapter, we have concisely introduced a systematic modeling framework, building on top of the goodness of pronunciation (GOP) measure, for Mandarin Chinese mispronunciation detection and diagnosis. This modeling framework not only adopts the state-of-the-art DNN–HMM acoustic models in replace of the conventional GMM–HMM acoustic models, but also integrates an effective maximum evaluation criterion training (MECT) based approach for training acoustic models, which optimizes an objective that is closely related to the ultimate evaluation metric of CAPT. Experimental evidence indeed supports the effectiveness of this modeling framework. The ways in which more acoustic and prosodic features, as well as other different kinds of speaking style information cues (Escudero-Mancebo et al. 2017), are integrated into the processes of mispronunciation detection and diagnosis would be a critical factor for the empirical success of CAPT. In addition, the development of different evaluation metric-related training criteria, in conjunction with more sophisticated DNN–HMM-based acoustic models and decision functions, for use in mispronunciation detection and diagnosis has emerged to be an important and appealing research direction. Finally, we remark that we have implemented a Mandarin Chinese CAPT prototype system with the modeling techniques described in this chapter, which aims to collaborate with Chinese as foreign language teachers in actual teaching and learning situations. Investigation on the impact of this CAPT system is left to future work.

Acknowledgements This research is supported in part by the "Aim for the Top University Project" of National Taiwan Normal University (NTNU), sponsored by the Ministry of Education, Taiwan, and by the Ministry of Science and Technology, Taiwan, under Grants MOST 107-2634-F-008-004, MOST 105-2221-E-003-018-MY3, MOST 104-2221-E-003-018-MY3, and MOST 104-2911-I-003-301.

References

Bishop, C. M. (2006). *Pattern recognition and machine learning*. New York: Springer.

Chen, L. Y., & Jang, J. S. R. (2015). Automatic pronunciation scoring with score combination by learning to rank and class-normalized DP-based quantization. *IEEE/ACM Transactions on Audio, Speech, and Language Processing, 23*(11), 787–797.

Chen, N. F., & Li, H. (2016). Computer-assisted pronunciation training: From pronunciation scoring towards spoken language learning. In *Proceedings of the Asia-Pacific Signal and Information Processing Association Annual Summit and Conference*. Jeju: Asia-Pacific Signal and Information Processing Association.

Escudero-Mancebo, D., Gonzalez-Ferreras, C., Aguilar, L., & Estebas-Vilaplana, E. (2017). Automatic assessment of non-native prosody by measuring distances on prosodic label sequences. In *Proceedings of the Annual Conference of the International Speech Communication Association* (pp. 1442–1446). Stockholm: International Speech Communication Association.

Gales, M., & Young, S. (2007). The application of hidden Markov models in speech recognition. *Foundations and Trends in Signal Processing, 3*(1), 195–304.

Gibson, M., & Hain, T. (2006). Hypothesis spaces for minimum Bayes risk training in large vocabulary speech recognition. In *Proceedings of the Annual Conference of the International Speech Communication Association* (pp. 2406–2409). Pittsburgh: International Speech Communication Association.

Goel, V., & Byrne, W. J. (2000). Minimum Bayes-risk automatic speech recognition. *Computer Speech & Language, 14*(2), 115–135.

Goodfellow, I., Bengio, Y., & Courville, A. (2016). *Deep learning*. Cambridge: The MIT Press.

Harrison, A. M., Lo, W.-K., Qian, X.-J., & Meng, H. (2009). Implementation of an extended recognition network for mispronunciation detection and diagnosis in computer-assisted pronunciation training. In *Proceedings of the Symposium on Languages, Applications and Technologies* (pp. 45–48).

Hinton, G., Deng, L., Yu, D., Dahl, G. E., Mohamed, A. R., Jaitly, N., et al. (2012). Deep neural networks for acoustic modeling in speech recognition. *IEEE Signal Processing Magazine, 29*(6), 82–97.

Hsiung, Y., Chen, B., & Sung, Y. (2014). Development of Mandarin annotated spoken corpus (MAS Corpus) and the learner corpus analysis. In *Proceedings of the Workshop on the Analysis of Linguistic Features*. Taipei: National Taiwan Normal University.

Hsu, Y. C., Yang, M. H., Hung, H. T., & Chen, B. (2016). Mispronunciation detection leveraging maximum performance criterion training of acoustic models and decision functions. In *Proceedings of the Annual Conference of the International Speech Communication Association* (pp. 2646–2650). San Francisco: International Speech Communication Association.

Hu, W., Qian, Y., & Soong, F. K. (2013). A new DNN-based high quality pronunciation evaluation for computer-aided language learning (CALL). In *Proceedings of the Annual Conference of the International Speech Communication Association* (pp. 1886–1890). Lyon: International Speech Communication Association.

Hu, W., Qian, Y., & Soong, F. K. (2015a). An improved DNN-based approach to mispronunciation detection and diagnosis of L2 learners' speech. In *Proceedings of the Symposium on Languages, Applications and Technologies* (pp. 71–76). Madrid: International Speech Communication Association.

Hu, W., Qian, Y., Soong, F. K., & Wang, Y. (2015b). Improved mispronunciation detection with deep neural network trained acoustic models and transfer learning based logistic regression classifiers. *Speech Communication, 67,* 154–160.

Huang, H., Wang, J., & Abudureyimu, H. (2012). Maximum F1-score discriminative training for automatic mispronunciation detection in computer-assisted language learning. In *Proceedings of the Annual Conference of the International Speech Communication Association* (pp. 815–818). Portland: International Speech Communication Association.

Huang, H., Xu, H., Wang, X., & Silamu, W. (2015). Maximum F1-score discriminative training criterion for automatic mispronunciation detection. *IEEE/ACM Transactions on Audio, Speech, and Language Processing, 23*(4), 787–797.

Kim, Y., Franco, H., & Neumeyer, L. (1997). Automatic pronunciation scoring of specific phone segments for language instruction. In *Proceedings of the European Conference on Speech Communication and Technology* (pp. 645–648). Rhodes: International Speech Communication Association.

Kingsbury, B. (2009). Lattice-based optimization of sequence classification criteria for neural-network acoustic modeling. In *Proceedings of the IEEE International Conference on Acoustics, Speech, and Signal Processing* (pp. 3761–3764). Taipei: Institute of Electrical and Electronics Engineers.

LeCun, Y., Bengio, Y., Hinton G. (2015). Deep learning. *Nature, 521*, 436–444, London: Nature Publishing Group.

Lee, A., Zhang, Y., & Glass, J. (2013). Mispronunciation detection via dynamic time warping on deep belief network-based posteriorgrams. In *Proceedings of the IEEE International Conference on Acoustics, Speech, and Signal Processing* (pp. 8227–8231). Vancouver: Institute of Electrical and Electronics Engineers.

Li, W., Siniscalchi, S. M., Chen, N. F., & Lee, C.-H. (2016). Improving non-native mispronunciation detection and enriching diagnostic feedback with DNN-based speech attribute modeling. In *Proceedings of the IEEE International Conference on Acoustics, Speech, and Signal Processing* (pp. 6135–6139). Shanghai: Institute of Electrical and Electronics Engineers.

Li, K., Qian, X., & Meng, H. (2017). Mispronunciation detection and diagnosis in L2 English speech using multidistribution deep neural networks. *IEEE/ACM Transactions on Audio, Speech, and Language Processing, 25*(1), 193–207.

Lo, W., Zhang, S., & Meng, H. (2010). Automatic derivation of phonological rules for mispronunciation detection in a computer-assisted pronunciation training system. In *Proceedings of the Annual Conference of the International Speech Communication Association* (pp. 765–768). Makuhari: International Speech Communication Association.

Luo, D., Qiao, Y., Minematsu, N., Yamauchi, Y., & Hirose, K. (2009). Analysis and utilization of MLLR speaker adaptation technique for learners' pronunciation evaluation. In *Proceedings of the Annual Conference of the International Speech Communication Association* (pp. 608–611). Brighton: International Speech Communication Association.

Povey, D., Ghoshal, A., Boulianne, G., Burget, L., Glembek, O., Goel, N., et al. (2011). The Kaldi speech recognition toolkit. In *Proceedings of* the *IEEE workshop on Automatic Speech Recognition and Understanding*. Waikoloa: Institute of Electrical and Electronics Engineers.

Qian, X., Soong, F. K., & Meng, H. (2010). Discriminatively trained acoustic models for improving mispronunciation detection and diagnosis in computer aided pronunciation training (CAPT). In *Proceedings of the Annual Conference of the International Speech Communication Association* (pp. 757–760). Makuhari: International Speech Communication Association.

Qian, X., Meng, H., & Soong, F. K. (2012). The use of DBN-HMMs for mispronunciation detection and diagnosis in L2 English to support computer-aided pronunciation training (pp. 775–778). In *Proceedings of the Annual Conference of the International Speech Communication Association*. Portland: International Speech Communication Association.

Qian, Y., Fan, Y., Hu, W., & Soong, F. K. (2014). On the training aspects of deep neural network (DNN) for parametric TTS synthesis. In *Proceedings of the IEEE International Conference on Acoustics, Speech, and Signal Processing*. Florence: Institute of Electrical and Electronics Engineers.

Qian, X., Meng, H., & Soong, F. K. (2016). A two-pass framework of mispronunciation detection and diagnosis for computer-aided pronunciation training. *IEEE/ACM Transactions on Audio, Speech, and Language Processing, 24*(6), 1020–1028.

Rand, W. (1971). Objective criteria for the evaluation of clustering methods. *Journal of the American Statistical Association, 66*(336), 846–850.

Wang, Y. B., & Lee, L. S. (2015). Supervised detection and unsupervised discovery of pronunciation error patterns for computer-assisted language learning. *IEEE/ACM Transactions on Audio, Speech, and Language Processing, 23*(3), 564–579.

Wei, S., Hu, G., Hu, Y., & Wang, R. (2009). A new method for mispronunciation detection using support vector machine based on pronunciation space models. *Speech Communication, 51*(10), 896–905.

Witt, S. M., & Young, S. J. (2000). Phone-level pronunciation scoring and assessment for interactive language learning. *Speech Communication, 30*(2–3), 95–108.

Yu, D., & Deng, L. (2014). *Automatic speech recognition—A deep learning approach*. New York: Springer.

Zhang, F., Huang, C., Soong, F. K., Chu, M., & Wang, R. H. (2008). Automatic mispronunciation detection for Mandarin. In *Proceedings of the IEEE International Conference on Acoustics, Speech, and Signal Processing*. Las Vegas: Institute of Electrical and Electronics Engineers.

Resources and Evaluations of Automated Chinese Error Diagnosis for Language Learners

Lung-Hao Lee, Yuen-Hsien Tseng and Li-Ping Chang

Abstract Chinese as a foreign language (CFL) learners may, in their language production, generate inappropriate linguistic usages, including character-level confusions (or commonly known as spelling errors) and word-/sentence-/discourse-level grammatical errors. Chinese spelling errors frequently arise from confusions among multiple-character words that are phonologically and visually similar but semantically distinct. Chinese grammatical errors contain coarse-grained surface differences in terms of missing, redundant, incorrect selection, and word ordering error of linguistic components. Simultaneously, fine-grained error types further focus on representing linguistic morphology and syntax such as verb, noun, preposition, conjunction, adverb, and so on. Annotated learner corpora are important language resources to understand these error patterns and to help the development of error diagnosis systems. In this chapter, we describe two representative Chinese learner corpora: the HSK Dynamic Composition Corpus constructed by Beijing Language and Culture University and the TOCFL Learner Corpus built by National Taiwan Normal University. In addition, we introduce several evaluations based on both learner corpora designed for computer-assisted Chinese learning. One is a series of SIGHAN bakeoffs for Chinese spelling checkers. The other series are the NLPTEA workshop shared tasks for Chinese grammatical error identification. The purpose of this chapter is to summarize the resources and evaluations for better understanding the current research developments and challenges of automated Chinese error diagnosis for CFL learners.

L.-H. Lee
National Central University, Taoyuan, Taiwan
e-mail: lhlee@ee.ncu.edu.tw

Y.-H. Tseng (✉)
National Taiwan Normal University, Taipei, Taiwan
e-mail: samtseng@ntnu.edu.tw

L.-P. Chang
National Taiwan University, Taipei, Taiwan
e-mail: lchang@ntu.edu.tw

X. Lu and B. Chen (eds.), *Computational and Corpus Approaches to Chinese Language Learning*, Chinese Language Learning Sciences,
https://doi.org/10.1007/978-981-13-3570-9_12

1 Introduction

Learning Chinese as a foreign language (CFL) has become increasingly popular around the world in recent decades. The number of CFL learners is expanding, as the Greater China Region becomes more and more influential in the global economics. This has driven an increase in demand for automated learning tools designed to assist CFL learners in mastering the language. Examples include the so-called MOOCs (Massive Open Online Courses) platform which promises huge numbers of learners to simultaneously enroll in a (CFL) course, and which, in turn, drives the demand for automatic proofreading techniques to help CFL instructors review and respond to the sheer number of assignments and tests submitted by the enrolled learners.

CFL learners usually make various kinds of errors, including character-level spelling errors and word-/sentence-/discourse-level grammatical errors, during their language acquisition and production process. However, whereas many computer-assisted learning tools have been developed to help learning English as a foreign language, such support for CFL learners is relatively sparse, especially in terms of tools designed to automatically detect and correct Chinese spelling and grammatical errors. As an example, while Microsoft has integrated robust English spelling and grammar checking functions in Word for years, such tools for Chinese are still quite primitive.

In our observations, the first barrier in studying this research topic for computer scientists is the lack of sufficient Chinese learner corpora to analyze error characteristics. Learner corpora are important collections of CFL learners' linguistic production for machine learning. The second barrier in studying spelling and grammatical errors written by CFL learners is the lack of a public platform for performance comparison. With the help of shared tasks, various techniques using the same data sets and evaluation metrics can be compared in a meaningful way and such knowledge could advance the techniques at a faster pace.

Therefore, we introduce existing Chinese learner corpora to reveal real case usages and error types. In addition, we investigate a series of international shared tasks that solicit various approaches to tackle this problem, most of which are held by us. The purpose of this chapter is to summarize the resources and evaluations for better understanding the current research developments and challenges of automated Chinese error diagnosis for CFL learners.

The rest of this chapter is organized as follows. Section 2 describes two representative Chinese learner corpora, including the HSK Dynamic Composition Corpus constructed by Beijing Language and Culture University and the TOCFL Learner Corpus built by National Taiwan Normal University. Section 3 introduces a series of SIGHAN bakeoffs for Chinese spelling checkers, and the other series of the NLPTEA workshop shared tasks for Chinese grammatical error identification. Conclusions are finally drawn in Sect. 4.

2 Resources

Chinese Learner corpora are the collections of linguistic responses produced by CFL learners. Annotating learners' inappropriate usage errors is an important task for learner corpus research (Díaz-Negrillo and Fernández-Domínguez 2006). From the linguistic perspectives, annotated learner corpora are valuable resources for research in second language acquisition (Swanson and Charniak 2013), foreign language teaching (Wang and Seneff 2007), and contrastive interlanguage analysis (Granger 2015). From the viewpoint of engineering, such language resources can be employed to develop natural language processing techniques for educational applications, such as verb suggestion (Sawai et al. 2013), automatic essay scoring (Yannakoudakis et al. 2011), assessment report generation (Sakaguchi et al. 2013), and native language identification (Malmasi and Dras 2015). In this section, we introduce two major Chinese learner corpora that are publicly available: they are the HSK Dynamic Composition Corpus and the TOCFL Learner Corpus, as follows.

2.1 HSK Dynamic Composition Corpus

Hanban/Confucius Institute Headquarters (http://english.hanban.org/), as a public institution affiliated with the Chinese Ministry of Education, China, is committed to offer Chinese language and cultural teaching resources and services worldwide. One of the functions of Hanban is to promote Chinese language popularity internationally. Hanyu Shuiping Kaoshi (HSK), organized by the Chinese Testing International Co., Ltd. (CTI) sponsored solely by Hanban, is the Chinese proficiency test to assess non-native Chinese speakers' abilities in using the Chinese language in their daily, academic, and professional lives. The HSK test consists of six levels. We describe the writing part of the corresponding levels as follows.

- *HSK Level I*: test takers have to understand and use very simple Chinese phrases, meet basic needs for communication, and possess the ability to further their Chinese language studies. There are no writing sections of this level.
- *HSK Level II*: test takers are asked to have an excellent grasp of basic Chinese in communicating simple and routine tasks requiring direct exchange of information on familiar and routine matters. No writing test is included in this level.
- *HSK Level III*: test takers need to communicate in Chinese at a basic level in their lives and manage most communications in Chinese when traveling in China. The writing test contains two parts. There are five items in the first part. Each item lists several words. The test takers should construct a sentence using the words provided. In the second part, there are five items as well. Each item provides a sentence with several blanks. The test takers should fill in the blanks with the appropriate characters.
- *HSK Level IV*: test takers should be able to converse in Chinese on a wide range of topics and communicate fluently with native Chinese speakers. The first part

of the writing section has 10 items. Each item consists of several words. The test taker should construct a sentence using these words. There are also five items in the second part. Each item consists of a picture and a word. The test takers need to write a sentence based on the picture and the word.

- *HSK Level V*: test takers have the abilities of reading Chinese newspapers and magazines, enjoying Chinese films and plays, and giving a full-length speech in Chinese. Regarding the writing section, there are eight items and two items in the first and second part, respectively. For part one, each item consists of several words from which the test takers should construct a sentence. For part two, the first and second item includes several words and a picture, individually. The test takers are then asked to write an article about 80 characters long using the word/picture provided for each item.
- *HSK Level VI*: test takers are able to easily comprehend written and spoken information in Chinese and effectively express themselves in Chinese, both orally and on paper. The test takers will be asked to read a narrative article of about 1000 characters within 10 min, and then rewrite it into shorter article of about 400 characters within 35 min. A title of the article should be also created. The test takers should recount the article without expressing personal opinions.

The HSK Dynamic Composition Corpus (Cui and Zhang 2011; Zhang and Cui 2013) was constructed by Beijing Language and Culture University, including original essays written on papers by CFL learners and their typing version with annotated errors. Besides learners' written texts, metadata such as learners' nationality, gender, evaluated score, and so on, are also retained. The tag sets used for corpus annotation are shown in Table 1. In total, there are 45 error types distributing into character-level errors (11 cases), word-level errors (5 cases), sentence-level errors (28 cases), and the discourse error (1 case). The newest version 1.1 contains 11,569 essays contributing by learners from 101 different countries. About 4.24 million characters were collected and annotated covering 30 different topics. This learner corpus is available online at http://202.112.194.56:8088/hsk/Login.

2.2 TOCFL Learner Corpus

The Steering Committee for Test of Proficiency-Huayu (SC-TOP) (http://www.sc-top.org.tw/english/eng_index.php) aims to develop and promote the Test of Chinese as a Foreign Language (TOCFL), which is the official test to assess the proficiency of Chinese language learners in Taiwan. The TOCFL writing test is designed according to proficiency levels of the Common European Framework of Reference (CEFR) (Little 2006). The testing principle is task orientation, which evaluates learners' ability to express their thoughts in the context of real-world situations. There are four available levels of the TOCFL writing test, which are described as follows.

- *Waystage level* (A2): test takers have to write a note and describe a story after looking at four pictures.

Table 1 Tag sets used for error annotation of the HSK Dynamic Composition Corpus

Character-level	nonexisting character (C), spelling error character (B), missing character (L), redundant character (D), traditional character (F), variant character (Y), pinyin character (P), non-identifiable character (#), incorrect punctuation (BC), missing punctuation (BQ), redundant punctuation (BD)
Word-level	incorrect word (CC), incorrect separable word (CLH), foreign word (W), missing word (CQ), redundant word (CD)
Sentence-level	把 sentence (CJba), 被 sentence (CJbei), 比 sentence (CJbi), 連 sentence (CJl), 有 sentence (CJy), 是 sentence (CJs), "是…的" sentence (CJsd), existential sentence (CJcx), pivotal sentence (CJjy), sentences with serial verbs (CJld), double-object sentence (CJshb), adjective-predicate structure (Cjxw), missing-constituent sentence (CJ−), redundant-constituent sentence (CJ+), missing/redundant subject (CJ∓zhuy), missing/redundant predicate (CJ∓wy), missing/redundant verb (CJ−/+sy), missing/redundant object (CJ−/+zhby), missing/redundant complement (CJ−/+zhbuy), missing/redundant attribute (CJ−/+zhdy), missing/redundant adverbial (CJ−/+zy), missing/redundant head-phrase (CJ−/+zxy), word ordering error (CJX), mixture error (CJZR), reduplicated error (CJcd), pattern error (CJgd), incomplete sentence (WWJ), ambiguous sentence (CJ?)
Discourse-level	discourse error (CP)

- *Threshold level* (B1): test takers are asked to write relatively detailed personal letters that describe their experiences and feelings about events they have encountered.
- *Vantage level* (B2): test takers are asked to write a functional letter highlighting definite purposes or to develop an argument to express personal opinions of specific events.
- *Proficiency level* (C1): test takers are asked to write an essay or report that gives reasons in support or against a particular point of view or explains provided figures and tables.

Test takers can freely choose one of the levels that may meet their Chinese proficiency. The proficiency-level evaluation is based on the appropriateness of the test takers' responses to situational tasks, compositional structure and completeness, syntax correctness, and the use of a suitably wide range of appropriate vocabulary. Each evaluation is conducted by at least two Chinese teachers and then scored on a point scale from 0 to 5, where an average score of 3 is the threshold for passing the test.

In addition to learners' written texts from the TOCFL test, all accompanying metadata, such as the corresponding CEFR level, evaluated score, and learner's native language, are also collected and kept in the built learner corpus.

The TOCFL writing test is online (i.e., computer-based), and therefore Chinese-typing ability is a requirement for all test takers. When annotating the TOCFL corpus, the spelling (character confusion) errors were manually tagged and corrected in a preprocessing phase. Then, the hierarchical tag sets designed by our team were used to annotate the grammatical errors (Chang 2016). Table 2 shows two kinds of error classifications used simultaneously to tag grammatical errors. The first capital letter

Table 2 Hierarchical tags for grammatical error annotation of the TOCFL Learner Corpus

Target modification taxonomy	
Missing (*M*), Redundancy (*R*), Incorrect Selection (*S*), Word Ordering Error (*W*)	
Linguistic category classification	
Word-level	action verb (*v*), auxiliary (*aux*), stative verb (*vs*), noun (*n*), pronoun (*pron*), conjunction (*conj*), preposition (*p*), numeral (*num*), demonstrative (*det*), measure word (*cl*), sentential particle (*sp*), aspectual particle (*asp*), adverb (*adv*), structural particle (*de*), question word (*que*), plural suffix (*plural*)
Grammatical Function-level	subject (*sub*), object (*obj*), noun phrase (*np*), verb phrase (vp), preposition phrase (*pp*), modifier (*mod*), time expression (*time*), place expression (*loc*), transitivity (*tran*), separable structure (*vo*), [numeral/determiner + measure] phrase (*dm*)
Sentence Pattern-level	complex noun clause (*rel*), 把 sentence (*ba*), 被 sentence (*bei*), 讓 sentence (*rang*), 是 sentence (*shi*), 有sentence (*you*), other patterns (*pattern*)
Mixture	formation (*form*), ambiguity of syntactic or meaning (*sentence*)

denotes the coarse-grained surface differences, while the subsequent lowercase letters denote the fine-grained linguistic category. The coarse-grained error types originate from target modification differences from comparing a sentence surface structure with the correct usages. There are four coarse-grained error types: word ordering, redundancy, missing, and incorrect selection errors of linguistic components (also called PADS error types, denoting errors of Permutation, Addition, Deletion, and Selection, correspondingly). The fine-grained error types focus on representing linguistic concepts. A total of 36 error types are distributed into word-level errors (16 cases), grammatical function-level errors (11 cases), sentence pattern-level errors (7 cases), and mixture errors (2 cases).

The TOCFL Learner Corpus (Lee et al. 2016a; 2018) was constructed by National Taiwan Normal University. Native Chinese-speaking annotators were trained to follow our annotation guidelines before conducting the error-tagging task. The annotators were asked to provide one of the corresponding corrections using a tagging editor (Lee et al. 2014). A total of 2837 learner essays scoring at least 3 (i.e., a passing grade) were included. The low-scoring essays were ignored because it was difficult to interpret the meaning intent of the test takers and to annotate the possible errors. The B1 level occupies near half of the corpus. In total, about 1 million characters were collected and annotated covering 62 different topics.

In the TOCFL Learner Corpus, there are 46 different mother tongue languages, with the top 10 languages accounting for 88%, and 36 languages accounting for the remaining 12%. Slightly more than 1/4th of the sample spoke Japanese as their first language, followed by English and three other Asian languages, i.e., Vietnamese, Korean, and Indonesian.

The top 10 error tags in the corpus occupied about 47% of the total 33,835 errors. The most common errors were related to the incorrect selection of verbs (Sv) and nouns (Sn). Half of these errors belong to missing of word-level linguistic components. A specially purposed retrieval system for the TOCFL Learner Corpus, which is available online at http://tocfl.itc.ntnu.edu.tw, was developed and implemented to help interlanguage analysis for second language acquisition (Lee et al. 2015a).

2.3 *Corpus Summary*

According to the statement of the Association of Chinese Teachers in German Speaking Countries (Fachverband Chinesisch e.V. 2010), Table 3 shows the correspondences between the levels of proficiency of both learner corpora. All levels are associated with the corresponding CEFL levels for comparisons. The HSK level I and level II are under CEFR A1 level because about one-third of vocabulary size would be needed to achieve the same levels of proficiency. The HSK level III is equal to CEFR Al level. In the TOCFL, the corresponding level is not available. The HSK Level IV, level V and level VI correspond to TOCFL Waystage level, Threshold level, and Vantage level, respectively. The TOCFL Proficiency level is the same as CEFR C1 level. There is no such corresponding level in the HSK. Both TOCFL and HSK do not have the level of proficiency corresponding to the CEFR C2 level.

Different tag sets were developed to annotate the errors in the corpora. In the HSK, error categorization focuses on linguistic categories from character-level to discourse-level errors. The TOCFL applies a hierarchical concept to tag an error with coarse-grained surface structure differences and fine-grained linguistic categories simultaneously. The former contains relatively large number of error tags, while the latter reflects more information in each error tag.

Table 4 summarizes the characteristics of both learner corpora. The size of the HSK is obviously larger than the TOCFL in terms of the number of essays and characters collected, while the TOCFL covers slightly more topics. Both corpora have been adopted in the shared tasks designed for using NLP techniques for educational

Table 3 The correspondences between the levels of proficiency of both learner corpora

CEFR	The corresponding levels of proficiency	
Under A1	HSK Level I & HSK Level II	Not available
A1	HSK Level III	Not available
A2	HSK Level IV	TOCFL Waystage level
B1	HSK Level V	TOCFL Threshold level
B2	HSK Level VI	TOCFL Vantage level
C1	Not available	TOCFL Proficiency level
C2	Not available	Not available

Table 4 Summary of the HSK Dynamic Composition Corpus and the TOCFL Learner Corpus

	HSK Dynamic Composition Corpus (Cui and Zhang 2011; Zhang and Cui 2013)	TOCFL Learner Corpus (Lee et al. 2016a; 2018)
Variety	Simplified Chinese	Traditional Chinese
Essays	11,569	2837
Characters	4,240,043	1,002,288
Topics	30	62
Error Tags	45	36
Errors	Not available	33,835
Shared Tasks	Chinese grammatical error diagnosis	Chinese spelling checking & grammatical error diagnosis
Web Access	http://202.112.195.192:8060/hsk/login.asp	http://tocfl.itc.ntnu.edu.tw

applications. Both learner corpora are valuable and complementary to each other for the study of linguistic differences or similarities among learners around the world.

3 Evaluations

Both the above learner corpora, either in parts or as a whole, were utilized to organize a series of shared tasks to solicit various techniques to deal with spelling check and grammatical error diagnosis in the sentences written by CFL learners, and the resulting data sets and scoring scripts were publicly released for further study. These evaluation campaigns would be able to: (1) explore more technological possibilities from the participants over the world; (2) make techniques comparable based on the same data sets and performance metrics to know the state-of-the-art techniques; (3) advance the techniques for Chinese error diagnosis at a faster pace to make some educational activities possible, such as MOOCs of CFL.

In this section, we describe two kinds of shared tasks for automated Chinese error diagnosis. One is a series of SIGHAN bakeoffs for Chinese spelling checkers. Another is a succession of the NLPTEA workshop shared tasks for Chinese grammatical error diagnosis.

3.1 Chinese Spelling Check

Chinese spelling errors frequently arise from confusion among multiple-character words that are phonologically and visually similar but semantically distinct. The first Chinese Spelling Check (CSC) bakeoff was organized as part the Seventh SIGHAN

(Special Interesting Group on Chinese Language Processing of the Association for Computational Linguistics) workshop, which was held in conjunction with IJCNLP 2013 (Wu et al. 2013). This shared task is the first open evaluation for automatic Chinese spelling checkers. A second version of this bakeoff was collocated with the Third CIPS-SIGHAN Joint Conference on Chinese Language Processing (CLP 2014) (Yu et al. 2014b). A third one was organized in conjunction with the Eighth SIGHAN workshop at ACL-IJCNLP 2015 (Tseng et al. 2015). The main purpose of these bakeoffs was to provide a common setting so that researchers who approach the tasks with different linguistic factors and computational techniques can compare their results. Through such technical forums, researchers can exchange their experiences to advance the field and eventually find the best solutions to the tasks.

Different from the initial edition in SIGHAN 2013 adopting the data sets written by Chinese native speakers, the second and third bakeoffs used the TOCFL Learner Corpus as the data source. This is considered a greater challenge in detecting and correcting spelling errors as the sentences written by CFL learners can contain errors that are hard to predict. Table 5 lists the similarities and differences of both bakeoffs. The goal is identical to evaluate the capability of a Chinese spelling checker. A sentence consisting of several clauses with/without spelling errors was given as the input. The checker should return the locations of incorrect characters and suggest the correct characters. Each character or punctuation mark occupies 1 spot for counting location. Both tasks were conducted as an open test. That is, in addition to the data sets provided, registered participant teams were allowed to use other publicly available data, but the use should be specified in their system description reports.

For CLP 2014 bakeoff, 13 teams of 19 registered participants submitted their testing results, and in which 10 teams provided their system description papers. Various techniques were adopted to tackle this problem. We briefly describe them as follows: The most frequently used approaches are n-gram model and language model. The SCAU system developed a character-based trigram model to determine the best sequence for detecting and correcting possible spelling errors (Huang et al. 2014). The SUDA system proposed a 5-gram language model to judge each character whether it can be formed an identified word with its neighbors (Yu and Li 2014). The joint system of NCTU and NTUT used a trigram language model along with word segmentation and part-of-speech tagger (Wang and Liao 2014). In addition to the *n*-gram language model, the NTOU system trained a rule-based classifier and an SVM-based classifier to identify spelling errors and then expanded the confusion sets by Shouwen and Four-Corner codes to find proper corrections (Chu and Lin 2014). The NJUPT system presented 2 and 3-gram based character models and a Conditional Random Field (CRF) model for detecting and correcting spelling errors (Gu et al. 2014). The NCYU system adopted *n*-gram models to induce rules for spelling error correction (Yeh et al. 2014a). The BIT system used *n*-gram models to retrieve nonwords by word segmentation and further combined them with heuristic rules for spelling error correction (Liu et al. 2014). The NTHU model proposed a noisy channel model to select appropriate correction for Chinese spelling errors (Chiu et al. 2014). The SJTU system proposed an improved graph model for generic errors and utilized two independently-trained CRF models for specific errors (Xin

Table 5 The similarities and differences of both SIGHAN bakeoffs for Chinese Spelling Checking

Shared Task	CLP 2014 CSC Bakeoff (Yu et al. 2014b)	SIGHAN 2015 CSC Bakeoff (Tseng et al. 2015)
Examples	Input: (pid = B1-0201-1) 我一身中的貴人就是我姨媽,從我回來台灣的時候, 她一只都很照顧我,也很觀心我。 Output: B1-0201-1, 3, 生, 26, 直, 35, 關	Input: (pid = B2-1670-2) 在日本,大學生打工的情況 是相當普偏的。 Output: B2-1670-2, 17, 遍
Data Source	TOCFL Learner Corpus	
Training Set	This set included 1301 sentences with a total of 5284 spelling errors	This set included 970 sentences with a total of 3143 spelling errors
Test Set	This set consisted of 1062 testing sentences, each with an average of 50 characters. One half contained no spelling errors, while the other half included at least one spelling error each for a total of 792 spelling errors	This set consisted of 1100 testing sentences. Half of these sentences contained no spelling errors, while the other half included at least one spelling errors
Evaluation Metrics	False Positive Rate, Detection-level Accuracy/Precision/Recall/F1, Correction-level Accuracy/Precision/Recall/F1	
Registered Teams	19 teams (10 from China, 8 from Taiwan, and 1 private firm)	9 teams (4 from China, 4 from Taiwan, and 1 private firm)

et al. 2014). The CAS system was based on extended Hidden Markov Model (HMM), ranker-based models, and a rule-based model to construct a unified framework for Chinese spelling error correction (Xiong et al. 2014).

Regarding performance evaluation, none of the submitted systems accomplished superior performance in all metrics, though those submitted by KUAS (without offering its system description paper), NCYU, and CAS achieved relatively best performance in different metrics.

For SIGHAN 2015 bake-off, of 9 registered participants, 5 teams had submitted their test results and system papers. All teams had joined the previous edition and improved their systems to participate again. The CAS system proposed a two-stage filter model to re-rank correction candidates efficiently and accurately (Zhang et al. 2015). The KUAS system adopted a linear regression model to integrate a rule-based method, parameters of similarities and syntax rationality (Chang et al. 2015). The NCTU&NTUT team used a word vector and CRF-based detector to find potential spelling errors and provide their suggested corrections (Wang and Liao 2015). The NTOU system added three preference rules to their previous system architecture for dealing with simplified Chinese characters, variants, sentence-final particles, and de-particles (Chu and Lin 2015). The SCAU system presented a model based on joint bigram and trigram language model and Chinese word segmentation for spelling error corrections (Xie et al. 2015). Among these systems, the CAS and NCTU&NTUT systems achieved relatively best overall performance when different metrics are considered.

3.2 *Chinese Grammatical Error Diagnosis*

Unlike the English learning setting for which many learning technologies have been developed, those to support Asian language learners are relatively rare. In response, the NLPTEA (Natural Language Processing Techniques for Educational Applications) workshops were organized to provide a forum where international participants can share knowledge on the computer-assisted techniques for Asian language learning and teaching. The initial workshop was held in conjunction with the 22nd International Conference on Computer in Education (ICCE 2014). The second and third edition of NLPTEA workshop was organized in conjunction with the ACL-IJCNLP 2015 and COLING 2016 conference, respectively.

In NLPTEA workshops, a series of shared tasks for Chinese grammatical error diagnosis was hosted (Yu et al. 2014a; Lee et al. 2015b, 2016b). Table 6 compares the differences between all three shared tasks. The goal of these tasks is to develop NLP techniques to automatically diagnose grammatical errors in Chinese sentences written by CFL learners. The grammatical errors are broadly categorized into four error types: word ordering, redundant, missing, and incorrect selection of linguistic components (also called PADS error types, denoting errors of Permutation, Addition, Deletion, and Selection, correspondingly). In the first edition in NLPTEA 2014 workshop, a sentence with/without one of grammatical errors is given, and the developed system should indicate whether it contains a grammatical error and further identify the error type if any error occurs. In the second edition in NLPTEA 2015 workshop, in addition to detecting whether a given sentence contains a grammatical error and identify the error type, the system should also indicate the range of occurring errors. In the third edition in NLPTEA 2016 workshop, the task is basically the same, except that a sentence may contain more than one errors and the HSK learner corpus is also included for the task. Besides the provided data sets, participants are allowed to adopt the other language resources which should be manifested in their system description papers. Among all registered participants, there are 5, 6, and 7 teams, respectively, submitting their testing results and system papers. We briefly describe them as follows.

For the NLPTEA 2014 shared task, the KUAS&NTNU system used manually constructed and automatically generated rules to identify grammatical errors (Chang et al. 2014). The UDS system designed an n-gram frequency-based approach to detect grammatical errors (Zampieri and Tan 2014). The NTOU system defined several features to train SVM classifiers for error detection (Lin and Chan 2014). The NCYU system adopted word segmentation and part-of-speech tagging techniques to identify missing and redundant error types (Yeh et al. 2014b). To overcome the insufficient data for supervised machine learning, the TMU system extracted a Chinese learner corpus from the Lang-8 website, and used it as a parallel corpus for phrase-based statistical machine translation for grammatical error identification (Zhao et al. 2014).

For the NLPTEA 2015 shared task, The HITSZ system presented an ensemble learning based method to detect and identify grammatical errors (Xiang et al. 2015). The SCAU system adopted a hybrid model by integrating rule-based and n-gram statistical methods for grammatical error diagnosis (Wu et al. 2015b). The CYUT team built an error diagnosis system based on the CRFs (Wu et al. 2015a). The NTOU system proposed two sentence likelihood functions based on frequencies of Google n-grams to diagnose grammatical errors (Lin and Chen 2015). The NCYU system also used statistical word and part-of-speech patterns based CRFs to detect grammatical errors (Yeh et al. 2015). The TMU examined corpus augmentation and explored syntax-based and hierarchical phrase-based translation models to participate in this task (Zhao et al. 2015).

For the NLPTEA 2016 shared task, the ANO system and CYUT-III system diagnosed grammatical errors based on the CRFs (Chen et al. 2016a; Liu et al. 2016). In addition to the CRF, word order sensitive embedding approaches were applied to this task (Chou et al. 2016). The NTOU system generated and scored correction candidates for grammatical error diagnosis (Chen et al. 2016b). The HIT system adopted long short-term memory (LSTM) neural networks to identify grammatical errors (Zheng et al. 2016). The PKU system presented a model based on bidirectional LSTM (Huang and Wang 2016). The NCYU system proposed the structure of the recurrent neural network using LSTM to detect grammatical errors (Yeh et al. 2016). The YUN-HPCC system built single word embedding based convolutional neural networks and LSTM neural networks for this task (Yang et al. 2016).

From the viewpoint of performance, a good system should have a high F1 score and a low false positive rate. Overall, none of the abovementioned system provided

Table 6 The similarities and differences of all NLPTEA shared tasks for Chinese Grammatical Error Diagnosis

Shared Task	NLPTEA 2014 (Yu et al. 2014a)	NLPTEA 2015 (Lee et al. 2015b)	NLPTEA 2016 (Lee et al. 2016b)
Examples	Example 1: Input: (sid = C1-1876-2) 對社會國家不同的影響 Output: C1-1876-2, Missing Example 2: Input: (sid = A2-0775-2) 我起床很早 Output: A2-0775-2, Disorder	Example 1: Input: (sid = B2-0080) 他是我的以前的室友 Output: B2-0080, 4, 4, Redundant Example 2: Input: (sid = B1-1193) 吳先生是修理腳踏車的拿手 Output: B1-1193, 11, 12, Selection	Example 1: Input: (sid = A2-0011-1) 我聽到你找到工作。恭喜恭喜! Output: A2-0011-1, 2, 3, S A2-0011-1, 9, 9, M Example 2: Input: (sid = 00038800464) 我真不明白。她们可能是追求一些前代的浪漫。 Output: 00038800464, correct
Data Source	TOCFL Learner Corpus	TOCFL Learner Corpus	TOCFL Learner Corpus & HSK Dynamic Composition Corpus
Training Set	1506 writings (5607 errors)	2205 sentences (2205 errors)	TOCFL Track: 10,693 sentences (24,492 errors) HSK Track: 10,071 sentences (24,797 errors)
Test Set	1750 sentences; half error-free and half with one grammatical error	1000 sentences; half error-free and half with one grammatical error	TOCFL Track: 3528 sentences (1703 correct & 1825 errors) HSK Track: 3011 sentences (1539 correct & 1472 errors)
Technical Challenges	Error Detection Error Identification	Error Detection (binary class categorization) Error Identification (multi-class categorization) Error Position (sequence labeling)	
Evaluation Metrics	False Positive Rate Detection-/Identification-level Accuracy/Precision/Recall/F1	False Positive Rate Detection-level Accuracy/Precision/Recall/F1 Identification-level Accuracy/Precision/Recall/F1 Position-level Accuracy/Precision/Recall/F1	
Teams	13 teams (4 from Taiwan, 3 from China, and 1 each from Germany, Japan, New Zealand, Russia, UK, and USA	13 teams (4 from Taiwan, 3 from China, 2 from USA, 2 from UK, 1 from Japan, and 1 from Poland)	15 teams (8 from China, 4 from Taiwan, 1 from Dublin, 1 from Germany, and 1 private firm)

satisfactory results when different metrics are measured, indicating the difficulty of developing systems for effective grammatical error diagnosis, especially in the CFL contexts.

3.3 Evaluation Summary

Based on the evaluation results of Chinese Spelling Check bakeoffs, exploiting feature-based conditional random fields is a good choice for achieving relatively better performance. In addition, integrating heuristic rules to correct commonly confused characters can usually enhance the performance easily.

Recently, neural networks based deep learning techniques were adopted to diagnose Chinese grammatical errors and accomplished promising results. However, a large-scale of instances are needed to train and fine-tune parameters of complicated networks. Besides, the biased distribution of error types in the training instances reflecting real errors that may be caused by CFL learners is also a challenging issue.

All evaluations encourage the proposal of unorthodox and innovative approaches which could lead to a breakthrough. All data sets with gold standards and evaluation tool after the bakeoffs are publicly available as follows for research purposes.

- CLP 2014 Bakeoff for Chinese Spelling Check: http://ir.itc.ntnu.edu.tw/lre/clp14csc.html
- SIGHAN 2015 Bakeoff for Chinese Spelling Check: http://ir.itc.ntnu.edu.tw/lre/sighan8csc.html
- NLPTEA 2014 Shared Task for Chinese Grammatical Error Diagnosis: http://ir.itc.ntnu.edu.tw/lre/nlptea14cfl.htm
- NLPTEA 2015 Shared Task for Chinese Grammatical Error Diagnosis: http://ir.itc.ntnu.edu.tw/lre/nlptea15cged.htm
- NLPTEA 2016 Shared Task for Chinese Grammatical Error Diagnosis: http://ir.itc.ntnu.edu.tw/lre/nlptea16cged.htm.

4 Conclusions

This chapter introduces two precious Chinese learner corpora: the HSK Dynamic Composition Corpus and the TOCFL Learner Corpus. We also describe two kinds of shared tasks based on these corpora for automated Chinese error diagnosis. One is a series of SIGHAN bakeoffs for Chinese spelling checkers. The other is a succession of the NLPTEA workshop shared tasks for Chinese grammatical error diagnosis. The hope is through our description the researchers could easily follow the development of Chinese error diagnosis by analyzing representative leaner corpora and using publicly released datasets as benchmarks to advance the techniques by enhancing system performance.

Acknowledgements This study was partially supported by the Ministry of Science and Technology, under the grant MOST 103-2221-E-003-013-MY3, MOST 105-2221-E-003-020-MY2, MOST 106-2221-E-003-030-MY2, and the "Aim for the Top University Project" and "Center of Language Technology for Chinese" of National Taiwan Normal University, sponsored by the Ministry of Education, Taiwan.

References

Chang, L.-P. (2016). Error classification and annotation of the TOCFL learner corpus. In *Proceedings of the 3rd International Conference of Interlanguage Corpora* (pp. 131–159). Beijing, China.

Chang, T.-H., Sung, Y.-T., Hong, J.-F., & Chang, J.-I. (2014). KNGED: A tool for grammatical error diagnosis of Chinese sentences. In *Proceedings of the 1st Workshop on Natural Language Processing Techniques for Educational Applications* (pp. 48–55). Nara, Japan.

Chang, T.-H., Chen, H.-C., & Yang, C.-H. (2015). Introduction to a proofreading tool for Chinese spelling check task of SIGHAN-8. In *Proceedings of the 8th SIGHAN Workshop on Chinese Language Processing* (pp. 50–55). Beijing, China.

Chen, P.-L., Wu, S.-H., Chen, L.-P., & Yang, P.-C. (2016a). CYUT-III system at Chinese grammatical error diagnosis task. In *Proceedings of the 3rd Workshop on Natural Language Processing Techniques for Educational Applications* (pp. 63–72). Osaka, Japan.

Chen, S.-H., Tsai, Y.-L., & Lin, C.-J. (2016b). Generating and scoring correction candidates in Chinese grammatical error diagnosis. In *Proceedings of the 3rd Workshop on Natural Language Processing Techniques for Educational Applications* (pp. 131–139). Osaka, Japan.

Chiu, H.-W., Wu, J.-C., & Chang, J. S. (2014). Chinese spelling checking based on noisy channel model. In *Proceedings of the 3rd CIPS-SIGHAN Joint Conference on Chinese Language Processing* (pp. 202–209). Wuhan, China.

Chou, W.-C., Lin, C.-K., Liao, Y.-F., & Wang, Y.-R. (2016). Word order sensitive embedding features/conditional random field-based Chinese grammatical error detection. In *Proceedings of the 3rd Workshop on Natural Language Processing Techniques for Educational Applications* (pp. 73–81). Osaka, Japan.

Chu, W.-C., & Lin, C.-J. (2014). NTOU Chinese spelling check system in CLP bake-off 2014. In *Proceedings of the 3rd CIPS-SIGHAN Joint Conference on Chinese Language Processing* (pp. 210–215). Wuhan, China.

Chu, W.-C., & Lin, C.-J. (2015). NTOU Chinese spelling check system in SIGHAN-8 bake-off. In *Proceedings of the 8th SIGHAN Workshop on Chinese Language Processing* (pp. 137–143). Beijing, China.

Cui, X., & Zhang, B.-L. (2011). The principles for building the "International Corpus of Learner Corpus". *Applied Linguistics, 2011*(2), 100–108.

Díaz-Negrillo, A., & Fernández-Domínguez, J. (2006). Error tagging systems for learner corpora. *Revista española de lingüística aplicada (RESLA), 19,* 83–102.

Fachverband Chinesisch e.V. (2010). Statement of the Fachverband Chinesisch e.V. on the new HSK Chinese Proficiency Test. http://www.fachverband-chinesisch.de/sites/default/files/FaCh2010_ErklaerungHSK_en.pdf. Accessed December 26, 2017.

Granger, S. (2015). Contrastive interlanguage analysis: A reappraisal. *International Journal of Learner Corpus Research, 1*(1), 7–24.

Gu, L., Wang, Y., & Liang, X. (2014). Introduction to NJUPT Chinese spelling check system in CLP-2014 bakeoff. In *Proceedings of the 3rd CIPS-SIGHAN Joint Conference on Chinese Language Processing* (pp. 167–172). Wuhan, China.

Huang, S., & Wang, H. (2016). Bi-LSTM neural networks for Chinese grammatical error diagnosis. In *Proceedings of the 3rd Workshop on Natural Language Processing Techniques for Educational Applications* (pp. 148–154). Osaka, Japan.

Huang, Q., Huang, P., Zhang, X., Xie, W., Hong, K., Chen, B., & Huang, L. (2014). Chinese spelling check system based on tri-gram model. In *Proceedings of the 3rd CIPS-SIGHAN Joint Conference on Chinese Language Processing* (pp. 173–178). Wuhan, China.

Lee, L.-H., Lee, K.-C., Chang, L.-P., Tseng, Y.-H., Yu, L.-C., & Chen, H.-H. (2014). A tagging editor for learner corpus annotation and error analysis. In *Proceedings of the 22nd International Conference on Computers in Education* (pp. 806–808). Nara, Japan.

Lee, L.-H., Chang, L.-P., Liao, B.-S., Cheng, W.-L., & Tseng, Y.-H. (2015a). A retrieval system for interlanguage analysis. In *Proceedings of the 23rd International Conference on Computers in Education* (pp. 599–601). Hangzhou, China.

Lee, L.-H., Yu, L.-C., & Chang, L.-P. (2015b). Overview of the NLP-TEA 2015 shared task for Chinese grammatical error diagnosis. In *Proceedings of the 2nd Workshop on Natural Language Processing Techniques for Educational Applications* (pp. 1–6). Beijing, China.

Lee, L.-H., Chang, L.-P., & Tseng, Y.-H. (2016a). Developing learner corpus annotation for Chinese grammatical errors. In *Proceedings of the 20th International Conference on Asian Language Processing* (pp. 254–257). Tainan, Taiwan.

Lee, L.-H., Rao, G., Yu, L.-C., Xun, E., Zhang, B., & Chang, L.-P. (2016b). Overview of the NLP-TEA 2016 shared task for Chinese grammatical error diagnosis. In *Proceedings of the 3rd Workshop on Natural Language Processing Techniques for Educational Applications* (pp. 40–48). Osaka, Japan.

Lee, L.-H., Tseng, Y.-H., & Chang, L.-P. (2018). Building a TOCFL learner corpus for Chinese grammatical error diagnosis. In *Proceedings of the 11th International Conference on Language Resources and Evaluation* (pp. 2298–2304), Miyazaki, Japan.

Lin, C.-J., & Chan, S.-H. (2014). Description of NTOU Chinese grammar checker in CFL 2014. In *Proceedings of the 1st Workshop on Natural Language Processing Techniques for Educational Applications* (pp. 75–78). Nara, Japan.

Lin, C.-J., & Chen, S.-H. (2015). NTOU Chinese grammar checker for CGED shared task. In *Proceedings of the 2nd Workshop on Natural Language Processing Techniques for Educational Applications* (pp. 15–19). Beijing, China.

Little, D. (2006). The Common European Framework of Reference for languages: Content, purpose, origin, reception and impact. *Language Teaching, 39*(3), 167–190.

Liu, M., Jian, P., & Huang, H. (2014). Introduction to BIT Chinese spelling correction system at CLP 2014 bake-off. In *Proceedings of the 3rd CIPS-SIGHAN Joint Conference on Chinese Language Processing* (pp. 179–185). Wuhan, China.

Liu, Y., Han, Y., Zhuo, L., & Zan, H. (2016). Automatic grammatical error detection for Chinese based on conditional random field. In *Proceedings of the 3rd Workshop on Natural Language Processing Techniques for Educational Applications* (pp. 57–62). Osaka, Japan.

Malmasi, S., & Dras, M. (2015). Large-scale native language identification with cross-corpus evaluation. In *Proceedings of the 2015 Conference of the North American Chapter of the Association for Computational Linguistics—Human Language Technologies* (pp. 1403–1409). Denver, CO, USA.

Sakaguchi, K., Arase, Y., & Komachi, M. (2013). Discriminative approach to fill-in-the-blank quiz generation for language learners. In *Proceedings of the 51st Annual Meeting of the Association for Computational Linguistics* (pp. 238–242). Sofia, Bulgaria.

Sawai, Y., Komachi, M., & Matsumoto, Y. (2013). A learner corpus-based approach for verb suggestion for ESL. In *Proceedings of the 51st Annual Meeting of the Association for Computational Linguistics* (pp. 708–713). Sofia, Bulgaria.

Swanson, B., & Charniak, E. (2013). Extracting the native language signal for second language acquisition. In *Proceedings of the 2013 Conference of the North American Chapter of the Association for Computational Linguistics—Human Language Technologies* (pp. 85–94). Atlanta, GA, USA.

Tseng, Y.-H., Lee, L.-H., Chang, L.-P., & Chen, H.-H. (2015). Introduction to SIGHAN 2015 bake-off for Chinese spelling check. In *Proceedings of the 8th SIGHAN Workshop on Chinese Language Processing* (pp. 32–37). Beijing, China.

Wang, Y.-R., & Liao, Y.-F. (2014). NCTU and NTUT's entry to CLP-2014 Chinese spelling check evaluation. In *Proceedings of the 3rd CIPS-SIGHAN Joint Conference on Chinese Language Processing* (pp. 216–219). Wuhan, China.

Wang, Y.-R., & Liao, Y.-F. (2015). Word vector/conditional random field-based Chinese spelling error detection for SIGHAN-2015 evaluation. In *Proceedings of the 8th SIGHAN Workshop on Chinese Language Processing* (pp. 46–49). Beijing, China.

Wang, C., & Seneff, S. (2007). Automatic assessment of student translations for foreign language tutoring. In *Proceedings of the 2007 Conference of the North American Chapter of the Association for Computational Linguistics—Human Language Technologies* (pp. 468–475). Rochester, NY, USA.

Wu, S.-H., Liu, C.-L., & Lee, L.-H. (2013). Chinese spelling check evaluation at SIGHAN bake-off 2013. In *Proceedings of the 7th SIGHAN Workshop on Chinese Language Processing* (pp. 35–42). Nagoya, Japan.

Wu, S.-H., Chen, P.-L., Chen, L.-P., Yang, P.-C., & Yang, R.-D. (2015a). Chinese grammatical error diagnosis by conditional random fields. In *Proceedings of the 2nd Workshop on Natural Language Processing Techniques for Educational Applications* (pp. 7–14). Beijing, China.

Wu, X., Huang, P., Wang, J., Guo, Q., Xu, Y., & Chen, C. (2015b). Chinese grammatical error diagnosis system based on hybrid model. In *Proceedings of the 2nd Workshop on Natural Language Processing Techniques for Educational Applications* (pp. 117–125). Beijing, China.

Xiang, Y., Wang, X., Han, W., & Hong, Q. (2015). Chinese grammatical error diagnosis using ensemble learning. In *Proceedings of the 2nd Workshop on Natural Language Processing Techniques for Educational Applications* (pp. 99–104). Beijing, China.

Xie, W., Huang, P., Zhang, X., Hong, K., Huang, Q., Chen, B., & Huang, L. (2015). Chinese spelling check system based on n-gram model. In *Proceedings of the 8th SIGHAN Workshop on Chinese Language Processing* (pp. 128–136). Beijing, China.

Xin, Y., Zhao, H., Wang, Y., & Jia, Z. (2014). An improved graph model for Chinese spell checking. In *Proceedings of the 3rd CIPS-SIGHAN Joint Conference on Chinese Language Processing* (pp. 157–166). Wuhan, China.

Xiong, J., Zhang, Q., Hou, J., Wang, Q., Wang, Y., & Cheng, X. (2014). Extended HMM and ranking models for Chinese spelling correction. In *Proceedings of the 3rd CIPS-SIGHAN Joint Conference on Chinese Language Processing* (pp. 133–138). Wuhan, China.

Yang, J., Peng, B., Wang, J., Zhang, J., & Zhang, X. (2016). Chinese grammatical error diagnosis using single word embedding. In *Proceedings of the 3rd Workshop on Natural Language Processing Techniques for Educational Applications* (pp. 155–161). Osaka, Japan.

Yannakoudakis, H., Briscoe, T., & Medlock, B. (2011). A new dataset and method for automatically grading ESOL texts. In *Proceedings of the 49th Annual Meeting of the Association for Computational Linguistics* (pp. 180–189). Portland, OR, USA.

Yeh, J.-F., Lu, Y.-Y., Lee, C.-H., Yu, Y.-H., & Chen, Y.-T. (2014a). Chinese word spelling correction based on rule induction. In *Proceedings of the 3rd CIPS-SIGHAN Joint Conference on Chinese Language Processing* (pp. 139–145). Wuhan, China.

Yeh, J.-F., Lu, Y.-Y., Lee, C.-H., Yu, Y.-H., & Chen, Y.-T. (2014b). Detecting grammatical error in Chinese sentence for foreign. In *Proceedings of the 1st Workshop on Natural Language Processing Techniques for Educational Applications* (pp. 62–68). Nara, Japan.

Yeh, J.-F., Yeh, C.-K., Yu, K.-H., Li, Y.-T., & Tsai, W.-L. (2015). Conditional random field-based grammatical error detection for Chinese as second language. In *Proceedings of the 2nd Workshop on Natural Language Processing Techniques for Educational Applications* (pp. 105–110). Beijing, China.

Yeh, J.-F., Hsu, T.-W., & Yeh, C.-K. (2016). Grammatical error detection based on machine learning for Mandarin as second language learning. In *Proceedings of the 3rd Workshop on Natural Language Processing Techniques for Educational Applications* (pp. 140–147). Osaka, Japan.

Yu, J., & Li, Z. (2014). Chinese spelling error detection and correction based on language model, pronunciation, and shape. In *Proceedings of the 3rd CIPS-SIGHAN Joint Conference on Chinese Language Processing* (pp. 220–223). Wuhan, China.

Yu, L.-C., Lee, L.-H., & Chang, L.-P. (2014a). Overview of grammatical error diagnosis for learning Chinese as a foreign language. In *Proceedings of the 1st Workshop on Natural Language Processing Techniques for Educational Applications* (pp. 42–47). Nara, Japan.

Yu, L.-C., Lee, L.-H., Tseng, Y.-H., & Chen, H.-H. (2014b). Overview of SIGHAN 2014 bake-off for Chinese spelling check. In *Proceedings of the 3rd CIPS-SIGHAN Joint Conference on Chinese Language Processing* (pp. 126–132). Wuhan, China.

Zampieri, M., & Tan, L. (2014). Grammatical error detection with limited training data: The case of Chinese. In *Proceedings of the 1st Workshop on Natural Language Processing Techniques for Educational Applications* (pp. 69–74). Nara, Japan.

Zhang, B.-L., & Cui, X. (2013). Design concepts of the construction and research of the interlanguage corpus of Chinese from global learners. *Language Teaching and Linguistic Study, 2013*(5), 27–34.

Zhang, S., Xiong, J., Hou, J., Zhang, Q., & Cheng, X. (2015). HANSpeller++: A unified framework for Chinese spelling correction. In *Proceedings of the 8th SIGHAN Workshop on Chinese Language Processing* (pp. 38–45). Beijing, China.

Zhao, Y., Komachi, M., & Ishikawa, H. (2014). Extracting a Chinese learner corpus from the Web: Grammatical error correction for learning Chinese as a foreign language with statistical machine translation. In *Proceedings of the 1st Workshop on Natural Language Processing Techniques for Educational Applications* (pp. 56–61). Nara, Japan.

Zhao, Y., Komachi, M., & Ishikawa, H. (2015). Improving Chinese grammatical error correction with corpus augmentation and hierarchical phrase-based statistical machine translation. In *Proceedings of the 2nd Workshop on Natural Language Processing Techniques for Educational Applications* (pp. 111–116). Beijing, China.

Zheng, B., Che, W., Guo, J., & Liu, T. (2016). Chinese grammatical error diagnosis with long short-term memory networks. In *Proceedings of the 3rd Workshop on Natural Language Processing Techniques for Educational Applications* (pp. 49–56). Osaka, Japan.

Automated Chinese Essay Scoring Based on Multilevel Linguistic Features

Tao-Hsing Chang and Yao-Ting Sung

Abstract Writing assessments make up an important part of the learning process as one masters the important linguistic skill of writing. However, this process has not been implemented effectively or on a large scale because the task of essay scoring is very time-consuming. The solution to this problem is AES, where machines are used to automatically score essays. In fact, the application of AES to English learning has been successful. Due to differences in linguistic characteristics, a redesign is needed before AES can be applied to Chinese learning. The purpose of this chapter is to introduce ACES, an automated system for scoring Chinese essays, and explain the basic framework, design principles, and scoring accuracy of the system. Unlike some end-to-end AES systems, ACES' basic framework is designed to provide more interpretative features. The experimental results show that the performance of the ACES system is stable and reliable, and on par with other commercial English AES systems.

1 Introduction

Writing is an important part of language education, and writing assessments are an important tool for assessing the effectiveness of writing instruction. However, difficulties related to scoring exams greatly restrict the implementation and development of writing assessments. In addition to studying in the classroom, students must also often engage in a lot of after-class studies. However, for teachers, correcting students' compositions is an extremely time-consuming task; if a teacher is responsible for a relatively large number of students, then the job of correcting compositions becomes

T.-H. Chang (✉)
National Kaohsiung University of Science and Technology, Kaohsiung, Taiwan
e-mail: changth@nkust.edu.tw

Y.-T. Sung
National Taiwan Normal University, Taipei, Taiwan
e-mail: sungtc@ntnu.edu.tw

X. Lu and B. Chen (eds.), *Computational and Corpus Approaches to Chinese Language Learning*, Chinese Language Learning Sciences,
https://doi.org/10.1007/978-981-13-3570-9_13

a significant burden. As such, the amount of writing practice assigned by teachers must often be restricted within a range that the teacher can cope with.

These problems also create difficulties for organizations that conduct large-scale writing assessments. With regard to scoring writings, these organizations must consider the following three factors: speed, cost, and reliability of raters. After examinations, the participants hope to quickly receive exam results; however, the only current means of increasing the pace of exam scoring is to increase the number of raters. Because raters must go through training and certification, increasing the number of raters also greatly increases assessment costs. Furthermore, if a composition is only reviewed by one rater and this rater is not reliable, then this will result in that participants do not trust the examination results. To increase the credibility of assessments, it is necessary to increase the number of raters and to increase the scoring capabilities of raters; this includes improving raters' understanding of scoring rubrics. However, these solutions cause significant increases in assessment costs. These large examination fees are very burdensome for nonprofit organizations or educational studies with limited funding. This means that fee-taking commercial organizations can transfer costs but must also recruit and train a sufficient number of qualified raters to overcome issues of scoring speed and scorer consistency. These issues are difficult to resolve. As such, the question of how to rapidly and effectively conduct writing scoring with low costs has become an important research topic.

One method for resolving the problems mentioned above is the use of Automated Essay Scoring (AES) technology, developed using natural language processing (NLP) and information retrieval (IR) techniques. NLP and IR are primarily the study of how to use computers to analyze the structure and linguistic meaning of human speech and text and to extract meaningful information for further applications. Beginning in the 1990s, resulting from substantial advances in NLP and IR, many researchers proposed usable AES systems. These systems have been widely applied to large-scale international language assessments, such as SAT and GMAT.

Although the development of AES systems has been successful, they are rarely applied to Chinese language writing. The primary reason for this are the different linguistic characteristics between Chinese and English. Many comparative linguistic studies have noted that although there are significant similarities in the frameworks for scoring Chinese writing and English writing, the intrinsic features of writing in these two different languages vary greatly. For example, Kaplan (1966) first proposed the idea that in different languages, writing not only varies with regard to grammar, vocabulary, and sentence pattern, but the usage of figure of speech also varies significantly across languages. Cai (2006) systematically organized and compared English and Chinese writing, noting many levels of differences. These variations can be divided among the four levels of topical, organization, sentence pattern, and rhetorical differences.

In both Chinese and English writing, emphasis is placed on the need to choose appropriate materials and for articles to fit the writing; however, cultural differences lead to different perspectives towards themes and writing materials. Many studies (Cai 2006; Kaplan 1966; Scollon and Kirkpatrick 2000) have explained the effects of cultural differences on writing. For example, when Chinese students choose writing materials for their works, they prefer to refer to authority or antiquity and rarely express personal opinions or feelings. Their criticisms of opposing viewpoints are more indirect and mild and may even be supportive of these opposing viewpoints. In contrast, Western students prefer to raise a large number of examples to support their viewpoints, do not shy away from sharing their own viewpoints, and directly and aggressively criticize opposing views. As such, scoring models must consider cultural differences when scoring narrative writing.

Many studies have also noted the relatively large differences in structure between Chinese and English writing. Kaplan (1966) noted that the structure of English writing is usually linear; English paragraphs usually begin with a topic sentence, which directly explains the central idea of the paragraph, while subsequent sentences develop this idea in sequence and each sentence is used to describe the topic. Chinese writing structures are usually helical; first, the topic is discussed and developed from different perspectives, and then this form is repeated in a parataxical form to express the writing theme. Scollon et al. (2000) noted that Western culture is accustomed to the use of deductive methods such as inference and argumentation, while Eastern culture leans towards the use of inductive argumentation. These differences in custom cause differences in writing structure. Zeng (1997) noted that the subject-predicate form does not exist in Chinese paragraph structures. These structures are dispersed only use few conjunctions to link paragraphs. Paragraphs are only one part of the overall layout of Chinese writing; sometimes, paragraphs are only used to describe latent or minor topics. English paragraph structures are consistent with principles of article organization; it is necessary to adhere to the principles of unity, coherence, and completeness. Liu (1999) also states that tree diagrams for writing structures show that in English writing, subordinate structures are generally used to link topics, while Chinese writing tends to use parallel structures to link topics.

Sentence structure variations also cause similar difficulties for AES in different languages. Many studies have pointed out that Chinese sentence structures are looser when compared to English sentence structures. Jiao (2002) argues that there are three major differences between Chinese and English sentence structures. First, English sentences use a tree-type structure, while Chinese sentences often use a linear pattern. Second, English sentences emphasize hypotaxis, while Chinese sentences emphasize parataxis. Third, there are clear restrictions for English sentences; when the main objects appear in the sentence, the sentence is complete. That is, a sentence is usually used to express an event. In Chinese sentences, however, the clauses often possess complete sentence structures and semantic meaning, but only after a series of events and actions has been completed does the sentence truly end. It is difficult to determine the actual boundaries of sentences. Lee and Zeng (2001) note that both Chinese and English sentence structure consists of three fundamental elements but there are variations between the two languages with regard to sentence patterns. For example, Chinese verbs and adjectives can act as subjects, but in English, a verb must take the infinitive or gerund form to act as a subject. Similar restrictions also appear with regard to predicates and objects. Furthermore, regarding the transformation of sentence structures, in Chinese, the object can be moved to come before the subject, but this is not possible in English sentences.

Intuitively, differences in rhetoric across languages should be relatively limited. However, Lee (1999) and Cai (2006) analyzed and compared many types of figures of speech in Chinese and English and noted that there are quite large differences in figures of speech between Chinese and English. For example, Lee (1999) used the example of similes in English and Chinese; although they look relatively similar, and are basic and common figures of speech, the use of vehicles and the selection of connectives varies across these languages. Bai and Shi (2002) analyzed 16 types of figures of speech in Chinese and 26 types of figures of speech in English; in both Chinese and English, there are six types of figures of speech that are rarely seen in the other language. This means that even for similar figures of speech, the technique and timing of their use is different.

Because of the differences in the language characteristics described above, Chinese AES requires a new design to analyze writing. Automated Chinese Essay Scoring (ACES) is a relatively successful form of Chinese AES, and this chapter mainly introduces the principles of ACES and the performance of its practical application. In the second section of this chapter, we will introduce some current AES systems and analyze their frameworks to help readers understand the common framework of AES systems. In the third section, we will explain the basic framework and principles of ACES. In the fourth section, we will show the accuracy of using ACES to grade compositions written by Taiwanese junior high school students. In the fifth section, we will discuss the future development of Chinese AES.

2 Research Related to AES

The Project Essay Grader (PEG) was the earliest developed AES system. Its design is based on a hypothesis called trins-proxes: an article's intrinsic variable can be quantitatively measured using its approximation. For example, an article's length can be used to represent its level of fluency and the number of prepositions and relational pronouns can be used to represent the article's sentence structure complexity, while variation in the length of words can indicate the author's ability to use vocabulary. Experimental results have shown that the correlation coefficient for PEG predicted scores and expert scores is 0.87. This result is similar to the correlation coefficient for two different individual raters. The trins-proxes hypothesis has significant effects on the development of AES; almost all real AES products use many approximations (also called "features") to measure the quality of a composition. This is similar to a doctor's combined use of blood pressure, blood sugar, and medical imaging to assess a patient's health. Some AESs even use many hundreds of approximation measurement results to assess the level of writing ability demonstrated in an essay. This method is also called the feature-based method.

The e-rater (Atali and Burstein 2006; Burstein et al. 1998) is the most representative feature-based AES system. It uses three modules to assess three types of linguistic features: discourse, syntactic, and domain. The discourse module uses the conceptual framework of relational connection to determine organizational structure;

these relational connections may be clue words, phrases, or grammatical patterns. The syntactical module first constructs the grammar trees of sentences. Then, it is employed to determine the subject, verb, and clause structure of a sentence, such as infinitive clauses or subordinate clauses. With these results, the e-rater can use a variety of grammatical elements to assess writing quality. The domain module is used to analyze the usage of vocabulary in a composition. The e-rater argues that when the word choice and variety of vocabulary used in two pieces of writing are similar, they should exhibit similar writing quality. As such, the domain module will use the words used in a theme for an unscored essay to search for a scored essay with similar domain words from a training corpus. The domain score of unscored essay will refer to that of the scored essay. Systems similar to e-rater are BETSY (Runder and Liang 2002), and IntelliMetric (Elliot 2003), etc.

Another kind of AES technique is based on semantic similarity analysis techniques. This type of method converts each essay into a mathematical form, called a “semantic vector.” A semantic vector represents the position of the essay in the semantic space. When the semantic vectors of two essays approach each other, this indicates that the contents of the two essays are similar. This technique assumes that for two essays with increasingly similar semantic descriptions, the writing qualities of these two essays should also be increasingly close to one another. A classic example of this is the Intelligent Essay Assessor (IEA) system. It uses latent semantic analysis (LSA) techniques to construct a semantic space and to convert essays into semantic vectors. Some AES studies aimed at Chinese or Japanese writing (Peng et al. 2010) also adopt this technique. Although in early periods of research, semantic similarity was only used to predict writing scores, currently, many feature-based AES systems also include semantic similarity as a feature for comprehensive writing assessment.

3 Framework of the ACES System

ACES is a system capable of automatically analyzing the content of Chinese writing and predicting the writing ability level of the author (below, this level will be referred to as the writing score). Similar to most AES systems, ACES uses a feature-based framework, as shown in Fig. 1. It is composed of three principal modules: preprocessing, feature extraction, and the scoring model. The following subsections will introduce the principles and applications of these modules.

3.1 Preprocessing

Because ACES must analyze vocabulary and sentence structures in the text when assessing writing, every sentence must first be processed in four steps: unknown word extraction, word segmentation, part-of-speech tagging (POS tagging), and grammar

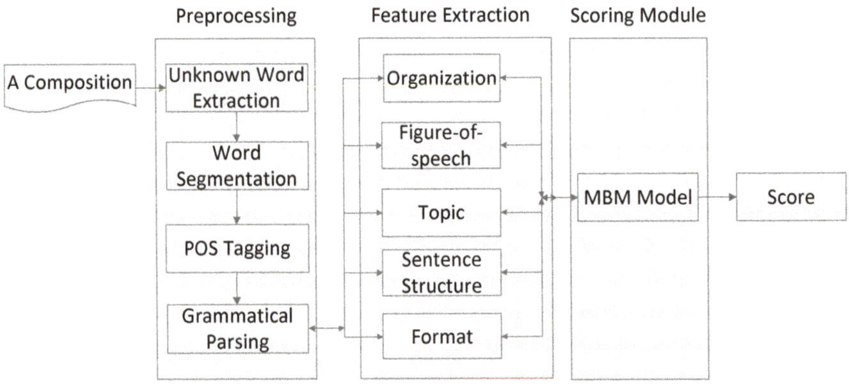

Fig. 1 ACES System framework

parsing. In English sentences, two words are separated with a blank. However, there are no spaces between words in Chinese sentences. This causes two problems. First, the word segments of Chinese sentences must first be identified to conduct POS tagging and grammar parsing. This step is also called word segmentation. Second, in English, words that do not appear in the dictionary are unknown words. However, in Chinese, unknown words are composed of known character components, and often, Chinese character components can be used alone to form a word, and so it can be quite difficult to identify whether a sentence contains unknown words.

There are a lot of studies on the identification of Chinese unknown words. However, many studies focus on the identification of the names of people and organizations, while there are a broad range of unknown word types that appear in students' writing, such as popular catchphrase. As such, ACES uses an unknown word identification method called SPLR (Chang and Lee 2003) to extract the Chinese unknown words of students' essays. This method assumes that there is difference between the statistical characteristics of unknown word strings and meaningless strings in a training corpus, and so the statistical characteristics of a string in essays can be transformed into several indices. The correlations between these indices can be used to identify whether a string is an unknown word or not.

Similarly, a lot of Chinese word segmentation and POS tagging tools have been developed and proposed. ACES uses a Chinese word segmentation and POS tagging tool called WECAn (Chang 2015) to process sentences in essays. WECAn utilizes both of the maximum matching model and conditional random field (Lafferty et al. 2001) model to segment sentences into words. Moreover, it also employs an improved hidden Markov model (Manning and Schütze 1999) to tag the POS of words. Compared with other tools, WECAn has a comparable accuracy for word segmentation and POS tagging in typical texts. In addition, WECAn also provides different functional options for different application environments, making it such that word segmentation results allow for greater accuracy in the analysis of Chinese writing. For instance, WECAn provides the function to revert reduplicated Chinese words into their original forms; for example, the reduplicated word "輕輕鬆鬆" (qingqing song-song; relaxed) can be converted into its original form, "輕鬆" (qingsong; relaxed). Because this kind of word reduplication is common in Chinese writing, WECAn provides a variety of functional options so that word segmentation and POS tagging can be adjusted for more appropriate analysis of Chinese writing.

In addition to WECAn, ACES also uses a tool called HanParser (Sung et al. 2016) to analyze sentence structure. This tool can use parsing trees to represent sentence structures of sentences on which word segmentation has already been conducted. The grammar inference rules for this tool are derived from Chinese TreeBank 3.0 (Chen et al. 2003) training. The definitions of symbols in sentence structure trees are the same as in CTB. Readers interested in WECAn and HanParser can refer to the web services offered at http://islab.kuas.edu.tw/HanParser.

3.2 Feature Extraction

Textual features can be divided into four levels: lexicon, syntax, semantics, and discourse (Sung et al. 2015). In writing, these four levels can correspond to the following four writing abilities: topics, rhetoric, sentence structure, and organization. ACES has designed various features and the method of extracting these features for essays. These features are also divided into two categories. The features of the first type can be treated as the approximations of the trins-proxes hypothesis, such as number of words, number of punctuations, or number of paragraphs. These features each represent one or multiple features of writing ability and are therefore called indirect features. The features of the second type are also used during human assess an essay; hence, these features are called direct features. For example, whether an essay uses rhetorical skills is one factor affecting its score, and so rhetoric in writing can be used as a direct feature. Below, we provide examples that explain how ACES extracts the direct features of these three writing abilities: organization, rhetoric, and topic. Furthermore, the number of misspelling words is an important indirect feature for scoring Chinese writing, and some studies believe that it is a direct feature of the lexicon level. In this subsection, we will also explain the misspelling words identification module of ACES. The details of these feature extraction methods can be found by consulting relevant references.

3.2.1 Topics

For writing in all types of languages, it is a difficult challenge to determine whether a composition conforms to a theme. This issue consists of two major difficulties. The first is the question of how to determine the degree to which a composition departs from the theme. For example, if there is a section with detailed descriptions of types of goods sold by snack bar and their prices in a composition with the topic "class break," although the circumstances of the snack bar are within the range of the topic, the described content is unrelated to the topic. Furthermore, if this irrelevant content is only present in a portion of the text, it becomes more difficult to score. Often, human raters determine the degree to which a composition departs from the prescribed domain based on their own background knowledge and the proportion of the writing that is unrelated to the topic, but this method presents the second difficulty to AES systems.

The ACES method for extracting topic features of a composition (Chang et al. 2009) is derived from the observation that some high-scoring compositions will describe some specific things addressed at a specified domain, but these things rarely appear in low-scoring writing. These things do not necessarily use the same vocabulary when mentioned but belong to the same semantics. For example, for writing on the topic "class break," many high-scoring compositions will mention vocabulary such as paeonia flowers, coconut trees, or sod; these words do not appear many times, but it can be seen that they belong to the category "plants," and are generally used to describe the campus landscape. It is interesting that in low-scoring writing on the topic "class break," vocabulary related to plants is rarely present. This phenomenon may result from two possible causes. The first is that only students with good writing skills are able to think of vividly describing the campus landscape in their writing, while the second is that for students with poor writing abilities, it is difficult to include descriptions of the campus landscape in their writing, and so these students choose not to write about this content. This kind of semantic categories that appears only in high-scoring writing is called the "discrimination type."

Another phenomenon that occurs in writing is that when the discrimination type of vocabulary is present in larger numbers within a composition, the writing score is often higher. As a result, ACES uses the number of discrimination type words appearing in writing as a topic feature. The method for constructing discrimination types is applied HowNet (Dong and Dong 2003) to convert the vocabulary that appears in training data into semantic categories. HowNet is a semantic thesaurus that records the semantic categories of each word. ACES takes count of each semantic category that appears in high-scoring writing and all writing respectively. Assuming that a semantic type appears a times in high-scoring essays, and b times in all essays, the probability that this semantic type is a discrimination type is $p = a/b$. When p is greater than a threshold t, then this semantic type is considered a discrimination type.

3.2.2 Rhetorical Features

ACES can recognize 12 types of figures of speech common in Chinese, including similes, parallelisms, repetition, metaphor, etc. Chang et al. (2007a) found that although compositions that use similes and parallelisms are not guaranteed to have high scores, they have much higher likelihoods of being high-scoring compositions when compared to works that do not use these figures of speech. This phenomenon does not exist only for these two types of figure of speech. ACES identifies specified figures of speech and designs a detection module for determining whether these figures of speech appear in a composition. The detection module is generally based on keywords, parts of speech, and structural patterns. Taking the example of similes, ACES can detect whether a simile is present in a sentence; if a connective is present, then ACES will proceed to determine whether typical nouns are present at specific locations surrounding the connective. If so, the nouns may be the tenor and vehicle of a simile. ACES will judge that the sentence contains a simile if these conditions are simultaneously met.

ACES' detection of figures of speech uses a relatively unique detection method for metaphors. In addition to meeting the conditions of a simile clause, a metaphorical clause must also meet the conditions of insufficient similarity to metaphorical vehicle and tenor. ACES uses the word2vec model as a basis for establishing a semantic space for vocabulary, further calculating the semantic similarity of two typical nouns in specific locations surrounding the sentence; if the degree of similarity is below a threshold, then the clause is viewed as a metaphorical clause. We can see from training data that compositions that contain metaphors have a higher probability of being high-scoring works than compositions with other figures of speech.

In addition to the phenomenon in which compositions that contain metaphors are extremely likely to have high scores, there is a different likelihood that typical figures of speech tend to appear in high-scoring writing. A possible reason for this difference is that some figures of speech are easier to use (such as repetition), while some require good writing skills to use. Different usages of some figures of speech also represent different levels of writing skills. For example, compositions containing the literary simile structure "如…一般" (ru…yiban), meaning "as…as a," have a higher probability of being high-scoring writing when compared to compositions that contain the typical simile structure "像…一樣" (xiang…yiyang), meaning "just like…." ACES also distinguishes between two features of these figures of speech, increasing the accuracy of using rhetorical features to predict writing scores.

3.2.3 Structural Features

The objective of writing is to express the personal ideas of the author. ACES assumes that the structure of a composition reflects the order and logic by which an author develops a relevant concept, where they express desired contents in sequence. This is similar to a movie script, where characters and locations will be presented in sequence while the story is developed. Furthermore, good writing structure involves appropriate organization of introductions of new topics, allowing readers to easily understand and accept the information transmitted by the author. Chang and Lee (2009) propose a method for extracting the previously described writing structure from a composition; this writing structure is called the C-L structure. ACES uses the C-L structure of a composition to serve as the structural feature of the writing.

This method first uses training corpus to establish a term co-occurrence matrix, whereby this matrix is converted into what is called an asymmetric relation matrix. This matrix can be used to determine the dependence relationship of any two concepts in a writing theme, and the dependence relationships between all concepts can determine the major concepts within the theme and whether these major concepts are correlated. For a composition, ACES extracts the major concepts expressed in the writing and then converts these concepts and their locations into a directed graph according to the order of their appearance and their correlation. This graph is the C-L structure of the composition.

Chang and Lee note that for a given writing theme, similar writing structures have similar scores. As such, ACES can extract the C-L structure of an unscored composition and then measure the similarity between the C-L structures of the composition and that of all writing in a training corpus. Next, it identifies the compositions that are most similar in this regard. The scores of these compositions can be used to estimate the score of the unscored writing.

3.2.4 Misspelling Word Feature

ACES uses a HanChecker tool (Chang et al. 2015) to detect misspelling words in writing. Generally speaking, essays with more misspelling words will have lower scores. As such, ACES uses the number of misspelling words as a feature. HanChecker distinguishes between two types of Chinese words. The first type is Chinese characters that are individually for words, such as the character and word "我" (wo, I); this type is called the single-character word. The other type is long words composed of more than one character, such as the two-character word "工作" (gong zuo, work). Assuming that an incorrect character appears in a long word, then the word segmentation tools will segment the word into its component Chinese characters in the form of a "successive singular character series" (SSCS). Therefore, HanChecker will analyze SSCS to determine whether an incorrect character was used. For each individual character in an SSCS, HanChecker first assumes that each character is not used incorrectly but that it is a component character of a long word. As such, HanChecker refers to all long words containing the character in question as "candidate words," while the original character sequence corresponding to the candidate word is called the "questionable character set."

Because questionable character sets do not necessarily include misspelling words, it is necessary to use a screening process to confirm whether the candidate word or questionable character set constitutes proper use. HanChecker has designed four indices to determine whether a questionable character set should be replaced by a candidate word. These four indices are the character's phonetic similarity, the character's visual similarity, frequency ratio, and probability ratio for POS. HanChecker assumes that one reason for the formation of misspelling words is confusion of a character's sound and of its visual appearance. If the candidate word's visual appearance and sound are dissimilar to the questionable character set, then the candidate word will not indicate the corrected form of the questionable character set. Therefore, the character sound similarity and visual appearance similarity indices are used to measure the similarity between a candidate word and questionable character set.

Furthermore, many questionable character sets are, in fact, frequently seen SCSS and do not include any incorrect characters; rather, there happen to be candidate words with character sounds and character visual appearances that are similar to the questionable character set. For this reason, HanChecker also determines whether the candidate word or questionable character set constitutes correct usage from the perspective of syntactical structures in a linguistic corpus. HanChecker calculates the frequencies of the questionable character set and candidate word within the linguistic corpus and compares the two. If the questionable character set's frequency is significantly lower than the candidate word, then the index "frequency ratio" will be large, indicating that the questionable character set may be a misspelt word. Conversely, if the index value is insufficiently large, this indicates that the questionable character set may not include an incorrect character. Furthermore, HanChecker can also use the Hidden Markov Model (HMM) to calculate whether the questionable character set or candidate word is more appropriate to use in a complete syntactical structure. To determine this, HanChecker compares the part-of-speech serial probability of each, and this result serves as the index "probability ratio for part of speech." If the probability of the questionable character set is much lower than the candidate word, then the index will have a large value, indicating that the questionable character set may contain an incorrect character.

3.3 Scoring Model

Each feature used by ACES has a corresponding index value. This index value is further converted into the probabilities corresponding to each score. However, sometimes, the information provided by features is contradictory. For example, an essay may be highly likely to receive a high score based on its topic features but may have a low likelihood of receiving a high score based on its structural features. As a result, it is necessary to possess a model that can combine these potentially contradictory feature values and generate a predicted score for the essay. Chang et al. (2014) designed a scoring model based on the multivariate Bernoulli model (MBM). This scoring model can combine the probability of each score for different features of an essay. Assuming that there is an essay e, then the probability that e will receive a score c_j can be calculated using the below equation:

$$P(d_i|c_j) = \prod_{t=1}^{V} \left[B_{it}P(w_t|c_j) + (1 - B_{it})(1 - P(w_t|c_j))\right] \tag{1}$$

where d_i represents essay i; c_j represents score j; $B_{it} \in \{0, 1\}$ indicates whether feature t appears in essay i; V represents the number of features; $P(w_t|c_j)$ represents the probability that feature w_t appears in an essay scored with c_j; $P(w_t|c_j)$ can be calculated by Eq. 2.

$$P(w_t|c_j) = \frac{1 + \sum_{i=1}^{D_j} B_{it}}{J + D_j} \quad (2)$$

where D_j is the number of essays in the training corpus scored c_j; J is a constant term which is assigned by 1 in this thesis. Based on Eqs. 1 and 2, essay d_i can be graded with c_h which generates the maximum of the probabilities in Eq. 1.

The principles of MBM are very straightforward. That is, the probability that an essay receives a certain score is equal to the product of the probabilities that each of the essay's features receives that score. However, the calculation of MBM may cause some practical mathematical problems (such as where the sum of each score probability do not equal 1). Chang et al. (2014) further propose a modification for the above-described equation, which allows the scoring model to be practically applicable. A detailed description of this modification can be found in the study (Chang et al. 2014).

4 Accuracy of ACES

Assessment of ACES accuracy is conducted using four data sets established using writing examination data from Taiwan's Comprehensive Assessment Program for Junior High School Students in 2010, 2011, 2012 and 2014. Each year, about 300,000 students take this examination. The exam's writing scores range from 1 to 6 points, with 6 being the highest possible level. At each examination, there is a unique writing theme, and so there are four different themes in our data sets. For each writing theme, we have taken 1200 compositions for our sample, which have each been scored by two trained experts. The scores of these 1200 compositions are evenly distributed over all six score levels such that there are 200 compositions assigned to each score from 1 to 6 points. These compositions were chosen from each test year and each score level using a random sampling method.

With the essay data sets of the four aforementioned themes as the basis, a 10-fold cross validation was used to analyze ACES' accuracy rate. For one theme, 200 essays of each score level were randomly divided into 10 folds, with each fold containing 120 essays. In the cross-validation procedure, each fold would be used as a test subset in turn, meaning that each essay would have a machine-predicted score assigned when it was being used as the test data. The scores of all 1200 essays were then used to calculate ACES' scoring accuracy for that theme.

The accuracy of ACES is shown in Table 1. The hit rate in Table 1 refers to the number of machine and human scores that are consistent with one another as a proportion of all scores. The adjacent rate refers to the number of machine and human scores that vary by one level or less as a proportion of all scores. Because in real-life exam scoring, where two experts' scores vary by one point or less, this affirms that the scores of each expert are acceptable, the adjacent rate of ACES is

Table 1 Accuracy of ACES

Data sets	Adjacent rate	Hit rate
2010	0.99	0.67
2011	0.97	0.61
2012	0.96	0.57
2014	0.98	0.61

determined using the same conditions as real-life testing. Table 2 shown the reliability if ACES. For each data set, the recall rate, precision rate, and F1-measure value at each level are shown in Table 2. In fact, recall rates in this table were the hit rates at each level. Tables 1 and 2 show that ACES exhibits a very stable hit rate and adjacent rate performance across different writing themes. Furthermore, these hit rates and adjacent rates are very similar to those of the two expert raters, in addition to being similar to the efficacy of existing English AES systems discussed in the second section of this chapter.

It was difficult to obtain details for all of the systems and test data used in previous studies, and some systems could not process Chinese. As such, it was not possible to make direct comparisons between the performances of different systems. The respective adjacent and hit rates for e-rater (Ramineni et al. 2012) and IntelliMetric (Rudner et al. 2006), as determined by previous studies and stated in the literature, are shown in Table 3. In the table, ACES' accuracy is the average value of the various systems. Its accuracy was very close or even superior to those systems.

Table 2 Recall rate, precision rate, and F1-measure of ACES

		1	2	3	4	5	6
2010	Rec.	0.79	0.61	0.75	0.77	0.58	0.50
	Pre.	0.80	0.65	0.68	0.62	0.52	0.78
	F1	0.79	0.63	0.72	0.69	0.55	0.61
2011	Rec.	0.71	0.51	0.66	0.70	0.57	0.50
	Pre.	0.74	0.55	0.60	0.56	0.51	0.78
	F1	0.72	0.53	0.62	0.62	0.54	0.61
2012	Rec.	0.71	0.52	0.57	0.66	0.51	0.49
	Pre.	0.79	0.52	0.52	0.49	0.48	0.78
	F1	0.75	0.52	0.54	0.56	0.49	0.60
2014	Rec.	0.71	0.52	0.57	0.66	0.51	0.49
	Pre.	0.79	0.51	0.52	0.49	0.48	0.78
	F1	0.75	0.52	0.54	0.56	0.49	0.80

Note: *Rec.* recall rate, *Pre.* Precision rate, *F1* F1-Measure

Table 3 Accuracy of various AES systems compiled from the literature

System	Adjacent rate	Hit rate
e-rater	0.92–0.99	0.52–0.60
IntelliMetric	0.96–0.98	0.54–0.62
ACES	0.96–0.99	0.57–0.67

5 Future Development of ACES

ACES has four unique attributes. First, ACES' performance to predict writing scores is similar to the existing English AES system. ACES' prediction results do not vary significantly from the scoring results provided by two human raters. Second, the tools and modules employed by ACES are designed with consideration of the characteristics of Chinese writing and effectively avoid errors in subsequent analyses resulting from errors in preprocessing. Third, ACES utilizes many innovative direct features, with some direct features exhibiting language independence (e.g., topic features or structural features). This shows that AES systems for other languages can also make use of this. Fourth, some innovative features are difficult to deliberately imitate in writing, such as structural features. During scoring, the ACES system simultaneously considers all features, and so imitating multiple features is increasingly difficult. This avoids the problem of test takers deliberately and maliciously composing compositions that fit high-score conditions for each feature but that are, in fact, incomprehensible.

Chang et al. (2007b) note that based on AES accuracy and subjects of application, AES has four stages of application. In the first stage, AES can correctly analyze changes in the writing abilities of a group. For example, the U.S. National Assessment of Educational Progress (NAEP) project utilizes annual records of AES assessments of American students' writing ability to monitor fluctuations in writing ability over time. In the second stage of application, AES is used as a third rater in high-risk assessments, thus increasing the reliability of scoring. In the third stage, AES is used to replace one expert in the process of scoring high-risk exams such that the exams are scored by one expert and an AES system. In the fourth stage of application, AES can be used as a direct scoring source for non-high-risk exams. For current AES systems that include ACES, all of them satisfy the demands of the third stage of application.

Currently, when ACES is practically applied, it faces two primary difficulties. The first is that if one wishes to use this system, it is necessary to have a sufficient amount of scored essays. This is a relatively difficult condition for teachers. The second difficulty is that essays that express unique viewpoints are easily underscored. Unique views may be interpreted as departing from the domain of the writing theme. For example, if the theme is "class break," students may write about how they would like to use their class breaks to read; this will often be judged as completely departing from the topic. By comparison, essays that focus on descriptions of their feelings toward class breaks rather than events and scenes of these breaks are viewed as demonstrating creativity and unique thinking. However, ACES is currently unable to distinguish these two kinds of writing. At present, ACES is only capable of using a multiple feature model to avoid misinterpreting some unique views expressed in works, and it remains unable to correctly identify different works with comprehensive material selection or those with general and common material selection. Although there are a few such essays as a proportion of all essays, this issue can still lead to the serious error of awarding the lowest scores to the highest scoring essays, and so the problem must be overcome.

Therefore, the primary objectives for the future development of ACES are to resolve the two problems mentioned above. In addition, the question of how to provide students with additional feedback represents another important research orientation. Currently, ACES is capable of correctly predicting writing scores, but it cannot advise users on how to improve their writing skills. To reach this objective, it is necessary to investigate the specific relationship and mutual influence of approximate and intrinsic characteristics.

Acknowledgements This study was partially supported by the Ministry of Science and Technology, under the grant 107-2511-H-003 -022 -MY3; 104-2511-S-003 -018 -MY3; 107-2511-H-992-001-MY3; 104-2511-S-151-001-MY3, and the University Sprout Project—Chinese Language and Technology Center of National Taiwan Normal University, sponsored by the Ministry of Education, Taiwan.

References

Attali, Y., & Burstein, J. (2006). Automated scoring with e-raterV.2. *The Journal of Technology, Learning and Assessment, 4*(3), 1–30.

Bai, S. T., & Shi, A. W. (2002). A comparative study of figures of speech between Chinese and English. *Journal of Xinzhou Teachers University, 18*(1), 70–71.

Burstein, J., Kukich, K., Wolff, S., Lu, C., Chodorow M., Braden-Harder, L., & Harris, M. D. (1998). Automated scoring using a hybrid feature identification technique. In *Proceedings of the 36th Annual Meeting of the Association of Computational Linguistic*s (pp. 206–210). Montreal, Canada.

Cai, J. G. (2006). *Contrastive study of writing and rhetoric in English and Chinese*. Shanghai, China: Fudan University Press.

Chang. T. H. (2015). The development of Chinese word segmentation tool for educational text. In *Proceedings of the 7th International Conference on Information* (pp. 179–182). Taipei, Taiwan.

Chang. T. H., Chen, H. C., & Yang, C. H. (2015). Introduction to a proofreading tool for Chinese spelling check task of SIGHAN-8. In *Proceedings of the 8th SIGHAN Workshop on Chinese Language Processing* (pp. 50–55). Beijing, China.

Chang, T. H., & Lee, C. H. (2003). Automatic Chinese unknown word extraction using small-corpus-based method. In *Proceedings of IEEE International Conference on Natural language processing and knowledge engineering* (pp. 459–464). Beijing, China.

Chang, T. H., & Lee, C. H. (2009). Automatic Chinese essay scoring using connections between concepts in paragraphs. In *Proceedings of the International Conference on Asian Language Processing* (pp. 265–268). Singapore.

Chang, T. H., Lee, C. H., & Tam, H. P. (2007a). On issues of feature extraction in Chinese automatic essay scoring system. In *Proceedings of the 13th International Conference on Artificial Intelligence in Education* (pp. 545–547). Los Angeles, CA.

Chang, T. H., Lee, C. H., & Tam, H. P. (2007b). On developing techniques for automated Chinese essay scoring: A case in ACES system. In *Proceedings of the Forum for Educational Evaluation in East Asia* (pp. 151–152). Taipei, Taiwan.

Chang, T. H., Lee, C. H., Tsai, P. Y., & Tam, H. P. (2009). Automated essay scoring using set of literary sememes. *Information: An International Interdisciplinary Journal, 12*(2), 351–357.

Chang, T. H., Liu, C. L., Su, S. Y., & Sung, Y. T. (2014). Integrating various features to grade students' writings based on improved multivariate Bernoulli model. *Information: An International Interdisciplinary Journal, 17*(1), 45–52.

Chen, K. J., Luo, C. C., Chang, M. C., Chen, F. Y., Chen, C. J., Huang, C. R., et al. (2003). Sinica Treebank. In A. Abeillé (Ed.), *Treebanks: Building and using parsed corpora* (pp. 231–248). Dordrecht: Springer.

Dong, Z., & Dong, Q. (2003). HowNet—A hybrid language and knowledge resource. In *Proceedings of International Conference on Natural Language Processing and Knowledge Engineering* (pp. 820–824). Beijing, China.

Elliot, S. M. (2003). IntelliMetric: From here to validity. In M. D. Shermis & J. C. Burstein (Eds.), *Automated essay scoring: A cross-disciplinary perspective* (pp. 71–86). Mahwah, NJ: Lawrence Erlbaum Associates.

Jiao, C. Y. (2002). A syntactic comparison and transformation between English and Chinese. *Journal of Yancheng Teachers College, 22*(2), 83–87.

Kaplan, R. B. (1966). Cultural thought patterns in intercultural education. *Language Learning, 16*(1–2), 1–20.

Lafferty, J., McCallum, A., & Pereira, F. C. (2001). Conditional random fields: Probabilistic models for segmenting and labeling sequence data. In *Proceedings of the 18th International Conference on Machine Learning* (pp. 282–289). Williamstown, MA.

Lee, G. N. (1999). *Contrastive studies of figures of speech in English and Chinese*. Fuzhou, China: Fujian People's Publishing House.

Lee, X. L., & Zeng, K. (2001). Heterogeneity and homogeneity of sentence structure in English and Chinese. *Journal of Shenyang University, 12*(1), 52–55.

Liu, L. J. (1999). A contrastive study of discourse structure in English and Chinese. *Modern Foreign Languages, 86*(4), 408–419.

Manning, C. D., & Schütze, H. (1999). *Foundations of statistical natural language processing*. Cambridge, MA: MIT press.

Peng, X., Ke, D., Chen, Z., & Xu, B. (2010). Automated Chinese essay scoring using vector space models. In *Proceedings of the 4th International Universal Communication Symposium* (pp. 149–153). Beijing, China.

Ramineni, C., Trapani, C. S., Williamson, D. M., Davey, T., & Bridgeman, B. (2012). Evaluation of the e-rater® scoring engine for the GRE® issue and argument prompts (ETS RR–12-02). https://www.ets.org/Media/Research/pdf/RR-12-02.pdf. Accessed August 31, 2017.

Rudner, L. M., Garcia, V., & Welch, C. (2006). An evaluation of IntelliMetric™ essay scoring system. *The Journal of Technology, Learning and Assessment, 4*(4), 1–22.

Rudner, L. M., & Liang, T. (2002). Automated essay scoring using Bayes' theorem. *The Journal of Technology, Learning, and Assessment, 1*(2), 1–21.

Scollon, R., Scollon, S. W., & Kirkpatrick, A. (2000). *Contrastive discourse in Chinese and English: A critical appraisal*. Beijing: Foreign Language Teaching and Research Press.

Sung, Y. T., Lin, W. C., Dyson, S. B., Chang, K. E., & Chen, Y. C. (2015). Leveling L2 texts through readability: Combining multilevel linguistic features with the CEFR. *The Modern Language Journal, 99*(2), 371–391.

Sung, Y. T., Chang, T. H., Lin, W. C., Hsieh, K. S., & Chang, K. E. (2016). CRIE: An automated analyzer for Chinese texts. *Behavior Research Methods, 48*(4), 1238–1251.

Zeng, X. H. (1997). Enhancing English writing ability by comparing the difference of organization in paragraphs between English and Chinese. *Journal of Nanchang Vocation-technical Teachers College, 4,* 75–77.

Lightning Source UK Ltd.
Milton Keynes UK
UKHW012018120219
337112UK00003B/127/P

9 789811 335693